The Kaiser's
Reluctant Conscript

The Kaiser's Reluctant Conscript

My experiences in the War 1914–1918

Dominik Richert

Translated by
David Carrick Sutherland

Pen & Sword
MILITARY

First published as Beste Gelegenheit zum Sterben:
meine Erlebnisse im Kriege 1914–1918/Dominik Richert.
Published by Angelika Tramitz and Berndt Ulrich – Munich:
Knesebeck and Schuler 1989 with ISBN 3-926901-15-2.

Published in Great Britain in 2012 by
Pen & Sword Military
an imprint of
Pen & Sword Books Ltd
47 Church Street
Barnsley
South Yorkshire
S70 2AS

ISBN 978-1-78159-033-1

Typeset in 10/12pt Palatino
by Concept, Huddersfield.

Printed and bound in England by
CPI Group (UK) Ltd, Croydon, CRO 4YY.

Pen & Sword Books Ltd incorporates the Imprints of Pen & Sword Aviation, Pen &
Sword Family History, Pen & Sword Maritime, Pen & Sword Military, Pen & Sword
Discovery, Wharncliffe Local History, Wharncliffe True Crime, Wharncliffe
Transport, Pen & Sword Select, Pen & Sword Military Classics, Leo Cooper, The
Praetorian Press, Remember When, Seaforth Publishing and Frontline Publishing.

For a complete list of Pen & Sword titles please contact

PEN & SWORD BOOKS LIMITED
47 Church Street, Barnsley, South Yorkshire, S70 2AS, England
e-mail: enquiries@pen-and-sword.co.uk
Website: www.pen-and-sword.co.uk

Contents

Introduction

In 1871 after the defeat of France in the Franco-Prussian War the region of Alsace was incorporated into Germany. In common with the rest of the German Empire, its young men were routinely conscripted for military service. Dominik Richert was one of these young men. He was born in the Saint Ulrich in the Sundgau, close to the Swiss border in 1893 and grew up in a German-speaking environment where French was banned. He proved to be an able pupil at the local school, and when he was due to leave, the local teacher visited his father and tried to persuade him to let him continue his education. However, his father needed his help on their small farm and Dominik's formal education finished at the age of thirteen.

At this time a railway line was being built in the area, and Dominik was able to find employment as a messenger. Later, he loved to tell his family of the pride he felt the first time he came home with his pay – a 20 Mark gold piece. As well as bringing in some well-needed cash to the family income, this job also gave him contact with people from very different backgrounds. There were a number of Italians working on the railway, and one of them encouraged Dominik to be sceptical of people in authority. He was learning to think for himself.

Dominik was called up in 1913, and did not return home till 1919. By this time, as a result of Germany's defeat, Alsace had once again become part of France. After his return, he started to write his memoirs, eventually filling nine notebooks with a very detailed and lively account of his experiences in the First World War. His ability to recall the events of the war in detail is very remarkable.

In 1922 Dominik married Adele Kayser and they had two sons, Marcel and Ulrich. They had reached manhood by the time that, in 1940, Germany invaded Alsace. By 1942, young men from Alsace were being conscripted for the German army. Given his experience of the First World War, Dominik encouraged his sons to escape across the border to Switzerland.

As a result of this act of civil courage, Dominik and Adele were deported to do forced labour in Germany in 1943.

When they heard that their parents had been deported, Dominik's sons joined the French Resistance and took an active part in fighting in France.

Dominik and Adele were dreadfully exploited, having to work fourteen to sixteen hour days on a farm in the Palatinate, but survived and returned home in 1945. The health and morale of both had suffered as a result of their ordeal. Alsace once again became part of France.

In the early 1960s Jean-Claude Faffa, a young man who had known Dominik in the village and had read his notebooks, decided to type them up in the hope that they would be published. He sent one copy of the typescript to Heinrich Böll, the German writer, but unfortunately Böll was not willing to lend his support. He sent the copy he had received to a military archive in Freiburg.

Dominik died in 1977 at the age of eighty-four in St Ulrich and is buried in the village churchyard.

In 1987, Bernd Ulrich, a postgraduate student of modern history from Berlin, discovered Faffa's typescript in the military archive and quickly realised its importance. He showed it to his friend Angelika Tramitz, and together they managed to establish contact with Dominik's sons, and to check the authenticity of the manuscript and its contents.

They sought and found a publisher and were actively involved in editing the book for publication. It was published in German in 1989, and a French translation was published in 1994.

One reason for the book's interest is its sheer scope. Dominik Richert was involved in the war from its outset until he deserted to the French in 1918, and his war service saw him fighting on both the Western and Eastern Fronts. His experience on the Eastern Front will be of particular interest to English speaking readers who are less likely to have read about the conflict from this perspective. His book provides a continuous autobiographical narrative – almost like a diary – for the entire period from the start of the war until his eventual return home in 1919.

It will also be of particular interest to English speaking readers to read his account of the fighting with Indian troops in 1914, and of the battle at Villers-Brettoneux in 1918, where many Australian troops were involved, and some of the first German tanks were in action.

Wherever he went, Dominik was interested in his environment and curious to learn more, visiting cities and towns, looking at the landscape and the way people lived.

However, the most important and valuable aspect of the book is the author himself. From the outset, it is clear that Dominik was a reluctant soldier who questioned authority and was willing to stand up for himself. There is also a clear development in his willingness to act independently as the narrative progresses, and he refuses to accept the propaganda which he encounters. He continues to fight to survive, but he still feels pity for his enemies, and has little respect for the upper echelons of his own army, or the society which sent it to war. He has a clear sense of humanity which transcends national boundaries. In this, he is a very modern hero.

Note on the Text

The translation is based on the published German edition and on Jean-Claude Faffa's typescript. I have added some of the footnotes from the German edition, and a few of my own where I felt it necessary to do so.

As it was not originally intended for publication, the original book was simply entitled *My Experiences in the War 1914–1918*. The title for the English edition was chosen in agreement with Mr Ulrich Richert and the publisher.

Acknowledgements

I am very pleased that all the people who were involved in my project were helpful and cooperative. In particular Angelika Tramitz was consistently supportive and helped me contact Ulrich Richert, the son of the author.

Ulrich Richert has given me a great deal of help and support. In particular I would like to thank him for sending me his copy of Mr Faffa's typescript, which enabled me to provide a complete translation, and for his provision of photographs of his father.

My interest in German was first encouraged by teachers at my Scottish high school – Madras College in St Andrews. I greatly respect their decision to promote the teaching of German and foster contact with Germany in the years following the Second World War.

My brother-in-law, John Walker encouraged me to study for a German degree at Birkbeck in 2002. Thanks to John, and to Eckard Michels, who taught me German history, I discovered the book and the need for a translation.

I would also like to thank Henry Wilson and Matt Jones of Pen and Sword. It is thanks to Henry's appreciation of Dominik Richert's story that it will be published, and he helped guide me to find the right title – not an easy task! Matt Jones has painstakingly guided the text through the proof stages and has been consistently helpful, enthusiastic and co-operative.

Finally I would like to thank my wife Sheila for all her help and encouragement in getting the translation right.

David Carrick Sutherland

Note on Map

There are a large number of places named in the book and many have had their names changed since the time of writing. In order to help the reader, in addition to the map printed on the previous page, we have also set up a more comprehensive map which is freely accessible on the internet using the following url: http://goo.gl/maps/hZFAF.

For those who have internet enabled smart phones, the map can also be viewed by scanning the QR code below.

Diary of a Conscript

At the age of Twenty

On the 16th of October 1913, at the age of twenty, I was called up for military service and assigned to the First Company of Infantry Regiment 112 which was stationed in Mülhausen (Alsace). After about half a year we recruits had been trained by the German Army's usual drill to become soldiers ready for war. In the middle of July 1914 our Regiment was moved to the military training ground in Heuberg on the border between Baden and Württemberg in order to take part in a large-scale combat exercise. While we were there we were often rushed around and drilled in the most mean and nasty way.

On the 29th of July 1914 we had a brigade drill in the morning, and in the afternoon the field artillery had target practise. As we were allowed to see what was happening, I decided to go along, as it seemed to me that I would never again have the opportunity to see something like this. I found it really interesting. I stood behind the guns and was able to see how the shrapnel exploded and how the shells hit the ground at the targets which had been erected. None of us soldiers had any idea that war was imminent.

On the 30th of July 1914 we went to bed early as we were exhausted. About ten o'clock in the evening the door was suddenly opened and we were ordered to get up by the Company Sergeant as the declaration of war was imminent. We struggled to wake up. To start with, nobody was in a fit state to say anything. War, where, with whom? Naturally everyone soon came to the conclusion that it would be the French. Then one of us started to sing 'Deutschland, Deutschland über alles'. Almost everyone joined in and soon hundreds of soldiers' voices boomed it out in the night sky. I really did not feel like singing, because I thought straight away that the most likely thing that can happen to you in a war is that you will be shot dead. That was a really unpleasant prospect. In addition, I was worried about my relatives and my home, because they were near the border and therefore at risk of being destroyed.

We all had to hurry to get packed, and that same night we went down to the station in Hausen, which was located in the Danube Valley. As there was no train there for us we then had to return to our barracks until the

1

following evening. Then they packed us into an overcrowded train – like salt herrings in a barrel – to transport us back to Mülhausen where we were garrisoned. At six o'clock in the morning on the 1st of August 1914 we arrived there and marched to the barracks. We were supposed to be allowed to rest until midday, but instead I was wakened by some of my comrades at nine o'clock and we were issued with our combat equipment from the stores – all brand new from head to foot, together with one hundred and twenty live bullets each. Afterwards we had to go to the armoury where our bayonets were sharpened.

My father and my sister came to see me, to bring me money and to bid me farewell. The order had been given that civilians were not allowed in the barracks, but I was given permission to talk to my relatives outside the gates. It was a difficult farewell because we did not know if we would ever see each other again. All three of us were crying. As he left, my father warned me to always take care and never volunteer for anything. This warning was not strictly necessary as I did not feel particularly patriotic, and the thought of dying a so-called hero's death horrified me.

After this, eight soldiers and I were ordered to perform guard duty at the cashier's office at the station. Others were guarding the station itself, or patrolling in all directions along the track. On the 3rd of August a French plane circled high above the town. All the soldiers tried firing at it. We anticipated that at any minute it would crash to the ground, but instead it continued to circle at a leisurely pace. A number of civilians had gathered outside the station to see what was happening. Suddenly one of them called out 'a Bumma!'.[1] The crowd quickly dispersed and disappeared into the station and the surrounding buildings. I too ran into the station and expected that in any minute a bomb would go off. Everything remained silent. Then I risked going out, looked into the sky, and saw an object falling to earth with something flapping on it. That's not a bomb, I thought to myself. In fact, it was a beautiful bunch of flowers, consisting mainly of forget-me-nots, wrapped in a red, white and blue ribbon. It was a greeting from France to the people of Alsace.

On the 4th of August two trains filled with German civil servants left Mülhausen in the direction of Baden. We made the most of the bottles of wine which they gave us. Then we heard that it was not simply a war between Germany and France, but one involving Germany, Austro-Hungary and Turkey on the one side, and France, Russia, Belgium, England and Serbia on the other. Oh yes, I thought to myself, that really will be something. On the 5th of August I marched with a small section to Exbrücke. We spent two days on the hill called the Kolberg, north of the village. On the 7th of August I saw my first French troops making their way on patrol

---

[1] Alsace dialect for 'a bomb'.

2

through the cornfields. We shot at each other, but there were no losses on either side. At the start, the noise of the bullets whistling by made me nervous. Then we got the order to retreat across the Rhine to Neuenburg, and marched off in that direction. We crossed the Rhine Bridge at daybreak, set up our tents near the cemetery in Neuenburg, and lay down to rest and recover from the march. We spent two days there – until the 9th of August. By then several regiments had gathered, and it looked impressive from a military standpoint.

On the morning of the 9th of August, we were told: 'Get ready! Form up!' We had to cross back over the Rhine Bridge and into the Hardwald forest. They did not tell us what was up or where we were heading. During the day we lay in the Hardwald forest. All the NCOs had to go to the Captain to receive their orders. Then each group leader passed on the order to his group: the French have occupied the line from Habsheim – Rixheim – Ille Napoleon and so on. This evening we have to attack and drive them back. Our Regiment has been given the task of taking the villages of Habsheim and Rixheim and the vine-covered hills between them by force. Suddenly all laughter stopped and nobody felt like joking any more, because none of us felt that he would survive the night, and there was heartily little of the famed enthusiasm for battle or victory which you find described in patriotic writings. We had to march on, and at the edge of the road we saw our first corpse – a French dragoon whose chest had been pierced by a lance. It looked horrible: the bleeding chest, the glazed eyes, the open mouth and the clawed hands. We all marched silently by.

We left the road and marched off to the left along a forest path. In the vicinity of our posts lay six dead German infantrymen – all on their faces. We were given the order to spread out, advance to the edge of the woods and then lie down flat. I was in the second line of riflemen. In front of us, on the edge of the woods we could see the hangars at the Habsheim parade ground. So we would have to cross the parade ground which was one thousand two hundred metres broad. I thought to myself: the Frenchmen will blow us away the moment we move. The command came: 'On your feet! March! March!' The first line got up and ran out of the wood. A warrant officer from the reserve remained lying there. I do not know whether it was cowardice, or whether he had fainted from fear.

The Battle near Mülhausen

As soon as the first line of riflemen left the woods they came under fire from the bushes about one thousand two hundred metres away. The bullets flew over us and whistled into the leaves or bounced off the trees. With thumping hearts we nestled as close as we could to the forest floor until the command came: 'Second line! On your feet! March! March!' We got up and

3

jumped out of the woods. Immediately the bullets whizzed past our ears. The soldiers in the first line were now lying down and directing a steady fire at the bushes. Already a number of dead and wounded were to be seen behind the first line. People with lesser wounds ran back between us into the cover of the woods. Our artillery was firing shrapnel into the vineyards between Rixheim and Habsheim. The whoosh of the shells was a new experience for us. The crashing, crackling and whizzing sounds brought on a nervous excitement. Suddenly we heard two shells whizzing very close to us: two French shells exploded less than twenty metres behind us. While still running I took a quick look back and when I saw the smoke and the tufts of grass flying through the air, I thought to myself: if one of those should land between my legs – oh dear!

We heard the command: 'Join the first line'. We jumped forward and lay down, filling the gaps in the first line. Now it was our turn to fire on the bushes opposite. How often we had practised attacks like this in peacetime, but then the enemy was marked by red flags. This time it was, unfortunately, quite, quite different. The soldiers on either side of me told me that Armbruster had fallen. He was a soldier the same age as me.[2] Ping, a bullet shot past me along the ground and kicked up some grass. If it had been thirty centimetres further to the left my life would have been over.

'Jump up! March! March!' Everyone rushed forwards, and once again trouble was crackling in our direction. Once again, individuals were hit and fell to the ground, often with terrible cries. 'Take position. Start firing. Groups 1, 3, 5, 7 and 9 are to jump, while groups 2, 4, 6, 8, and 10 give rapid fire!' It alternated in this way from now on. When we were close to the bushes, the French soldiers stopped firing. When we had made our way through them, we could see the last of the French soldiers disappearing in the direction of the station at Habsheim. That was the first time I had seen any Frenchmen during the attack. I only saw two dead people in the bushes.

We advanced across open country towards Habsheim and came under heavy fire from the station and from the vineyards on the hill, but only a few of us were hit. When we stormed the station the Frenchmen had cleared out again. There were just too many of us. Our next task was to storm the vineyard on the hill. To start with we had to face heavy fire, but as soon as we got up there, the French troops fled among the vines and disappeared. The French position only consisted of a trench about fifty centimetres deep, behind which we found a large stock of white bread and a small barrel of wine. Both the bread and the wine were quickly consumed. Even the greatest patriot found that the French white bread was better than the army issue.

[2] According to the official records of the 112 Regiment, Armbruster, a 23-year-old joiner, was not actually killed on this day, but he was shot in the chest and severely wounded.

The French continued to defend the village of Rixheim on our left, and we could hear the crackling noise of lively firing. We had to attack Rixheim from the flank. In the meantime it had grown dark. Amongst the vines we found a young Frenchman. He was unconscious. By striking matches, we were able to see that he had been hit on his thigh. A chap from Mannheim wanted to beat him to death. My comrade Ketterer from Mülhausen and I had some difficulty in stopping the monster from carrying out his plan. As we had to move on, we left the Frenchman lying there.

When we stormed into Rixheim cheering, the French soldiers had to pull back to avoid being taken into captivity. Despite this, on searching through the houses we found and took some prisoners, who had hidden there because they were afraid. Most of the soldiers were behaving a bit madly and thought they could see Frenchmen hiding everywhere in the dark. People started shooting wildly, hitting trees and everything, even chimneys became targets. Bullets were flying everywhere, so that nobody was safe. The tallest soldier in the regiment, the two metre tall Hedenus,[3] collapsed and died when he was hit by a bullet. Some of the houses had caught fire, and lit up the surroundings. The injured of both sides were brought in. The dead were left lying.

We had to get together and marched in the direction of Mülhausen. Then we had to spend the night in a meadow about one kilometre from Rixheim. As we were all wet from sweating, the cool of the night was unpleasant, and we longed for the comfort of our bunks in the barracks. However, as we were so tired, we soon fell asleep. We were frightened into wakefulness by the sound of shot and shell. 'What's up?' we called to each other in the darkness. As the firing, which could be seen to our rear in the village of Rixheim, continued to increase in volume even a machine gun joined in and people said: 'The French have outflanked us.' The chaos was indescribable. The wounded screamed for help. Our officers ordered us to form a line, to lie down, and to fire at the origin of the shots.

We fired for several minutes, and then word came in that they were Germans. 'Cease fire!' We had to sing 'Deutschland, Deutschland über Alles' so that the soldiers in Rixheim would realize that we were Germans. My God, how we sang! Almost all of us pressed our faces into the grass, to get as much cover as possible. The officers shouted and cursed, but they could not bring the poor people who had been hit back to life. We had lost as many men to the German bullets as we had lost to the French.

The next morning we marched towards Ille Napoleon. Everywhere you could see corpses lying around, Germans and French – a gruesome sight.

---

[3] Hedenus was a 19-year-old high school pupil. According to the records he died on the 10th of August 1914 at 10.30am, hit by a bullet in the chest.

We marched as far as Sausheim, turned round, and returned by the same route to Mülhausen, which we entered to the sound of martial music. The inhabitants behaved quietly, and it seemed to me from their expressions, that they did not welcome us back. For the next two days we were given emergency quarters in our barracks and were able to get a rest. Most people claimed that they had carried out God knows what kind of heroic acts and had shot a huge number of Frenchmen dead. The people who were loudest were those who had been most afraid during the fighting.

On the 12th of August we marched in the direction of Baden, crossed the Rhine at the Isteiner Klotz, and were quartered in barns in the village of Eimeldingen. The next day we boarded a train to Freiburg. There we were given many gifts by members of the public – mainly chocolate, cigars, cigarettes and fruit. Then we travelled on, but nobody knew where we were going to. All kinds of rumours started to spread: to Northern France, Belgium, Serbia, Russia and so on. But everyone was wrong, because we crossed the Rhine again at Strasbourg and had to leave the train at daybreak in Zabern. Straight away we had to march up from Zabern to Pfalzburg (Lorraine). It was a splendid, clear summer's morning, and at some points the view across the plain of Alsace was wonderful. We remained on high alert – we were not even allowed to take our boots off. In the distance, we could hear artillery fire. So, here too, there was action.

In the evening we headed on towards Saarburg. On a raised piece of ground we had to dig trenches. This was a real struggle as it was a huge effort to shift the hard, dry, chalky ground with our small spades. Ahead of us in a dip lay the village of Rieding, further back lay the little town of Saarburg. As night fell, there was a heavy thunderstorm in the area. It grew very dark, and there was a downpour. We were soaked through. Even our boots had filled with water, so that we were able to pour it out again. We were sitting or standing around in the open and started chattering like geese as a result of the wet. 'Everyone head for Rieding, and look for quarters.' We made our way across the soaking wet field and eventually reached a street which led to the village. The whole place was so full of soldiers that it took us a long time before we found anywhere to shelter.

Ketterer from Mülhausen, Gautherat from Menglatt and I stuck together. Ketterer said: 'In the church there's sure to be room.' We went there, but it was the same as elsewhere. The soldiers had lit the altar candles, so that the church was fairly well lit-up. There were soldiers everywhere – on the pews and in the aisles. The soldiers lay or sat around on the altar. We left the church and reached a house at the end of the village with a locked door. There were hussars camping in the barn. We rattled the door-handle of the house – nobody came. Ketterer started to bang on the door with the butt of his rifle, first gently, then harder and harder. Eventually someone asked: 'Who's out there?' I said 'Three soldiers – from Alsace – seeking a billet. We

6

will be happy if we can just sleep on the floor.' The door opened. We had to go into the kitchen. My God, said the woman, you are soaking wet. Without our asking, she made us warm milk and gave us bread and butter, all of which was greatly appreciated. The friendly woman said she had only one free bed. We all undressed and crept into the bed. The good woman took our clothes and dried them on the oven. When we awoke the following morning, all the other soldiers had left the village. The woman brought us our dry clothes and gave us breakfast. Each of us wanted to give the woman a Mark for her effort[4] – but she did not want to take anything. We thanked her and said goodbye. We went looking for our Company, and we found them on the hill where we had dug the trench the evening before.

At midday we marched to the village of Bühl, stopped, marched on, stopped again, and so on. From ahead, several regiments of Bavarians – infantry, artillery and cavalry – marched past us going in the opposite direction. Nobody understood what was going on. Eventually we marched back too, and had to dig a trench in a muddy hollow at the edge of a wood near the village of Rieding. Wherever you looked you could see soldiers digging trenches. Batteries were mounted and camouflaged. It was soon clear to us that we would have to stop the French here. Several days passed uneventfully. On the 18th of August, some French shells landed. The ones which landed in the soft ground in our area failed to explode, while those which hit hard farm land did detonate with a loud crash.

19th of August 1914 – Battle at Saarburg (Lorraine)

In the night of the 18th to the 19th of August the French troops occupied the villages and the territory next to our lines. In the early morning the order was given for a general attack on the French. At a stroke all laughter, all humour, seemed to have vanished. Everyone had the same serious, tense appearance. What will the day bring? I do not believe that anyone thought of the Fatherland, or of any other patriotic swindle. The concern for one's own life pushed everything else into the background.

On the road which led down to the village of Rieding about five hundred metres from our position, we saw the Cycle Company of our Regiment, which consisted of about eighty-nine men, speeding towards the village. As soon as they reached the first houses people started firing madly. All but four of the Company were killed. Suddenly the German artillery fire started. The French replied. The battle had started. With backpacks and loaded guns we kneeled in the trench and awaited orders, with our hearts pounding. 'The Battalion will creep along the trench towards the road. Pass it on!' We crept

---

[4] The soldiers' pay was 53 Pfennigs a day.

forward, keeping as low as we could. Several French shells landed close to the trench, causing us to throw ourselves on the ground. We reached the road and crept – mainly on all fours – along the ditch at the side of the road. All too soon, the French artillery had seen us. Suddenly we heard a noise above us, there was a flash, and a shrapnel shell had exploded, but nobody was injured. Sst-boom, boom they now came flying over. There were screams here and there. The man but one ahead of me screamed fell to the ground, rolled over and cried out wailing for help. That raised the tension.

'Forwards! March! March!' We all ran forward in the ditch, but the French shells were faster. The losses increased. 'Battalion spread out to the left and form into lines by company with four steps between each person. March! March!' In less than two minutes the battalion had spread out and we continued at a trot. Now the French infantry, which we could not see at all, opened a lively fire at us. Our hearts were beating wildly as a result of the excitement and the running. We stormed the station at Rieding. As we outnumbered them, the French troops were forced to retreat. We took some prisoners. We had to lie behind the railway embankment and were able to get our breath back. From all directions we heard the boom of the guns, the bursting and crashing of the shells, and the cracking of the infantry fire and of the machine guns. Oh, if only we could spend a long time lying here like this, I thought to myself! A piece of cake! Another battalion moved in on us from behind. 'The first battalion of Infantry Regiment 112 move under cover to the left.' We reached a hollow then we came to a wood and circled round it for about two kilometres in order to attack the village of Bühl, which was being bravely defended by the French soldiers, from the side. Our first line had hardly left the protection of the wood before the first shells arrived. They were well aimed and the clods of earth flew about our heads, without, however, causing much damage. We had to cross a flat valley, through which flowed a stream. As the meadow did not afford us any cover, we had no alternative but to take cover behind the bank on the other side of the stream. We spent nearly two hours up to the waist in water, pressing ourselves close to the bank, while the shrapnel shells tore the alders and willows above our heads to shreds. We were given reinforcements from the woods and had to attack the heights. A crackling infantry fire rattled in our direction. Many a poor soldier fell in the hay. A further advance was impossible. We all threw ourselves down and tried to dig ourselves in with our spades and our hands. Shaking, nestling close to the ground, we lay there, expecting death at any minute. Then I heard terrible explosions up above. I lifted my head and looked up. Big black clouds of smoke billowed up there, and new clouds shot into the sky. Clods of earth were flying around. The German artillery was keeping the heights under heavy fire. We managed to capture the heights and the village without incurring heavy losses. We sought shelter from the French artillery in a dug-out cellar on a building site. Next to me lay an army reservist from Baden, a man who was the father of two children. He pulled out a cigar and said to me: 'who knows, it might be my last.' No sooner had he said this than a shrapnel shell burst overhead. A splinter penetrated the webbing of his pack on his chest and bored into his heart. He let out a loud scream, stood up, and fell down dead. Two other soldiers and our sergeant were wounded.

We stayed in the cellar until evening. Then we continued to advance, without encountering any resistance and occupied the farms to the south-west of Bühl. We were supposed to spend the night there. Dead tired and exhausted, wet from sweat and stream water, we all lay down. I fetched some sheaves of oats which were standing nearby. I spread two of them out in a furrow, and covered myself with two more. I soon fell asleep. Suddenly there was a shout and the sound of gunfire. 'Form three lines! First line lying, second line kneeling and third line standing! Rapid fire straight ahead!' Most of us ran into position and in no time at all the lines were formed and the Frenchmen who were making a counter-attack were welcomed with a furious rapid fire. Despite this, some of them were able to make their way into the German lines, where people fought with bayonets in the darkness. Eventually the Frenchmen withdrew, and silence returned.

I had not taken part in the whole thing, and had hidden myself as much as possible in my oat sheaves. For a long time I was unable to get to sleep. I found the wailing and groaning of the wounded and their cries for help really upsetting. Eventually I managed to sleep again. At long last, at 2.00am the field kitchen caught up with us and we got something to eat: hot coffee and bread. The hot coffee tasted splendid, we had got cold in our damp clothes. As about half of the men were missing, we were able to take as much as we wanted. I filled my canteen for the following day. Then I crept back to my oat-sheaves and did not waken up until the sun was shining in my face. I got up. What a sight I was faced with! In front of us lay dead and wounded Frenchmen, as far as the eye could see. The dead Germans were also still there, but the wounded had been taken away. I went to the nearest French wounded and distributed the coffee from my canteen among them. How these poor people thanked me! German ambulances arrived and trans-ported the wounded Frenchmen away. It was horrible to look at the dead. Some of them lay on their faces, and some on their backs. Blood, clutching hands, glazed eyes, distraught faces. Many still held their guns tightly in their hands. Others were clutching earth or grass which they had ripped out as they were fighting for life. I saw a group of soldiers standing together at one place and found something terrible. A German and a French soldier lay, half kneeling, against each other. Each had stabbed the other with his bayonet, and then they had collapsed together.

Now an order of the day was read out: yesterday the French were attacked across a front of one hundred kilometres from Metz to Donon, and despite a

9

brave defence they were driven back. So and so many prisoners were taken. Artillery was captured. The losses on each side were estimated to be forty five thousand men. Our soldiers have earned full praise for their courage and heroism. The hearty thanks of their Fatherland are owed to them – and so on and so forth.

Bravery, Heroism – does it exist? I doubt it very much, because all that I saw when under fire was fright, fear and desperation written in every face. But I did not see courage or bravery at all, because in reality it's only the fearful military discipline, the force, that drives the soldier forwards to his death.

20th of August 1914

An NCO and ten of us were sent to Bühl to fetch ammunition to replace what had been used up. Near the village a wooden crucifix which had stood in a field had been hit by a shell. The horizontal spar was missing and the vertical spar had been cut off at knee height, leaving the figure of Jesus undamaged, with his hands outstretched. It was a horrifying image, and we went on without speaking.

At about ten o'clock in the morning, the order was given: 'Get ready to advance'. Now, once again we had to advance abreast on the French in multiple lines. Soon we came under shellfire and one of them hit a farmhouse, which almost immediately started to burn brightly. Nobody thought of putting it out. Ahead of us I saw a horse standing in a barley field with his head hanging down. On getting there we saw that he was standing near the body of his rider, a French cavalryman, and that he had been seriously injured in his stomach and on his rear leg. I shot the horse through the head to put an end to his suffering. He fell down dead. A few steps further on I stood on something soft in among the barley. It was a severed hand, to which some scraps of the sleeves of a shirt were still attached. Nearby, near a shell-hole lay the torn-up corpse of a French infantryman with a missing hand.

As we continued to advance we came under heavy shellfire. We ran at the double to the shelter of a hill which was about the height of a house. Now the shells either hit the top of the hill or shot past us. Then they changed to shrapnel shells, which burst directly overhead. Oh these cursed 75mm field-guns. The shells flew at us as fast as the devil. You didn't even have time to throw yourself to the ground. Within one second they were fired, zoomed towards us and left us dying. Out of fear, we held our packs over our heads, but still several people were hit. Our major, by the name of Müller, was remarkably unafraid. Smoking a cigar, he walked among us, ignoring the exploding shrapnel shells, up and down, encouraging us not to be afraid.

Behind us, to the left, a German battery was brought up. Within a few minutes it had been taken out by the French artillery. Only a few of the artillerymen were able to escape by running away. Gradually the firing ceased, we advanced and spent the night in the woods near the village of Hatten.

21st of August 1914 – Battle near Lörchingen

In the morning the advance continued in a valley, heading towards the town of Lörchingen. As our captain had been injured, Lieutenant Vogel, a morose, ugly, hoarse human being had sole command of the Company in our advance on Lörchingen. On reaching the village, the patrols which had been sent on ahead reported: 'Up on the height to the left of the village, almost in our backs, French infantry is withdrawing'. We entered the village in double time and occupied a market garden which was surrounded by a strong wall. The Frenchmen were about four hundred metres from us, and were advancing unsuspectingly towards us when they were suddenly overwhelmed by a fearful wave of fire. Many fell, while others lay down and fired back, but they were unable to do us any harm as we were protected by the wall. Then they started to hold their rifle butts in the air as a sign that they wanted to surrender. We stopped shooting. Then several of the French-men jumped up and tried to escape. They were shot down. I felt sorry for the poor people. I could not bring myself to shoot at them. 'Forwards, March! March!' shouted Lieutenant Vogel. 'We want to catch the rest of the gang!' We all climbed over the wall and ran towards the Frenchmen. They were not firing any more. Then suddenly from behind us we heard a whistling sound. Boom. A large shrapnel shell exploded directly overhead. As if they had been hit by lightning, several men fell to the ground. We all wanted to run back and find cover, as we were being shelled by our own artillery. Lieutenant Vogel shouted 'Advance!' When some of the soldiers hesitated, he shot four of them down without further ado. Two were dead, two were wounded. A good comrade of mine, by the name of Sand, was one of the wounded. (Lieutenant Vogel was shot dead by his own soldiers in northern France two months later.)[5]

Now the French soldiers, shaking with fear, came running towards us with their hands up. We took them back to Lörchingen at a trot and found cover in cellars and places like that. In the evening we went back to the

---

[5] According to the regimental records, the 23-year-old sugar factor worker Sand was wounded on his right shin on the 21st of August 1914 in Lörchingen. Lieutenant Vogel, whose civilian role was that of a senior postal assistant, was not shot dead at the end of 1914. Two days after the battle he was sent behind the lines to Belgium, where he remained until 1917.

village of Hessen, taking our prisoners with us, where we spent the night sleeping in a garden of fruit trees.

22nd to the 24th of August 1914

Early in the morning. Alarm. Drink coffee. March to the front. Damn, I thought, every day we have to go hunting for death. I cannot describe how reluctantly I moved off. After marching for a few kilometres we reached the French border. The post marking the German border with the eagle on it had been broken by the Frenchmen. I thought that they might expect us to cheer as we crossed the border, but we crossed silently. Everyone was probably wondering if he would ever cross back again. We marched on until after dark and camped in an open field.

A French aircraft wakened us from our slumbers by dropping a couple of bombs. Fortunately nobody was hurt. There was no sign of the field kitchen, so we went hungry. There was a village nearby. We were hoping that we would be able to find some food there, but we had to march close by without entering it. We pulled out some yellow turnips from where they had been planted and managed to shake some small plums from the trees. That was our breakfast. However, hunger is the best cook – that was a lesson we would often learn. The consequence of this food was that we suffered from diarrhoea – and how! More than half of the troops were suffering. As a result lots of people reported sick in the hope of being transferred to the field hospital instead of running around playing the hero. Oh yes, field hospital! All you got was a drop of opium on a lump of sugar from the battalion doctor and then – march – get the enemy! Oh how we would now love to be drilled back in the barracks! And the beds! Oh you straw mattresses, how happy we would now be, to be able to stretch our warm dry legs on you! Carry on, without a break.

At midday we stopped in a village. A real hunt for chickens began. Rabbits were fetched from boxes and stalls, together with wine from the cellars and bacon and ham from the fireplaces. I went looking for eggs, and emptied the contents of about six to eight of them. Then I went into a house. In the living room on a shelf I discovered rows of milk jugs. I reached up and found one filled with cream. It tasted excellent, sweet and cool! While I was enjoying drinking, I noticed an elderly lady standing pale and trembling in the doorway. Although I had not committed a crime, I was ashamed to take the cream with me without paying. I offered her half a Mark, but she did not want it, and gave me a big piece of bread as well. The woman was the only civilian I saw in the village. The inhabitants had either crept into hiding or run away.

Form up. On you go. Several companies went forwards in loose formation, while we formed the reserve. Bang, bang it started up again ahead of us.

12

It was the French rearguard, who put up a limited resistance. Our Company did not have to take part. As we continued forwards we saw several dead Germans lying around. We went on and spent the night in a large wood on a hill. We could tell from the restlessness and excitement of the officers that something was in the offing for the following day.

25th of August 1914 – The Crossing of the Meurthe

In the early morning the German batteries started uninterrupted shelling. You could hear the shells landing on the other side. We stood at the ready in the woods and waited. The company commanders now got us to spread out. My company was in the second firing line. 'Forwards, march!' Everyone started moving. Ahead of us sunlight shone brightly through the trees, this was the edge of the woods. Almost as soon as the first line showed itself at the edge of the woods, the French infantry opened sweeping rapid fire. The French artillery shelled the woods with shells and shrapnel. These things started bursting between and above us. We ran like mad from place to place. Quite close to me a soldier had his arm torn off while another one had half of his throat cut open. He collapsed, gurgled once or twice, and then the blood shot from his mouth. He was dead. A pine tree which had been hit in the middle collapsed to the ground. We didn't know where to hide. 'Second Line Forwards!' Arriving at the edge of the woods I was able to see a fairly deep valley through which passed a river, a road and a railway line – the valley of the Meurthe. The village and the hills on the other side of the river were heavily occupied by the French. You could only see a few individuals, as they had taken cover. Everywhere you could see the clouds of smoke shooting skywards from the German shells. On both sides of us German troops advanced in lines out of the woods and the French artillery shells flew over and found their victims. In the explosions and rattling it was almost impossible to hear commands. We rushed down the hill and were able to find cover at the side of the road. As we moved further forward we all headed for the bridge, and the French poured down a hail of shrapnel, infantry and machine-gun fire on it. Masses of the attackers were hit and fell to the ground. There was no prospect of getting across. I lay shaking without cover on the meadow next to the road near the river. I thought my last hour had come, and I didn't want to die. I prayed to God for help, as one can only do when one's life is in danger. It was a fearful, quivering plea from the bottom of my heart, a deep, painful plea to him. How different a prayer like this is, coming as it does from a situation of extreme need, compared with others which one carries out as a matter of routine or thoughtless repetition.

Bang, close to me a shell had exploded. Crackling splinters and clods of earth fell around. In one jump I was in the shell-hole! Bump – another soldier also seeking cover had landed on top of me. But I was underneath and I was not going to give up my position. 'Forwards, attack across the river.' We heard the commands through the din. Everyone jumped up, without taking too long to think about it and jumped into the river heading for the cover of the opposite bank. The water was chest-high but nobody minded. Several people were hit by shrapnel and washed away. Nobody helped them; each of us was preoccupied with his own survival.

At the edge of the village several houses had been set on fire by the shooting; driven by the heat, the French were forced in places to give up the defence of the village. We now had to attack with bayonets and the French were forced to give way. Prisoners were taken. Soaked through and exhausted we sought cover behind the houses to get some rest. Gradually the shooting came to a complete stop. Towards evening we had to attack the wooded hill to the left of the village. We returned to Thiaville to spend the night. I lay with a large number of comrades in a barn with soft hay. It was a stormy night. The rain poured down on the tiles on the roof. As a result of the noise of the collapsing houses, which had been set on fire by the shelling, it was difficult to sleep even though we were exhausted. Many cattle were still tied up in the burning stalls and were bellowing loudly from the fear of death. It was dreadful! Eventually I fell asleep. After midnight I heard a call: 'The Heuchele Group should come here immediately!' That was my group. We climbed down. Our wet clothes were still sticking to our bodies. We eight soldiers and the NCO had to do sentry duty a few hundred metres from the village. We stood or crouched there in the pouring rain and stared and listened out into the blackest of nights. Eventually the morning came grey in the east. What would the next day bring?

26th of August 1914 – The Fight in the Woods near Thiaville

As it grew light, we expected to be relieved, but no-one came. A few steps ahead of us we could see a small house which we had not been able to see in the dark. In a hedge nearby lay the body of a dead German infantryman which had been soaked through by the rain. In the yard of the little house lay two French infantrymen. Next to one of them lay a purse. I picked it up. It contained two 20 Franc pieces in gold. However, I was not interested in money, so I threw it away. Probably one of the Frenchmen had been hoping to be spared by giving away his money. A section of dragoons rode up to us from the village and went on past us along the road towards the woods which were about four hundred metres away. They were followed by companies of infantry. We had to join our company and plod along behind them in our wet clothes. Nobody asked us if we had had anything to eat or drink. Ahead of us in the woods, shots rang out. Damn, the same thing

14

again! The dragoons who came galloping back out of the woods told our brigadier, Major-General Stenger that they had encountered the French. The general now issued the following order, to the company commanders,[6] who read it to their companies: 'Today, no prisoners are to be taken. Wounded and captured Frenchmen should be executed.'

Most of the soldiers were struck speechless, while some of the others were pleased by this despicable breach of international law. 'Spread out. Forwards, march!' Carrying our guns, we headed towards the wood and entered it, with my Company in the second row. No shot fell. We were already hoping that the French troops had withdrawn, as they had been fired on by the dragoons. Bang, bang, bang it started. Some bullets reached us and loudly collided with the trees. In the early morning our Company had been allocated some raw recruits to make up our losses. These soldiers, who had never heard the whistle of a bullet, had questioning, fearful faces. As the intensity of the fire increased, we had to move up to join the front line. Using every tree and every bush for cover, we moved forwards. We were followed by several further lines of troops. To start with, although the French mountain troops fought bravely, they were forced to give way. They kept on taking up new positions behind trees and ditches and firing on us. The losses increased. The wounded Frenchmen were left lying there and became our prisoners. To my horror, there were some monsters among us who either bayoneted or shot these poor defenceless men while they pleaded for mercy. An older regular NCO from my Company, by the name of Schirk, sneeringly shot a wounded Frenchman lying in his own blood in the backside. Then he held his gun to the head of the poor unfortunate man who was pleading for his life and shot him dead. I will never forget the man's distraught expression as he faced his death. A few steps further on lay another wounded man, a handsome young fellow, in a ditch in the wood. NCO Schirk ran towards him and I followed. Schirk wanted to bayonet him. I parried the blow and shouted out: 'If you touch him, you're dead!' He looked at me with a baffled expression, and since he did not know what to expect from my threatening attitude he mumbled something and followed the other soldiers. I threw my gun to the ground, and kneeled down beside the wounded man. He started to cry, took hold of my hands, and kissed them. As I did not know any French, I pointed to myself and said 'a comrade from Alsace'. By making signs I managed to explain to him that I wanted to bandage him up. He did not have any bandages. Both his calves had been shot through. I removed his puttees, cut open his red trousers with my pocket knife and bandaged up his wounds using my first aid kit. Then I stayed, lying beside him, partially from sympathy and partially because the

[6] There is no trace of this in the military records.

ditch gave me cover. I raised my head slightly but was unable to see the advancing troops any more. Bullets continued to whiz through the woods. They snapped off twigs and bored into trunks and branches.

Near by there were some bilberry branches, which were laden with ripe berries, so I picked and ate them. That was the first food for more than thirty hours. Then I heard steps behind me. It was the Company Sergeant Penquitt, a man who had been a dangerous pest in the barracks who stuttered every time he started to speak: 'Y-y-ou lazy bugger, make your way to the front!' What could I do? I took my gun and went. After going a short distance I hid behind a tree to see whether he was going to attack the wounded man. I was determined to shoot him down if he tried to kill the Frenchman. He took a look at him, and then went on. Now I rushed on to stay ahead of him and forced my way through a thick bramble bush. In the bush there were six to eight Frenchmen all lying face downwards. I immediately noticed that they were only pretending to be dead. They were no longer able to flee as the German lines had advanced beyond them. I touched one of them with my bayonet and said 'Comrade'. He looked at me fearfully. I indicated to him that he should continue to lie there, which he agreed to do, nodding his head keenly. Corpses and wounded men lay spread throughout the woods. The rattling and banging kept on and on. Injured soldiers ran backwards past me. I crept forwards, always seeking cover, to reach the front line. Once again, cheering, we continued to attack, and the losses mounted. Schumacher and I were standing behind a tree which did not offer enough cover for the two of us. He set out to get behind a pine tree about five metres away, but he fell on his face after only a couple of steps and did not move any more. He was dead. On advancing further we reached a broad ravine. The Frenchmen were retreating up the opposite bank. Many of them were shot down like rabbits. Some of them rolled back down the slope. When we had crossed the ravine we suddenly came under fearful fire from a hill which had been planted with young pine trees. We all took cover or threw ourselves to the ground. Some fled. Major Müller waved his dagger, shouting 'forwards children!' – and dropped down dead.[7] Now, up among the young pine trees, things started to get moving. A host of mountain troops started running towards us with fixed bayonets. We turned and headed back as quickly as possible. I was running together with about six men. Four of them fell screaming to the ground. I didn't take the time to look round to see how they were. Almost all our wounded were left lying. While continuing to run, I undid my pack and threw it away. When I had got further back I heard someone calling my name two or three times. On looking round I saw my good barrack-room comrade Schnur, who was the son of a farmer

---

[7] Major Müller, born in 1863, fell in this battle after thirty-one years of service.

from Wangen on Lake Constance. He was lying on a tent which had been fastened to poles by ambulance men. The ambulance men left him lying and ran away. I got three other comrades to come and help. We put the poles on our shoulders and retreated at a trot. This was a real torture for poor Schnur. The strings on the tent pulled together. Schnur was sitting with his bottom in the lowest part of the tent, with his legs and his head peeking out the top. In the process the tent swung backwards and forwards between us. 'Stop! For God's sake slow down!' he groaned, but we ran on to get out of range of the bullets. Here the officers stopped all the retreating soldiers and got them to form a line to drive off the French troops. The four of us were allowed to carry the wounded man to a field dressing station which had been set up in a small farm at the edge of the woods. The farm was so full of wounded that we had to lay Schnur down in the yard. He had been shot in the back and was greatly weakened by loss of blood. As it started to rain again, I went looking around and found a space for him in the kitchen. We carried him in. God, what it looked like in this house! Blood, groans, moans, prayers! Wishing my comrade a speedy recovery, I left this house of suffering. (Three months later, Schnur died in a military hospital in Strasbourg.)[8]

My room-mate Wöltje from Hanover, who had always been a jolly chap, came hobbling out of the woods. He was supporting himself on his gun. 'What's wrong Wöltje,' I called. 'A shot has gone through both my legs.' 'There is a dressing station over there,' I said to him, but he was so agitated and fearful that he did not want to be stopped and he hobbled on towards the rear.

As I had not eaten anything more than a few bilberries for about thirty hours, I was now feeling very hungry. As it was not possible to get anything to eat at the farm, I went back into the woods to look for bilberries. There I found a dead Frenchman. I opened his pack and took out a tin of meat and a packet of cigarettes. A short distance away lay a dead German. I removed his pack and used it to replace the one I had thrown away. In this pack I found iron rations and a clean shirt. I pulled off my dirty sweaty shirt and replaced it with this one. Then I ravenously ate the Frenchman's tin of food. The shooting in the woods died down. Gradually it became evening. The companies regrouped at the edge of the wood. My Company now consisted of about forty people. More than a hundred were missing! My comrades Gautherat and Ketterer had also survived. They had been more cunning than me and had hidden in the bushes right at the start of the battle. We

---

[8] According to military records Schnur was injured in the upper thigh on the 26th of August 1914 and died on the 2nd of December 1914 as a consequence of his injury, amputation and blood-poisoning.

spent the night on the slope of a hill in the pouring rain. We lounged around with deadened senses, dog-tired and half-despairing.

27th of August 1914

In the morning a patrol consisting of a lieutenant and eight men was to be sent to fetch the body of Major Müller from the woods. Soon we heard shots from the direction which they had chosen. None of them returned. According to other soldiers, Major Müller had shot two wounded Frenchmen with his pistol. It's good that fate caught up with him. NCO Schirk was also missing,[9] together with another soldier from the reserve who had shot a wounded man.

I now went to Thiaville to collect some water in canteens so that we would be able to brew some coffee. Next to the road there was a battery of the 76th Field Artillery Regiment. The men were being fed by a field kitchen. 'Richert, where are you wandering to?' called out one of the men. It was Jules Wiron from Dammerkirch. 'Are you hungry?' he asked me. When I told him that I was, he fetched me a big portion, which really suited me, and then he filled up my canteen with a good white wine from a demijohn which was standing on the gun limber. I thanked him, filled the other canteens with water and went back to the rest of the Company. There Gautherat, Ketterer and I drank the wine.

About midday we went back across the Meurthe and marched about five kilometres down the valley to the little town of Baccarat, which had been conquered by the Germans two days before. It must have been a fierce fight, especially at the bridge across the Meurthe. The business area on the western side of the river was totally burnt out and the church tower was full of holes. We were told to pitch our tents in the town park, and were allowed two days' rest. Next to our tent was a mass grave in which more than seventy Frenchmen had been buried. Next to it was the grave of a Bavarian major.

Despite the complaints of various inhabitants, all the chickens, rabbits and pigs which could be found were stolen and slaughtered. Any wine which was still available was stolen from the cellars, and drunk soldiers could be seen everywhere.

Once again the companies were brought up to compliment with new recruits from Germany, and then we had to advance once again – initially upwards in the direction of Ménil. On both sides of the road lay large quantities of equipment discarded by the French – packs, guns, a drum and trumpets. As we went through a wood further up, we encountered dead

---

[9] According to the records, the 22-year-old butcher was badly wounded in this action.

German and French mountain troops in the undergrowth. They had already started to decompose and gave out a horrible smell. On a rise on the other side of the wood we had to dig trenches. As it was hot, my NCO sent me off with a number of mess tins to collect water. I found some in a roadside ditch in the hollow behind us. I drank three or four cupfuls and filled the canteens. After drinking, it occurred to me that the water had a rotten offensive taste, but I assumed that this was caused by the fact that it was flowing slowly. Then when I went a bit further along the ditch a horrible smell reached my nose. Next to a willow bush I saw a dead Frenchman who had already started to decompose. His forehead, which had been split open by a shell, was facing towards the water and was covered with maggots and little worms. I had drunk the water which was trickling through the corpse! It made me feel so disgusted that I vomited repeatedly. Then I emptied the canteens and filled them with fresh water from further up. When I returned, the soldiers drank the water eagerly. We stayed in the trench for three days. Apart from the occasional shrapnel shell, things were quiet. Ahead of us in a dip lay the half burnt-out village of Ménil, with the village of Anglemont further back, and the village of St Barbe over to the right.

On the fourth day, in the early morning, several battalions of reinforcements arrived. We were to attack and capture the villages of Ménil and Anglemont and the woods behind them. We were all afraid. People exchanged addresses and looked at photos of their loved ones. Many of us prayed quietly. Each face was earnest, fearful and full of horror.

The Attack on Ménil and Anglemont

At ten o'clock in the morning officers and messengers ran around and brought the command to attack immediately. 'Get ready. Put on your packs. Company spread out in lines.' Six lines were formed. 'Forwards, march!' Everyone set off. Our artillery shelled the two villages. We reached Ménil before the French fired a single shot. We pushed into the village. No Frenchmen were to be seen. The village was not occupied. A horrible smell caused us to go through Ménil at a trot. In many of the houses the cattle had been burned in their stalls and the summer heat had caused them to decompose. We went on in the direction of Anglemont. In front of us bullocks, cows and calves ran back and forth. A number of cattle had eaten too much fresh clover and had died of distended stomachs. Others had been killed by shells. When we approached the village of Anglemont we suddenly came under shrapnel fire from the French artillery. The infantry fire started at the same time. We were only able to advance in jumps. We gathered behind a bush and then attacked the village at double time with fixed bayonets, cheering as we went. The Frenchmen put up a spirited defence, but they had to give way to our greater numbers. At one of the first houses a wounded French-man was sitting on a wheelbarrow. A soldier from my Company wanted to shoot him dead. When I earnestly objected, he changed his mind. An ambulance man who came up bandaged his wound.

The French artillery concentrated their fire on the village. I jumped behind the high, stone-built gable end of a barn where a number of other soldiers had already sought cover. Suddenly there was an explosion directly above us. The stones from the walls fell down and hit a number of soldiers, knocking them to the ground. A shell had flown through the roof and burst against the wall, blowing a large hole in it. Nowhere was safe any more. I placed myself under the trunk of a thick apple tree which stood at an angle. Then we were given the order to advance again. We had hardly left the cover of the village before the French troops began shooting like mad at us. Shells were landing from all directions. Shrapnel shells distributed their hail of lead from the air. Whooshing, hissing, banging, smoke and clods of earth and people who had been hit flew around. A shell hit about three metres away from me. I involuntarily bent down and raised my arm to cover my face. I was hit by smoke and clods of earth. A splinter had broken off the butt of my rifle down by the breech. The two men next to me lay dead on the ground. As if by a miracle, I remained uninjured, so I picked up the rifle of one of the people who had been hit and jumped into the shallow shell-hole, because I was quite shocked. 'Come on, Richert – on we go!' It was an NCO from my Company. What could I do? I had to go on. We headed on through clover, potato and turnip fields. The French infantry poured bullets at us from the woods. We sought cover in the furrows of the fields, but still had to keep moving on. One of the bullets bored a deep ridge in the wood of my rifle, close under my hand. As a result of the ever-increasing fire and the losses we were sustaining, it became impossible to advance any further. I threw myself in a ditch where several others were already lying. Fortunately for us, the fields ran at right angles to the woods so we had some cover.

In the course of the advance, the regiments and companies had become mixed up. Next to me lay a soldier from the Baden Grenadier Regiment. I pulled out my spade to dig myself in. The ground was hard and dry, and it was only with great effort that I was able to dig myself a hole while lying down. A soldier who was lying near me got the idea that it would be easier to dig a hole in a furrow in the next field which was planted with potatoes than in the field of clover where we were. 'Stay here and don't show yourself!' I said. 'The moment that anyone moves, the Frenchmen will fire at it, because they can't see anyone any more in the field.' 'What's the odds – I'll be over there in a single jump!' With his gun in his hand, he jumped up. Bang, splat. More than twenty shots fell. Bullets whizzed over me. The soldier fell on his face and did not move any more. I could only see his legs.

The upper part of his body lay in the next furrow. Now the reserve soldier Berg nudged me. 'Richert, give me your spade,' he said. I gave it to him. A grenadier said to Berg: 'When you are finished with the spade, would you give it to me?' I curled myself up in my hole and nodded off until I was awakened by a shell landing near me. Berg was now lying in his hole, and the grenadier was working with the spade. I nodded off again. 'Richert, look at what the grenadier is doing!' said Berg. The grenadier was kneeling in the trench with his back to me, his head was down, but he was not moving. 'Hi, comrade!' I called, and then I crawled to him and shook him. He fell on his side and groaned. A bullet had drilled through his head above his ear and his brain was sticking out like a pencil for about three centimetres. I wound a bandage round his head although I knew that I could not really help him. Gradually the groaning changed to a rattle, which became ever weaker. After about two hours, he was dead.

We remained lying there until it got dark. Then we were given the whispered order: 'Everyone is to withdraw and regroup in Anglemont!' Now everyone tried to reach the village as quickly as possible. You heard wounded men pleading for help: 'For God's sake don't leave me here. I have a wife and children at home!' Some were taken, others were left lying. Here it was a case of 'everyone is his own nearest and dearest'. In Anglemont there was complete chaos. 'Infantry Regiment 112 assembles here!' I heard our Company commander calling. I went there and others came, but very many people were missing. 'First Company, Infantry Regiment 112 assemble here!' called the Company commander once again. One more person turned up. Nobody said anything. Everyone thought about their lost comrades. 'Break step, march!' The reformed companies moved out into the night, retreating. The village was completely evacuated.

On high ground behind the village we had to dig a trench. This was a rough task in the hard limestone. At about midnight I was sent on a patrol with another man and an NCO to find out whether Anglemont had already been reoccupied by the French. The night was dark. As we crept forwards in the roadside ditch we heard steps coming in our direction. We hid in the bushes at the edge of the road. A French patrol of eight men went slowly along the verge of the road, hardly a metre from us, without noticing us. We stayed calm, and didn't move. In the village we heard people running and people speaking French. Thus we could be sure that the village had been reoccupied. Shortly after that we heard shooting in the vicinity of the Germans. Six Frenchmen came panting back. Two were missing. We went back and reported what we had seen.

There was no question of getting any sleep that night. At long last, towards morning we were able to get food from the field kitchen. The following morning, when the French saw our trenches, they fired shells at us. One of the first ones was a direct hit, which tore three men apart. We remained there for several days. A battery of German field artillery which was brought up under cover was blown to bleeding bits by the French artillery in a few minutes. It was a dreadful sight when you had to pass by it on bright moonlit nights. Soon we made a big detour to avoid the battery as the stink was unbearable. Nobody seemed to think of burying them.

One night the French tried to attack our trench, but they were driven back. On the following day my comrade Camill Rein from Hagenbach was killed when his head was split open by a splinter from a shell.[10] Roger Alfons from Obersept was badly injured in the leg. The French had withdrawn to the woods again. One evening the order came: 'Attack!' My room-mate Uts said: 'Richert, I'm not going to make it home, I can feel it.' I tried to talk him out of it, but he insisted that it was true. We advanced in two thin lines of troops. I was furious. What was the point in sending a few men like this to be shot dead? We headed off more to the right and passed Anglemont in the direction of the woods. Single shots fell. Ping, the bullets whizzed past our ears. The man next to me fell silently to the ground. 'Ooooh!' shouted NCO Liesecke, throwing his gun away and shaking his hand. One of his fingers had been shot off.[11] Tack, tack, tack rattled a machine gun over there. 'Lie down. Dig in.' We fell to the ground and started digging. My comrade Uts was sent with two others to a clump of alder and willow bushes about three hundred metres ahead of us to check whether it was still occupied by French troops. It was beginning to get dark. The patrol had not yet returned. The Company Commander said: 'The next three people' – I was one of them – 'should advance to the bush to find out what has happened to the three men.' We were quite afraid, but we had to go. We very carefully crept towards the bush, lying down frequently to listen. We could not hear anything. In the darkness we could see the outline of the bushes. Eventually we got there and crept into the bushes with our fingers on the triggers and our bayonets at the ready. Then we heard a quiet rattle. In front of us lay Uts – dead[12] – and a few steps further on lay the soldier who was making the noise in his death-throes. He had been shot in the stomach. There was no sign of the third man. We ran back and reported to the Company Commander. Then we lay back down in the line.

An order came from the left: 'Everyone withdraw quietly! Pass it on!' This was good news. We all got up and hurried backwards. In the meantime it

[10] According to the records, Rein, who had worked in a brickyard, died of a shell splinter on the 5th of September 1914.

[11] According to the records he was wounded by a shot to his left hand on the 10th of September 1914.

[12] According to the records he fell after being shot in the chest on the 10th of September 1914 at 7.00am while on patrol.

had become pitch black. We were stumbling around in furrows and shell-holes, and some of us fell over, but we still knew the direction to our trench. Several times soldiers walking ahead of me suddenly broke into a run. What's up, I thought – then I started running too. The horrible stench of corpses assailed my nostrils. 'Hold your breath! Run away!' This smell came from dead bodies which had already started to decay, but which could not be seen in the dark. Eventually we reached our trench and occupied it. We regained a sense of security. Almost all the soldiers grumbled: 'What a stupid thing to do! Advance, get a few blokes killed, and then retreat again, without any goal or purpose.' 'Is everyone there?' asked the Company Commander. 'Yes sir!' 'The Company is to withdraw with all its equipment and meet up at the church in Ménil.' Now, what's that supposed to mean? asked the soldiers. We put our packs back on, took our guns, climbed out of the trench and groped our way towards Ménil in the dark. Poor old comrade Uts, I thought to myself, now you're lying there dead in the bushes, but at least you have put the suffering of war behind you – you are almost more fortunate than I am.

When we arrived in Ménil it was crawling with soldiers. Everyone was asking the same question: 'What's up?' The order: 'Companies are to assemble' sounded through the night. We went on, while several battalions marched past us in the opposite direction. 'Break step, march!' We stopped in the woods above Baccarat. In the woods we heard the artillery drivers calling out as they urged their horses on. Several batteries of baggage retreated past us. 'The first Company of Infantry Regiment 112 is to act as a rearguard.' So now we could be certain: the area for which thousands of poor soldiers had given their lives was to be evacuated. When everyone else had marched past us we marched off too. I toyed with the idea of staying behind to wait for the arrival of the French and surrender. But the dammed discipline stopped me. And maybe the Frenchmen might shoot me or stab me to death when they see their pillaged and destroyed villages. So I went on.

When we crossed the Meurthe Bridge in Baccarat several military engineers were preparing to blow it up. We had hardly left the town before a massive explosion blew it into the air. We retreated for about another twenty kilometres until we reached a village where we stopped and were given coffee and bread. Then we had a few hours of rest, after which we went to one of the hills above the village with entrenching equipment and dug a trench. We were looking forward to staying here for a while. Far away from us we could hear the boom-boom of the French artillery. So they had not heard anything about our retreat, and were firing at our empty trenches. As night was falling we once again heard the order: 'Get ready!' We sat and waited. What's happening now? Advance or retreat? From the rear we heard troops arriving. It was a reserve regiment coming to relieve us.

23

We marched back for the whole of the night. At daybreak at Deutsch-Avrincourt we crossed the border between Lorraine and France. We were given quarters in barns in the village of Azoudange. During the following six days we marched through the whole of Lorraine via Mörchingen, Rémilly and Metz to Vionville. From Metz we once again heard the sound of shellfire and by evening we were quite near to it. Brr, goose pimples ran over my back, for fear of what the future had in store for us. We spent the night in Vionville. I hauled a bundle of straw into a looted food shop and lay down on it with my comrade Gautherat.

Before dawn, alarm. Everybody leapt up out of their sleep. Packs on. Form up outside with your gun in your hand – all in a few minutes. We were each given a mug of coffee and a piece of dry army bread. When we had eaten it was 'Forwards! March!'

The morning was unfriendly, rainy and foggy. We had marched for about an hour when the order came: 'Spread out!' The fog disappeared, the sun appeared. About four hundred metres ahead of us we could see a wood. That's where we were heading. Ping, ping the bullets were whizzing about our ears. 'Forwards, March, March, to attack!' yelled the officers. We ran towards the woods with our bodies bent forwards. Some men fell. It was well-aimed shrapnel. Those accursed 75mm field guns! The Frenchmen withdrew. We occupied the wood. Then it continued in a narrow hollow in a meadow between woods. Nearby stood the fat battalion doctor and he kept shouting 'The Fortress of Maubeuge has fallen', probably with the intention of encouraging us. Crash, bang, shrapnel shells exploded over the hollow. We went on at the double to get away from the danger. Then we heard: 'The battalion doctor has fallen.' We were getting strong rifle fire from a small wood on a hillock straight ahead of us. We jumped back into the wood and then crept to the edge of the wood and all fired at the little wood. The French fire dwindled and then stopped completely. We advanced and took possession of the wood. The French troops had disappeared.

Towards evening we had to bury the dead Frenchmen who were lying in the wood. They were all older soldiers, about the age of forty. I really felt sorry for these poor chaps, almost all of whom were fathers. Due to the terrain, it was not possible to dig them respectable graves. Thirty centimetres down we hit chalk. When we laid them in, their bodies were level with the ground. We covered them with some earth. The work was over. Nobody looked to find their names or other means of identification, with the result that these poor chaps would be counted among the missing. We spent the night in the wood. A cold wind was blowing, and there was a shower of rain, with the result that we got soaked and felt really cold. What for? For whom? I was overcome by an impotent rage. That didn't help. With my teeth chattering, and near to despair, I sat on some pine branches which I had bent down, and stared out into the night, thinking of my home, my family, and my bed. I was overcome with an incredible longing for my home and my loved ones. I had to cry. Will I see them again? Hardly. The end of the war? Hard to think when. The thought came to me: do I actually still have a home, are my parents still alive? Or where are they? Since the outbreak of war I had received one letter from them, dated the start of August. What might have happened since then! So near to the border! Possibly everything might have been shot to pieces or burnt, and my relatives might have fled. Where to? This uncertainty was a terrible torture to me. Now my cup of sorrows was full, with the uncertainty about my future and the worry about my home and my relatives. I was no longer able to think about sleep. I got up, ran out of the wood, and beat myself with my hands to try to get warm. Eventually the dawn came. What I would give for a hot cup of coffee! No field kitchen. Nothing. We went to the village of Flirey, which lay ahead of us. As usual, rabbits and chickens were slaughtered. Everything was taken as if the owners were not there. We saw practically no-one; almost all of them had hidden when we arrived. I went into a stall in the hope of finding a cow, so that I could get myself some milk. With a lot of effort I managed to get about half a litre. In the meantime other soldiers fetched the rabbits and chickens from the stall. Then the door opened, and an old farmer came into the stall. When he saw the empty rabbit hutches and the chicken run he beat his head with his hands and said: 'Mon Dieu! Mon Dieu!' I felt sorry for him, and went out feeling ashamed.

Now each of us was trying to cook something. Some people were cooking rabbits; some were plucking chickens, while others were plundering a bee stand, turning the baskets upside down and boring out the honey with their bayonets, with the result that they squashed a number of bees to death as they were not able to fly in the cool morning air. Other people were shaking the plums from the trees. I fetched myself a few. After that I pulled some potato plants from the ground, took the potatoes, peeled them and put them in my canteen with some water and salt and started to cook them. As I really wanted some honey too, I took some and put it in the lid of my canteen. When I had just got my water warm, I heard the order 'Get ready! On we go!' Nobody asked whether we had eaten or not. I poured away the hot water but left the potatoes in the canteen, in the hope that I would be able to finish cooking them later on. Then I put the lid on my canteen, and we headed out of the village in the direction of the French.

We passed the village of Essey. We had hardly left the village before the dance started once again. French shrapnel shells flew towards us; fortunately to start with they flew over our heads. Soon we were getting light infantry fire from a wood ahead of us, and some people were hit. Our artillery shelled the wood, and the French infantry withdrew. We occupied the wood. Through the wood ran a narrow meadow valley, about two hundred metres wide, and a fairly high railway embankment had been built along it.

We occupied it. Suddenly, from the wood opposite we came under heavy infantry fire. The reserve soldier Kalt who was standing next to me was hit and rolled down the embankment. Several others suffered the same fate. We could not see any of the French troops, but soon their fire was so strong that nobody tried to raise his head to shoot. After a heavy bombardment by our artillery, the French shooting subsided.

About another hour later came the order that acting officer Bohn[13] should take four men to search the wood; it was my misfortune to be selected for this patrol. With fearful hearts, we entered the wood, constantly in danger of being laid low by a bullet. We crept carefully through the low dense copse and then came to a straight path (firebreak) in the wood, from which you could see to the edge of the woods on the other side. We could see no signs of Frenchmen. Hiding as far as possible in the undergrowth we advanced along the path. All at once I saw something red in the bushes about twenty metres away. I got ready to fire, but as it did not move we advanced slowly towards it. In front of us, near a shell-hole we found an older French soldier whose leg had been torn off at the knee. The stump of his leg was bound up with a shirt. As a result of the loss of blood the poor chap's face had already turned quite yellow and he was very weak. I knelt down beside him, put my pack under his head and gave him a drink from my water bottle. He said 'Merci' and indicated with his fingers that he had three children at home. I felt very sorry for the poor chap, but I had to move on. I pointed in his direction and said 'Allemand Hospital'. He smiled weakly and shook his head, as if to say that that was no longer possible. Gradually we crept to the other side of the wood. Acting officer Bohn sent me back with one of the others with the message that the wood was clear. As we passed the wounded man once again I saw that he had a rosary in his hand and was praying. With one hand he pointed to his tongue to indicate that he was thirsty. I gave him the rest of the water from my bottle. When we returned about half an hour later with the Company, he was lying there dead, with his rosary still in his hand.

We occupied the edge of the woods. I stood at the entrance to the firebreak and looked across the hilly area in front of us. Then I saw a French soldier about five hundred metres away. When he saw me he lay down; then I saw the smoke from his shot rising, and a bullet hit the ground about a metre ahead of me. Now I crept into the undergrowth as quickly as I could and tried to dig a hole for cover, but the ground was a mass of roots, so this was not possible. We heard the rattle of a salvo, and the bullets whizzed crackling through the bushes. As we had no cover, we soon had dead and wounded. The private from our barrack room, Mundiger, caught a bullet

---

[13] Bohn was a trainee teacher, aged thirty-two, who had joined in 1908 as a volunteer for one years' service.

through his artery on the upper half of his left arm which caused the blood to shoot out of the front of his sleeve like it would out of a pipe.[14] I quickly applied a tourniquet above the wound, cut off the sleeve, and bandaged the wound. In order to get away from the fire, I led him back together with another comrade. Now the heavy artillery from the Forts of Toul sent us their sugar cones.[15] They whizzed gurgling over us and exploded with a fearful crash back in the woods. When we reached the railway embankment where our dead from the morning were still lying, I wanted to follow the railway line to the village of Essey, but the wounded man insisted that we should go to the road which passed nearby. I did not want to quarrel, so went along the embankment in the direction of the road. We had hardly gone any distance before one of the large shells exploded on the tracks with a terrifying roar. Earth, splinters, stones and sections of rail flew over our heads and we were covered in smoke and dust, but remained unharmed. If the wounded man had followed my advice, all three of us would have been torn to pieces. The wounded man, who had previously collapsed from weakness several times, now hurried along so fast that I could hardly keep up with him, until he collapsed once again on the meadow. Towards evening we reached the village of Essey, where we took him to the doctor.

As I did not feel like going back to the front, I decided to spend the night in the village. I went to a woman and asked for some *pommes de terre*. When I got them, I gave her two Nickel. How astonished the woman looked! Never before had she been paid for anything by a German soldier. They just took whatever they wanted. Now I set a small fire in the yard and cooked the potatoes. The woman then also brought me out a litre of milk. When I offered to pay, she did not take the money, but just indicated that I should drink it in peace. As I was really hungry, it tasted excellent. Afterwards I lay down in the barn to spend the night. It was a pleasure to sleep in safety, dry and warm.

In the night I was wakened by the sound of troops marching back on the road. I got up and asked who they were. It was my battalion. I quickly put on my pack and joined them. About a kilometre behind and above the village we stopped, formed a line, and started to dig a trench. This was difficult work as we could not see anything, and because at a depth of about thirty centimetres we hit hard chalk. Despite this, by morning we were one metre deep. Our trench ran through a field of vines. I ate some of the half-ripe grapes. As a consequence I had stomach pains and diarrhoea.

Half of the troops were permitted to sleep in the wood to the rear; it was the last days of September 1914. About midday, post was distributed and I

[14] According the records, the mason Mundiger, who was twenty-three at the time, was wounded by a shot in the upper arm at Essey on the 25th of September 1914.
[15] Soldiers' terminology for heavy shells.

was given the first letter from my home town, which had been occupied by the French since the start of the war. How happy I was to read that my relatives were still healthy and living at home. As my home village was only about eight kilometres from the front, I was always afraid that it would be evacuated.

On the following evening we had to go back to the trench. The French attacked at night; without seeing anything, we shot out into the night. As people believed that they were close to our positions, our artillery also fired very close to us. When the morning dawned and the four men from the outpost situated in a short trench about fifty metres ahead of us did not return, I was sent forward with another man to find out what had happened. We crept out there. All four of them were lying there dead, some of them with their guns still at the ready. They had been killed by the German artillery firing too close, as could be seen by the fact that their wounds were on the backs of their heads and on their backs. My comrade from the barracks, Sandhaas, was one of them.[16] We left them lying, crawled back and reported.

During the day half of the men stayed in the trenches, while the others went back to build shelters for the reserve troops. As it was a warm afternoon, we were working in shirts and trousers. Soon we saw a French plane circling over us. He had seen us in our white shirts, then he flew away again and nobody thought any more about it. But suddenly we heard shells approaching and about eight of them landed among us and close to us. Immediately there were screams of pain, as many people had been hit. Most people ran away in all directions. I tried to hide as deep as I could in the hole I had been digging. Then the second wave of shells hit. One of them exploded in the heap of earth above me, which I had dug out myself. Another one landed among the rifles which had been laid to one side, destroying a number of them. Now I ran away as fast as my feet could carry me, with my hands in front of me, through the bushes. The third wave of shells exploded behind me. Soon I reached a railway embankment where I crawled into an underpass in which several other comrades were cowering. After the end of the shooting, we cautiously approached the place we had been working. There lay the torn corpses of several comrades, and a number of seriously wounded men. A good comrade of mine by the name of Kramer had had his stomach torn open and his guts were hanging out. He asked me and pleaded with me to shoot him dead as he could not bear the pain any longer. With the best will in the world, I was unable to fulfil his request. Now the battalion doctor came. To start with he bandaged up the Company Commander, who had had one leg torn off at the calf. Then he dealt with

[16] According to the records, the 22-year-old cigar maker Sandhaas was killed near Essey by a shot in the stomach.

Kramer. He sorted out his intestines, sewed him up, and gave us the order to carry the wounded man back. We made a stretcher from some poles, laid coats and tents on it and then lifted the wounded man carefully onto it, and carried him back. He was immediately transported further by an ambulance. Two months later he wrote to me that he was completely cured, as his intestines had not been damaged and only his skin and his stomach wall had been torn open.[17]

The next night it was my turn to collect the food. Several of us were making our way along a path in the woods. Suddenly an infantry shell tore the brass sheet on the top of my helmet, to which the spike is fitted, in two. If it had been two centimetres lower then I would have had it. In the last night of September we were relieved by other troops and marched thirty-five kilometres back to Metz. We arrived at daybreak and were quartered in a cinema. We were allowed three hours sleep, after which we were to clean our rifles, followed by an inspection. I made up my mind to have an easy day, so I boarded the tram and went into the town. I really wanted to have a good meal as I hated the monotonous food from the field kitchens. It was so good that I had lunch in three different places. Afterwards I went to a pastry shop where I had a piece of cake and a milky coffee. Then I had a look around the town, especially the beautiful cathedral, bought a stock of chocolate and sausage, and rejoined the Company in the evening. The sergeant had a go at me: 'Well, where did you get to today?', to which I calmly replied: 'I had a look around Metz.' During the day, new troops had come from Germany to replace the significant losses. Among them was August Zanger from Struth. As we had been good friends in the past, we were really pleased that we had met up again. We went straight to the sergeant and asked to be put in the same group, and he agreed to this.

The Journey to Northern France

On the 2nd of October 1914 we were entrained and travelled along the Mosel to Trier. A beautiful journey through the rear of the Eifel, through Belgium via Liege, Brussels and Mons to Northern France. Belgium is a beautiful, wealthy country with a lot of industry and a large number of coal mines. The land is crossed by numerous railway lines and canals. I also saw my first windmills there. The population looked at us in a hostile manner, which was not too surprising. We left the train between Valenciennes and Douai and then entered the town of Douai, which had been evacuated by the French shortly before. We were quartered in the Cuirassier Barracks. The

---

[17] According to the records, Kramer died on the 27th of September 1914, two days after being wounded.

commander of our regiment made a speech in the yard of the barracks in which he said that the worst of the war was over for us now as we would only have to fight Englishmen and Blacks. We soon discovered differently.

From Douai we then advanced through a beautiful, rich area – coal mines, sugar factories, towns, villages and workers' settlements, one after the other. The country roads were almost all paved. In the area of Richebourg we had our first encounter with the English. We were to creep up on them through a filthy roadside ditch. At the entrance to a field we had to run across in order to reach the ditch on the other side. The English soldiers soon noticed us, and everyone who tried to jump across came under a hail of bullets. Soon there were several dead at the entrance. The last five had all fallen. Now it was my turn. As it would have been certain death, I refused to go, although my superior shouted at me. An NCO gave me a direct command to jump. I cold-bloodedly said to him that he should show me how to do it, but he also lacked the courage to do so. So we remained there until it got dark.

The next morning we attacked Richebourg and the English troops were forced to retreat. With the exception of their wounded, we did not take any other prisoners. In almost all the houses we were able to sit down for a meal that the English troops had cooked for us. There was a pig being cooked in a big cauldron, so we shared it out between us.

All around the fields lay German cavalrymen with their horses. They had been killed in skirmishes while on patrol. Towards evening we formed a line outside the village and dug foxholes which were occupied by one to four men. About midnight my friend Zanger, an 18-year-old volunteer and I were sent to an outpost. We three crouched in a trench near a farm track. I was looking straight ahead, while the other two looked to the left and the right. All at once we heard footsteps to the left. Three shapes appeared out of the dark. Each of us drew a bead on one of them. The two younger warriors wanted to shoot, and it took some effort to dissuade them. But I wasn't sure, whether it was Germans or Englishmen. I waited until they were about ten metres away. With my gun at the ready I called out 'Halt! Password!' How shocked the three of them were! However, they knew the correct password. It was three men from my Company, who had occupied the listening post to the left of us. They had been relieved and had then lost their way in the dark. We were very happy not to have shot.

Soon afterwards, we too were relieved. After I had spent a while sleeping in my foxhole the man from the outpost ran back saying 'The English are coming!' Now a wild period of firing started. Our young soldiers fired off their ammunition as fast as they could. I fired five shots. However, as I neither saw nor heard any of the English I saved my ammunition. In the morning a patrol was sent out to search for dead Englishmen. What did they find? Two dead cows and a calf. This attack was naturally easily repulsed.

Then we all had to show our ammunition, and anyone who had none left was thoroughly told off by the people in charge.

Now half the men in the trenches were sent off to aid Regiment 114. This left our position very weakened. In addition, lots of people had gone off to the village to look for food. Suddenly the English artillery started to shell us heavily. Large numbers of artillery and shrapnel shells exploded, scattering death and destruction. Soon lines of English infantry appeared and approached us by leaps and bounds. We fired heavily at them, but as they outnumbered us we withdrew. Quite a lot of us fell before we could reach the houses. We withdrew at the double through a drainage ditch which had been planted with willow stumps, while the English shrapnel shells continued to burst overhead. A number of us fell before they were able to reach the houses. A shrapnel shell cut off the upper part of a rotting willow stump above my head. As a result of the explosion and the shock, I fell flat into the dirty ditch, but then I got up again immediately to get out of the dangerous line of fire. Now the English took over the village, but they did not try to chase us any further. We dug ourselves in and spent several days facing the enemy. We had to be very careful, because the Tommies – as we called the English – were good shots. As soon as one of us showed himself he would lose something.

Then we were relieved and were given three days' rest in the village of Douvrin. Straight away the usual slaughter of rabbits, chickens and pigs started. In short, everything that could be eaten or drunk was taken. Our unit was quartered in a school. Directly opposite us there was a big wine and liqueur shop. The officers had posted a sentry in front of it to prevent the troops from entering. And naturally, to keep it all for themselves. We noticed that the sentry often disappeared into the cellar. Eventually he was so drunk that he sank down at the entrance and fell asleep. Taking advantage of the situation, Zanger and I helped ourselves to several litres of Anisette.[18] Soon the path to the cellar was going like a fair, and by the evening there was nothing much left for the officers.

On the third day, at about midday, we had to march off once again. First we went to the church, where the whole of Regiment 112 gathered together. As the church was already full to overflowing, several companies formed up outside. A padre made a short speech and gave us general absolution. Then we went on. We went past several villages whose inhabitants had fled. Then we reached a canal. The bridge across it had been destroyed, but nearby there was a laden coal barge. Using long poles we managed to shove it across the canal so that the ends were touching the opposite banks and we could get across. We marched on and as it got dark, we stopped at a field of

---

[18] Aniseed liqueur.

sugar beet to spend the night there. None of us anticipated that this might be the last night of our lives. As the night was fairly cold, we were happy to go on as the morning approached. Soon we were able to make out rows of houses in the darkness. We were in the small town of La Bassée, and could hear soldiers working in the gardens building shelters. Then we heard a voice from the darkness: 'Which regiment is that? Which company?' '112, the First.' 'Is Zanger with you?' When the answer yes was given, he came running, and two brothers embraced each other, crying. What a reunion! All three of us were crying, because none of us had heard any news of home for ages. Charles accompanied us to the other end of the town, and then bade us farewell. Soon we heard the command: 'Halt!'

22nd of October 1914 – The Attack on the Village of Violaines

In a field they got us to form up in lines abreast while it was still dark. Then we advanced. As the dawn approached, we started to see houses and fruit trees. It was the village of Violaines. We attached our bayonets to our rifles and headed towards the village at the double. Instead of keeping silent, our young soldiers shouted 'Hurrah' as they had been trained to do. As a result of their shouts, the English troops in the village were alerted. Soon single shots fired towards us, one minute later shots crackled out of all the windows and doors and from behind hedges and walls. One of the first bullets hit the man next to me in the stomach. He plunged to the ground uttering a terrifying scream. August Zanger turned to me and called: 'Nick, have they hit you?' Just at that moment, three bullets ripped through his pack and his canteen, without injuring him. The man next to him was shot in the shoulder and fell to the ground. We ran behind a thorn-bush as quickly as possible. We all hid behind the hedge, so the English soldiers concentrated their fire on it. Soon several comrades lay motionless. Together with further lines of advancing troops we charged through the hedge and stormed through the gardens towards the houses, in the course of which more of our people were hit. As we had superior numbers, the English troops withdrew. We jumped between the houses to the road beyond and just managed to catch an Englishman who was trying to climb over the wall of the church-yard, which ran parallel to the road. As the bullets were whizzing around us, we were forced to take cover. The Englishman thought we were going to kill him, but we let him know that we did not intend to harm him. He was very pleased and wanted to give us his money, but we did not take it. A lieutenant who came up made us advance. Further down on the road stood an English ammunition waggon. Underneath it lay an English soldier who was firing at the German soldiers who were advancing from the other side of the village. I touched him from behind with my bayonet. He looked round and was very frightened, but instead of surrendering he jumped out from the other side of the waggon and tried to escape. We shouted 'Halt!' but he ran on. Then Drummer Richert from Reichweiler[19] shot him down. A bit further back in a roadside ditch was an English autocannon which was pouring projectiles at us. A few well-aimed bullets laid the gun crew low.

The regiment gathered in the village, and now the task was to storm the English trench which lay about three hundred metres behind the village. We were met by a fearful barrage of machine-gun and infantry fire. Despite heavy losses we stormed the trench. Some of the English soldiers surrendered, while many of them fled, but were almost all gunned down due to the lack of cover on the flat ground. In order to escape the artillery fire, Zanger and I took a wounded soldier back to the village and carried him to the doctors. Then we hid in the cellar of a house which had been stocked with food by its inhabitants. In one corner sat a woman and a girl of about twenty. They were very afraid of us. By using gestures we were able to explain that they did not need to be afraid of us. We spent three pleasant days together. We set up a stove in the cellar, with a chimney leading out of it, and the two women cooked the chickens and rabbits which we fetched in the evenings from the village. The village was continuously under English artillery fire. Our house suffered several hits, and on one occasion bricks fell down the steps to the cellar. On the evening of the third day we heard footsteps crashing down the stairs. It was a lieutenant, the Adjutant of the Regiment. 'You dammed cowards get a move on out of here!' he yelled at us. The girl, whose name was Céline Copin, gave us some medallions depicting the Holy Mother of God as mementos. In the street there were about sixty men who had all hidden in the cellars. The Adjutant of the Regiment led us all to the Commander of the Regiment who read us a real lecture, but we did not mind that. In the meantime, our Regiment had advanced by about five kilometres and was occupying the village of Rue Du Vert. We learned that the day when Violaines was taken had cost our Company over one hundred men, more than two thirds of the total number. As the losses had been replaced by new recruits from Germany, there were many new faces. We lay in a barn for the night. Our new Company Commander held a speech, which I can still remember exactly: 'I am First Lieutenant Nordmann.[20] I have taken over command of the 1/112. I expect everyone to do his duty. To hell with anyone who does not! Dismiss!'

The following morning, while it was still dark, we were organised into groups and then we advanced under cover to a farm which was located

---

[19] Three days later, Drummer Richert, a 'cementer' who was born in 1891, was wounded. In May 1915 he fell in a battle at Liévin.

[20] Nordmann, who was born in 1885, had been in the army for nine years by this stage.

about two hundred metres from the village. From there we were to advance across the field in groups of eight to some willow trees and dig ourselves in. We did not know where the English troops were. The first group jumped. Soon we heard shots. We saw straight away that three men fell. The others ran behind a heap of wheat sheaves standing in the field. Now the second group, to which Zanger and I had been allocated, had to jump. I can't describe to anyone what my feelings were as I forced myself to do so. But the terrible force of circumstances prevailed. There was no argument. Just a quick prayer and off we went. We had barely become visible, when it felt like we were surrounded by a swarm of buzzing bees. The man ahead of me stumbled, threw his arms in the air, and fell on his back. Another man fell on his face. Then I noticed that no-one from the first group apart from NCO Luneg was still alive. We threw ourselves to the ground and pressed our faces into the soft ground of the field. All the English soldiers in the trench now concentrated their fire on us. The bullets hit the ground all around us, showering us with earth. Now an English machine gun started up too. The bullets flying over us were less than a hands-breadth above us, and one after the other, people were being killed. I too felt that my final hour had come, thought of my loved ones at home and prayed. Zanger, who was lying near me, said 'We can't go on lying here'. He raised himself slightly and noticed a farm track with ditches on either side about fifty metres ahead of us. In one leap we jumped up and rushed towards the safety of the ditch. Although the English troops directed a rattling fast fire at us, we miraculously arrived unharmed. NCO Kretzer, the leader of our group arrived right after us. As the trench at this position was very shallow, we crept on our stomachs towards some foxholes which had been abandoned by the English soldiers. While we were creeping forward, NCO Kretzer was hit in the back, he said 'Please greet ...' to me, and was dead.[21]

Zanger and I were now the sole survivors of our group. As the rest of the Company, which had remained at the farm, had seen our fate, nobody else dared to advance across the field, and so the two of us stayed lying in the foxholes on our own all day. Although the English artillery shelled the village all day, not a single shell was fired in our direction. As night fell we were preparing to return to the Company at the farm, when it arrived to occupy the position which it had been ordered to in the morning. The men were very astonished to find us alive.

We had to draw up a line and dig a trench. Everyone worked as hard as possible to get into the ground as quickly as possible, as single English shots whistled through the air at a regular pace. Now it started to rain. I wrapped

[21] According to the records, the mason Kretzer died on the 23rd of October 1914 at Violaines as a result of a bullet to the head. The entry was apparently recorded on the 22nd of April 1914.

an English cape I had found around my shoulders. When the ditch was deep enough I fetched two sheaves from a heap of straw for Zanger and myself. On the way there, I stumbled over dead bodies. When I had slept for a while in the trench, I woke up because I was feeling cold. I found out that I was lying lengthways in water which had accumulated in the trench as a result of the pouring rain.

Now Sergeant Hutt came along. Zanger, two other men and I were to bury NCO Kretzer, who had been a good friend of his.[22] We searched for a long time in the pitch darkness before we found the corpse. We scraped the sticky wet earth of the field away with our spades, detached his cape from his pack and wrapped him in it, laid him in his grave, which was barely thirty centimetres deep, and covered him up. When we thought we were finished, Zanger felt with his hands to see whether Kretzer was fully covered with earth. It turned out that his nose and his boots were still sticking out, so we covered them. Zanger took the dead man's bayonet and stuck it through the leather scabbard to form a cross, which he placed at the head of the grave.

We had hardly got back to the trench before we got the order to advance quietly. Then we came through an area of low ground overgrown with reeds as tall as a man. By the time we had made our way through the reeds we were all soaked to the skin. The rain fell non-stop. We were given the order: 'Halt! Dig in!' Zanger and I quickly dug a hole. When we were finished we had to advance about ten metres, as the line was not straight. As the English bullets were whizzing over us from the front, the left and the right, we threw the earth up around us to provide better cover. As dawn approached I looked carefully over towards the English and saw their trench about one hundred and fifty metres ahead of us. When the English soldiers spotted our mounds of earth they fired like mad at them for a while. They eased off and I saw that one of the young soldiers who, with two others, had occupied the hole next to ours was cautiously looking towards the English lines. I quickly called to him to take cover, which he did. But his curiosity was too great. After a while he wanted to look across again. Almost as soon as his head was visible, he fell down dead, shot through the forehead. His two comrades wanted to put his corpse into the field behind them as there was not enough room in their foxhole. One of them got up too high and was shot in the back. He fell down dead in the hole and the corpse tumbled down on top of him. Now there were two corpses and one living person in the foxhole. The English fired shrapnel shells at us, but nobody was injured. It was very boring, spending the whole day sitting in a hole in the ground. We were in a field of mangelwurzels.[23] In order to pass the time I fitted my bayonet to my

---

[22] The mason Hutt did not survive the war either; he was wounded in March 1915 and died three months later at the age of twenty-three.

[23] A root vegetable that nowadays is primarily used for feeding cattle and pigs.

rifle, pierced a mangelwurzel, and pulled it into the hole. Then I stuck the bayonet into the mangelwurzel from below, put my helmet on top and raised the contraption up above the cover of the trench. The English soldiers thought it was a head and shot at it wildly. Very soon, both the mangelwurzel and the helmet were full of holes like a sieve.

The following night we finished a continuous trench. Towards the morning the 3rd Battalion came as reinforcements with the order to attack the English position. This was a mad venture. The officers drew their revolvers and drove us out of the trenches. No sooner were we visible than the English troops started to fire at us. Many of us fell to the ground immediately. The rest turned round and ran back into the trench. The heavily wounded were left lying. Many groaned and wailed until nightfall, until they too died. Despite this, two days later, when further reinforcements arrived, another attack was made. Despite heavy losses we got as far as the English trench, but it was not possible to get into it, as the English troops stood man to man and shot us down. There was nothing else for it but to get back to our trench as quickly as possible. The part of the field between the two trenches was now strewn with corpses and with wounded men who could not be helped. Once again, Zanger and I survived uninjured. The following days passed peacefully. As it rained frequently, and the rain water gathered in the trenches, there was so much mud that it was soon impossible to move.

All of a sudden, we were informed that the English trench was occupied by black people – Indians. And sure enough, here and there we noticed a turban – their head-cover. As we did not trust them, half of us had to do sentry duty at night. One dark night, suddenly one of the Indians jumped into our trench and held his hands in the air. Nobody had heard him coming. He kept pointing towards the English lines and made a sign of cutting their throats. A soldier who had signed up for a year, who understood English, was fetched, and as the Indian could also speak some English, the two of them could make themselves understood. The Indian said that he and his comrades hated the English and that they all wanted to cross over to us and fight against them. We believed him and let him go to fetch his comrades, as he had said he would do. We listened out into the night to find out whether they were coming. Soon a peal of mocking laughter showed us that the black man had really fooled us.

The next day our heavy artillery was meant to bombard the enemy trenches, but the shells fell short. The first one exploded in the middle of our trench. Three soldiers were torn apart by them and their body parts were flung high into the air. The Indians laughed and yelled with joy when they saw this. The second shell exploded several metres behind the trench. Now we were told that if someone would volunteer to go back to the village to phone the battery and let them know that their shells were falling short then he would be awarded the Iron Cross. Only one man volunteered, Lance

Corporal Himmelhahn. He started to crawl back along a drainage ditch, which was not deep enough to give him cover. He had not gone fifty metres before the Indians saw him. A number of shots were fired. We saw the dirt fly up near him. Soon he lay motionless. In the evening when we pulled him into the trench we were able to see with our torches that he had been hit by two bullets. We put him in a shell-hole behind our trench and covered him up.

One morning after a rainy night six rifles were missing. The Indians had pulled them out through the loopholes and fled with them without being observed by the sentries. We were there for about fifteen days without being relieved. As it rained frequently there was so much mud and dirt that you kept getting stuck. We had nowhere to lie or sit down, and we were constantly soaked to the skin. Our feet were never warm, and many soldiers suffered from colds, coughs and sore throats. The nights seemed endless. In short, it was a desperate life. Every day we suffered several losses to shrapnel shells. Fetching food at night-time was particularly dangerous as the terrain was very flat and the English sentries fired their rifles and machine guns at the area behind our trench. One night, the man who was fetching the food for our group went missing. We waited until it was nearly morning. When he still had not arrived, some of our men went to look for him. They soon found him lying dead. The canteens were lying half empty beside him. The following night another poor comrade lost his life. He had fetched a bundle of straw from the village and decided to slide down into the trench not knowing that someone had left a rifle with a fixed bayonet there. As he slid down, he impaled his body onto it from below, up to his neck. He let out a terrible shriek and died. Then, unexpectedly we heard: 'We are going to be relieved'. And really, the next night Infantry Regiment 122 took over the trench, and we marched back. It was a beautiful, free feeling for us when we were out of shooting range. Then we stopped and fetched food from the field kitchen. When day broke, we went further back.

On the battlefield of Violaines lay the bodies of English soldiers who had fallen three weeks before. We saw a number of ravens sitting on them, having a meal. All the Germans who had fallen had been buried. We took up quarters in the small town of La Bassée. But what did it look like! If you haven't seen it you can't imagine it. None of the inhabitants remained. In all of the houses and rooms everything was topsy-turvy. Clothes, hats, photographs – in short: everything which was in the rooms was lying all over in disorder. You also saw a quantity of immoral pictures and texts lying around. Most of the furniture had been smashed up and used as firewood. In a shop selling material for making clothes soldiers had torn strips of the rolls of material to make themselves puttees. In a hat shop I was hoping to find a cap with ear-flaps to protect me from the cold when I was in the trenches. In the shop it was the same picture: caps, hats, straw hats and top hats. Everything lay on the floor to a height of about half a metre, and the soldiers were walking across this in their filthy boots. The house next door had been a shop selling china and glassware. Everything was in broken fragments on the floor. I could not see anything that remained intact apart from some little brandy glasses in a corner.

There were eight of us in a room, in the vicinity of the church. In the night we were wakened by a fearful banging. The house was shaking as in an earthquake. The church tower, which had previously been hit by a number of artillery shells, had collapsed. We were in La Bassée for three days and used the time to dry our clothes and to rid them of dirt as far as possible. Then we went back to the trenches. We were about one kilometre further north than we had been before. Opposite us lay the villages of Festubert and Givenchy. Once again we had Indians opposite us at a distance of about eighty metres. Soon we had a number of dead and wounded who had been hit from their loopholes. For this to happen there must have been an Indian constantly at the ready who would shoot at us the moment we moved. Zanger and I did all that we could to find the chap. However, we were unable to find his position. Then one night, it snowed. Through the English loopholes we were able to see the snow at the back of the trench. Now, as soon as an Indian stood at the loophole, the white patch of snow disappeared. Zanger lay in wait. Soon the white patch disappeared. The Indian was observing us again. Zanger shot, the Indian was hit. Now we had a bit more peace.

We got the order to storm the Indians' trench. Our pioneers dug saps – zigzag trenches – reaching close to the Indians' position. One night I was sent with eight others to cover the pioneers who were working out front. We stood about six metres behind them with our guns at the ready and listened out into the dark night. We could not see or hear anything. Suddenly two dreadful screams, which came from our pioneers, sounded through the night. We shot quickly into the darkness and then jumped to help our pioneers. But both of them lay on the floor of the sap, the one dead, and the other seriously wounded. Both had been stabbed by Indians who had crept up on them.

On the 21st of November we conquered the Indian trench. From the saps, hand grenades, which I saw in use for the first time, were thrown into the Indian trenches. Then we jumped across and drove back the Indians in the trench. In a dead-end trench leading to the latrine we were able to take more than sixty of the brown fellows. One of our young lieutenants, who had only been in action for a few days, climbed out of the trench and called to the Indians 'Hands up!' in English. But some shots were fired and the lieutenant tumbled head over heels into the trench. My Company, which had been brought back up to a strength of two hundred and forty men, only lost three men and the lieutenant. In the trench lay several dead Indians; the older ones had long hair, while the younger ones' hair had been cropped short. They were all wearing new clothes and had really only been in the trenches for a short time. Scattered around in the trench were lots of new woollen blankets and lots of their food, which I could not identify. We took the English loopholes and built them in on the opposite side, facing the Indian troops, who had occupied another trench about two hundred metres further back. Whenever we saw a turban, we shot right at it, and soon nobody dared to raise his head.

End of 1914 into 1915

22nd of November 1914 – Terrible Night Battle with Indian Troops

As it was getting dark, we came under a deluge of rifle fire, but we fortunately only had a few casualties as we all lay down in the bottom of the trench. Some men were buried; some of them were able to free themselves, in the case of the others we were able to dig them out. As we anticipated a counter-attack, half of us had to do sentry duty. Zanger and I took it in turns. While one of us stood, the other slept, wrapped in several Indian blankets. I was on duty between four and six o'clock in the morning. As I did not trust the Indians, I peered out into the night. Suddenly I thought I heard a noise ahead of me. The next sentry to me, who was only two metres away, asked me whether I had had heard anything. When I said that I had, we undid our safety catches, got ready to fire and tried to penetrate the darkness with our eyes. For about half an hour we did not see or hear anything and we were feeling more relaxed again.

Suddenly the loud sound of a whistle pierced the peace of the night. At the same moment, a salvo burst close to us and with a fearful, shrill scream the Indian soldiers stormed towards us. We were completely surprised and many of us lost our wits. I quickly fired off my five bullets and then fitted my bayonet and placed myself at the front wall of the trench. Zanger staggered awake and to start with, in the agitation, he was unable to find his gun. When he got it, he took up a position next to me. The Indian soldiers were firing down into the trench, but as we pressed ourselves forward against the wall of the trench, their bullets flew over us. They could not see us in the dark trench, while we could see them clearly as they were outlined against the sky. We shot and stabbed above us and none of the Indians dared to force his way into the trench. Soon, however a terrible yelling told us that about thirty metres away from us the Indian soldiers had made their way into the trench. This led to a confused muddle. The crowd shoved us from our places and pushed us so close together that I was hardly able to reach into my ammunition pouch to reload my rifle. In the confusion and the darkness many of us shot their own comrades in the head. After the Indian troops had won over a stretch of our trench, a number of them climbed out

40

the back of the trench, ran along the outside, and fired into our trench from behind. We really were in hell. The Indian soldiers fired into the trench from ahead, from behind, and from the side. We all rushed towards the communication trench leading back to our previous position. The people who were hit fell and were trampled to death. Everyone was screaming and shouting. There was a terrible crowd at the entrance to the trench; everyone wanted to get through first, but the entrance was so narrow that people could only get in one at a time. Eventually Zanger and I managed to get into the trench. We had hardly run back ten metres before we could go no further, because the few reserve troops who had been stationed in the old position wanted to come to our assistance. Soon we were tightly packed in as the people behind us were desperate to get back. Then we heard the call: 'Every man for himself!'

Zanger and I threw our rifles out of the trench and ran back across the field. Several times I had to bend down to the ground to avoid being seen by the Indian soldiers. Soon I lost sight of Zanger. Suddenly I heard him utter a muffled call for help. I leapt in his direction and quickly saw two figures wrestling with each other in the darkness. I was able to identify the Indian by his turban and rendered him unable to fight. We ran to our old position as quickly as possible. Zanger wanted to quickly load his gun, but his magazine did not fit. When he looked more closely he realized that he was holding the Indian soldier's gun, and that this was the reason that his magazines did not fit. Every so often, individual soldiers ran back. We fired on any Indian soldiers who could be seen on the field, and they soon disappeared into the trench. Suddenly they appeared a few metres from us in the communication trench. Our shots felled the people in front. We barricaded the communication trench with sandbags and had peace. We were very tired and weary, and our nerves were all shot up. What a state we were in! Filthy from head to foot, my trousers were torn open from the knee to the top and my backpack together with all my possessions was gone as I had not had the time to put it on when the Indian troops attacked. I had also lost my helmet and my ammunition pouches were empty. Zanger and the others were more or less in the same state. About midday our Lieutenant Hüssler, a good officer from Alsace, came and wrote down the names of all the people from the Company who were still there. He counted twenty-four men: so ninety per cent of the Company were gone. Terrible! As I later heard, only sixteen men from 4th Company survived.

The following night we were relieved by another regiment and marched back in the communication trenches. In places we could hardly make any progress and often sank up to our knees in the mud. We were happy when we had a firm road under our feet, marched back to La Bassée, and waited for the dawn. We were given coffee and dry army bread. Not much of a breakfast. We felt that we deserved a better one. When we had eaten, we marched further back. There was no question of marching in line or of discipline. Each of us went as he wanted. Now the Battalion Commander gave the order to sing. A general murmuring was the answer, but nobody sang. We also passed the town of Courièrres where 1,400 miners were killed in a disaster a few years ago.[24]

We were quartered in the town of Hénin-Liétard. Zanger and I were allocated to an older married couple. When we arrived the wife was alone. When she saw us, she clapped her hands together above her head, because she had never before seen such dirty, ragged soldiers. We were unshaven as well. She indicated that we should follow her into the yard at the back, and gave us soap, warm water and brushes. After we had got ourselves relatively clean, she got each of us a pair of trousers, a jacket, socks and slippers. How pleasant it was, at long last, to have dry feet once again! The woman was very kind to us, although we could not even communicate with each other by speaking. Then she gave us warm coffee, cognac and bread and butter.

Afterwards I took my rags to the Company Sergeant and asked him for new clothes. After he had checked them, he gave me an authorisation to have new clothes issued at the quartermaster's store. There I was given new trousers, a jacket, boots and a cap. Then I went for a haircut and a shave. After that I returned to my quarters. The woman did not recognize me any more. We spent the evening in the living room. Then the husband came home. He did not seem at all pleased to see us, and looked at us with the most unfriendly expression in the world. Then I said, pointing to us, 'Alsaciens', but he did not believe us. We showed him our pay book in which our home address was recorded. Now he became somewhat friendlier. Afterwards I gave him several cigars. This broke his resistance and he even fetched a bottle of wine. As we were both very tired we indicted that we wanted to sleep. We would have been happy to lie on a bundle of straw, but instead they led us upstairs and the woman showed us a good bed in a friendly room. What a joy it was for me to be able to sleep in a bed! During the past four months I had only slept in a bed once. We soon fell asleep, but I woke up again, and it was impossible for me to keep my feet from moving. My feet, which for weeks had been cold and wet, were now warmed up again and felt as if they were crawling with hundreds of ants. Soon, how-ever, the sweat ran out of my feet, making that part of sheet quite wet. Then I was able to sleep. We stayed for fourteen days with that family and each day we got on better with one another. We ate together, as many a rabbit had to learn. In return, we brought the family new shirts, underpants, laced shoes, a good quantity of cigars and tobacco, and so on. At that time, there was a surfeit of everything.

[24] The accident occurred in 1906.

We only had a few duties to perform, mainly sentry duty. On one occasion I also had to act as guard of honour to a prince of Hohenzollern, who lived in a castle. These birds certainly know how to survive in a war! They filled their chests with medals without ever hearing the whistle of a bullet, ate and drank to excess, and chased the girls. In addition they took big salaries while the ordinary soldier got 53 pennies a day for his dog's life. One day we did sentry duty on a bridge. We were stationed in a house of ill repute. Until then I had never believed, that women's morality could sink so low. In general, in that area there were many girls and women who had sunk very low. Soon the sick bays filled up with soldiers with sexually transmitted diseases.

We were given new replacement teams from Germany, including a number of volunteers younger than twenty. Once again the order was: 'March to the front!' And it was with regret that we said farewell to our good hosts. Then we got into a better position, with the French about eight hundred metres away. Immediately behind the French position lay the village of Vermelles. Further in the distance lay the town of Béthune. Although that town was within range of German artillery, work in the coal mines continued, as we could see from the smoke. We spent three days in the trench followed by three days in reserve in a workers' settlement one kilometre behind the front, and then we had three days' rest five kilometres further back. Three weeks passed like this without very much happening. Occasionally we would come under heavy artillery fire and there were always some losses. When we were in reserve, we had to work each night digging communication trenches and positions. As the area there is free of woods, we could not build any dugouts as we had no timber, and so we lived the whole time out in the trench, exposed to the rigours of the weather. Our position ran close to a coal mine, Shaft 8, near which a workers' settlement – all beautiful, attractive houses – had been built. There was plenty of coal for building fires. However, as there was no wood, first the shutters, then the doors, furniture, floors and roof battens were taken in order to be able to build fires. In a short time, only the bare walls remained. Our artillery observers were stationed in the mine's tall chimney. The French soon found this out and did not leave us in peace until they had demolished the chimney.

The French started to dig a trench towards us at night. I was delegated to go with two others to the artillery to be trained for three days in the use of a small-calibre Belgian gun. The artillerymen brought the gun into position in a gravel pit about 200 metres behind the infantry trenches; only the barrel stuck out above the level of the ground so the gun was fairly well hidden. The following day we were supposed to fire into the French trench. The first shot fell close, but the cartridge, which belonged to an old system, was filled with loose powder, and as soon as we fired a large cloud of smoke gave away our position. We had hardly fired our second shot, which hit the French trench, when a French shell came flying over, landing about a hundred metres behind us. Now came one shell after another. We fled down into the gravel pit and hid behind the high steep side. Soon our gun got several direct hits and tumbled down into the pit where it came to rest, totally wrecked. We stayed in the pit until it got dark. Then we returned to our Company to resume our duties as infantrymen. So our service as artillerymen quickly came to an end.

Just at this time Lidy Theophil from Struth was killed in action. Zanger and I often visited his grave in the cemetery of the village of Hulluch. At this time Walter Theophil from Struth and Joseph Walch from Merzen joined my Regiment as replacements.

Now came Christmas, the first Christmas of the war. Our Company celebrated it in Vendin-le-Vieil. A large number of presents for the troops had arrived. As Zanger and I, and Gautherat from Menglatt, did not have any contact with home and could therefore not receive any parcels, the leader of our Company gave us some extra presents. Then we got a share of the rest of them like everyone else. In addition, Zanger and I got a big case containing good and useful things donated by a rich lady industrialist in Mannheim who wanted to bring some happiness to soldiers who had lost their homes. We were hardly able to carry our stuff to our quarters at one go. We had a whole table full of chocolate, sugared rolls, sweets, cigars, cigarettes, German salami, sardines in oil, pipes, braces, scarves, gloves and so on. I shared out the sweets and chocolate with the children I met in the street. Soon they all knew me and whenever I showed myself they came running and asked me for sweets. But I was only able to give them some until my stock ran out.

We were ordered to march off in the direction of the Loretto Ridge about twelve kilometres away to the left. We marched through the town of Lens. As night fell we passed through the villages of Louchez, Ablain and St Nazareth which were all within firing range of the French artillery. We dug ourselves in amongst the bushes on the slope, above which lay the ruins of the chapel of Notre-Dame-de-Lorette which had been shelled to pieces. Round the summit lay trenches occupied by French alpine troops. As our position formed a curve, we soon came under heavy-calibre artillery fire. On all sides the large shells crashed in. A foxhole occupied by four men suffered a direct hit; the torn bodies of the occupants were thrown in all directions. There was no chance of running away as anyone who dared show himself was immediately shot down by the alpine troops. There I lost a good comrade by the name of Sand.[25]

[25] See also page 11. According to the records, having returned to the front on the 1st of January 1915, Sand was shot in the head on the 21st of January 1915 and died two days later.

One night, snow fell, and I and four others were sent on a patrol up the hill with Sergeant Hutt. We had pulled on white shirts on top of our uniforms in order to be less visible in the snow. I still do not know what we were supposed to look for up there, it was sheer madness. We were soon spotted and some bullets flew past our ears. One man was shot in the chest. We ran as quickly as we could down the hill to our position. Sergeant Hutt submitted a report which was a pack of lies and was awarded the Iron Cross some days later.

After three days our Company was given a rest in the so-called castle in the moat, a large building which lay in the middle of a stream. Nobody dared to let himself be seen as it was within firing range of the French infantry. One day the building was shelled so heavily by the French artillery that we all fled into the strongly arched basement. There was a terrible thundering and crashing above us and the entrance to the basement was blocked by the falling beams and rubble from the walls. With great difficulty we managed to make an exit and in the evening we crept out one after the other. I happened to find out that the 111th Infantry Regiment was stationed next to us on the left. The reserve soldier Emil Schwarzentrüber, from my home village, was serving in the 11th Company of that regiment. I immediately decided to look for him in the hope of finding news from home, as I had had no news for several months. I went to the village of Saint Nazaire and met some soldiers of the 111th Regiment, who told me that the 11th Company was in position up the hill. They described the route to me and I went to find them. I soon reached the communication trench which led up to their position. As the snow was melting, there was a flow of dirty water running down the trench. Despite all this, I splashed my way upwards through the dark night and eventually reached the position. I asked a sentry about my comrade. He did not know. I asked another, and he directed me to the group where my comrade was. I went there and when I asked I was only given evasive answers. I said goodbye and left. Then someone came running after me, a man from Alsace, and asked if I was a good friend of Emil. When I told him that I was, he said that Emil had deserted two days earlier.

I now returned to my Company and had to help bury a number of the fallen. It was sad work, especially as we never knew how soon it would be our turn. We remained at the Notre Dame de Lorette Ridge for another ten days. Then we were given the order to march back towards our old quarters in Vendin-le-Vieil. I travelled ahead in a baggage waggon as I was foot-sore. As the road at Souchez was constantly bombarded at night time we galloped through safely. When we arrived in Vendin-le-Vieil I set a fire to warm the room, and made coffee for my comrades. The next evening, when mail was being distributed, I received a letter from my parents. As I did not know if they were even still at home I tore the letter open and read: 'St Ulrich, the ... Dear son! We are all well and still at home ...' I could not get any further. Tears of joy and longing welled up in my eyes and I could not read on. As I felt embarrassed in front of my comrades, I went outside. I soon calmed down and was able to read the letter to the end. It only contained good news, and now I was reassured about the fate of my relatives.

We remained in Vendin-le-Vieil for several days and then we were ordered to march in the direction of a place from which we could hear a steady sound of shelling. At night we reached the village of Auchy which was almost completely in ruins. Through a communication trench, which had been partially shot up, we reached the outermost position. At daybreak our artillery and mortars started a fearful bombardment of the trenches, which were occupied by English troops. We were to storm them. We had hardly left our position before the English welcomed us with rapid fire. Despite heavy losses we captured two English trenches – one close behind the other. Almost all the English soldiers who tried to escape through the communication trench were shot down. We were also supposed to capture a third English trench. However, in this trench the English stood close together and shot us down. Soon there was a whole line of dead and wounded in front of their trench, and the rest of the Company fled back to the second English trench. Here, Walther Theophil from Struth fell. It was a terrible sight; there were dead and wounded everywhere, Germans and English all mixed up, and blood trickled out of the wounds. When you looked into the trenches you saw nothing but legs in puttees and clawed hands sticking upwards. The bottoms of these trenches were full of dead Englishmen.

We had to bury the dead who were lying in the positions. We removed some earth at the rear wall of the trench, laid down the dead, and covered them with earth. As there was no other place to sit in the trench, these little hills were used as seats. It started to rain again. The trenches soon filled up with water and mud, and soon we were so filthy that you could not see anything of us but the whites of our eyes, there was so much dirt. Then I was sent to collect ammunition; everywhere I saw the toes of boots, clutching hands, and hair stuck together by mud sticking out of the earth. It was a gruesome sight, which nearly made me despair. It put me off so much that I did not want anything more from life. The fighting there had gone on since October and the fallen from that time were still lying in the field between the trenches. It was impossible to bury them. A bit to the right of my loophole lay a German soldier on his face, with his head towards me. As he fell, his helmet had fallen off, as a result of rotting, the skin and the hair had slipped down, and his cranium, bleached by the sun, was exposed for about the area of a hand. In one hand he still held his rusty rifle with its bayonet, the flesh had already rotted off his fingers, and the bones were sticking out. Especially at night it was quite sinister to see the white skull right in front of me. As a result of the bullets that frequently whizzed around, especially at night, the body had been punctured like a sieve. The next night, the 26th of

January 1915, we were moved about four hundred metres to the right, behind the so-called buffers. We lay on a railway embankment and fired over the tracks towards the English trenches. Soon their artillery started to fire on us. We hid behind the embankment. The shells either exploded on the track above us or flew closely past us into the open country. The following night we were moved two hundred metres to the left again. Right in front of our trench there were several house-high piles of bricks, as there had been a brickyard there, but it had been flattened by the shooting. When it got dark, English soldiers would climb up these piles of bricks from behind and if they caught sight of someone in the trench they would shoot him down. One evening Zanger, comrade Kopf and I were standing chatting about something. Zanger and I were covered by the shoulder protection while Kopf was standing leaning against the back of the trench. Suddenly a shot was fired down from the pile of bricks, and behind the head of our comrade, it shot some of the earth away. He sank groaning to the ground with a hole in his forehead. He was carried back, but he died while being transferred further back in an ambulance.[26]

Of the two hundred and eighty men who had been taken to war with the Company, there were now only five of us left who had taken part in all the action. In addition, the sections had also lost a hundred men who had joined as replacements during the campaign. During an attack which we made on a salient section of English trench, Zanger was injured in the forehead and was sent back.[27] Soon he wrote to me that he was in a military hospital in the town of Douai. In the Company, they used to call us 'the two inseparables'. Now that he was gone, I felt even more put off and I thought of ways to escape this miserable dog's life.

Another comrade of mine, a man from Baden by the name of Benz, was also fed up with the whole thing and we discussed what we should do. All at once, Benz said: 'I've got it!' He took his false teeth out of his mouth and trampled them into the mud with his boot. 'So, now I will report sick with stomach pains and will get sent back to the hospital,' he said. Then it occurred to me that I had a number of bad teeth in my mouth. Although I did not have any toothache, I wound my scarf, which was stiff with mud, round my head and went to the Company Commander and reported sick; I couldn't bear the toothache any more. Then Benz came with his problem. The Company Commander said that he could not send us back. He had received orders that he should keep all the soldiers who still had some

[26] According to the records, the 24-year-old cigar maker Kopf, who was wounded by being shot in the head at the pile of bricks in Auchy on the 29th of January 1915, died on the 31st of January 1915.

[27] According to the records, the 22-year-old mason Zanger was injured in the right eye by a shell splinter at Auchy.

ability to fight in the trenches, as they constantly feared an English attack. Despite our request he refused to give us an authorisation. And without an authorisation by the Company Commander you would not get very far. We went back to our places. The English were constantly firing small mortar shells into our trench. We had to withdraw from the outermost stretch of trench, as it was only sixteen metres from the trench occupied by the English, and they kept throwing hand grenades into it.

Now Benz and I decided to go back without authorisation. We put on our packs, took our guns, and crept to the communication trench leading to the rear. In the dirt there were several dead bodies of soldiers who had fallen while collecting ammunition. We stepped carefully over them and after about four hundred metres we reached the end of the trench, which led into the road. When we wanted to round the corner we encountered a military policeman who demanded our papers. Despite all our talking he did not let us through, and sent us back towards our Company. We went back into the communication trench; after we had gone about fifty metres back, we climbed out of the trench and ran through between some houses in order to get to the road further on. English soldiers saw us and shot at us, but fortunately they did not hit us. We went looking for the Battalion Doctor and found him in a cellar. As we had no authorisation he said 'Cowards!' and sent us on to the Regimental Doctor, who was also in a cellar. When we entered he said: 'What's wrong?' I said that I was suffering from bad tooth-ache. He looked in my mouth and when he saw my bad teeth he immediately gave me an authorisation for Military Hospital II, Dental Department in Douai. My comrade Benz had the same good fortune and the two of us waltzed off. We were euphoric to have escaped the misery in the trenches for some time. In Hénin-Liétard we boarded the train and travelled to the town of Douai. On arrival, I went straight to the Military Hospital. Straight away they pulled two teeth. For each of the next three days they pulled two teeth more. The pain was not trivial, as it was done without injections.

As we were allowed to go out, I went to visit Zanger, who was in another hospital. The wound on his forehead was close to being healed. When we said goodbye, neither of us expected that we would not see each other for another two years. After three days I was let out of the Dental Department and had to report to the Cuirassier Barracks.[28] There, all the people who were released from the hospital were medically examined and either sent back to the front or to Germany. In my case the doctor diagnosed that I had a deep-seated catarrh, which had been caused by a cold, and I was sent back to the Reserve Battalion of Infantry Regiment 112 which was located in Donaueschingen in Baden. How happy I was, to get right away from the

---

[28] According to the records, Dominik Richert was in the hospital for eighteen days, from the 8th to the 26th of February.

48

front! And yet I did not feel completely comfortable, as I had to leave behind my comrade Zanger.

I went straight to the station in Douai and travelled with a Bavarian hospital train through Belgium to Aachen. There we had to alight and were given something to eat. I then travelled on in a passenger train to Cologne. I stayed there for a day, looking at the town and the Rhine. Then I boarded the fast train and travelled first class through the splendid Rhine Valley. A man in the same compartment pointed out the most interesting places to me, such as the mighty Niederwald Memorial, the Ehrenbreitstein Fortress located up on a hill, the Lorelei Rock, the place where the Mosel joins the Rhine, the Memorial to Blücher at Kaub, and so on. It was a beautiful, interesting journey, although it was winter. In my opinion the Rhine Valley from Mainz to Cologne is one of the most attractive places you can find. I travelled with the express to Offenburg in Baden and arrived at night time. As the last train on the Kinzig Valley Railway had left, I spent the night in Offenburg Station. The following morning, I caught the first train to Donaueschingen and reported to the Reserve Battalion, which was accommodated in barracks. Soon I met several comrades from my Company, who had been shot to half-cripples and having recovered, were awaiting their discharge. Our active Captain was there and spent a long time talking to me. The following day I reported sick and was sent to the Karl Hospital. There we were taken care of by Catholic nuns who were very friendly and good to us. I really felt splendid there, and wanted to stay there for a long time. All too quickly the splendour came to an end, because after five days came the order: everyone from Alsace in the Reserve Battalion 112 is to go to Freiburg to join the Reserve Battalion of Infantry Regiment 113. So I had to take my leave of the kind nuns. We travelled down the Höllental Railway to Freiburg. On the way, the soldiers from Alsace cursed the Prussians and people said things which did not sound very patriotic. In Freiburg we were accommodated in a factory hall. For a bed I had a sack of straw which lay on the ground. I immediately reported sick again. Several young doctors checked me, and the result was that I was fit for service again. Altogether I was in Freiburg for about seven days.

One evening, after end of duty, quite a number of us from Alsace were sitting together. There were lots of young soldiers who had never been on active service. They asked me to tell them something about my experience of war. Among other things, I told them about the events of the 26th of August, about the order given by General Stenger, not to take any French prisoners and to kill them all, and that I had seen with my own eyes how French wounded had been killed and so on. All at once the Company Clerk came into the hall and said 'Richert should come to the orderly room!' I had no idea why. Soon I would find out. The Company Sergeant said to me: 'Well, you can tell pretty stories. What were you just telling the men?' I said that

I had told them about my experience of the war. Then he barked at me: 'What, you really want to assert that a German general gave the order to kill French wounded?' 'Sergeant, the order was actually given as an order to the Brigade on the 26th of August 1914 and General Stenger was in command of the Brigade.' Now the sergeant shouted: 'Withdraw this assertion immediately or you will face the consequences!' I replied 'I cannot withdraw my statement as it is factually correct'. 'Sooo, clear out, you'll find out what happens next!' yelled the Company mother.[29]

On the following afternoon we were to go on a training march in the hills of the Black Forest with our backpacks packed as for war. The Company had formed up. Then I was called to the orderly room once again. There the strict Company Captain awaited me. His eyes flashed like those of an irritated wild animal: 'You despicable, nasty animal. You are asserting that a German general gave the order to kill enemy wounded, aren't you?' This is how he received me. I stood to attention in front of him and answered: 'Yes indeed, Captain!' In a rage he now went for me and shouted: 'You damned traitor to the Fatherland! Even in front of me you dare to make this assertion. You pig! You camel! You rhinoceros!' Now followed the names of all the wild animals and some of the tame ones and the conclusion of this litany was: 'Go to the devil, you damned scoundrel!' I turned round and went down to join the assembled Company. We marched off. As we were marching up a mountain road the Captain, who until then had been riding behind the Company, came to the front. I soon noticed that he was looking for me.

When he saw me he said 'Well, you rascal, come here!' I left the unit and stood to attention in front of him. 'Well, unpack your backpack!' I did so but there was nothing wrong. Then he said: 'I will catch you yet!' With that he rode after the Company. I packed my things again and had to run at the double up the hill in order to catch up with the Company.

The next morning the sergeant sent me back from the unit to the quarters. There, nobody bothered with me and I did not know what it was all about. On the following day a NCO came into the hall with two men and asked for me. I reported. 'Come with us.' 'Yes', I said, 'In a minute, I just want to buckle up.' 'You do not have to do that,' he said, 'you are under arrest.' I was not really surprised and went along. We went through a number of streets, the two soldiers with their guns on the left and the right, and the NCO behind me. Many passers-by stopped and looked at us. Several times I heard people saying quietly: 'A spy'. Thus we came to the Barracks of Infantry Regiment 113. We had to wait for a long time in a corridor. Then I heard an order from a room: 'Enter!' There sat a major with his clerk. The major looked at me for a long time and studied me from top to bottom. I

---

[29] Soldier's slang for the Sergeant.

stood still and looked him straight in the eye without embarrassment. Now the interrogation started. Name, company, home, parents, whether my father had actively served with the German army and so on. I answered all the questions. 'Now to the main question,' he said. 'You have made a monstrous statement concerning an order made by the General Stenger of your brigade. How do you come to do that? Tell me exactly what occurred.' I now told the major exactly how things happened and gave as witnesses the names of several comrades who were still serving with the Company in the field. The clerk recorded everything. Then the major wrote a note, gave it to the NCO who had accompanied me, and told him to return me to the Company. Then the major said to me 'You can go!'

We went back to the Company. There it was soon a case of 'Richert is back on duty'. The next day a transport to the front was being organized. Naturally, I was one of those selected although I did not yet feel fit. At the medical examination I was put right at the front and when the doctor was about to check me I heard the sergeant who stood beside him quietly saying: 'That's Richert!' Then the doctor immediately said 'KV'.[30] That is, fit for service.

So now they had punished me; I would much rather have ended up in prison than back at the front. But what could I do? I was, like thousands of others, an impotent tool of German militarism. We were given new uniforms, and as we had to go to the station at 5.00am, we were given time off until 11.00 pm We headed for the pubs. As I had no connection to my relatives, my purse was rather empty. I had all of five Marks. I paid out half of it for beer. The young soldiers sang boisterous songs and talked big about how they wanted to beat the enemy. I thought: just wait, all too soon your high spirits will be dissipated. Half befuddled by beer, I then lay down on my paliasse and thought with horror of how I might be spending the night camping at the front, as it was still winter. In the morning, we went to the station. We were one thousand two hundred men – half of us from Baden and half from Alsace. We travelled down the railway to a barracks in Karlsruhe, where we were given rifles. Then we went back through the town to the station. The mood among the chaps from Alsace was not good. When a woman asked 'Where are you all going to?' a fellow from Mülhausen replied 'Go and kick it, you damned ...'

At the station, the Grand Duke of Baden gave a speech to embolden us. He said that we were heading to the Carpathians, and that there, together with our Austrian comrades, we would soon drive the Russians out of Austria. I thought to myself: he can talk! Then we resumed our journey; we travelled in third-class carriages, with six men per compartment. From Karlsruhe we went to Mannheim, from there to Heidelberg and then on

[30] The German word is *Kriegsverwendungsfähig*.

through the beautiful Neckar Valley to Württemberg. In the Bavarian town of Würzburg we were given coffee, sausage, butter and bread. Then we went on through the snow covered Franconian Jura, through the Fichtelgebirge via Hof to Saxony, via Chemnitz, Freiberg to Dresden. The journey was very interesting. I sat at the window, watched the regions flying past, and smoked one cigarette after another.

In Dresden our train remained stationary until near morning. Then we went on and when I awoke we were already in Austrian Bohemia. We went on through the Valley of the Elbe to Prague, the capital of Bohemia. There we were once again given something to eat. The inhabitants of Prague gave us hostile looks as the Bohemians are no friends of the Austrians – or of the Germans. Then we travelled on past the beautiful city of Brünn to the Austrian capital, Vienna. There they gave us something to eat again. Afterwards we had to form up in two ranks, an Austrian regimental band played, and an Austrian grand duchess and her entourage distributed framed photographs of herself to us. This did not please me very much, as I hated these ceremonies. Then it went on from Vienna via Pressburg to Budapest, the capital of Hungary. The valley of the Danube between Vienna and Budapest is very beautiful and interesting. There were quite a number of steamers on the river, and everywhere the population cheered us and called: 'Hail, and Victory!' In addition, when the train stopped we were often given presents, especially things to smoke. From Budapest we travelled for two days across the large Hungarian plain. In the two days it took, I never saw a hill higher than ten metres – everything was as flat as a board. Everywhere we encountered the same picture: villages and free-standing farmsteads, all the little houses painted white and with roofs of straw or tiles and a well nearby. For a change, you often also saw windmills. Several times I saw herds of up to ten deer standing or lying in the fields. The River Thiess was in flood, and the large areas of surrounding countryside had been flooded.

In the town of Debrecen we were fed once again: soup, roast meat and potatoes with sauce. But it was almost impossible for us to enjoy any of it as it had all been flavoured too strongly with paprika, the red pepper which is so popular in Hungary. It burnt like fire in our mouths and throats. Then we went on to the town of Tokaj. Vines were growing everywhere you looked. This is where the famous Tokaj wine comes from. Travelling on, I could see the snow-covered Carpathian Mountains appearing in the distance. In Hungary we saw lots of very pretty dark-skinned girls. They wore coloured bodices, short skirts and cavalry boots reaching up to their knees. They blew us loads of kisses, and we naturally replied in the same way. When the train ran slowly, large numbers of gypsy children came begging for bread. Often we would throw a bit out and it was fun to see how they scrapped over it. There were quite different breeds of cattle and pigs there. The adult bullocks had huge horns with a span of at least one and a half metres, and there were pigs which looked like our sheep, with woolly coats. We reached the town of Munkács, which lies at the foot of the Carpathians. We had to alight there. We were quite stiff and whacked out as a result of having been sitting for so long, as the train journey had lasted for seven days and nights. When our young soldiers saw the high, snow-covered mountains in the grip of the cold they soon lost a lot of their enthusiasm. I thought with longing of my loved ones who were now more than three thousand six hundred kilometres away. Would I ever see them again, or would I find my grave in the big mountain range ahead of me? We spent the next night in army camps. The following morning we boarded the train and travelled about eight kilometres into the mountains to the village of Volocs. The place consisted of a few miserable huts. We alighted and went into barracks to spend the night. As there was no stove to provide heating, we froze terribly for this first night. The walls of the huts were made of pine trunks piled on top of each other, with moss in between and clay filling the gaps. The roofs consisted of straw. I had never before believed that people in Europe would live in accommodation like this. I did not see any of the inhabitants.

The next morning, we set off. We marched up a high mountain on a zigzag road. There I saw my first Russians. They were prisoners who were working on the roads, all of them big strong men. Their coats were the colour of clay. They wore tall fur hats on their heads, and their feet were stuck into large boots which reached up to their knees. As we continued upwards, it started to snow, so that it was not even possible to see for a range of fifty metres. Soon we looked like snowmen. Eventually, the road led downhill again. The snow stopped and deep below us we saw about twenty miserable houses. The village was called Verecky. A soldier asks 'Am I going to kick it?[31] That is the question.' We marched on and soon reached another equally miserable village. On a sign was the name 'Also Verecky'. Now the soldier said: 'Is there no hope for us. There it says. So I am going to kick it.' Despite the seriousness of the situation we had to laugh. We were quartered in Also Verecky. I went with another comrade to an Austrian field kitchen which was still standing there and asked for something warm to eat. Although he did not understand a word of German,[32] he gave each of us a cup of very good tea with rum. We thanked him and went to the hut that had been allocated to us, but it was so packed with soldiers that we could not find any free space in it. It was the same picture in the next hut.

[31] A pun on the German word *verecken*, which means to die miserably.
[32] In the multi-ethnic Austro-Hungarian Empire only a minority spoke German. Even in the Austrian part of the Dual Monarchy only thirty six per cent spoke German.

Now I asked one of the Austrian soldiers coming from there if he could not find anywhere for us to stay. He said all we had to do was to follow his footsteps. Then we would reach a hut located at the back of a little pine forest in a quarter of an hour. As we did not want to spend the night out in the snow, we went there and soon reached our objective. I opened the door and found myself in a room which was impossible to name. It was a living room, a stall and a larder. I was quite flabbergasted, as was my comrade. In the corner in front of us stood two cows; the water from them ran across the clay floor to the entrance. Two half-naked children were squatting there, scratching out bits of the clay floor, which had been softened by the water, and turning them into little round balls, something like our marbles. Next to the cows stood a goat, tethered to a post which had been beaten into the ground. There was not a bed to be seen – not even a table. There was a shelf fitted to the wall, which obviously served as a place to sleep for the four Austrian soldiers who were sitting on a bench playing cards. Underneath the shelf I noticed the family's stock of potatoes. But how poorly they were dressed! The man was wearing torn boots, and was wearing his shirt hanging over his trousers, as was usual in this area. Over his shoulders hung a sheepskin coat and his wife was wearing a similar garment. The man had a powerful-looking beard, and the hair on his head hung down to his chin. His head was covered with a pompom cap. The two of us just kept looking and looking.

Neither the soldiers nor the inhabitants of the house could speak a word of German, and they used signs to indicate that we should sit down. I took of my pack and placed it next to the enormous stove, which took up about a quarter of the total space and provided heat and a means of cooking as well as acting as an oven. Then I took off my helmet and put it on top of my pack. Splash; something had hit me on the back of the neck while I was bending down. I reached up with my hand and – oh horror! – my neck and my hand were covered in hen's dirt. Now I looked up and observed about ten hens which were sitting peacefully upon sticks which had been nailed to the beams, and if they needed to go they just let it fall down to make a mess in the room. That was a nice billet! But even so, it was better than spending the night outside in the snow. We brewed some coffee on the stove and ate some army bread with it.

As we were exhausted from marching, we indicated that we wanted to sleep. They indicated that we should use the shelf. We lay down on it and covered ourselves with our blankets. Each soldier had been issued with a blanket on leaving the barracks so that he could get some protection from the cold. As it was now getting dark, the man took a long pinewood spill down from the oven, stuck it between two pine trunks in the wall, and set it alight. That was the lighting. Two of the Austrians now came and lay beside us, while the two others got a handful of straw and laid it on the floor. That

54

was where they were going to sleep. Now I found myself wondering where the family would go to sleep. Soon this problem was solved. The woman climbed on top of the stove, her husband passed the two children up to her, and then climbed up himself. They all lay down and covered themselves with their sheepskins. There was no sign of a duvet or of an underlay. Soon we were all sleeping peacefully next to each other: we two Germans, four Austrians, four Ruthenians, two cows, one goat and the chickens. However, something was awake and that was a dangerous enemy: the lice. Already at night time I was wakened by being bitten, but I did not realize that it was lice as I had never had any before. In the morning we rejoined our troop. On the way I felt quite a biting on my chest. I scratched away, but soon it bit even more. I undid coat, jacket, under-jacket shirt and vest and saw the source of the biting. Three lice, full up, were sitting on my chest. I pinched them between my fingernails and crack, they were gone. I now started to get bitten – on the back, on the legs, and on certain other parts of the body. But that was just a prelude of what was to come.

When we reached our troop it had already formed up to move on. In the distance we heard the boom, boom, boom of artillery fire at the front. I cannot describe how reluctantly I marched on. What awaited us there? Snow, cold, lying outside at night, mortal danger. We marched past several barracks which acted as field dressing stations. I tried to report sick and went into the first barrack. This was full of wounded and half-frozen soldiers, half German and half Austrian. Almost all had faces that were grey and yellow and they looked very despondent. You could see from their appearance that they had been through a lot. I now reported to the doctor. He asked me what I wanted. I told him that I was suffering from catarrh and that I was debilitated. He laughed in my face and said: 'Well, my friend, you have been at the front already and you are sick fed up with it. Just get out of here and join your unit!' What could I do? I marched behind them and caught up with them when they next had a break. Once again we marched uphill and downhill all day. You often lost your footing on the icy roads. Entire caravans of sledges, laden with ammunition and food, passed us by, heading for the Front. They came back empty. Single sledges brought the wounded back. Towards evening we reached some barracks where we were to spend the night. You could see that there had previously been a village built at the side of the road. The houses were burnt down to ground-level, only the big ovens and the chimneys remained. On the snowed-up slopes of the hills you could see barbed-wire barriers sticking out of the snow. I also saw a number of bayonets. I asked one of the German-speaking Austrians who was on guard duty at the barracks what was going on. He told me that there had been heavy fighting in this area. The Russians had pushed through to here, and had then been forced to withdraw. There were still many dead lying under the snow, and it would only be possible to bury them when it thawed in the spring. When the young soldiers heard this, their courage vanished. And they pulled long faces.

Once again, next morning, we carried on. We climbed a high hill. Up on the ridge, we had a rest-break. This place was on the border between Hungary and Galicia. The view from up here was splendid. All around were snow-covered mountains and gorges and on the slopes we could see a number of splendid pine forests. From up ahead, the thunder of shellfire rumbled clearly over to us. We went downhill once again on a zigzag path. Down in a deep valley we saw a gun lying with its horses tethered to it. It had probably started slipping on the icy road, fallen off, and pulled the horses down with it. In the valley below us was the place where the sledges stopped. From this point, everything was transported to the front on narrow paths using donkeys. We went one behind the other along one of these paths, which led us into the meanders round the mountain. When we met one of the donkeys we had to squeeze up close to the side of the mountain as the path was so narrow. Eventually we reached the village of Tucholka. Once again, the houses looked miserable, and their dirty inhabitants stood between them in their sheepskin coats. After we had rested in Tucholka for about an hour we had to form up in two rows. The Company Sergeants of the 41st and 43rd Infantry Regiments arrived, and we were allocated to companies. Together with about fifty comrades, I was allocated to the 7th Company of Infantry Regiment 41. My address is now: Musketeer Richert, 7th Company, 41st Infantry Regiment, 1st Brigade, 1st Division, 1st Army Corps of the Imperial and German Southern Army.

Fighting and Exertion in the Carpathians

As darkness approached, we marched towards the front, led by the sergeants. The route we took was impassable during the day as it lay within range of the Russian artillery. We reached the village of Orava, which consisted of about twenty huts and a church. The church was covered with metal and the tower had the form of a cupola. The cross at its top had three cross-spars, with the lowest one at an angle, the sign of the Greek orthodox religion. The village lay at the foot of a mountain called Zwinin, which was about eight kilometres long and one thousand two hundred metres high, shaped like a roof and very steep in places. The Germans had dug themselves in on the slope, about two hundred metres below the summit and one thousand metres above the valley floor. As morning approached, we were led up to our position. The snow was generally about seventy centimetres deep, while in the hollows and ravines it had drifted to a depth of several metres. It was impossible to move around during the day as the Russians were able to spray the slopes with rifle and machine-gun fire from some prominent locations.

We joined our Company. Most of the men came from Eastern Prussia and spoke a dialect which was difficult to understand, while others were German Poles.[33] As it dawned I was able to see that they were all very run-down and looked in a bad state. They told us how much they had suffered from the cold, and warned us that it was very dangerous to raise your head above the snow as the Russians, Siberian marksmen, would shoot anyone who dared to do so. Then I saw, about thirty metres away, a German leaving the trench to go down the hill. A number of shots rang out from above. The man threw his arms in the air and fell down into the snow. He was the first casualty from our replacements, a strong, overconfident lad who, during our journey, had sung the following popular song at least a hundred times: 'The stork is a bird with a beak, he brings the little children. But he's only here in the summer. Who does it in the winter?' Now the poor devil had sung his last. As I subsequently found out, he had wanted to fetch some dried out pine twigs to make coffee.

The East Prussians then told us that they had already made several attacks on the Russian positions, but that they had been beaten back each time with heavy losses. Their dead were still lying up there and had been buried by the snow. I raised my head for a moment and was able to see a number of rigid hands and bayonets sticking up out of the snow. I also saw a number of mounds in the snow, under which lay the bodies of the fallen. Food could only be fetched at night-time. As it was not possible for a field kitchen to get up here, the cooking was done down in the valley in small portable pots. By the time that the people who had been given the task of collecting the food had climbed back up the one thousand metres, both the food and the coffee were cold. Thus we only got something warm to eat every third day. When I was responsible for collecting the food I ate my share down at the bottom. The army bread was practically frozen solid, so that you could hardly cut a bit off with your pocket knife. I put the piece of bread which I had cut off onto my chest between my jacket and my vest to get it to thaw out. As a result of the cold conditions, almost everyone was suffering from stomach pains and diarrhoea. Most people had blood in their stools. It drove you to despair, and there was no way out; we were threatened either by death, injury and frozen limbs or by being taken captive. There was an incredible lack of courage among the soldiers, and it was only the terrible force of circumstances which forced us to bear it. In particular, there was no end to the bitter cold nights. There was little point in thinking about sleep as we were all stamping from one foot to another and beating ourselves with our hands in order to warm up a bit. Sometimes the Russians would suddenly shoot a number of salvoes down at us. When this happened

---

[33] Approximately ten per cent of the inhabitants of Prussia were Poles. They suffered from discrimination.

most of us held our hands up above the snow in the hope of being shot in the hand and being transferred to a hospital.

On particularly cold nights several soldiers would have frostbitten feet, noses or ears. One morning they found two sentries in a listening post who had frozen to death in the snow. One day a terrible snowstorm started. Instead of snowflakes, the snow consisted of needles which were frozen solid. The trench was soon filled by a snowdrift and we had to keep on shovelling out the snow. The cold really went right through us, and you could not see even thirty paces ahead because of the snowstorm. This lasted for two whole days. The supply route was completely disrupted and for several days we got very little to eat. For three days we did not get any bread but only Austrian rusks, as hard as stone. Then, on several successive days, eight of us had to share one army loaf weighing three pounds between us.

One day we were given lard to spread on bread. Our group leader, NCO Will, a rough East Prussian, kept half of it for his own consumption and put it in a tin. He wanted to distribute the other half to the eight of us. I told him he could not do that and that the lard should be distributed in nine equal portions. When he yelled at me about it I got really angry and gave him a piece of my mind. From then on, the NCO bullied me whenever he could.

As I was powerless against him, I became even more demoralized and I decided to injure myself in order to escape. In order to do this I tied a little board to my hand. The board was meant to catch the residue of the gunshot so that the doctor who would bandage me would not be able to see that the shot had come from close range. I was waiting for the right moment. I put the loaded gun to my knee, held my hand with the board in front of it about twenty centimetres from the barrel, held on to the trigger with my right thumb, gritted my teeth and – did not fire, as my courage failed me at the last moment.

We were all suffering from lice, and it seemed a mystery where they had all come from. As it was impossible to get undressed because of the cold, the lice were able to nest and breed in our clothes. I caught at least four of them whenever I scratched my chest reaching to my armpit.

Each day the Company's strength was reduced as people were wounded or taken seriously ill. Then one night we were given a Battalion of the 43rd Regiment as reinforcements. In the morning we were ordered to attack. I thought: 'Our leaders are mad. Attacking with us half-dead, exhausted soldiers!' At 10.00am we had to leave the trench. Prior to that, we had had to dig short exit trenches.[34] No sooner were we out than we heard shots from above. It was difficult to make progress in the deep snow. Soon people who had been hit started falling in the snow. People who were lightly wounded

---

[34] Rudimentary trenches from which the assault would take place.

turned round and ran back to the trench. Then, as if an order had been given, everyone ran back to the trench. The dead and wounded were left lying, and some of the wounded wailed until nightfall, when they died.

The following night, at long last, we were relieved and went down to the village of Orava. We had been up there for sixteen days without being relieved. How glad we were to be in a warm room and to be able to stretch out on a dry floor and go to sleep! On the following day, we were paid. We were given one Mark extra per day, making 1.53 per day. After the three days' rest, we went back to our positions for three days, followed by three days' rest, and so on. One day, everything suddenly started to thaw. A mild wind wafted across the hills. The snow started to melt and the mess in the trenches was indescribable. We had to deepen the trench as we lost cover as the snow melted. As the snow melted, you could see the fallen between the positions, and lots of them lay around in all kinds of places.

9th of April 1915 – The Conquest of Zwinin Mountain

In the morning we returned to our positions before dawn. We had been sent two battalions from Infantry Regiment 43 to act as reinforcements. Nothing was said about mounting an attack before we went up, but we suspected it. No sooner had we arrived than we had to dig exit trenches. At eight o'clock on the dot it started. The order was: 'The Mountain must be taken whatever the cost!' As soon as we left the trench the Russians appeared above us and welcomed us with rapid fire. Despite this, everyone ran and climbed upwards. While running, we could see the heads of some Russians and fired our rifles at them. That put them off and they did not aim so well. I hid behind a hill of earth for a moment. Looking to the side I could see that the Germans were attacking along the whole side of the mountain. In places, they had already reached the summit. There was so much yelling and shooting that it was not possible to hear commands, or anything else. Suddenly a Russian machine gun began firing at our flank. Many people were hit and they fell between those who had fallen during previous attacks. At particularly steep places, the people who were hit tumbled quite a way back down the hill.

At last, out of breath, we reached the Russian positions. Some of the Russians continued to defend themselves, and they were stabbed to death using bayonets. The others either apprehensively held their hands in the air or ran off down the other side of the hill. The Russian positions had not been well manned as they had been busy cooking breakfast in the shelters which were located behind their position. Now we crossed the brow of the hill and could see that the slope on the other side was crawling with Russian soldiers who were fleeing downwards. They were shot down in large numbers. As the northern slope of the mountain was quite bleak, they could not find cover anywhere. It was horrible to look at this slaughter. Only a few of them reached the foot of the mountain. Some of them rolled three to found hundred metres down the mountain. At some places there were deep snowdrifts. The Russians sank in them up to their waists and were unable to move quickly, so they were almost all shot dead or wounded.

We started to search their shelters for food. I pushed back a canopy at the entrance of a shelter and went in; only to crash backwards as I found eight Russians who had not dared to flee in there. They immediately raised their hands in the air. Two of them wanted to give me their money not to harm them. I was actually happy that they had not harmed me. I got them to understand that they should come out. They were taken by other soldiers and led to the summit of the mountain, where several hundred other prisoners had been gathered together. I had probably landed in the food supply for a Russian company, because in there I found a large piece of beef, a side of smoked bacon, several balls of butter and a number of rounds of sugared rolls. I quickly filled my bread bag and all my pockets with rolls. I cut the side of bacon in two and tied a large piece under the cover of my backpack, so that the ends were sticking out on both sides. Then I untied my mess tin and stuffed it full of butter. Finally I took some handfuls of sugar out of a sack and used it to fill every empty space in my pockets. In the meantime, other soldiers had come into the shelter and in a few minutes it was empty. Many soldiers only found bread and other small things. When they noticed the bacon sticking out of the sides of my backpack some of them took their pocket knives and cut themselves bits of it. Soon I was only left with the bit which fitted inside the backpack. Even then, I still had ten pounds of it. I gave my good comrade Hubert Weiland from Baden, who had been a theology student before the war, a good piece of it and also gave smaller pieces to several comrades from Alsace.

We were ordered to meet at the top of the hill. The wounded of both sides, who had been bandaged up in the meantime, were put onto stretchers and carried down to Orava by Russian prisoners. A section of Russians had to help us dig large holes; in these, the bodies of those who fell during the attack were buried, together with those who had lost their lives earlier. The latter looked dreadful. You had to summon up all your courage to help gather them up.

We remained in the Russian position. During the night a fierce snowstorm started, and in the morning the mountains, ravines and forests were once again covered in a white blanket. Ahead of us were two hills shaped like houses with the narrow sides pointing towards us. Looking through the gorge between them we could see a valley with several of the miserable huts, and in the background were three or four hilltops, one higher than the others. Patrols were sent to the hills opposite to determine whether the Russians had evacuated them. We soon got a signal that the Russians had

60

gone. We went down the northern slope of Zwinin; wherever you looked, lay dead Russians. Snowed in, at the foot of a hollow, about twelve men who had rolled down the steep side of the hollow were lying. In the stream at the foot of the hill a number lay dead in the water, while others were leaning against the side. It was a sad picture. The Russians were much better equipped against the cold than we were. They wore thick woollen coats with hoods, had tall fur caps on their heads, most of them wore felt boots, and their trousers and jackets were padded with cotton.

We went into the ravine between the two hills and waited for nightfall. As night fell we climbed up the hill on the right and half way up we dug a trench. It was a cold night. A comrade of mine by the name of Brüning, from Mülhausen, father of a family, who was also very fed up with it, asked me if I would hammer a bullet through his hand with the head of my axe. I told him that I could not bring myself to do it. The next morning, as the sun was rising, and we could not see anything of the Russians anywhere, we sat down on our packs behind the trench and each of us ate whatever he had. Suddenly there was a whizzing through the air and at the same moment we heard a fearful detonation. Earth, snow, smoke, everything whirled around. A large Russian shell had fallen less than five metres from our trench. We all leapt quickly into our trench. Then the second one hit. It hit under a machine gun and threw it into the air. Two men were killed. The third shell exploded close behind the trench, while the fourth landed in the middle of it, about seven metres from me. Now it was just going too far. I jumped out of the trench and ran along the slope to a low wood which was mainly composed of hazel bushes. Soon the people who had been hit were the only ones left in the trench. After a while, the shooting stopped.

We went carefully back to the trench to look after the wounded. Soon two men brought Brüning; pale as death he staggered away, held his arms out, and struggled for breath. There was no sign of any injury. Suddenly blood shot out of his mouth and nose. He collapsed and, after a few convulsive movements, he was dead. His lung had burst as a result of a shell exploding in close proximity to him. There were seven more of the dead lying in the trench, and several of them had been mutilated so badly that they were unrecognisable. We put them all into one of the big shell-holes and covered it up with earth. Then we tied two sticks together with willows in the form of a cross and put it on the grave. We then spent two more days in that trench but were not fired at as none of us dared show that we were there.

During the third night we left the hill, crossed a narrow valley, and dug ourselves in on the opposite side of the valley. The Russians were positioned opposite us on an elongated hill which was higher than our one. During the day we had to sit or lie the whole time as the Russians were able to shoot down into our trench from above. The slope in front of us was covered in bushes about the height of a man. One evening I was on sentry duty.

I was not paying attention, but was chatting with my comrades. Suddenly a Russian appeared in front of us on the edge of the trench, with his gun in his hand. I expected many more, and hit out at him with my gun. Then he held his hands up and jumped down into the trench. He was a deserter who had obviously had enough of war. We gave him some cigarettes. How happy the man was, to have brought his life into safety! That same evening we were allocated fresh troops from Germany. An NCO who joined our Company was killed that same night. We spent about three weeks there. Apart from being shelled by the Russians, nothing much happened.

On the 2nd of May we heard the muffled rumble of shellfire far in the distance. It was the breakthrough of the German Army at Gorlice-Tarnów. The 4th of May was my twenty-second birthday. In the afternoon, the Russians started to bombard our trench with shrapnel. We had placed boards over the trench and covered them with earth to protect ourselves from the shrapnel. Five of us were sheltering underneath. Suddenly a whizzing, a flash, a bang; I was hit on the head and lost consciousness. When I came to, everything seemed to go in circles. I was lying in the trench covered by pieces of board and by earth. I had an enormous lump on my head and on my face under the right eye the skin had been grazed off. One of my four comrades lay dead in the trench. Another was leaning against the side of the trench in a sitting position with his head hanging forwards, and groaning. When I looked more closely I saw that he had a piece of shrapnel stuck in his back. I yelled for the ambulance men, but nobody came, because everyone was cowering in the corners of the trench. After a while, when I turned round to look at him again, he had died. There was no trace of the two others; they had probably run away. Later I learned that my good comrade Weiland, who wore spectacles, had been lightly injured. The lenses of his spectacles had been smashed by clods of earth and the splinters cut his face underneath his eyes.

We did not get much to eat, and as my booty from Zwinin had long since been consumed I, like all the others, was suffering from serious hunger. One day about ten of us were sent back to Zwinin to fetch boards from the Russian dugouts. When we arrived at Zwinin we saw that the Russian corpses had still not been buried. Their heads were black and quite fat; in fact their whole bodies were so bloated that their uniforms were completely full.

We looked for something to eat. I saw how my comrades picked up crusts of bread which lay in the dirt, washed them in stream water and ate them. There was a Russian lying on his back in front of me with a rucksack on. I saw that he had been shot in the chest. I cut the straps with a pocket knife and pulled the rucksack out from underneath him, cut it open and found a little sack of sugar and a big piece of bread. Unfortunately his blood had seeped through the rucksack and the bread. But my hunger was such that I cut away the part which had been contaminated by blood and ate the rest.

We continued to hunt, but found nothing more. Each of us took a board, and we went back to our Company. When we got back, we heard that in all twelve thousand Germans had died at Zwinin.

Start of the Major Offensive in May 1915

On the 5th of May 1915 we left our position and marched eastwards through a little valley behind the Front. When we arrived the place was teeming with newly-arrived Austrian troops. We heard that it was planned to break through the Russian Front there. Once again, the Russians had built their front along the ridge of a mountain. We were afraid of the attack, but this time we were more fortunate; we were kept in reserve. We remained in cover in a small pine forest to avoid being seen. On the morning of the 7th of May the dance started. Several Austrian mountain batteries fired at the Russian position. Then the German-Austrian infantry went into the attack. The infantry and machine-gun fire crackled terribly. In between you heard the crashing of artillery and shrapnel shells. We were able to observe the progress of the battle. We saw that many people who had been hit were left lying behind the Germans and Austrians as they climbed higher. Despite that, they reached the summit and soon large columns of Russian prisoners were being led down the hill. But the fighting continued, a sign that on the other side of the hill the Russians were continuing to resist.

On receiving the order 'fall in, advance!' we gathered at the edge of the wood; suddenly a heavy Russian shell landed in the middle of the crowd of soldiers and killed or injured more than forty men. We all dispersed out of fear. More shells came, but they flew past us. We had to assemble again and then made our way uphill; between the German positions and the summit lay many dead and injured from our side. The wounded asked for our help but we had to go on. German ambulance men and doctors, assisted by Russian prisoners, were making efforts to bandage up the wounded and get them away.

In the Russian positions lay a large number of dead Russians who almost all had been stabbed to death. The far slope of the hill was also littered with the bodies of Russians who had fallen, together with some Germans bodies among them. At one point I saw an entire line of Russian troops lying dead. Some of them had their spades in their hands, while others had their rifles at the ready. They had probably been mown down by a machine gun. Behind the Russian position was a real mess. You could not see a latrine anywhere. As a result you could not get through without standing on human excrement.

It was not until we reached the summit of the next hill that we caught up with the troops we were chasing. The Russians had set up a strong reserve position there, but they had not had the time to offer any resistance.

We started to pursue them. For the whole day we went up and down hill, chasing the Russians. Every so often, individuals or small groups of Russians would come over to us voluntarily to surrender. They had also had enough of war.

As it was hot, we quenched our thirst in the clear spring water, of which there was an ample supply. When it came to food the situation was bad, as each of us had only one pound of tinned meat and a little sack of rusks (iron rations). They could only be used on the orders of the Company Commander. We spent a hungry night up on a hill. At daybreak we went on. Before we started we were allowed to eat half of the tin of meat and a number of rusks.

At midday, about twenty men, including myself, were sent to the hill ahead of us to look around. Almost as soon as the first people reached the summit of the hill they started firing and called to us to come up quickly. From the summit I saw a deep ravine below us. It was crawling with Russians who were in the process of withdrawing. We shot down at them as much as we could and several Russians hit the ground. Then they all threw their guns away and held their hands in the air. As we did not want to reveal our weakness, we stayed under cover and waited for the Battalion to arrive. The Russians had to assemble and were led to the rear. There were more than seven hundred men. We crossed the next mountain and entered a primeval forest which covered the whole side of the mountain. The ground was covered with the trunks of pine trees. The ones underneath were rotten, while those on top were hard and free of bark. At some places it was almost impossible to get through. In between the fallen trees were younger trees of all sizes, together with mature trees which were unbelievably tall and massive. The mountains here were very wild and rugged – no roads, bridges or human habitation anywhere. The pursuit went on without a break. As a result of the difficulty climbing up and down the hills and the lack of food we became very tired and worn-out, but despite that we had to carry on until night fell. We ate the rest of our food and slept in a forest.

The next morning we continued to advance on empty stomachs; as we were climbing down the slope of a hill we came under intense infantry fire from the hill opposite. Fortunately there were a number of large rocks nearby so we were able to take cover. It was the Russian rearguard, which had the task of covering their retreat. German units soon fired at them and the Russians withdrew. We then climbed the hill where the Russians had been and we were pleasantly surprised to see a beautiful valley through which passed a railway line, a road and a small river. There were a few little villages and farmsteads dotted around the valley. In the distance you could see the retreating Russians with the naked eye. As far as you could see, the road was filled with their convoys. We climbed down into the valley and by following the road we reached the small town of Skole. As we were tormented by hunger we went looking for food. Soon we found a supply. At the roadside were two barrack huts which were filled with Russian bread and salmon. We took them by storm. There was an unbelievable crush at the entrances. Soon we saw soldiers sitting and lying around with big bits of fish and Russian loaves, chewing away at them. We spent the next night in Skole. The next morning we set out along the road. At one stage, where the road crossed the river, the bridge had been blown up by the Russians. We took off our boots and tried to wade across with our trousers rolled up, as we did not think that the water was very deep. However it was deeper in the middle, and we got wet to the waist. A chap from Baden by the name of Maier had taken off his trousers so they remained dry. He really had a laugh at our expense, but when he reached the bank he realized that he had left his pack behind. Now he had to go back to get it and he had the misfortune to slip on a wet rock and fall on his side in the water. He was soaking wet when he came back with his pack. We had a good laugh at him. When we marched on, we soon encountered obstacles. The Russians had sawn down large pine trees on the slope, and placed them directly across the road. We had to clear them.

As a consequence of the uneven diet, I and many others suffered from bad diarrhoea. The East Prussian discipline demanded that, despite the exertions and suffering, you had to ask your superior each time you needed to go. I asked my platoon leader NCO Will for permission. As he still hated me, he sent me to the Company Commander – I should go and ask him. However he was riding at the head of the Battalion. I asked NCO Will for permission once again. And as it was impossible to wait any longer I left the line, laid down my backpack, rifle and webbing at the edge of the road and went into the nearby bushes. At exactly the same moment the column came to a halt as there were obstacles on the road again. Our Company Commander, a fearful coarse individual, rode back to his Company and when he saw my things lying at the side of the road he shouted out in a grating voice: 'Who do these things here belong to?' I called out from the bush: 'They belong to me, Musketeer Richert.' 'Now, come here,' he yelled. I sorted out my clothes and stood to attention in front of him. 'Have you asked permission to leave the column?' 'Yes sir, I asked NCO Will,' I replied. 'NCO Will, come here,' said the first lieutenant. 'Has this man asked permission to leave the column?' NCO Will now saw an opportunity to get one over on me and lied: 'No sir!' Now the first lieutenant yelled at me: 'You insolent, nasty lout! I hereby punish you with five days of strict detention for lying to a superior officer.' I now wanted to tell him that at least twenty men must have heard me asking NCO Will for permission. I had hardly started to speak before he raised his arm holding his riding whip and yelled: 'Will you shut up!' I almost exploded with anger but I was totally powerless. This was the first punishment I had received in nearly two years of military service. For several days I was so angry that I only did my duty with the greatest reluctance.

As there was no time to serve your sentence, and there were no detention cells, the punishment consisted of tying the offenders to a tree or a waggon-wheel. Two hours of being tied up were equivalent to one day's arrest. So I was to be tied up for ten hours.[35] This was a delightful prospect, especially when I thought about what I had had to put up with and go through for these Prussians. A letter from home which arrived at this time was a great comfort to me. My loved ones were getting on well and in good health, and despite being close to the Front they could still stay at home. As we marched on we left the mountains and saw before us the broad Galician Plain. It was green and blooming and it made us happy to have put the terrible mountains behind us. Looking out across the plain, everyone must have wondered if he would find his grave here. Sadly, for most of them, it turned out to be true. We passed a number of villages without encountering any Russians. The standard of the houses was better than in the Carpathians. As in the mountains, the farmers walked around with their shirts hanging out over their trousers, and the womenfolk looked dirty. They looked astonished to see us, as they had never seen any Germans before. We could not speak a single word to them as they spoke Polish. Once, I went into a house to purchase eggs. I showed the woman six fingers and clucked like a hen. The woman did not seem to understand. Then I drew the shape of an egg on the wall. It was no use she just did not want to understand me. Then I got out my wallet and pulled out a note. That helped. The woman pulled a basket out from the corner and gave me six eggs. She asked for 'one Kuronna' – that is one Austrian Crown, which had a value of eighty Pfennigs. I gave her one Mark. I was given two more eggs instead of the twenty Pfennigs.

On the following day we heard the thunder of shellfire to our left, from which we concluded that the Russians wished to halt our advance. Large clouds of smoke rose into the sky and villages burned. At night, the sky above that area was blood-red. The next day the advance continued. As a result of the long marches we were totally exhausted and longed for a rest day. All at once we heard firing ahead. A cavalry patrol came rushing back with the news that they had encountered smaller Russian units. It seemed that it would soon be getting serious again. About twenty of us were sent ahead with a lieutenant to check out the wood which lay ahead of us. However, we did not find a single Russian. From the opposite side of the wood we saw a village. Several houses had tiled roofs, while other roofs were covered with metal and wooden shingles. Along the edge of the wood was

[35] This was, at the time, a normal military punishment in all European armies.

a shallow ravine about five metres deep. We lay down on the edge of the ravine and observed the village. But there was not a Russian to be seen. All of a sudden a Russian came galloping quickly round a bend in the ravine. We immediately pointed our rifles at him. He threw away his lance, held his hands in the air and rushed towards us without holding the reins. Then he swung one leg over the horse's neck, jumped down and surrendered. We were all astonished by this feat of riding. We indicated to the Russian that he should stay with us and he seemed quite satisfied to do so.

Then one of the farmers from the village came out to work on the field. We called *'Panje, Moskali?'* That meant, roughly, 'Sir, are there any Russians here?' The man replied in fluent German: 'No, the last of them left half an hour ago.' He told us that the previous night the village had been full of Russians and as far as he could make out the intention was to defend the area. This was not good news for us. The village was called Bergersdorf and was occupied by Germans. After the lieutenant had sent several men to inform the battalion, we entered the village and were made welcome by the inhabitants. As we were all run-down and looked bad, the people felt sorry for us and gave us food: milk, bread and anything else they had. After the battalion arrived we had to dig a trench on the far side of the village through the middle of a potato field. The inhabitants of the village slaughtered a pig paid for by them, cooked sauerkraut and potatoes to go with it, and brought the food to us in the trench. How tasty it was! That was really something special after the eternal monotony of the field kitchen. Then we were told 'Tomorrow is a day off!'

We slept in a barn. In the morning the two daughters of the man who owned the house brought us boiled milk. They were two pretty, very friendly girls and I chatted with them several times in the course of the day. In the afternoon an NCO came to me and said that I was to be tied up to one of the apple trees in the yard in half an hour. I was to provide the cord myself. I was so angry that I felt like destroying the whole world. After about a half an hour I got out the string which I used to clean my rifle out of my backpack and was going to report to the NCO. Then the Company Messengers ran round the village and called out: 'Get ready to move off immediately!' Although we suspected that we would soon be in conflict with the Russians I felt a sense of relief that this time I would be spared the shame of being tied up.

We marched for several kilometres through a wood until we came to its edge. We spent the night there. During the night we heard continuous infantry fire and some of the bullets actually reached us. It was a very beautiful warm May night and sleeping in the open was not bad at all. Towards morning we had to advance and came through a large area which was completely covered with heather. Austrian troops had dug a trench there and we occupied it. At daybreak I saw that in front of us at a distance of about eight hundred metres there was a pine wood consisting of young trees which formed the semicircular edge of the heath. Suddenly to the right of us there was a burst of infantry fire. There, fighting had already started. Throughout the day we lay peacefully in the trench. In the evening the Company Commander got the NCOs to come to him and told them that a patrol of two men – if at all possible active people who had been on the campaign since the start – should go ahead to try to find out where the Russians were positioned. My NCO told him that he had a man like that in his section. As a result a chap from Baden by the name of Brenneisen and I were sent out. We went past the listening post out front and I asked them whether they knew the password as I did not want them to shoot me on the way back. The password for that day was 'Helene'. We crept carefully forward and then lay down again and listened out into the night. We progressed in this way for a while. In order to be sure of our direction I had a compass with a luminous dial. Brenneisen wanted to go even further, but I got him to lie down beside me in the heather and said: 'Man, just think that you have a mother. What do you think you can find out here? The most likely thing is death!' He whispered back: 'But we have to report where the Russians are!' 'Just you leave that to me; I will deal with the report.' Then we lay there quietly.

Suddenly, to the left we heard the heather rustling and right afterwards we heard people whispering softly. We quietly got our rifles at the ready and I murmured in Brenneisen's ear that he should avoid shooting if possible. Then eight Russians appeared near us. Peering carefully they went by less than twenty paces from us without seeing us. We held our breath, but we could not prevent our hearts from pounding. Continuing to lie quietly we listened out into the night. Then we were able to hear hammering and the sound of axes. Now there was no doubt about it, the Russians were building a barbed wire barricade in front of their position at the edge of the wood. The hammering sound was caused as they put in the posts, and the sound of axes came because they were felling young trees to make the posts. After about two hours we went carefully back. Soon the listening post called out to us: 'Halt! Who goes there?' We said 'Helene' and were allowed to pass. On arriving in the trench we went straight to the Company Commander who was lying asleep in a corner. I woke him and reported: 'Patrol back!' He got up and said: 'Now, what's the news from out there?' I told him: 'We crept to the edge of the woods directly in front of us. We nearly bumped into a Russian patrol of eight men, but they did not notice us. We lay down and heard the Russians felling trees and sharpening posts which they then hammered into the ground. We also heard the squeak of rolls of wire, which indicated that the Russians were building a barricade of wire in front of their position. We got so close to the Russians that we were able to hear them speaking. On the way back I stepped out the distance to the edge of the wood and it is about eight hundred metres.' In this last part, I lied to the Company

Commander in the hope that he might let me off my five days' arrest. When I had reported, he patted us both on the shoulder and said: 'You have performed this patrol in an exemplary manner. I am very satisfied with you. What are your names?' We told him our names. 'Richert? Richert? Are you not the man whom I punished with five days strict arrest?' 'Yes, sir, that's correct,' I answered. 'So,' he said, 'as you have carried out the patrol so well I will pardon you. Otherwise, I would have awarded you the Iron Cross!' I had achieved what I wanted and my times of being tied up were over. That same night the First Lieutenant called the Group Leaders together and ordered them to inform all the soldiers in the Company of the bravery with which Brenneisen and I had carried out the patrol. From that night onwards, the First Lieutenant really liked me. Otherwise he was quite a dangerous brutal person who was greatly feared in the Company. Once I saw how he hit a soldier, one of the older ones, in the face making his nose bleed. Another time I heard him telling off some wounded men who were moaning with pain, calling them big children and cowardly cissies.

Before dawn we left the trench and went across the heath to the right towards the woods. Right at the edge of the woods stood a forester's lodge consisting of a house and stables. At and near the house lay the bodies of many German soldiers who had fallen in an encounter with the Russians days before. We spent the whole day lying in the woods. A six-man Russian patrol bumped into us and was forced to surrender. They were strong fellows, probably from Eastern Siberia as they had yellow-brown faces, had somewhat slanted eyes, and prominent cheekbones (Mongolian race).

26th of May 1915

Round about midnight we were given the command to advance quietly through the wood until we came under fire. Then we were to lie down and dig ourselves in. The night was dark and we sometimes bumped into trees. When we had advanced about three hundred metres we saw short flashes ahead and heard shots coming towards us. We lay down, tried to form some kind of lines, and dug ourselves in. It was not easy as it was pitch black and the ground was full of roots, but eventually I managed to make a foxhole, crawled into it and fell asleep. It was always an unpleasant feeling to lie in a chilly foxhole, which felt like a grave, especially as the imminent prospect of death was always with us.

It was already broad daylight when I awoke. Then we were given an order which always filled me with dread: 'Get ready; fix bayonets, advance!' We put on our packs and fitted our bayonets to our rifles. I put five bullets in the magazine and one in the chamber. We advanced with fear and trembling, peering carefully ahead, but not seeing anything. Then we encountered a wire which had only been put up from tree to tree. It was easy to get across it. The wood consisted mainly of large beech trees and oaks, while the ground was covered with low bramble bushes. However hard I peered forwards, I could not see any sign of a Russian position. All of a sudden we heard the crash of a salvo about fifty metres ahead. Machine guns rattled; the shots went on and on. As the range was close, the effect of this fire was terrible. The first salvo shot about half of us down, dead or wounded. Those who were uninjured also dived down. Each of us tried to dig himself in as quickly as possible, but many of us were hit while doing so. Then everyone lay still, and the Russians pretty well stopped shooting. It was terrible to listen to the wailing and groaning of the poor wounded soldiers. I, too, had thrown myself to the ground immediately on hearing the first salvo and had crept behind the sturdy trunk of an oak tree. A chap from Baden who was lying about three metres away from me had been shot at an angle through his left cheek. He crept to me behind the tree, stood up, took out his pocket mirror and had a look at his wound. 'Not too bad,' he said to me, 'it's a home-shot.' That's what we called light injuries. All of a sudden he looked fixedly ahead, threw his hands in the air, and swayed. Blood shot out of his mouth and nose and he fell on his back across me, spraying me with his blood. I rolled him down off me; I was unable to tell whether he had been hit by a second shot or whether he had fallen as a result of the shot to his face, as I almost did not trust myself to move. I noticed that several shots seemed to be coming from the side and whizzing narrowly overhead. I raised my head a little and was able to see that the Russian position was off at an angle. Now I was able to see how skilfully it had been built. The trench was covered with boards, with earth on top, and this had been covered by foliage. The Russians had also stuck bushes on top to make the position almost invisible. Their loopholes were only small round holes just above the level of the wood. A bullet bored through the cover of my backpack and went diagonally through my wash bag. I expected to be drilled through by a bullet at any moment and called out to more saints than there are in heaven. I realized that I could not stay behind the oak any longer, so I pulled my backpack from my back, raised my head a little, and noticed a small dip in the ground, roughly the size of a man, about twenty centimetres deep and three metres to the right. Pressing my body flat on the ground I crept quite slowly to the dip, taking care to avoid shaking the low bramble bushes. I pulled my backpack by the strap behind me. In the dip there was damp, rotten foliage and mud. I now lay on my side and pushed it out of the hole with my hands. Then I took my spade and in a lying position, dug myself in deeper. As I threw the earth out, the bramble bushes moved and soon bullets were flying overhead. It did not take long before I had complete cover. I lay peacefully in my damp hole in the ground. From the right hand side a dead man's leg stretched up to the hole. I recognized him from his footwear. It was Lance Corporal Zink from Strassburg, who always wore lacing shoes and leather spats instead of boots. To the left behind me a Pole was rolling backwards and forwards in pain, uttering terrible wailing sounds. He had been hit in the stomach by the first salvo. While he was writhing in pain on the ground, a ricochet shot four fingers of his right hand off, and another bullet smashed his chin. It was terrible to be a witness to this. Despite his terrible injuries the pitiful fellow wailed and moaned until about three o'clock in the afternoon, when death freed him from his pain. A lightly wounded soldier crept forward from behind: he must be mad, I thought to myself. Then I saw that he was trying to get his backpack, which he had taken off after being wounded. At the moment when he reached for his backpack, a bullet hit him in the forehead. He slumped down and did not move any more. I lay there in the foxhole all day, all on my own. I did not know whether anyone else was alive or not. It was very frightening as I was afraid that the Russians might come and bayonet me while I was in my foxhole. Fortunately they stayed in their trench. I got very hungry so I took my iron rations and ate them all up. I was thinking of creeping back at nightfall and taking the iron rations of one of the people who had been killed. It seemed that the day was lasting forever. Towards evening, I heard a voice calling out softly: 'Hi there! Is nobody else there?' The voice came from less than three metres to my right. I quietly replied, 'I'm still here, it's me, Richert.' We now started, whilst kneeling, to dig a little trench to link up to each other, and in an hour we were together. I felt much better, to be together with another person. By and by other people indicated where they were and we all endeavoured to get in touch with each other by digging out little trenches.

As no officers could be heard or seen, I was intending to head for the rear when it got dark. As I was just about to make a run for it there was a rustling in the dry leaves behind us. Infantry Regiment 222 had come to provide reinforcements. As quietly as possible, we deepened the little trenches, but we often had to duck as the Russians heard us working and fired away merrily at us. At long last, the trench was complete. With the help of some dried-out branches I made myself a loophole so that I would be able to shoot from a covered position if the situation required it.

Petersen and Niederfellmann, two Westphalians who had joined the Regiment recently, and I were the only survivors of my group, which had consisted of eight men and an NCO. Half the men had to stay awake and do sentry duty, while the others, including myself, sat or lay in the damp, cold trench and slept. Suddenly a gun battle started and it was a case of: 'The Russians are coming!' I jumped right up, shoved my gun through the loophole and fired out into the darkness without seeing anything. The Russians, who probably thought that we wanted to attack, fired wildly back at us. They also threw hand grenades, which exploded loudly a short distance in

71

front of our trench. Petersen, who had not made a loophole, was shooting up over the mound of earth. All at once I noticed that he was not standing next to me. Turning round, I saw him cowering in the trench. I yelled: 'Come on, Petersen, shoot!' As he did not get up I assumed that he was scared of shooting because of the bullets whizzing overhead. I tried to shove his head with my hand to get him to shoot. To my horror, my hand stuck to his bleeding head. I reached into my pocket and got out my flashlight. Petersen was sitting collapsed and dead in the trench; a bullet had drilled through his forehead and the blood was running down over his face and chest. When, after a while, the gun battle stopped, Niederfellmann and I pulled Petersen's body out and laid it on the forest floor behind the trench. As the night was now peaceful, I got down into the bottom of the trench to sleep. Niederfellmann said: 'I'm going to lie down behind the trench on the forest floor. I will be sheltered well enough by the wall of earth at the front of the trench.' Then he lit his pipe and lay down beside Petersen's body. At daybreak, Niederfellmann lay there, apparently asleep, with his pipe in his mouth. I tried to wake him to get him to come into the trench, as he might otherwise be seen by the Russians. Although I called to him and shook him he did not move. On looking more closely I found that he was dead. A bullet had gone through the top of the mound of earth and hit him in the side, penetrating his heart. He had died in his sleep, without feeling any pain. Now all his suffering was over, and I almost envied him. I was very despondent as a result of the terrible things I had just experienced.

27th of May 1915

As it became light we saw a big notice in front of the Russian position. On it, written in German was the following message: 'You stupid German pigs, now Italy is on our side too!' It was the day after Italy had entered the war.[36] As it was very hot in the afternoon and none of us had anything to drink, we were really thirsty. Then I noticed that each of the soldiers to our right was being given a mug of water. They told us that about one hundred metres to our right there was a hollow which reached up to our trench, and that as a result it was possible to go back under cover to the well at the forester's lodge to collect water. I collected together several mess tins and went. In front of the stable at the forester's lodge lay a long row of seriously wounded men, who were lying there exposed to the full heat of the sun. I felt really sorry for the poor people. Ambulance men were busy carrying them away on stretchers one by one. Then I heard a quiet weak voice calling my name. I looked round, and recognized NCO Will, my former enemy who had been

[36] Italy actually entered the war on the 23rd of May 1915.

responsible for me unjustly being given five days' arrest. 'Richert, for God's sake give me some water!' he groaned. I went to the well. The mechanism for pulling up the water had been destroyed. There was a long cable next to it, which I used to lower a canteen into the well, and haul it up full of water. The water seemed very unhealthy and tasted putrid. Probably the Russians had washed their canteens there and then emptied the water back into the well. I went to Will, knelt down beside him, raised his head with my hand and gave him a drink. He drank at least a litre of this bad water. I now saw that he had been shot in the chest. 'Thank you, Richert,' he then said weakly, and I put his head back down. I could not bring myself to say a word to him. I filled my canteens and went safely back through the hollow to the trench. Everyone wanted water, but I only gave it to the soldiers who occupied the trench to the left and right of me.

On the following morning the order was given that the people who belonged to Regiment 41 should retire through the hollow and assemble at the forester's lodge. We left the trench and our dead comrades who were still lying in the woods and had not yet been buried. We gathered together. The Company consisted of thirty men, one hundred and twenty six had gone. We marched back about two kilometres and reached a small village, where the field kitchen was waiting for us. The Russian cavalryman we had captured at Bergersdorf had been given the task of helping in the field kitchen. He could not suppress a sneering smile when he saw how small our Company had become. We were given something to eat and were to have the day off. After the meal we had roll call and were paid. It was a very sad occasion; sometimes the sergeant read six to ten names and nobody came. We survivors reported what we knew about the fate of the others to the sergeant – whether they were dead or wounded. If nobody knew what had happened to someone, they were recorded as missing. I was paid forty six Marks for the thirty days, together with twenty Marks of prize money in payment for the Russian artillery and machine guns we had captured earlier.

I made myself comfortable, pulled off my boots and socks, and washed my feet, arms and head. Then I fetched a bundle of straw from a barn and lay down in the sun. However I was not able to lie peacefully as the lice tormented and bit me terribly. I took off my shirt and the hunt started. There were two kinds of louse: larger ones and really tiny ones which just looked like little red dots. The latter were the most dangerous. Afterwards I lay down and went to sleep. Towards evening we were given the order: 'Get ready immediately! Fall in!' Our rest was over. We marched off, arrived in a small village during the night, and slept in a barn. The next morning we had a religious service. We were given general absolution, a sure sign that there was a prospect of an engagement. The regimental band played for several hours and in the afternoon our Company was given more than one hundred replacement troops from Germany – all of them young soldiers who had never fought before. At nightfall we went to sleep in the barn once again. We were wakened at about midnight. Post had arrived. I got a postcard. I took my flashlight and read: 'On behalf of your former comrade August Zanger I have to inform you that he was hit by a shell on the Loretto Ridge and is here in a military hospital with a fatal wound. Nurse so-and-so; Reserve hospital, Schladern an der Sieg (Rheinland).' This news made me very despondent. Other than my relatives, August had become the most important person in the world to me since the time when we were together on the Western Front. I would not find it easy to find another comrade who was so loyal and upright.

We had to march off in the middle of the night. Fairly far away we could hear the thunder of artillery. From time to time we heard a really big gun being fired. After several kilometres we passed an Austrian 30cm heavy gun; the huge shells were loaded using a crane. The sound when they were fired nearby was so loud that you almost fell to the ground. At daybreak we reached a village in which a number of German batteries stood ready to fire. We had to occupy a hollow in a wheat field outside the village. Nobody knew what was actually happening. Suddenly the German batteries roared out a terrible salvo, and then the heavy barrage started. There was a terrible crashing and whizzing in the air. From up ahead we heard the detonation of the shells. Soon the Russians answered, firing shrapnel, and a number of men were wounded. We sat on the ground with our backpacks over our heads. The young soldiers who were experiencing their baptism of fire were all shaking like leaves. We were ordered to advance. The Russian artillery fell silent. On reaching the top we saw the Russian position along the edge of a wood at about six hundred metres from us. We spread out and advanced at the double. In the smoke of the exploding artillery and shrapnel shells the Russian position was almost invisible. Suddenly it got lively at the Russian position. First as individuals, then in greater numbers, and finally in masses, the Russian infantrymen came running towards us with their hands in the air. They were all trembling as a result of having had to endure the terrifying artillery fire. Now our artillery shifted its fire into the woods and we advanced into the Russian position without incurring any casualties. The ground round about the trench had been churned up by the shells, and mutilated Russian corpses were lying around in the position.

We received the order: 'Infantry Regiment 41 stays in reserve.' We remained where we were while other battalions advanced, and soon we heard intensive rifle fire which slowly got more distant. Then we had to catch up and reached the other side of the wood, which led to a downward slope. Ahead of us we could see the plain of Stryi spread out before us. Across the whole territory you could see lines of advancing German and Austrian infantry, and in between them were groups of Russian prisoners who were being led back. Everywhere, artillery and shrapnel shells exploded. The town of Stryi was situated further back. As a result of the shelling, several fires had broken out there and massive clouds of smoke climbed into the sky. To the right of Stryi the Russians were resisting fiercely. To the left of the town they had occupied a village in strength, and were defending it bravely. The lines of troops turned to left and right to attack the Russians' flanks, and it became the task of our regiment to fill the gap that developed. Several batteries started to fire at the factories, and the Russians pulled back. I had to go forward in a patrol of eight men, led by an officer, to find out whether the Russians had evacuated the town. A patrol of Austrian hussars rode past us into the town. Several shots were fired and the Austrians came galloping back. Just ahead of us, one of the hussars was hit and he toppled onto the road, smashing his head. When we advanced cautiously a while later, the Russians had disappeared and the town was free of them. The inhabitants brought us rolls, cigarettes and so on. An old Jew came up to me and said: 'We have prayed to our just God to give the Germans victory.' He immediately got down to business, pulling out a packet of tobacco and saying: 'Would you like to buy some very good Russian tobacco, German sir, it's not expensive – really cheap.' I told him that I hardly ever smoked, but he kept on following me for a while, pestering me to buy his tobacco. These Galician and Polish Jews were a real pest to us whenever we entered a town or a village.

We were hoping that we would at least be given a day off in Styri. Unfortunately this was not to be, for as soon as the Regiment arrived we left the town and camped at the side of the road. A battery of German field artillery drove up next to us and shot at the retreating Russians in the distance. One of the very first shells exploded as it emerged from the barrel of the gun and two artillerymen were killed by splinters.

We spent the night in the ditch at the side of the road and the following morning the advance continued. We came to a wooded area and were marching along a well made-up road. As it was very hot and there was not a drop of water to be seen, we felt terribly thirsty. Eventually we reached a well close to the roadside in that desolate area, and everyone rushed to it to quench their thirst. But what a disappointment we experienced! The surface of the water was covered in tar, which the Russians had thrown into the well, and two bones of a dead horse were sticking out of the water.

Despite marching all day, we did not see a single Russian. We reached a more fertile area with a number of villages in it, and I was able to see a small town in the distance. I now looked at a map (which I had taken from a dead sergeant) showing the region in detail and was able to see that it must be the small town of Zurawno, which lay on the River Dniester. The Dniester flows from west to east and as we were marching northwards the river represented a dangerous obstacle to us. It was certainly to be expected that the Russians would try to prevent us from crossing. During the night we occupied the town. It was rumoured that we would have to force a crossing of the river in the morning.

Crossing and Fighting on the Dniester

The Dniester, which was about one hundred metres wide, had been crossed by a wooden bridge at Zurawno, but the Russians had burnt it down. On the other side of the river were meadows about two hundred metres wide. Behind this was a wide steep rocky hill about eighty metres high. There the Russians had constructed three rows of trenches: one was situated on the upper ridge, the second had been blasted out of the rock on the slope, while the third ran along the foot of the hill. Hiding behind a hedge, using the NCO's binoculars I was able to observe the Russian position. It seemed to me that it would be impossible to carry out this crossing without incurring enormous losses. As I had absolutely no desire to drown or to suffer a glorious hero's death I decided to keep out of the way. A comrade from the Rhineland by the name of Nolte and I sneaked away from the Company. We hid behind a house in a heap of wooden posts and waited for things to get going. At about eight o'clock in the morning the German artillery started to bombard the Russian trenches with artillery and shrapnel shells of all calibres. I looked round the corner of the house and saw that the hill, which was occupied by the Russians, looked like a volcano. Everywhere it was flashing and columns of smoke shot into the air. Soon the whole of the hill was hidden beneath black shell smoke. Several Russian shrapnel shells exploded close to me, forcing me to leave my observation post and seek cover behind the house. After about an hour the sound of rifle fire mixing in with the sound of the artillery told us that the infantry attack had started. As the Russian artillery shelled the town of Zurawno continuously I did not dare leave the protection offered by the house in order to observe the progress of the fighting. After about another hour the fire abated and large columns of Russian prisoners were being led back.

We spent the rest of the day in the town and bought some food from the few remaining inhabitants. The German troops must have advanced quite far that day, as you could only just hear the sound of the artillery by the time the evening came. We spent the night with a Jewish family and slept in their kitchen. The following morning, we both advanced to join our Company again, as we were very curious to find out how our comrades had fared during the attack. The German engineers had already built a bridge across the Dniester, which was sturdy enough to carry all the loads that needed to cross it. On the other side of the river the bodies of dead German infantry-men were spread out across the meadow. They were just in the process of burying them. For the most part, they were being laid in trenches which had been dug by the advancing infantry and covered with earth. 'What do you think, Richert?' said my comrade. 'If we had not kept out of the way, we might also be lying there!'

In front of the bridge a road led across the meadow towards a deep cleft in the rocky hill ahead of us. Just to the right of the road lay about ten dead Germans close together; several had horribly distorted faces and in their stiff hands they were still holding handfuls of grass or earth, which they had torn or scraped out while in their death throes. I thought I recognized one of the fallen as a comrade from my Company. In order to check, I took his pay book out of his pocket and discovered that I was mistaken. When I bent down to return the book to his pocket I saw that his clothes were crawling with lice which had left the cold dead body and were now warming themselves in the sunshine. We noticed the same thing on all the fallen who were lying there. We went on. It was terrible in the Russian positions on the hillside. The bodies of Russian soldiers, which had been torn up by shells, lay around among bushes which had been torn to shreds. The ground was covered with lumps of rock, which had been broken off, and clods of earth. I also saw shell-holes the size of a room which had probably been made by shells from the Austrian 30cm motorised artillery. We had marched several kilometres forwards when we saw a small unit of about thirty men coming towards us, led by a lieutenant. 'Hey, wait a minute!' he called to us. We stood still. The lieutenant asked us where we had come from and where we were going. We told him that we had been separated from our Company and were trying to find it. 'I've heard that before!' he yelled at us. 'You're just the same kind of cowards as this gang here!' Now we had to join the column and were led forward. In the evening the lieutenant handed us over to the Company who were busy digging a trench at the edge of a wood. I expected that we would get a real telling off but this time we got off relatively lightly. We spent the night in the trench. I had to do two hours of sentry duty with two other men. I discovered from my comrades that the Company had lost about thirty men in the fight at the Dniester.

At daybreak I was able to see a village about three hundred metres away. As the trench was undermanned, we were give Austrian riflemen as reinforcements. Several men were sent back to fetch coffee and bread from the field kitchen. On their return, we were just getting on with eating our bread and drinking our coffee when suddenly very strong Russian artillery fire started. Their target was our trench, and they shot well. We were completely surprised, dropped our mess tins, grabbed our rifles and lay down flat on the bottom of the trench. Several men were buried when shells burst right in front of the trench, but we were able to free them from the masses of earth without them coming to great harm. An Austrian rifleman who was lying next to me got up to look ahead. He had hardly raised his head above the trench before he called out: 'The Russians are coming!' We all jumped up. Several lines of Russians were coming towards us at a trot. We opened a crackling rapid fire at them, and I saw several of them fall, but they formed into new lines. We were facing an overwhelmingly superior force. The Russian artillery then started to attack us with lots of shrapnel. Some of us lacked the courage to shoot, and ducked down in the trench. Others were hit, among them the Austrian rifleman standing next to me, who got a full load of shrapnel in his head and chest and died immediately. The Russians, who used every opportunity to charge towards us, had got fairly close. Then I noticed how some of us were climbing out of the back of the trench and seeking safety by fleeing. As I had no desire to be run through by one of these semi-educated Russians I, too, left the trench, followed by my friend Nolte from the Rhineland. The Russians fired lots of bullets after us but after a few leaps we were covered by the bushes and they could not see us. To our good fortune, the path through the wood led downhill so that we were covered against rifle bullets, which only hissed through the tops of the trees. The balls of shrapnel which we heard hailing down through the wood were more dangerous. We hurried to get out of their range. As I looked round, I found that all the people from the trench were following. The wounded men, who could not run any more, fell captive to the Russians. Behind the wood we ran past a battery of field artillery. The battery commander asked what was wrong. 'The Russians have broken through!' we replied, whereupon he got the battery to limber up so that it would be able to resume firing from further back. Behind us, the rifle fire ceased, a sign that the Russians were not directly following us, while, to our right, the fighting was still in full swing. An uninterrupted rattle of rifle and machine-gun fire reached us from the village. A bit further back, near Zurawno, we reached the road which led back several kilometres to the bridge across the Dniester. Soon the whole road was crawling with retreating German infantry. The Russian artillery then started firing at the road and we were forced to take to the fields. Everyone chose his own route and nobody obeyed orders any more.

In this way – tired, wheezing and soaked with sweat – I once again reached the top of the rocky hill above the Dniester where the Russians had had their old positions. My plan was to cross the bridge across the Dniester in order to put the river between myself and the Russians. But the soldier thinks, while the officer commands! Several officers stopped us and commanded us to stop and form a group. I pretended not to hear because I was really hoping to reach safety across the bridge. However, when an officer with his pistol raised shouted at me to stop or - - -, I had no option but to join the other troops who had been grouped together. In a hurry we had to form a firing line and dig ourselves in. We were to stop the Russians if they forced their way as far as this until the last of us had crossed the bridge. 'We must, if necessary, sacrifice ourselves for the sake of our comrades!'

was the command. 'Good God!' said a Bavarian near me, 'this time we've really had it!' Five hundred metres away from us was a wood, out of which streamed the troops who had been positioned to the right of us and had also been forced to retreat. Some of the soldiers carried their wounded comrades on their backs. I also saw how a Hungarian hussar heaved a badly wounded German infantryman onto his horse in order to save him from captivity.

After about an hour only a few individuals, mainly people with minor wounds, came out of the wood past us. They told us that the Russian infantry was not far behind, but there was still nothing to see of them. Then suddenly things got lively at the edge of the woods. Shots rang out, and bullets whistled frighteningly past our ears. The Russians advanced out of the wood, shooting as they came. We answered with all that our guns could give. Then we were ordered: 'Withdraw, March! March!' Nobody waited for the order to be repeated. Each of us jumped out of his hole as quickly as possible in order to take cover behind the slope. A soldier running ahead of me was hit and fell on his face with a loud shriek but nobody took the time to look back at him, far less to help him. Each of us had only one idea; to reach the safety of the far side of the river by crossing the bridge. So we climbed, slid and jumped down the steep slope and ran as quickly as possible across the meadow to the bridge. Although it had been half torn apart by shells, almost all of us crossed it safely. By the time that the Russian infantrymen appeared at the top of the rocky hill we had found cover behind the houses in Zurawno. The bridge was blown up by our engineers. When it got dark we left the little town and marched to a village about five kilometres further back, accompanied by many refugees from Zurawno who took their most important possessions with them. Outside the village we met up with our Company's field kitchen, so we were able to satisfy our hunger.

Once again replacement troops from Germany joined us and were shared out amongst the Company. Afterwards the Articles of War were read out. Each ended with 'Shall be punished by imprisonment' or by 'Shall be punished by death'. There was nothing but punished and punished again. These Articles of War were read out to impress upon the soldier that he had no rights and was powerless with respect to his superiors. Afterwards we had to form a firing line with a space of one metre between us, and then we had to dig ourselves in. We lay down to sleep in the damp holes. Some of the soldiers wanted to go to the village to fetch straw, but the Company Commander forbade this. Although it was a warm summer night, I felt cold as I was still wearing a shirt that was soaked in sweat, and did not have another one to change into. The following day, we remained in the same position. It was rumoured that it was intended to entice the Russians to cross to our side of the river. Then the German pilots and the artillery would destroy the crossings and we would attack and take them prisoner. But the Russians were too clever to fall into the trap; only smaller units ventured across the river. The main force reoccupied the three positions one above the other on the rocky hill at the other side of the river. Our patrols in the forward area managed to take some Russians captive. They belonged to a regiment of guards. They were all very large, strong men, who made us look like boys. Apart from the odd shot between patrols, the day remained peaceful.

In the evening our artillery fired on Zurawno, and soon a number of columns of smoke showed that fires had broken out. During the night, the town became a sea of flames. It was a terrible but beautiful sight. The sky was blood red for quite a distance. During the night and the following day we remained in the same position.

The Second Crossing of the Dniester – mid-June 1915

As it got dark we were given the order: 'Get ready immediately!' In less than ten minutes our Battalion was assembled on the street, ready to move off. Extra ammunition was quickly handed out and each of us was given a tin of meat and a little sack of rusks in case we should get out of touch with our field kitchen. 'Quick march!' and off we went. We soon covered the five kilometres to Zurawno. Almost the whole of the little town had been burnt down. The fire still glowed underneath the rubble causing a horrible smell of smoke. We went down to the vegetable garden on the bank of the Dniester and dug ourselves in. Ahead of us on the river there were signs of activity. We could not see very much but we heard gentle tapping, and the sound of oars. Our engineers built two footbridges across the river. They tied together sturdy boards with clamps and wire. On both sides they drove poles into the bank and the footbridges were tied to them with wire to prevent them from wobbling too much. The crossing started at midnight. Our first battalion went first then we were the next. In order not to overload the swaying bridge we had to leave a gap of four paces between one man and the next. It started to rain too, and it got so dark that it was difficult to see the silhouette of the man in front. With each step that you took you had to check your feet to make sure that you did not miss the footbridge and plunge into the water. In the middle, the bridge sank down under our weight, causing the water to run into the top of our boots.

Everyone heaved a sigh of relief when he had the firm ground under his feet on the other side of the river. There a sergeant told each of us to go to the right and form a line. We lay down on the gravel at the side of the river and awaited orders. The Russians, who were occupying exactly the same places on the rocky hill as at the time of the first crossing, fired in the direction of the river all night, but almost all their bullets went over our heads. When the whole regiment had crossed, we were quietly given the command to advance slowly, and to dig ourselves in if we came under fire. As the meadow between the river and the Russian position was only two hundred metres wide, the Russians soon noticed us and fired a few shots off. I immediately threw myself to the ground, in order to dig myself in with my spade. In the darkness I could not even see the man next to me. Then I heard someone quietly calling my name: 'Richert, come here and we can dig ourselves in together!' It was my friend from the Rhineland who was calling. I had hardly gone three steps before I fell into a hole in the darkness. I felt around with my hands and discovered that I was in a foxhole which had probably been made during the first crossing. I called to the Rhinelander to join me. As the Russians began to shoot heavily we were both happy to have cover in the hole. A scream, followed by groaning, told us that a man near us had been hit. The order 'ambulance men to the left!' was now passed from man to man, and soon two of them went past us, but there was no need to bandage the young man as he had already died. It was a young volunteer from East Prussia. Now he had reached the end of his suffering. The Russian fire diminished so we enlarged our hole to enable us to lie at right angles to the Russian position. On the following morning we learned that we had done the right thing, as several of our men were shot in the leg from the Russian trench further up the steep hill. At daybreak, when the Russians noticed the heaps of earth close to them, they started firing at them. They hit our heap too – several times – sending the loose earth flying, but the two of us had good cover, so they could not harm us.

When the Russian artillery started to fire it became less comfortable. Three men from Lorraine had dug themselves in to the embankment of the road quite close to us. A shell landed in their hole and flung their mutilated bodies out onto the grass. It was a gruesome sight. Our artillery remained silent until, at about eight o'clock in the morning, we heard the crash of a gun. This heralded the bombardment that was going to soften up the Russian position in preparation for the attack. Suddenly a terrible din tore through the air as all the German batteries of different calibres hurled their shells at the Russian position. There was a crashing and a roaring and the earth shook. Lying there on the ground we were able to feel the impact of the heavy shells quite clearly. How they whooshed and roared over us! From the smaller calibres all we heard was whizz-bang. The shot was fired, flew over, and struck in a few seconds. You could recognize the middle calibres in flight by the longer drawn out sch-sch, while the large shells roared in with a loud sch-sch-sch. I lifted my head a little to watch the fearful spectacle. The whole of the rocky hill looked like a mountain breathing fire: shells were landing everywhere, throwing bushes, earth and lumps of rock all around. Various splinters and clods of earth flew over to us. Everywhere you could see the heads of our infantrymen sticking up out of their holes to watch the terrible sight. Some of them stood upright, offering the Russian infantrymen a good target, but the Russians were probably all lying in terror at the foot of their trenches, as they could not defend themselves while this hail of iron continued to drum down on them. After about half an hour there was movement in the front Russian trench, which followed the bottom of the hill. Making their way between the exploding shells all the occupants of the trench who were capable of marching came over to us with their hands in the air. They were almost all pale as death from fear and were shaking violently as a result of the terror they had survived. They were made to assemble and lie down on the meadow behind us to give them better cover from the Russian shells, which still flew over from time to time. The troops occupying the top Russian trench saved themselves by fleeing. That meant that only the middle trench, which was on the slope, was still occupied.

We were given the order: 'Get ready! Fix bayonets!' and had to pass it on. We put on our packs and fixed our bayonets to our rifles. As always, when advancing I put my little spade with the handle in my belt buckle in the hope of having some protection against a shot in the stomach. The German artillery moved its fire further forward. The command rang out: 'For attack, forwards. March! March!' We all shot out of our holes and, yelling 'hurrah', stormed off in the direction of the Russian trenches. But our artillery had already done most of the work; we only encountered minimal resistance. In the bottom trench there were only dead and wounded. A few shots came out of the middle trench and one of the bullets smashed our first lieutenant's knee. The man, who had previously called the moaning wounded 'big children' and 'cowardly cissies' now yelled and moaned as if he were possessed. With the best will in the world, I could not feel any sympathy for him. We climbed up the steep slope. Some of the Russians from the middle trench wanted to flee and climbed upwards as fast as they could, but they were shot down like rabbits and rolled back down into the trench. When we reached the trench, those who were still alive put their hands up and they were sent to join those who had been captured earlier down on the meadow. From above, some individuals climbed down to surrender. They could easily have escaped, but they preferred to go into captivity than to be involved in the war for any longer. We forced our way through tattered bushes and holes to the summit where our regiment gathered. From up there we saw how the Russian prisoners were making their way backward across the river. At least they were luckier than us, for they had put the murderous process behind them.

The Further Development of the Offensive

Now the Second Battalion had to advance slowly in extended order, and patrols were sent ahead. The First and Third Battalions followed in closed ranks. To the left and the right of us other regiments were advancing. We did not encounter any resistance all day. Here and there individual Russians would come out of hiding in the corn or the bushes, in order to surrender. We spent the night in the village from which we had been driven back by the Russians on our previous attack. For the next three days we did not see any Russians at all. According to the map we were nearing the town of Rohatyn.

One morning, while we were on a hill planted with grain, we were ordered to occupy the watermill which lay below us in the valley. About two kilometres away lay the small town of Rohatyn. We advanced towards the mill in open formation. Shrapnel shells came whizzing in and several men were wounded. We ran towards the mill at the double to get cover. I jumped into a wood shed with several comrades, while others entered the house and the outbuildings. On our arrival, the Russian battery directed its fire at the mill. Four shrapnel shells came whizzing in together. They all exploded around or over the mill. The buildings, which were built of wood with straw roofs, did not offer us much cover. Four men were wounded by a shrapnel shell which exploded above the shed, one of them being my friend from the Rhineland, who had been hit in the upper thigh by a projectile coming diagonally down towards him. I cut open his trousers and put both of his gauze bandages on the wound. Then, helped by another comrade, I carried him into the living room where there was more cover. The room was full of soldiers who were lined up against the walls lying on their packs. In all their faces was a look of fearful tension, as nobody knew where the next salvo would hit. Now each salvo consisted of two shrapnel shells which exploded in the air, and of two shells which exploded on contact with the ground. A soldier called Spiegel who was lying in the front corner of the room got up and went through the hallway to the door to pee. At the same moment a shell exploded at the front corner of the house, tearing a large hole in the wall. Splinters, pieces of wood, and soldier Spiegel's backpack hit the ceiling. The whole room was filled with the stinking smoke of gunpowder. Spiegel's backpack and his canteen were completely torn to pieces. When he came in and saw his kit he went deathly pale, and when one of the soldiers remarked that he had to thank a lucky chance that he had survived, he replied: 'I have a mother at home who prays for me every day.'

Just then, four more shells landed. One exploded in the yard, while the others landed behind the mill. We all got very stressed. Several soldiers put on their packs – but where should we go? Suddenly there was a terrible crash. I jumped to the broken window and looked out. Behind the barn rose a massive cloud of smoke. Clumps of grass and earth flew around. A large shell had hit. It was followed by another, which flew past the mill and landed in the mill pond further up, causing the water to be thrown up as high as a tower. A third shell exploded between the house and the barn. We all ran about, scared to death, without knowing where to go. Nowhere was safe. Then we were ordered to leave the mill immediately. We were to follow the stream, covered by the alders and the willow bushes, to the village which lay a few hundred metres further down. We carried the wounded with us. The Russians continued to shell the mill until evening, setting it on fire, although none of us were there any more. We spent the following night in the village, and I slept on a pile of straw behind a hut. Before daybreak we marched into a village about three kilometres away to the right of us.

At an open place in the village there were a number of cardboard boxes lying around. This was where the Russian infantry had been issued with ammunition. I went into a hut to buy a few eggs, and was lucky to be able to get half a dozen. As she had milk as well, I paid the woman to boil me up a litre. This took about half an hour. In the meantime, my Company had advanced to the far side of the village, where they came into contact with Russians, and the silence of the morning was broken by rifle fire. Right afterwards I saw some of our infantrymen running back on their own. I called out the window, asking them what was happening. They did not really know, and ran on. I quickly drank up my milk and put the rest of my eggs into my bread bag. As more and more soldiers ran back, I joined them, but I still did not know what was wrong.

We ran into a valley with a meadow and reached a stream. We took up a position in the dried-out bed of the stream. Within a short time, the whole Company was there, with the exception of a few men who had probably fallen or been wounded in the village. About midday we saw some Russians at the edge of the village, but when we started to shoot at them they disappeared behind the houses. In the afternoon, to our right, we heard heavy artillery fire. This was soon interrupted by the rattle of infantry fire and of machine guns. Towards evening they said that our troops had broken through the Russian front there. We spent the night in the dried out bed of the stream. The next morning, one of the soldiers said: 'That too was a bed – but a hard one!'

With no sign of the field kitchen, we went on with empty stomachs. I was fortunate because I still had three eggs in my bread bag, which I really enjoyed. After a few kilometres we reached a broad flat valley in the middle of which grew a patch of metre-high reeds about five hundred metres wide. On our side of the valley there were several farmsteads. As we approached the first one, we heard the whiz of approaching shells, and several shrapnel shells burst above us. I jumped behind the trunk of a willow tree, while the other soldiers ran behind the houses. A shrapnel shell tore several branches from the tree, which was uncanny. Then I heard the order: 'Second platoon – move behind the houses to the left!' I was a member of this platoon. When the first of them ran across, they were fired on from the other side of the valley. I peered across and was able to see that on the front edge of a wheat field, which climbed up gently from the reed bed, there was a long wall of earth – the Russian infantry position. I decided to stay behind the trunk of the willow tree and to dig myself in. I had hardly dug out the first few shovelfuls before our sergeant, who was standing behind the house, saw me and called across: 'Richert, would you please see to it that you join your unit!' I ran across the field towards the two houses as quickly as possible. Soon the bullets were flying around. One hit the ground right in front of me, causing me to involuntarily leap into the air. A few steps ahead, a soldier was lying dead on the ground. I reached the houses without being hit. There we were forced to dig ourselves in, as the Russian bullets were whizzing through the wooden walls and the low thatched roofs. We stayed in our holes until it got dark. We felt very thirsty as the sun shone brightly on us all day. There was a stream less than one hundred metres away from us, but nobody wanted to risk his life to fetch water. We continued to lie in the holes until it got dark.

As night fell, we had to make a bridge across the stream, advance on the other side through the reeds and then dig ourselves in about two hundred metres from the Russian infantry position. This was easier said than done. On starting to dig, the water immediately gathered in the hole, and there was no point in thinking of digging deeper. I got some lumps of grass and piled them up in front of me to get some cover. We spent the night squatting in the damp reeds. Despite this, I managed to fall asleep, but I awoke towards morning feeling cold and found that I was sitting in water, as were most of the others – the Russians had dammed the stream further down, raising the water level. All night long there were single gunshots from the Russian trench. When it had got light in the morning I heard a comrade calling: 'The Russians want to surrender.' I raised my head and peered across the reeds. Correct, I saw the Russians waving with their hats and with white cloths. However, as we did not really trust them, we sent some men over. When they reached the Russian position, the Russians – about twenty in all – climbed out of their trench and surrendered. They had been left behind in order to mislead us by their shooting while the main body of men retreated. In their trench there were still pieces of bread left lying around and we eagerly consumed them. Many soldiers pulled the grains from the green heads of wheat, blew away the chaff and ate them, in order to overcome their pangs of hunger.

A number of patrols were sent out to find out whether there were Russians in the area. I was sent with two men to a village about one kilometre away to find out whether it was free of Russians. We went carefully, bending down through the wheat fields towards the village. We got thoroughly soaked by the dew which was hanging on the heads and the stalks. At the edge of the wheat field we lay down and peered at the village, which was still about two hundred metres away. Some of the chimneys were smoking, but we could not see any Russians. As quickly as we could we ran to the closest house and peered down the dirty village street. There was no trace of any Russians. Then a door opened and a woman came out. On a stick which she carried on her shoulder she had hung two wooden water containers. She went to the well which was situated near us. As we were leaning on the gable end she only noticed us when she was about to pull up some water. She got a terrible fright, screamed out loud as if she had been impaled on our bayonets, dropped everything and ran like someone possessed back into the house where she locked the door. I went round to the back door, because we really wanted to know whether the Russians were still in the village. Just as I put my hand on the latch, the door opened. It seemed that the woman wanted to flee through the back door with a small child on her arm. When she saw me, she fell to her knees from fear and held her child towards me. She said something in her language – probably that I should spare her for the sake of her child. In order to calm her down I gave her a friendly pat on the shoulder, stroked her child and made a sign of the cross to it, so that she should see that I too was a Catholic, like herself. Then I pointed at my gun and then at her and shook my head to show her that I would not do anything. How happy that made her! She told me a great deal, but I did not understand a word of it. Now I had to call in my two comrades. She gave us boiled milk, butter and bread. It tasted really excellent! I asked '*Moskali?*' She went to the clock in the sitting room and pointed at twelve o'clock and then waved her hand to indicate that they had gone then. Now we knew that the Russians had left at midnight.

I went to the back of the house, climbed a mound of earth which was situated there, put my helmet on top of my bayonet and signalled to the Company to come. We marched together into the village. There we stopped, stacked our guns together, and waited for the field kitchen. Girls and women came from all directions and brought boiled milk, bread and other foodstuffs. They fixed flowers to our guns and helmets. We were quite astonished as we had not seen many friendly faces in other villages in Galicia. We discovered that before the Russians had left the village they had raped several women and girls. For this reason they viewed us as their liberators. At long last the field kitchen arrived. They had cooked good rice and beef and several chickens and the outcome was that that we all had more than enough to eat.

Once more, in the afternoon, we were given replacement troops, mostly people from Lorraine. They had been taken from the Western Front as several men from Lorraine had deserted. There were also some people from East Prussia. My good comrade Hubert Weiland, the theologian who had been slightly wounded in the Carpathians on the 4th of May also returned to his unit from the military hospital having recovered from his injury. We were both glad to see each other again, because he had not met many other former comrades. Most of them had died, been wounded or fallen ill. When the companies were reconstituted we asked the Sergeant to allocate us to the same group, and he did this. In this group there was also a young teacher and a rich student who was the son of a lord of the manor; both were from East Prussia. The group was led by NCO Hiller from Lorraine. We spent the night in the village. In the early morning we moved on. The following evening we stopped in a wood, where we stayed for two days, which gave us an opportunity to rest.

On the morning of the 30th of June we moved on again, encountering weaker Russian units, which withdrew quickly. We took several of their wounded into captivity. On the 1st of July 1915 we occupied a hill. We were forbidden to show ourselves at the top of the hill, so we stayed under cover on the rear slope until midday. I was very curious to find out what we were facing, so I crept to the summit, lay down behind the trunk of a massive hornbeam, took my telescope and looked at the region ahead of me. Directly below me was a valley with a village strung out in it, and a stream and a railway line running through it. On the opposite slope I could see another railway, which led from the first one about five hundred metres away to my left and into a side valley. I took my map. Soon I had determined where I was. The village ahead of us was called Livtira Gorna, while the stream was called the Zlota Lipa. There were several fields of oats stretching lengthwise along the opposite slope. Between the fields were embankments overgrown with bushes. Then I noticed something that filled me with fear: a freshly built wall of earth partially hidden by the bushes. That was certainly something which would have to be stormed, the best opportunity to die. I crept back and told my comrades what I had discovered and it made them all despondent, especially the young soldiers who had not yet taken part in a battle. There was no trace of the bravery or daring about which you could read every day in books and newspapers.

1st to the 2nd of July 1915 – Fighting on the Zlota Lipa

On the afternoon of the 1st of July we were ordered to get ready. We were to sneak down into the valley using all available cover and gather behind the high railway embankment. We were fortunate that a hollow filled with dense bushes led down to the valley. By going through it we got down behind the railway embankment without being seen by the Russians. The companies that had to occupy the embankment to the left of us were less fortunate in their route, as they had to run down the slope where there was an open field. They all ran individually. As soon as the first of them appeared at the top the Russians opened an intensive rifle fire at them. Soon the whole hill-side was covered with soldiers rushing downhill as fast as they could go. We could clearly see the impact of the Russian bullets, as each one stirred up a little cloud of dust. Despite this only about ten men out of the three companies were hit and left lying there. The Russians bombarded the railway embankment with shrapnel fire so we were forced to dig holes to get better cover. Weiland and I wrote postcards for home, but we did not have any opportunity to hand them in at the field kitchen that day. Towards evening we had to work our way forwards behind the railway embankment which led along the side of the opposite slope. Here too we were lucky; we got through without losses thanks to the cover offered by some bushes, which lined the side of a stream leading in that direction.

When the sun had already dipped below the horizon, I thought that we would be spending the night behind the embankment and that the attack would not take place until the following morning. It turned out that I was wrong. Behind us artillery shots could be heard; the shells whizzed over us and exploded further up at the Russian position. Four pieces of shrapnel whizzed down to us. 'Advance!' called the Commander of our Regiment from the back of the embankment. How these words made me shudder! Each of us knew that it would be the death sentence for some of us. I was most afraid of being shot in the stomach, as the poor pitiful people would normally live on, suffering the most terrible pain, for between one and three days before breathing their last. 'Fix bayonets! Forwards to attack! March! March!' Everyone ran up the hill. To start with we were covered by the bushes, but when we broke through their protective cover we were met by a roaring rapid fire, punctuated by screams here and there. A soldier who was running ahead of me suddenly threw his arms in the air and tumbled backwards. I nearly caught him in my arms but then we would both have hit the ground. It was terrible to hear the cries of the wounded. Those who had light wounds ran as quickly as they could back to the security of the railway embankment. Despite everything, we made progress. Amidst the roar of the infantry fire you could hear the rattle of the Russian machine guns. Shrapnel shells exploded overhead. I was so nervous that I did not know what I was doing. Out of breath and panting we arrived in front of the Russian position. The Russians climbed out of the trench and ran uphill towards the wood nearby, but most of them were shot down before they got there. We continued to advance to the edge of the wood, where we lay down to catch our breath.

Slowly it became dark, and the shooting almost stopped completely. Only occasionally did German shells whizz over us and explode in the wood. Suddenly, to our left infantry fire crackled out of a projecting part of the wood. Ping, ping the bullets whizzed past us. We could hear lots of voices cheering and in the darkness I was still able to see the Russians come charging out of the wood towards us with their bayonets at the ready. As they were attacking from the flank, most of us were unable to shoot for fear of hitting our comrades who were kneeling or lying in front of us. Some of us pulled back, and after firing a few shots I also pulled back. The Russians lay down and both parties shot at each other from close quarters. Hiding behind a bank, I waited to see what would happen. In the meantime it had become night, but you could still see the immediate environment quite clearly. A number of soldiers flitted past me and cleared out. The shooting continued, but it became steadily weaker. I heard someone approaching; a soldier slid down the bank and sat beside me, groaning. 'Are you wounded, comrade?' I asked, to which he replied: 'Yes, my arm and my chest are so painful.' I shone my torch and saw that he had a deep score in his neck, out of which blood ran. 'It is not bad,' I said, 'a graze on your neck.' 'I can't feel anything on my neck – just on my right arm and in my chest.' After I had bandaged his neck with a gauze bandage, I wanted to guide him down the hill, but he did not have the strength to walk. Only then did I notice that his right arm was hanging down loosely. I shone my torch again and saw an entry wound. The bullet had gone through his arm and had forced its way between his ribs into his chest. Just then, a number of soldiers ran past us. I called to them to help me carry the wounded man down, but they all ran on. A few minutes later, another man came, and he immediately agreed to help me. We put the wounded man on my rifle – one of us held the barrel while the other held the butt. The wounded man put his healthy arm round my neck and we headed down the hill, but we did not get very far. As the bank was steep, we both started to slide and we fell to the ground together with the wounded man. I said to the soldier that he should carry my rifle and pack and then took the wounded man on my back and carried him for as long as I could manage. Then we swopped round. In this way, we reached the village. Despite the darkness, I was able to identify an ambulance man by his white armband. As he came running up to us I asked him where to find the doctor. 'The third house on the left is the dressing station.' We went there and handed over our wounded man. We did not stay there for long, as the moaning and groaning and the blood got to us.

'Where shall we go now?' asked my comrade. I would really have liked to spend the night in a barn, but I could not rest without knowing what had happened to Weiland and my two East Prussian comrades, so we decided to go and look for the Company. On the way we met a soldier sitting at the side of the road who had been shot through the heel. He had hauled himself this far but he could go no further as a result of loss of blood, pain and exhaustion. The two of us carried him to the dressing station. The man we had brought in before lay unconscious on the straw and seemed near to death. By now it was midnight, and we set out once again to find our Company. We found them behind the railway embankment from which we had started our attack. The soldiers were lying or squatting there, some were asleep, while the others stared out into the night. I went along the embankment, asking everyone 'Is Weiland here?' until I came to the next Company – but I could not find him. Then a soldier told me that he had seen him stagger and fall, but that he did not know whether he was dead or seriously injured. This news really left me shattered. I would have happily gone to look for him, but there was no point in trying to do so in the dark, and in any case, as patrols had determined, the Russians had reoccupied their position. The dead and most of the wounded had been left lying up there and were in the hands of the Russians. I met my other comrade, the student from East Prussia. He told me that the young teacher had been hit by a sideways shot through his face which had knocked out some teeth and injured his tongue. So, only two of our four good comrades remained. Our Group Leader, NCO Hiller was missing too. The Company had suffered heavily.

Sitting near me was the Company Commander, talking to a young lieutenant who had just been ordered to our Company that night. I heard how the latter said that this would be the last night of his life, as he would probably fall tomorrow, since his unit was ordered to go first. The Company Commander, a nineteen year old in a rifleman's uniform, sighed too. He too was horrified by the prospect of the coming day. I made up my mind that I would, if at all possible, try not to take part in the attack at all.

The darkness slowly turned to grey. Several men were sent to the field kitchen and returned with food, bread and coffee. Some soldiers did not eat anything as they were afraid of being shot in the stomach, since this is naturally much more dangerous if your stomach is full. I heard a comrade shout: 'There's a wounded man coming down from up there.' I looked up over the tracks and sure enough there was the wounded man rolling over and over down towards us, coming to a halt in the ditch on the other side of the railway. Some soldiers ran across and fetched him back behind the protection of the embankment. He looked dreadful! He had been hit in the right calf by an explosive bullet. His calf was torn apart in three places from above his ankle up to his knee. It was a terrible sight. His lips were dry and split from traumatic fever. He kept asking for a drink, and consumed at least two litres of coffee. Using the bushes as cover, he was carried back.

As it was getting lighter, we all expected the order to attack. Then the German artillery started, but it was far too weak to threaten the Russian position. I cannot describe the mood of despondency in the troops. You felt like someone who had been sentenced to death and was waiting for the executioner to come and take you to the scaffold. You could not refuse to take part, as one of the Articles of War states: 'Anyone who disobeys orders in the face of the enemy will be punished by death.' So the only choice was to take part or to inconspicuously creep away to hide somewhere.

'Get ready!' We had to line up behind the railway embankment. One company was to remain in reserve at the embankment in order to fight off any possible counter-attack by the Russians. 'Forwards! March! March!' We crossed the tracks. No shots were fired. We were covered by the bushes. I intentionally stayed slightly behind and crept quickly under a stunted oak bush on the embankment. Further up the rattling and cheering started. I was

90

very tense about the outcome of the attack, but soon I was certain that the firing was diminishing and a number of Russian captives, accompanied by some of our soldiers, came down the hill. The attack had succeeded.

I was really quite surprised when our Company Commander came up the hill carrying supplies of ammunition – he had also shirked his duty. I thought to myself, if he can duck out of doing his duty when he is paid as a lieutenant[37] why shouldn't I when I am only paid 53 Pfennigs a day. I too went behind the railway embankment and collected ammunition to take up to the Company, in order to give the impression that I had been sent back to collect it. My absence had not been noticed. On the way, I stopped among the dead, of whom about half were lying on their faces, in the hope of finding Weiland, but I was unable to find him.

At the edge of the wood there were a number of places which were carpeted with flowers. Between them lay some of the Russians who had been shot down while fleeing. These poor innocent people who had been forced to leave their homes were victims of European militarism. What a contrast there was between them and their splendid surroundings!

The Company was busy digging itself in at the top of the hill. I went to the Company Commander and asked for his permission to go and look for Weiland, as he had asked me to inform his relatives if anything should happen to him. I was given permission and went back to the place where our Company had pushed forward, where I searched among the pitiful corpses. Many of them were lying face-down and I had to turn them over. Several times I was shocked to recognize good comrades of mine. I found a man called Wigieria from Silesia who had been popular with all of us. 'So, they got you too,' I said as I turned over another of the fallen. It was a chap from the Rhineland, a coarse, unreasonable fellow, a miner, who cursed a lot and was very proud of his powerful body. Whenever he had talked to me about my parents he always called them 'your old folks'. A bullet had tracked through his body from above through his chin, his neck and into his chest. His nose had been completely flattened as he fell. Right in front of the Russian position I found my group leader, NCO Hiller from Lorraine. He was lying on his back and had been shot in the stomach. He had pushed down his trousers, pulled up his shirt, and had wound his gauze bandage twice around his waist. Probably he had lost consciousness while doing so. His insignia had been removed from his collar and his sleeve: probably the Russians had taken them as a souvenir. Despite searching, I could find no trace of Weiland. The only explanation I could give was that he had been seriously wounded and that the Russians had taken him prisoner. I wrote to Weiland's parents to tell them what I knew of their son's fate.

[37] A lieutenant was paid about 280 Marks per month.

Further up the hill I investigated the contents of the rucksacks which had belonged to two dead Russians; I took a little sack of sugar and a piece of black bread from one of them, and out of the other I took another sack of sugar and a new shirt. I put it on straight away and threw away my dirty old shirt which was crawling with lice.

In the meantime, my Company had advanced further. I caught up with them at a battery of four guns which the Russians had abandoned. We spent the next night there. Early in the morning, other regiments took over the pursuit, and our Division had to assemble at Livtira Gorna in order to be deployed on another part of the Front. As we marched off, I seemed to hear a quiet sobbing sound. I looked round and saw a soldier holding back his tears. There had been two brothers serving in the Company: one was on active service, while the other was an eighteen year old volunteer. The latter was a popular cheery young chap who was only ever known as 'Bubi'. Bubi had fallen. His brother told me that he had buried him.

At midday I asked the Company Commander for permission to leave the ranks and intentionally stayed behind. When the whole Division had marched through I strolled along behind them. In the next village I met another soldier from my Battalion who had also had enough and wanted to duck out for a few days. We bought ourselves bread, milk and eggs in the village and spent the night in a barn. Then we strolled along behind the Division for several days. We were stopped by officers several times, and they asked us where we had come from and where we were going. I told them that we had been separated from our unit and were in the process of trying to find it. I knew quite clearly that if you were away from your Company for more than seven days then you would be considered to be a deserter and would face the prospect of severe punishment. So we went to some Austrian units who were stationed in the villages, reported to a Company Commander and asked him to be allowed to join their unit until we encountered German troops again. We were fed by their field kitchen. Then I asked the Company Commander to give me a document which I could show to my Company to prove where I had been while I was away. As soon as we had got this document, we disappeared at the next opportunity.

Slowly we approached the Front in the direction of the town of Brzeżany in the north-east of Galicia. Not far away from us in the direction we were going a heavy battle was in progress; all afternoon we heard the boom of the artillery, the rattle of the machine guns, and the sound of rifle fire. How good it was to be listening to a battle from a distance instead of taking part. Towards evening the shooting abated. Lots of soldiers with minor injuries walked past us – most of them with shots to the arm or the hand. There were soldiers from my Division, and many Austrians too. After a while a large column of Russian prisoners led by a few German soldiers passed us as well.

We did not go any further until the following afternoon. A bridge crossed a stream. I developed a strong desire to bathe, as I had not had a chance to do so for the whole of the summer. The two of us got undressed and cleaned ourselves thoroughly. I was shocked when I saw my naked body – it was yellow-grey in colour and had thinned down to look like a skeleton. The skin everywhere was scratched open because of the lice, especially down by the ankles. As far as the woollen socks reached, there were a number of sores caused by scratching. My comrade's body had the same miserable appearance. After bathing we sat down in the sunshine and caught the lice in our shirts and clothes. Each of us caught several hundred of these little pests.

Afterwards we went on. To the left and the right of the street were many willow bushes, and in between I saw lots of foxholes. When we had passed the area with the bushes we reached the place where the battle had taken place the day before. The Russian position had been located on a little raised piece of ground. Their trench had been protected by barbed wire, which had been shot up in places. Between the willow bushes and the Russian position there were flat meadows which had offered no cover, and there were a number of fallen Germans and Austrians scattered across them. In front there was a zigzag line of these poor chaps. We both went down from the road to take a closer look. A number of them had their spades in their hands; they had been hit as they were digging themselves in. The Germans were from the 43rd Infantry Regiment, so they were from our division. Many of them had new uniforms and equipment, so in all probability they had arrived from Germany a few days before and had then met their deaths here. At least they could be considered more fortunate than those who had endured the misery for years and fallen after that. At one place an access road led up to the main road, and behind it fifteen to twenty of the fallen were lying in a heap. In all probability, they had been shot up by a Russian machine gun, which had been able to hit them from the flank. I unfastened a new canteen from one of the backpacks and threw my rusty dirty old one away. Then we carried on. In the Russian position we only saw very few dead.

We came to a village, half of which had been set on fire by the German artillery. The inhabitants were standing around bemoaning the loss of their burnt out homes, from which smoke was still rising. Most of the inhabitants of the village were German settlers. A woman who was standing by her burnt out house told us that her house had already been burnt out the previous autumn when the Russians advanced. They had rebuilt it in the spring, and now she was homeless again. Her crying was heartbreaking. Her husband had been serving in the Fortress of Przemyl, but she had not heard any news from him since the Russians captured it. What misery and heartache a war like this brings to humanity!

Two days later, we reached our Company. I wanted to slip in unnoticed but the Company Sergeant soon found me out. Once again we had a new Company Commander, who was unknown to me. The Sergeant took me to him. He gave me a real dressing down, and I had naturally lost my good reputation in the Company. I could not care less, I had become so indifferent. The Sergeant raged, 'You deserve an exemplary punishment!' I pulled my wallet out of my coat pocket, hauled out the document and showed it to the Sergeant. 'What's this note about?' he shouted. 'Proof of where I have been during my absence from the Company,' I replied. When the Sergeant had read it he said: 'You seem to be a cunning bastard, but I'll catch you out yet. Get out of my sight!' I asked which group I should join, and then left him. There were a lot of unfamiliar faces – new replacements who had come from Germany – and the Company had suffered a number of losses during my absence. By chance I joined the group to which my comrade, the student from East Prussia, belonged. 'Well, Richert, where have you come from? Where have you been for all these days? I thought something must have happened to you,' he said. I replied: 'I have just had a few days of rest and recuperation behind the front,' and we both laughed.

We marched on. As a result of the intense heat, we suffered greatly from thirst. As a result of the dry weather, there was a great deal of dust on the poorly made-up roads and tracks; the marching columns of men stirred it up so much that we were advancing in a real cloud of dust. The dust landed on your uniform and pack, and worked its way into your nose, eyes and ears. As most of us were unshaven, the dust gathered in our beards, and the sweat ran down continuously, forming streams in the dust-covered faces. On marches like this, the soldiers looked really disgusting.

As a result of the lack of regular feeding, the exertion, the dirty drinking water, the heat and the exhaustion, the troops began to fall ill with dysentery, typhus, and gastro-enteritis, resulting in many losses. I personally suffered a lot from diarrhoea. I reported sick on a number of occasions, and was given medication, but I was not hospitalized as I was still fit enough to soldier on. We were often inoculated against infectious diseases, and this could be painful. The place where you were inoculated on your chest would sometimes swell up. After these injections, lots of soldiers would collapse on the march and have to be carried along behind us on waggons requisitioned from farmers.

We marched for two days until we were near the town of Brzeżany. On the evening of the 18th of June we were hiding behind a hill which had been planted with wheat, waiting for nightfall. During the day we had heard continous shellfire. As night fell, looking over the top of the hill we could see that the sky was blood-red; massive fires seemed to have broken out. We were ordered to occupy the hill. We passed several groups of Austrian troops, who were busy burying their dead. As we passed them I asked what

94

was going on, but nobody could answer as none of the Austrian troops spoke German. When we got over the top of the hill we saw, far below us, a number of villages and isolated farms up in flames. It looked to us as if the fires had been lit deliberately. We were ordered to dig ourselves in in a wheatfield which sloped down ahead of us, with about ten metres between one man and the next. We were strictly forbidden to let ourselves be seen after daybreak as the Russians had a good view into our position. So we spent the whole day lying in our holes, each of us on his own. The sun burned remorselessly down on us all day, resulting in tormenting thirst and we all longed for the cool evening in the hope that it would then be possible to fetch coffee – or at least water – from the field kitchen. I had fallen asleep in my foxhole when I was startled by a loud noise. Right afterwards a cloud of smelly black shell smoke passed over me. A shell had burst a short distance ahead of me. Probably the Russians had discovered us in the wheat. Now came shell after shell, some of which burst behind me while others burst to the side of me. It was quite frightening and I even forgot my tormenting thirst. Eventually the shooting stopped and it gradually became evening. Dew formed on the grass and the stalks. In order to get some coolness and moisture in my mouth I licked the dew off. We were hoping to leave in the evening, but we had to stay until early the next morning. Then we heard that the Russians had withdrawn. We got up and looked around. Not a shot was fired, and there was no trace of the Russians. The field kitchen rolled up and we were given food, coffee, bread and tobacco. Then we had to advance through the burnt-out villages which the Russians had intentionally set alight.

In the afternoon we caught up with the Russian rearguard again. We had to form lines and advance on the Russians. They soon withdrew, but we were subject to lively fire in the flank from a round hill about one and a half kilometres off to our right. As they were quite far away, the fire only had a limited effect. Suddenly the man next to me let out a bloodcurdling scream, dropped his gun, clutched both his hands to his face and screamed continuously in a heartbreaking way. I rushed to him and saw the blood running between his fingers. 'What's wrong, comrade?' I shouted. 'The eyes! The eyes!' he shouted, crying. 'I can't see any more.' I pulled his hands from his face and was terribly shocked. The poor chap had been shot blind. A bullet had torn open both his eyes, so that they ran out. It was a pitiful sight, the likes of which I had seldom seen before. Although I was hardened to suffering, my comrade's wailing touched my heart so much that I cried. 'Oh, if only a bullet would kill me!' he moaned. As bullets were still whizzing around us, I pulled him down to the ground, wrapped my two bandages round his head, consoled him as far as possible, and promised him that I would stay with him and lead him back as soon as the gunfire abated. After a while, two ambulance men who had seen us lying there came and led him back, while I ran on to rejoin the others.

We rested on a hill from which we had a good view ahead. We could clearly see the lines of withdrawing Russians. In a shallow valley ahead of us was a village, and it was our job to occupy it. The inhabitants had dragged out their few bits of furniture and the windows and doors from their huts into the open, in case their village should be shot into flames. As I passed, a woman gave me a large piece of bread. Three of us went between two houses to reach the road. Then we heard horses galloping along the road towards us, and three Cossacks appeared about five metres from us. As we saw them they all swung down to the right hand side of their horses and hid themselves from us, so that all you could see was their left arms holding the reins. It felt like being in the circus, and we were all so surprised that none of us thought of shooting to start with. We did fire a few shots after them but did not hit them, and they soon disappeared round the next corner. We spent the night in the village.

The next morning the Regiment had to assemble. It was said that we were going to be transported to another front. Some people said that we would be going to Italy, some said it would be France, while others said we would be going down to Serbia. I would have preferred to go to France for two reasons: firstly, during the journey there would be no risk of getting shot dead, and secondly, I was hoping that I might find an opportunity to run away and go into captivity. I did not trust the Russians, and the authorities lied to us that captured Germans were sent to Siberia to work in the mines until most of them died of cold and deprivation. It soon became clear that we had misunderstood what was to happen to us.

The March into Russian Poland

For the rest of the following day we marched along behind the Front towards the West, reaching the small town of Przemylany, where we stopped. We had to form up in units and march the goose step past some Austrian generals. That was just what we needed! With our tired limbs. I was ordered to position myself on the right wing of the group, because, as an active soldier, I had been trained in the goose-step according to the regulations. An Austrian military band started to play. 'Quick March!' We were supposed to switch to the goose step when we were about thirty steps away from the generals, but when I saw the overfed fatsos with their chests full of decorations and medals watching us with the coldest expression in the world I felt so angry that I could not bring myself to change to a goose step and I marched past normally. A sergeant who was behind me at the head of the third unit then said to me: 'Well, Richert, why did you not march properly?' I answered: 'I was too tired.' 'You were quite right,' he replied. 'We don't need stupidity like that during wartime.' We spent the night and the following day in a village. Some of the soldiers slept in the houses, while others slept outside.

Instead of being allowed to rest we had to practise all kinds of stupid drill: saluting, marching the goose step, normal marching – in short: as on a barrack square.

From this point on we had to march at night to prevent the Russian aircraft from seeing our troop movements. We set off at nightfall and marched along a good broad road, counting the large white kilometre stones as we went. After about fifteen kilometres, I left the line to read what was written on a milestone. I read 'Lwow 13 Km'. Lwow is called Lemberg in German, and is the capital of Galicia. I would like to see this town, I thought to myself, and I would be able to buy all kinds of things. It was quite clear to me that we would not be quartered in such a large town, so it was up to me to go there on my own. I left the ranks and asked the Company Commander to be excused. 'Yes,' he replied 'but make sure that you get back in line as soon as possible!' 'Yes sir,' I replied. I jumped across the ditch, went behind a bush, put my backpack on the ground and sat on it. The march past of the Division went on and on. As I had been sweating underneath my backpack my back became quite cold in the cool of the evening. Eventually, after about two hours, the last of the baggage waggons went past. I swung on my pack, hung my rifle round my neck and walked on comfortably behind them.

After about half an hour I came to a farm standing on its own. The door to the barn was unlocked. I went in, crept into the straw and soon fell asleep. I awoke to find the sun shining in my face through a hole in the shingle roof. A woman who was feeding the chickens in the yard was quite surprised to see a German soldier coming out of the barn. I greeted her in Polish: '*Tschen dobra, madka.*' To which she replied: '*Tschen dobra, pan.*' That is the same as 'Good morning, madam, good morning, sir'. I now asked her about '*milka, jaika, masla and kleba*' (milk, eggs, butter and bread), pointed to my wallet and said '*pinunze*', which means to pay. The woman waved to me to come in and soon put what I wanted onto the table. She had to smile when she saw how much I consumed. When I was full up, I put some bread and several eggs into my bread bag, paid, thanked her and went out, as I heard the sound of waggons coming from the direction we had travelled along the previous evening.

A baggage train approached, led by a lieutenant. Although I was perfectly well, I hobbled to the road and asked the lieutenant if I might be allowed to travel with them as I had pain in my foot and had been unable to keep up with my unit. The lieutenant, who seemed to be kind-hearted, called back that people should make room for me in one of the waggons. I got on board the second waggon in the train and lay down on some sacks behind the driver under the curved canopy. We chatted for a while. The friendly baggage-train soldier let me have a drink from a bottle of cognac; I made the most of this opportunity and then fell asleep. I was wakened by a strange humming noise. I crept out from the canopy and saw that we were in a town. That could only be Lemberg, and the sound had come from a tram passing by. We were just passing a market where all kinds of things were being sold on stalls. I quickly took my leave of the soldier and climbed down from the waggon. I started shopping – chocolate, sausage, sweets from the confectioner, and so on. Then I went into an inn and ordered a good midday meal. After lunch, I had a look round the town. There were some splendid streets and very attractive buildings, which I had not expected to find in Galicia. By chance, I found a military information office, so I went in and asked where the second battalion of Infantry Regiment 41 was currently located. They told me they were in the next village north of Lemberg. The road leading past the office went straight there. On my way I met a farm cart and got a lift. I reached my Company just as they were getting ready to march off. I sneaked back into my group. 'Tonight we are going to the town of Rava-Ruska, thirty five kilometres away!' they told us. Outside the village we were stopped. Once again we were to parade in front of some German and Austrian generals and senior officers. From the rear we heard the command: 'Move over to the right!' A convoy of trucks drove slowly past us. 'Where are you going?' I heard a soldier behind us call out to a driver, to which he replied 'To Rava-Ruska'. Immediately a number of soldiers, myself included, climbed onto the lorries despite the angry calls of the officers and NCOs.

It took about one and a half hours to reach Rawa Ruska. Some of the inhabitants had not yet gone to bed. We went to a bakery and bought bread rolls. We boiled up some milk to have with them in a farmhouse, and then lay down to sleep in straw, while our comrades struggled to join us through the dark night. In the morning we went to find our Company, which was sleeping in an orchard. Each of us lay down beside his group. In the evening, we headed on. It appeared that there had been heavy fighting at Rava-Ruska. There were foxholes, shell-holes and the graves of soldiers everywhere. We often encountered sections of Russian prisoners who seemed very happy to have gone into captivity. We marched for six days and then heard shellfire ahead. We were once again approaching the Front. We were now in Russian Poland on the left bank of the River Bug. Almost all the villages and farms here had been burnt down and only the masonry ovens and the chimneys were still standing. The region was almost completely flat. During the day we could see fires and the clouds from shrapnel shells not very far away. 'Tomorrow morning we will be deployed to break through the strong Russian position' they said – a pleasant prospect!

Fighting in Russian Poland at the end of July 1915

We had to advance during the night. We passed a large number of German batteries, which were mainly situated at the edges of woods. In a big potato field we had to dig ourselves in. The shots of the infantry came from further ahead, so I was hopeful that we would remain in reserve when the attack took place. The German artillery started to bombard the Russian position shortly before daybreak. We could not see where it was, but it probably ran along the edge of a large estate, as we could see the smoke from the shells rising in the air there. After an hour, the whole estate was in flames. Quite suddenly, ahead of us, rifle and machine-gun fire started. The German infantry was going on the attack. Lots of bullets whizzed past us, so we kept our heads down. The Russian artillery scattered shells in the area round about us. The rifle fire lasted a long time, so that we could not tell what the outcome of the fighting was. Eventually large numbers of Russian prisoners came walking past us with their hands in the air. I saw a number of them who came doubled up, holding their stomachs and groaning. They were ill, with dysentery or gastro-enteritis. These poor devils also had a good chance of being well looked after. 'Get ready! Advance!' Backpacks were put on, and off we went.

Soon we reached the Russian position. God, what it looked like there! Large numbers of fallen Germans were lying in front of and in the wire entanglement, which had partly been torn apart by shellfire. The Germans must have attacked unsuccessfully a number of days before, as many of the dead had already started to decompose and gave off a ghastly stench. They were Bavarian troops; I could tell this from the lions on the buttons of their uniforms. The Prussian regiments had crowns on their coat-buttons. There I saw bodies with ghastly rotting head wounds which had already started to crawl with worms and maggots. Each of us pushed his way across shell-holes and the confusion of barbed wire to escape from the smell. Directly in front of the Russian position lay a Russian. He looked like a sack of potatoes with a leg. His head, both his arms, and one leg had been torn off. His wounds were also covered with worms.

The Russian position was very strongly built, roofed-over with beams with boards on top, and covered with earth. It was only at the front above the surface of the earth that the open gun ports were visible. The Russians had only had a few losses, some of which had suffered from direct hits while in their position. We continued to advance in extended order. Ahead of us we saw the town of Grubeschow. We were expecting to meet resistance there, but were able to take possession of it without fighting. It did not take long before Russian shrapnel shells flew towards us. We looked for cover behind the houses. Two women, who were probably refugees, went out in the open to try to catch hold of a large calf which had been driven wild by the whizzing and banging of the shrapnel. Although the balls of shrapnel were hitting all around them the two women did not let go of the calf. We called and waved to them to come to us to seek cover, but to no avail. Then there was a cry. One of the women had been shot through the arm by a shrapnel ball. Now the other woman let the calf go and it ran off jumping madly. A comrade and I jumped to help the woman. We pulled her behind the cover of the houses and an ambulance man bandaged her up.

Towards evening, the firing ceased. I looked round the end of a house and saw the Russian infantry position at the edge of a wheat field about seven hundred metres away. Between us and the Russians was a hollow through which flowed a stream. Whatever happens, we will have to attack here, I thought to myself. As it started to rain at night, we went into the houses. They were so packed with soldiers that I had no alternative but to lie in the front of a bed in which a Jewish refugee girl was sleeping at the back. I quietly prayed the Rosary in order to get through the following day's attack safe and sound.

The Attack at Grubeschow on the 30th of July 1915

The following morning we had to go behind the houses and build a number of narrow portable bridges, as patrols in the night had found out that the stream between ourselves and the Russians was deeply filled with quick-sand making it impossible to stride through it. I thought to myself: that will have consequences, if we have to carry the bridges across such open terrain and then have to cross them in Indian file. This seemed a reckless undertaking to me. Towards evening it started; the bridges were carried to the stream at the double, followed – also at the double – by the infantrymen. But, what a miracle, no shots were fired from over there. I thought: either the Russians have pulled back, or they want us to get closer in order to wipe us out with rapid fire. Only when we had crossed the bridges were some shots fired. A soldier fell, shot through the forehead, while another had his jawbone shattered. Then no more shots were fired. We ran cheering towards the Russian position. Nothing moved.

When we arrived in front of the wire entanglement we suddenly noticed a number of rifles with fitted bayonets waving backwards and forwards with Russian caps perched on them or white cloths tied to them. None of the Russians was even willing to raise his head above the parapet. We climbed happily over the entanglement. When I looked into the trench, the rifles were standing around the walls but there was no sign of the Russians. I called down into the trench. Then I saw a fearful face visible down below me. There were dugouts facing forwards underneath our feet and the Russians had crawled into these out of fear. I gave the Russian a friendly laugh, and indicated to him that he should just come out. Now they came out, one after the other. Some of them wanted to give us money, while others offered bread or butter and so on, if we would not harm them. However, we were very grateful to them, as they had effectively given many of us our lives back by behaving as they had. We now lined them up and counted them. There were four hundred and fifty men, five officers and four machine guns. If they had chosen to defend themselves, not one of us would have made it to their trench. We spent the night in the Russian position. To make sure, various outposts were set up but all remained calm.

When it got light the next morning, the East Prussian soldier, another soldier, and I were sent to check a wood about a kilometre away. Orders like this were seldom easy to carry out. We reached the wood without noticing anything. The student acted very boldly here. Ignoring any need to take care, he went ahead of us with his gun on his arm, as if he were chasing rabbits. At the opposite side of the wood, we looked through the bushes and saw, at a distance of about one thousand five hundred metres, how Russian infantry were busy constructing trenches. 'My God, once again there is a Front ahead of us. Where do the Russians get all these soldiers from?' The student and I stayed hiding behind the edge of the wood while the other soldier went back to the Company to report. We now took turns to observe the Russians with my binoculars. A number of them were pulling out oats or grass and spread them on the freshly dug earth in order to camouflage the position. Then the soldier came back with the order that we should stay lying at the edge of the wood until we were relieved by troops. About midday a reserve infantry regiment occupied the wood.

In the afternoon several companies were to occupy a hollow to our right, which was overgrown with bushes. The soldiers ran out of the woods at the double. Immediately, Russian shrapnel shells flew over. As if struck by lightning, I saw how a soldier at the edge of the wood plunged to the ground. A lieutenant and his orderly were lying behind an oak tree. From a long distance away large artillery shells started coming in. One of them hit next to the tree behind which the two of them were lying. They were thrown sideways and lay there dead. The three of us ran back, seeking cover behind the tree trunks from time to time. A company commander pointed his pistol at us and shouted that if we went one step further backwards he would shoot us down. He thought we were soldiers from his regiment. I ran to him and told him about the command we had received from our Company. Then we went back to the Russian position where we had left our Company, but it had moved on, and we had no idea where they had gone. We went back to Grubeschow, bought some food, and spent the night with a Jewish family, sleeping on the floor in a room.

We searched for two days before we found our Company. Three companies from the battalion were camped by a farm, while the fourth one was camping several hundred metres away on open ground. We soon found out the reason. There had been two cases of cholera in that company, and both had been fatal. Many of the soldiers who had diarrhoea were being taken in to military epidemic hospitals for observation. Cholera – that's all we needed to make the list of suffering complete. This epidemic was more dangerous than the Russian bullets, because you could not take cover.

101

We were inoculated against it several times. We spent the night and had the following day off in a poor, dirty Polish village. I went into a house to buy some eggs. As I opened the living room door I stepped back in horror. In the room lay two dead women on the floor; they were probably victims of cholera. One of the two cooks on our field kitchen, who had still been handing out the coffee in the morning, was lying dead in a wooden shed by the time we went to collect lunch. On the same day, two more soldiers died of cholera. It was a terrible death; they writhed backwards and forwards on the floor, doubled up like worms and pushed their stomachs hard with their hands. They vomited constantly and their stools flowed continuously as well. Their eyes had already taken on the colour of death, when these miserable people were still fully conscious. Towards evening we were ordered to assemble. The Commander of our Regiment, a full baron, made a speech from horseback: 'Comrades, I am not feeling well. Tomorrow I will have to go to a military hospital for a few days to recover. It is my wish and hope that I will meet you all again fit and well on my return. Dismiss.' The following morning we were informed that the Commander of the Regiment had died – a victim of cholera. It was becoming sinister for all of us. As most of us had stomach trouble and often had diarrhoea we were always afraid that we might have caught the disease. It was strictly forbidden to drink any water which had not first been boiled.

Fighting at Chelm (Russian Poland) at the beginning of August 1915

Very early in the morning we left the village which was contaminated with cholera. We had only marched about two kilometres when we heard firing ahead. Our advance guard had encountered Russians. We had to lie down and await developments. Apparently the Russians were stronger than it first appeared, because we were suddenly ordered: 'Spread out and advance!' To start with we were still sheltered by a hill, which was planted with oats and sloped gently upwards. Having reached the top, I could see undulating hilly countryside, mainly planted with oats, with a widely scattered village in between. I could not see anything of the Russians, although we immediately came under rifle fire. 'Lie down! Dig in!' We had hardly dug more than a few spadefuls before four shrapnel shells burst above our heads. Several men were wounded, none seriously. They were all able to run back without assistance. The battery shot at least twenty salvos but they all went just a bit too far over our heads. We all worked as hard as we could to get under cover as soon as possible. Then we sat in our holes, while the sun shone down mercilessly upon us. 'Becker, have you got anything more to drink?' I asked a comrade who had dug himself a hole about one and a half metres from me.

No reply. I thought he had fallen asleep and crept over to him. But what a scene awaited me! Becker was sitting in his foxhole staring at me. I saw that he wanted to say something but he could not make a single sound. He had to vomit again and again. His jacket and trousers were covered in it. I examined him and found that he had been shot in the neck. The Russian bullet had bored through the soft earth which he had dug up and then forced its way into his neck, where it had then probably lodged in his throat. I bandaged his neck; there was nothing more I could do. He weakly held my hand and looked pleadingly at me. I understood his gesture and said: 'Yes, Becker, I will stay with you.' I stuck our two bayonets into the earth to the left and right of him, undid his coat from his pack, and spread it over the bayonets so that he was sheltered from the heat of the sun. From the left we heard the order: 'Prepare to advance.' I asked three of my comrades to stay behind to help carry Becker back in the evening. They were happy to comply as they too preferred to stay in their holes instead of advancing. Our Group Leader had received a shrapnel wound earlier on and had run back, so there was nobody there to drive us on.

'Forwards! March! March!' came the command. The soldiers jumped out of their holes and the Russians started firing like mad. Many bullets whizzed over our heads and through the oats. We four did not know what was happening up ahead, and none of us felt brave enough to stick his head above the oats to have a look. So we lay in the holes until evening. Then we spread out Becker's tent on the ground and laid him on it. Two men pulled at the front corners, while two other men shoved him from behind. That was a form of transport! It all had to happen while creeping as we did not dare to be seen above the short oat stalks. Eventually, after a lot of effort and sweating we got behind the summit and were able to walk upright. For Becker this way was truly like the way of the cross.[38] He waved with both hands to show that he wanted to walk. I grabbed hold of him on one side, a comrade held him on the other. We picked him up and carried him for a stretch and then he collapsed again. We put him back on his tent and carried him into the village to the battalion doctor. In a room in which there were already many wounded, we laid Becker down on the straw. I asked the battalion doctor to take him on. He came, took a look at the wound, and let me know by his look that this was a hopeless case. Then he went on to the other wounded. We said goodbye to Becker, who seemed half unconscious, as he was lying very still.

As we came out of the house, a troop of Russian prisoners was being led back. Two of us put our bayonets onto our guns and went off as escorts. As it was now getting dark we went looking for somewhere to stay the night

[38] Dominik Richert is likening Becker's suffering to that of Christ on the way to the Crucifixion.

with the others. We hauled some straw into an empty room and lay down. However, my stomach started to complain and we did not have anything to eat. I got up, went to the back of the house and was able to fetch a canteen full of potatoes from the vegetable garden by the light of the moon. Now all we needed was water so that we could wash them and cook them. I went to a well at the side of the road. The mechanism was broken, but I found a telephone cable nearby, tied it to my canteen, and was about to haul up some water when a soldier came and said: 'Comrade, you should not take any water here, it is suspected of carrying cholera. Look, there is a warning on the frame of the well.' I heard straight away from his accent that the soldier came from Alsace, and his voice sounded familiar. I looked at his face in the moonlight and it really was Xavier Schorr from my neighbouring village Fülleren. 'Are you not Xeri Schorr from Füllera?'[39] I asked him. He almost fell on his backside when he heard someone speak to him like that. 'Yes, he replied, but who are you?' I shone my pocket lamp in my face, but he was unable to recognize me from my appearance as I was so emaciated. I was also unshaven. We now went together to my quarters. Schorr was an NCO and was the supervisor of the Company's machine gun waggon, so he did not have to take part in any fighting and always had enough food. He fetched an army loaf, a tin of meat, a little sack of sugar and rusks from his quarters. After we had eaten, we lay down on the straw and talked of home. I had recently had a letter from home in which I had learned that although they were near the front, the inhabitants of Fülleren were still able to live at home. Schorr was very pleased to hear this as he had not had news from home for a long time. We chatted away until the new day shone into the window. As Schorr now had to do his duty, we made our farewells. Then I slept until the afternoon. After that my comrade and I set out to find our Company. We passed through the region where the battle had taken place days before. Dead bodies were scattered around everywhere, first Germans and then Russians. In the field of oats ahead of us we could see a number of rifle butts. The Russians had stuck their bayonets in the ground as they surrendered. It took us two days until we rejoined our Company. We were in no hurry to do so. The following night we once again marched for several hours. Then we had to dig ourselves in by platoons, in rows on a gently rising hill.

Fighting at Wlodawa at the start of August 1915

In the darkness, several of our battalions went quietly forward past us. None of us knew what was going on. At daybreak several batteries behind us started shooting. The shells impacted quite far ahead of us, so once again we

---

[39] Dominik Richert spoke back to him in the local dialect.

were in reserve. Ahead of us the infantry engagement started, but it did not last long before the Russians surrendered without putting up much resistance. Their artillery scattered the area with small-calibre shells. Suddenly a heavy shell crashed down about three hundred metres ahead of us. Then the second one hit about two hundred metres ahead, while the third one landed one hundred metres from us. All three were following a direction towards us. 'Just you wait,' I said to the student from East Prussia, 'the next one will land in the Company!' It was an uncanny experience; we ducked down as low as we could into our hole. Then the fourth one whizzed in and landed in a foxhole about three metres from us where two soldiers of the first platoon were sheltering. When the smoke had cleared we saw their limbs scattered about, while pieces of entrails were hanging in a bush nearby – a terrible, but easy death. The next shell flew over our heads. Then the heavy guns stopped firing. Only random small-calibre shrapnel shells flew in every once in a while. Then the student said 'I will have to relieve myself' and went behind a bush nearby. A shrapnel shell exploded directly above him, and a ball of shrapnel passed through his temple into his head. He died instantly. With the help of my comrades we fetched his body and laid it in the hole which the big shell had made. The collected body parts of the other two soldiers had already been put there. We covered them up. I used my pocket knife to cut two thick sticks from the bushes and tied them up with a willow to make the form of a cross, which I then put on the grave. An NCO wrote their names on a piece of paper and tied it on to the top of the cross with a string. Now I had lost the last of my best comrades. I was so put off that I hardly knew what to do any more.

Then we were ordered: 'Forwards! March!' We went across the fields towards the Russian position, in front of which lay several fallen Germans. In the Russian position, which was very well located and built, I only saw two dead Russians. We continued to advance and followed the other soldiers, who had already taken up the pursuit. In a house that had been burnt right down we saw a gruesome sight which made almost all of us shudder. The house had probably been a Russian dressing station, and on the floor was a heap of completely charred corpses. One body was several metres away from the others and had only been burnt on one side. Probably it was a wounded man who had wanted to save himself but had not been able to creep any further. 'He died a hero's death for his Fatherland!' A hero's death – what a lie that is! I have experienced and gone through so much, but I have hardly met one hero in a thousand men.

The Russians had once again cleared out completely. We marched for several days without a shot being fired, until we reached undulating hilly countryside which was mainly planted with oats and barley. Here we encountered the Russians and advanced, swarmed out in extended order. Suddenly we came under heavy shrapnel fire, and my comrade Anton

Schmitt from Oberdorf was seriously wounded. He was hit by three balls through his shoulder and upper arm. I dragged him behind a nearby hut where I bandaged him with the assistance of an ambulance man who came to help. A sergeant ordered me to rejoin the line. A group led by NCO Walter from Alsace advanced in a line about one hundred metres ahead of us. The shrapnel fire continued incessantly. I could not see any Russian infantry. Suddenly we saw movement in the oats ahead. Masses of Russians were facing us and ran cheering towards us. Soon they reached Walter's group. His soldiers threw their guns away and surrendered to the Russians. They were led away immediately. We were all very excited, knelt down in the oats, and each of us shot as quickly as possible. We were outnumbered by about ten or fifteen to one. The Russians at the front shot regularly at us as they advanced. Our losses mounted. They were only about fifty steps away from us and I was about to throw my gun away to surrender – a frightening moment as you could not be sure whether they would bayonet you or not – when we heard cheering behind us and two companies of our regiment came storming out of a hollow. They immediately fired over our heads at the Russians. The Russians at the front stopped short. They did not know how powerful the new attackers were. Some of them turned, and they took the others with them. In a few minutes, they were all retreating. We fired at them as hard as we could and they suffered dreadful losses.

Afterwards, as we advanced through the oats we passed their dead lying there, almost all of them face down. The survivors had escaped through a hollow in the field. The wounded of both sides were bandaged up and carried to a road. We had to continue on. In extended order, we advanced towards a wood. Sporadic shots came towards us. Suddenly I felt as if I had been lashed on my right elbow. I dropped my gun, reached there with my left hand and saw a bullet hole in my jacket. I felt a strong burning feeling at my elbow. My first thought was: Thank God! Now I will get to a military hospital! I dropped to the ground to prevent myself from being a further target for the Russians, pulled up my sleeve, and experienced a great disappointment. I had only a graze: a bullet had only cut a groove in the skin. I bandaged myself with my left hand, helped by my teeth, and stayed lying there. When the shooting ahead of us stopped, I went back and went straight to the Battalion Doctor. I wanted to squeeze past him and go further back, but he called to me and said: 'Well then, what's wrong with you? Come here!' I went to him and removed my bandage. 'Yes, lad, that's not enough for the hospital! Go and join your Company's field kitchen for a couple of days, and then come back and see me!' Yes, field kitchen! Where are you? In the evening it arrived and I walked along behind it after I had loaded my backpack and my rifle onto it. The next time it stopped I got coffee and a meal.

After two days I went back to see the Battalion Doctor. 'So, you can rejoin your Company!' I waited until evening and went back with the people who had come to collect the food. On the following day we marched past the town of Brest-Litovsk and headed eastwards through the Rokitno swamps in the direction of Pinsk. For a number of days now I had once again been suffering from stomach pain and diarrhoea. This weakened me so much that I was hardly able to keep up. I reported sick again, but had to return to the Company and continue to do my duty. We came to a wooded area where our Company was marching on a bad forest track. Bang, bang, we heard shooting ahead. A scream! One of the soldiers had been shot through the middle of his knee. We had to lie down. The people from the Russian outpost had run away. We waited for orders from the Battalion Commander. When none arrived, a lieutenant took two of us and we set out to find the Battalion Headquarters to get our orders. We went along a footpath which was not often used. The lieutenant stopped and said: 'We have lost our path! Can you possibly read maps?' 'I understand them to some extent,' I replied. I was surprised when I looked at the map. Every footpath and every detail was marked. There were several footpaths leading through the wood. We just did not know which one we were on. 'Well, we'll just walk on,' said the lieutenant, 'and we're sure to come out somewhere.' We came to a hollow in which there was a fairly large boggy area, overgrown with reeds, in the form of an elongated triangle. I had noticed a triangle like that on the map. 'Sir, I know where we are now,' I said. 'So,' he said – astonished. I asked for the map and showed him where we were. We were on the nearest route to the headquarters. We got our orders and returned to the Company. We had to wait in the woods and dig ourselves in. In the morning, it was 'Advance!' It was a very hot day again. Some Russians who were in a hut on the edge of the woods surrendered to us. The others had retreated. We marched after them all day. The sweat poured down our bodies like little streams, and our backpacks were heavy. Our feet in our boots burned like fire. According to the regulations each of us had to carry three hundred bullets, but that was too heavy, so I simply threw two hundred of them away. My stomach pains increased so much that I was not going to be able to bear it much longer. At the next stop I reported sick. I was permitted to put my gun and my backpack onto the field kitchen waggon, but had to continue walking. We spent the night in a wood of bushes. There, the Battalion Doctor decided that I was ill: gastro-enteritis. My God, how happy I was! Nobody can describe it! Now I knew that I would leave the front and go to a military hospital.

The next morning I had to continue with the others because, as the Battalion Doctor explained, it was not possible to send an ambulance back just for me; I had to stay with them until a number of wounded and ill people had gathered. Now I was transported with the Battalion Baggage

Train. On an almost impassable forest track we encountered a column of refugees. The Russians had misinformed these poor people that we would massacre everyone when we arrived. In a hurry they had put some food-stuffs and other necessities onto waggons and fled from us. We had caught up with them there in the wood. It was a solitary, almost unpopulated area. The baggage train horses could hardly make any progress on the poor track. Then the horses belonging to the poor refugees were simply unhitched and taken for our use. The wailing and pleas of the poor people touched my heart. Many of the women fell on their knees in front of the soldiers and implored them to leave the horses. It was no use. Some of the roughest soldiers climbed onto the refugees' waggons and stole their food. Then we went on. The wailing refugees were simply left behind.

Up ahead, the patrols fired some shots. A soldier came to the Battalion Doctor with a shot in the arm. In the evening, two more soldiers were found to be ill. One had the same illness as me, while the other was vomiting blood. On the following night, our last at the Front, the four of us shared a tent. In the early morning an ambulance man came with a light waggon of the kind which was common in the area, pulled by two horses. We sat or lay on it and set off back from the Front. Despite the pain in my stomach I could have shouted out with joy. Now it was certain that for a time I would not be shot dead. I was also really looking forward to being able to sleep in a bed. The three comrades with whom I was travelling were also really happy, despite their condition. We travelled the whole day through a dismal land-scape. There were swamps and bushes, and here or there one or more human habitations. The houses were quite small, as everywhere in the Carpathians and Galicia with the exception of the towns, with wooden walls and roofs of straw. The ambulance man gave us army bread and tinned meat for lunch, but I did not dare eat as I was afraid that my stomach pains would return. In the evening we reached a village where a medical company was based. We slept in the village overnight and in the next morning about fifteen of us, mostly suffering from dysentery, travelled in a motorized ambulance to Grubeschow, where we arrived at night time.

In the Field Hospital at Grubeschow in Russian Poland

The new Russian infantry barracks in Grubeschow had been turned into a field hospital. A sleepy medical orderly received us. Each of us was given a cup of tea, and then we were allocated beds – soldiers' beds of the kind you usually find in a barracks. I lay down, exhausted, covered myself with the white woollen blanket and fell asleep straight away. I woke up. I was being bitten and itched all over my body so badly that I felt I was beyond helping myself. I was used to lice, but this sort of thing was almost unbearable. Despite this, I eventually managed to fall asleep again. When I awoke, it was already broad daylight. I looked at my blanket. Good Lord, it was crawling with lice! There were at least twenty as big as a five Mark piece. I would have preferred to stay in bed for longer, but it was impossible. I got up and got dressed – a task with which I was no longer familiar as I had not slept a single night without my clothes on since February, almost six months ago. Russian prisoners, who acted as orderlies, brought us tea and army bread. I went out to take a look around. Right behind the barracks was a new military cemetery. About ten Russians were busy digging graves. Two corpses were just being taken from the former drill house, which had been converted into a hospital for cholera patients, and being buried without ceremony by the Russians. All the graves had attractive black crosses painted with white inscriptions saying the name, regiment and company of the person who had died. On the Russian crosses, there was only 'Here rests a brave Russian' or: 'Here rest three brave Russians', depending on the number of soldiers buried in the grave. On one of the crosses I read: 'Musketeer Schneidmadl, 7 Company, 1 Regiment 41' – a soldier with whom I was good friends. I had already noticed that he was missing from the Company for a number of days – and now I found him like this. The field hospital was not good at treating our illness; it had not yet been set up properly. In the afternoon I went into Grubeschow. We were fortunate because each of us was able to buy a good loaf of white bread, which was at least much better for our ill stomachs than the army bread. On the way home we were approached by a Jew who was standing at the door of his house. 'Come into my house, sir and drink a cup of tea. You can ... with my daughter as much as you want for two Marks.' My comrade hit him quite hard in the face and we went back to the hospital. Many of these Polish Jews used all possible means to earn money; nothing was too base for them. Only money, nothing else seemed to matter to them.

Each day new wounded and ill soldiers came to the hospital, many of whom were near to death. A soldier in the bed next to mine was like this. His stomach pain caused him to writhe like a worm in the sun. He was called Simon Duka from Upper Silesia. When the doctor examined him he said to the attendant: 'Bring this man to Section C!' That was the drill house in which the cholera victims were treated. After two days I went across the cemetery. On the cross of a new grave I read the name Simon Duka. Cholera had taken one more victim. Now all I wanted was to get out of this place as quickly as possible. I had been in Grubeschow for six days when we were all medically examined. All those who were fit to travel were to be sent further back the following day. We travelled for a half a day on requisitioned farm carts and then we reached a narrow gauge military railway. The trains, consisting of little flat cars, were hauled by horses. We sat down or lay on the waggons and travelled on. The place was very boring and had few inhabitants. Most of the farms and villages had been burnt down. We spent the night in tents. Russian flyers attacked the camp with bombs during the night, but nobody was injured. Early the following morning we continued our journey and crossed the border between Russia and Galicia. At the station in the town of Unov we boarded the train which took us via Rava-Ruska to Lemberg, which we reached at night.

In the Military Hospital in Lemberg

The military hospital in Lemberg in which we were accommodated was a large building, a former school. In the hall, to which I was allocated, were lots of soldiers who were suffering from dysentery, gastro-enteritis and typhus. They were all poor people who spent half their time sitting on the toilet. Our accommodation consisted of straw sacks lying on the floor. The food was poor. There was no order: Austrian conditions! The days passed slowly. People did not talk much as almost everyone was suffering from terrible stomach pain. If someone moaned too much then the attendant would come and stick a thermometer under his arm to measure his temperature – as if that would do any good. One soldier was so annoyed by this that he threw the thermometer at the wall where it smashed into small pieces. When the doctor took him to task, the soldier said that he expected to be treated as a human being. We all waited for the day when we would be transported further.

Journey to Germany

Eventually after six days we went to the station. We travelled third class. The journey went through Galicia, past the Fortress of Przemyl, then via Jaroslau and Tarnów to Cracow. We travelled along a double track. Every five minutes a train from Germany would pass us with soldiers, war material and foodstuffs. The Russians had destroyed all the bridges as they retreated so emergency bridges made of wood had been built. The trains could only cross them at walking pace. A number of these emergency bridges crossed deep gorges, so that you could hardly trust yourself to look. We stopped in front of the Fortress of Cracow; thousands of Russian prisoners were working next to the track, shifting earth. There was a thunderstorm and it started to rain about as hard as I have ever seen. In a few minutes the Russians were soaked to the skin. It seemed that they were not permitted to leave the workplace. Travelling onwards, we crossed the border from Galicia into Germany. Our first stop in Germany was the station in Annenberg. We all had to alight and fall in and then we went to the delousing station. This was as big as a small village. Every day thousands of soldiers were freed from their lice there. We first all came into a large heated room where we had to undress. We were all in our birthday suits; most of the soldiers

110

were so thin that they looked like a frame of bones, but they all seemed happy to be back in their homeland and could look forward to a pleasant life in hospital. We moved on to the shower room. Warm water sprayed down on us in more than two hundred jets. Each of us positioned himself under a shower head. How good it felt as the warm water trickled down your body. There was enough soap, so we were soon all white from the lather. Once more under the shower, then we went into the dressing room. We were each given a new shirt, underwear and socks. In the meantime our uniforms had been collected into large iron tubes which were heated to ninety degrees. The heat killed the lice and nits in the clothes. The clothes came out crumpled and looked a bit yellow, but that did not matter to us. We were given something to eat. Those of us with stomach trouble were given gruel, which caused less stomach pain than more solid food.

We returned to the station. Only someone who has been tortured by these bugs can understand how good it felt to be free of the lice. At the station I drank a glass of beer; I also ate an apple that a woman gave to me. It was a very careless thing to do, and it might have killed me. I had such severe stomach pain that I writhed around in the compartment. It gradually improved, and it grew dark. We did not know where we were travelling through the dark. The following morning, the train stopped in each town. Each time, the number of ill and wounded who had to leave the train was determined by the number of spaces which were free in the military hospitals. The last to leave the train, myself included, left the train in Fraustadt (Province of Posen). Those who could not walk were fetched in waggons. The military hospital had been set up in the local infantry barracks, and it held more than two thousand wounded and ill soldiers. The people who were suffering from gastro-enteritis, dysentery and typhus were allocated to the epidemic section, which was located in the drill hall of the barracks. The large spacious drill hall had been divided up into several large rooms, and in these rooms stood white clean beds. Beside each bed there was a small bedside table. In the middle of the room was a large table with books, news-papers and magazines. Everything was immaculately clean. I can survive here, I thought to myself. The patients lying in the beds looked curiously at us. Each of us was allocated a bed. Then the doctor came and examined us again. I had to get into bed straight away. How good it felt to be able to lie undressed and free of lice in a soft clean bed!

However, I did often – very often – have to get up and go to the toilet. In doing so I had such pain in my intestines that I often fell unconscious. It felt as if several drills were at work in there. I was not allowed to eat anything apart from gruel or rice gruel. The doctor warned me not to try anything else as he would not be responsible for the consequences.

The treatment was very good. The nurses, doctors and attendants were very friendly. Each morning we would find an attractive bunch of flowers

111

on each bedside table, together with a glass of water with a mouthwash added to it. The doctor went through the ward twice a day. I gradually became so weak that I was unable to get out of bed. We were weighed each Saturday. The first time, I weighed 118 pounds in my jacket and trousers (without boots). The second time, in my shirt, I weighed 115 pounds, while the third time I weighed 114 pounds.[40] I lost a great deal of blood in my stool. I often had to spend hours on the bedpan in my bed. My comrades were not doing much better – some were doing worse. The relatives of many of the patients came to visit. I would really have liked mine to visit too, but this was not possible as the Western Front separated us.

One morning, the bed next to mine was empty. The patient who had occupied it, father of a family, had become so weak for several days that he could hardly speak any more. Now he had died in the night. The following night a man with dysentery died in the same ward. I awoke just as the attendants were carrying out his corpse. Although I always hoped to make it through, I was not always sure, but I just prayed quietly until my weakness caused me to fall asleep again. I was not even able to slurp my gruel by myself; the nurse had to hold the cup to my mouth and raise me up slightly, because I was so weak. How unpleasant that became! Whenever I saw the nurse coming with it, I felt more and more disgusted.

Once, during doctors' rounds, I pretended to be asleep. The doctor and the nurse stepped quietly to my bed. 'Well, doctor, what do you think of Richert?' asked the nurse quietly. 'I am really hopeful that I will pull him through. He has a very tenacious hold on life,' answered the doctor equally quietly. How happy I was to hear this! I was filled with new hope, because dying is always difficult when you are only twenty-two years old.

By and by I felt a bit stronger, and I could raise myself up in my bed. I had survived the worst. The nurse, who saw that things were improving, and who knew that I longed for something other than gruel, would often pass me a rusk made from fine wheat flour to me under the cover, although the doctor had not yet given his permission. Eventually I was allowed to eat something different. Like a child, they got me used to eating again; to start with I was given fine rusks soaked in milk, then rice pudding with apple purée, then grated potato and grated meat – all things that would not put great demands on my stomach. You would hardly believe what an appetite I developed – I was able to eat more and more. In the first week in which I was able to eat and was allowed to do so, my weight increased by seven pounds. My strength returned quickly, so that I was able to stand up again. We often sat out on comfortable couches and enjoyed the autumn sunshine. I was happier than I had ever been since the outbreak of war. In our ward nobody

---

[40] Dominik Richert was 1.78 metres tall. He would be using metric pounds, so, for example, 114 pounds = 57 kilograms.

was seriously ill any more, so we sometimes got quite loud. We played cards, draughts, dominos and all kinds of other games to pass the time. I really enjoyed it and yet I often thought that the fun might end badly as the war was still in full swing. Fit people who left the military hospital usually only spent a short time with their reserve battalion before being sent back to the Front. I dreaded that, as winter was approaching.

My comrade August Zanger, with whom I had kept up regular contact by post, would soon be back on his feet, but he was not fit to be a soldier again. He was still in a reserve military hospital in the Rhineland. He sent me an application form from his hospital. I was really happy that there was a chance that we might get together again. I showed the form to the doctor and asked him to let me travel there. However he told me that it was impossible because the Reserve Battalion of Infantry Regiment 41 was stationed in Speyersdorf near Königsberg in East Prussia. Then the doctor said to me: 'Richert, you can apply for four weeks' convalescent leave; I will support your application.' I replied: 'That's not possible for me, doctor. My nearest and dearest are all in the part of Alsace which has been occupied by the French, so I cannot get there.' 'I really feel sorry for you, Richert,' said the doctor. He asked whether I had had any news from home, then he continued on his round. The next day I asked the doctor whether it would be possible for me to spend four weeks in a convalescent home. 'Yes, that can be arranged,' said the doctor, and he brought me an application form for the convalescent home with the Grey Nuns in Frauenstadt. I thanked the doctor and the nurses and attendants and took my leave of them and of my comrades in the room, many of whom had become good friends. Then I left.

In the Convalescent Home in Fraustadt – end of September and October 1915

When I arrived I was made very welcome. The convalescent home was the former town hospital of Frauenstadt. Almost all the soldiers there looked well. They would soon be fit to be led back to the slaughter! The food was excellent and plentiful, and the sisters were very friendly and kind. Two young girls served the food with a friendly 'Here you are!' We slept until eight in the morning and then we got up and washed. For breakfast we were given coffee – good coffee with milk – and rolls cut in two and spread with butter or jam. At ten we were given a cup of bouillon. At lunchtime we had soup followed by either meat and vegetables or a roast with noodles. We were each given a bottle of beer to go with it. As a dessert we had apples, pears and – now and then – grapes. At four in the afternoon we had tea with rolls – with butter or jam as a matter of course, and sometimes with ham or sliced sausage – and at six in the evening we were given roast potatoes and sausage, followed by coffee with milk. We were all able to eat as much as we wanted.

That was a splendid time, but the days were soon over and the four weeks were approaching an end. Rich ladies and their daughters from the town often brought us presents and chatted to us. The sisters played dominos, draughts and so on with us. Those young soldiers who often went to mass in the little hospital chapel, and now and then took the holy sacrament, were particularly favoured by the sisters.

A doctor came to examine us – but only once a week. Each time he came, soldiers were declared fit for duty and sent to their reserve battalions. Now my four weeks were up. 'The doctor's coming tomorrow,' they said. That morning I did not eat anything. I smoked several cigarettes, drank a large amount of cold water, ran like mad backwards and forwards round the back by the toilets and then went to be examined. The doctor noticed that my heart was pounding too fast, and as a result of my smoking and drinking water I looked pale. 'You can stay here for at least another week,' said the doctor. I had achieved what I wanted for the time being, and could enjoy another seven lovely days. We were weighed once again during the last week. With my shirt and trousers on I weighted 157 pounds, so I had gained 43 pounds. When this week was over, I was declared fit and was given a travel permit to go to Speyersdorf near Königsberg. On the last night, I slept badly, and dreamt of doing drill at the barracks and of life at the Front. That night, the first snow fell.

The next morning, the 28th of October 1915, I got ready to go and said goodbye to the nurses who liked me and were sorry to see me go. They gave me a big pile of buttered cake for my journey. One last handshake and I was on my way.

At the station, I boarded the train in the direction of Königsberg. The journey was boring as it was cold and everything was covered in snow. I travelled the whole day and the following night. When the train arrived in Königsberg the next morning I went into a restaurant in town and drank several cups of hot coffee before asking my way to Speyersdorf. Although the restaurant owner gave me directions, I had to ask several people before I found the right way through the large town. Finally I passed out through the old defensive walls, and in a quarter of an hour I was in Speyersdorf.

In the Reserve Battalion of Infantry Regiment 41 at Speyersdorf and Memel

The Reserve Battalion of Infantry Regiment 41 was based in wooden barracks next to the road outside Speyersdorf. Some soldiers were just fetching coffee from the kitchen. I asked the way to the office and reported to the sergeant.

With his parents – as a
young man, prior to the
First World War.

eady for duty – 1913.
Iilitary service was seen as
significant stage in
rowing up and celebrated
ccordingly – hence the
icture. DR is second from
e right.

On manoeuvre in Heuberg 1914. DR is marked second from the right, second row from the front.

In the barracks in 1914. By the start of 1915, DR was the only one who was still serving. The others had been killed, injured, or driven mad by what they had experienced.

In Uniform – probably taken during the War.

n the hospital in Fraustadt in 1915.
ЭR is on the back row, second from
he right, near the door.

As an NCO with his Machine Gun Crew.

...ecuperation – Probably taken in Donaueschingen, 1915. DR is behind the garden gnome, on the left.

...n leave - with August Zanger. This ...hotograph was taken in Siegburg, October ...- November 1916.

A wartime picture in uniform: since a medal ribbon can be seen, it must be after he was first decorated in 1916. It may be the picture which was taken in 1918.

A family picture with his sons – probably taken in the 1930s.

RÉPUBLIQUE FRANÇAISE   N° 670583

CARTE DE PATRIOTE RÉSISTANT À L'OCCUPATION
DES DÉPARTEMENTS DU RHIN ET DE LA MOSELLE,
INCARCÉRÉ EN CAMPS SPÉCIAUX
délivrée par le Ministère des Anciens Combattants et Victimes de guerre

TITULAIRE : RICHERT Dominique

Né le 4 mai 1893
Domicile : ST. ULRICH N° 51
(HAUT-RHIN)
Période de contrainte du 1er 3. 1943
au 12. 5. 1945
Carte établie le 1 JUIL 1960
POUR LE MINISTRE
ET PAR DÉLÉGATION :   Le Titulaire,
LE DIRECTEUR INTERDÉPARTEMENTAL D. Richert

RÉPUBLIQUE FRANÇAISE   N° 670584

CARTE DE PATRIOTE RÉSISTANT À L'OCCUPATION
DES DÉPARTEMENTS DU RHIN ET DE LA MOSELLE,
INCARCÉRÉ EN CAMPS SPÉCIAUX
délivrée par le Ministère des Anciens Combattants et Victimes de guerre

TITULAIRE : RICHERT née KAYSER Marie Adèle

Née le 10 septembre 1902
Domicile : ST. ULRICH N° 51
(HAUT-RHIN)
Période de contrainte du 1er 3. 1943
au 12. 5. 1945
Carte établie le 1 JUIL 1960
POUR LE MINISTRE
ET PAR DÉLÉGATION :   Le Titulaire,
LE DIRECTEUR INTERDÉPARTEMENTAL Richert A

ostwar passes. These passes were issued by the French authorities to those people who had
uffered deportation by the Nazis.

As a grandfather, with his grandchild in his arms.

He sent me to a barrack room and told me that I should be examined by the doctor when he made his rounds at nine o'clock. I went to the hut, was allocated a bed, and was given coffee and army bread. When I took my first bite of army bread it felt as if I had a piece of earth in my mouth. I felt a great longing for the good food provided by the kind sisters at Frauenstadt. But that was over now, and I had to accept what I could not change. The doctor signed me off for ten days and I was allocated to the recuperation company. After the examination I went out for a walk in the yard. There were lots of soldiers who had been shot to half cripples there, waiting to be discharged. A soldier limped past me, supporting himself with two sticks. I thought to myself: he must have shot himself through both feet. As he went past he looked in my face and said: 'My goodness! Are you not Richert?' 'Yes, that's me,' I answered. 'Do you not recognize me any more?' he said, so I said no. 'We were in the Carpathians together, until both my feet froze on Zwinin Mountain!' Now I recognized him. His face was now about twice as broad as at that time in the Carpathians. That was why I did not recognize him immediately. He told me that all ten of his toes had been amputated, but he was happy about it and said: 'I would rather live without ten toes than be buried somewhere at the front with all my toes. The war is over for me and I will get a seventy per cent pension.' He really was to be envied, even though he would be half-crippled for the rest of his life. On that day I met several other soldiers from my Company when I was in the field. Several of them limped around with missing toes. One had lost an arm, and yet another had a stiff arm and leg, but they all seemed happy because they would soon be able to return home to their parents forever.

On the following day I met Anton Schmitt from Oberdorf, the chap whom I had bandaged in the field after he had been wounded by three shrapnel balls. He had to go to Königsberg each day to have his arm electrically stimulated and massaged. (He made a complete recovery, returned to active duty, and was killed.)

One day I also met the young East Prussian teacher who had been hit by a shot which went right through his face during the attack on Livtira Gorna on the 1st of July 1915. He had red points on each cheek where the bullet had entered and left. As his tongue had been injured, he could no longer speak as well as before. He had become a senior NCO as he had joined as a one-year army volunteer and served for a year.[41] He expected to become a lieutenant soon. He invited me to spend an evening in Königsberg. We really enjoyed ourselves, but for me it was the first and the last time as my wallet could not take the strain. I was still not earning more than thirty three Pfennigs a day and that was not enough for buying the bare necessities.

[41] An *Einjähriger* was a volunteer with higher education who would normally expect promotion after a year's service.

115

I could see that other soldiers who had normal contact with home would receive money and parcels of food, and could live it up, going to theatres, cinemas and pubs, while I was solely dependent upon my miserable army food and was reduced to looking at the moon with nothing in my pockets. Nevertheless, I felt myself fortunate when I compared my life now with life at the Front, and I wanted it to stay the same until the end of the war.

I had been in Speyersdorf about a week when the whole reserve battalion was loaded onto a train. We travelled via Insterburg, Tilsit and Heydekrug up to Memel, where the barracks of the 41st Infantry Regiment were located. We arrived at night-time. The barracks were situated behind the town. Life up there was more pleasant than in the huts. The rooms were warmer and easier to keep clean.

Memel is a port on the Baltic at the northeastern tip of Germany. As I had never seen the open sea before, I really wanted to do so. The following morning I went upstairs in the barracks to where I could look down from an attic window over the houses to the sea. But that wasn't enough. Without asking for permission, I walked past the sentry at the gate and walked through the town to the harbour. From there I went on to the mole, which had a concrete lighthouse at the end. The mole was a wall about four metres broad which stretched out into the sea and protected the harbour from the waves. The weather was stormy, and I was fascinated by what I saw. The whole time, waves several metres high rolled in, breaking on the mole and sending spray flying further. It was as if one wave was chasing the other. It was as if the water had been completely churned up. Suddenly I was showered with water so I hurried back off the mole. There were several ships in the harbour, so I went to look at them. One of them with a cargo of oats was being unloaded. The sacks were lifted up and over with small cranes and then loaded into railway waggons by the dock workers. Then I went back to the barracks.

The following day the sergeant called me. He had noticed in my pay book that I had been in the field since the start of the war and had not had any leave. He said that I could have fourteen days' leave. 'I cannot accept this leave,' I said 'because I have nowhere to go to,' and explained my situation to him. 'My word!' he replied. 'That's quite something. We'll see what we can do. You can live here too, and I will treat you with consideration!' This sergeant was an exception in the German army. During the following days I was treated lightly although the ten days free of duty which the doctor had ordered were already over.

Once I had to go with eight others on guard duty at the station for a period of twenty-four hours. I was back on duty from midnight until 2.00am. I was walking slowly backwards and forwards along the platform when I suddenly heard a terrible explosion. All the soldiers on duty, together with various railway workers, came and asked me what had happened. I didn't know, but believed that it must have happened at the harbour. The next morning we found out what had happened. A mine moored in the sea had broken loose and was washed into the mole, where it blew a large hole in the wall.

Another time, I was sent to guard the harbour. I had sentry duty on the gate through which all the people going into and out of the harbour had to pass, as the whole harbour was protected by a wire fence. There was a lot of work checking all the passes when the harbour workers left for lunch. The same was true when they came back. Most of them were mean, rough people who spoke a dialect which even the devil would not be able to understand. A number of them got rough with me when I asked for their passes, as I had seen them an hour before when they went to lunch. I would not have minded, but for the fact that I might have been observed by someone in charge. Then I would have had to spend three days in clink. I was able to get all of them to calm down apart from one of them, who seemed to be a really nasty human being. He absolutely refused to show his pass. I stepped two steps back, pointed my gun at his cheek and ordered him to show me his pass or to leave. He gave in, showed me his pass, and went through growling. In the evening a number of slovenly prostitutes wanted to go to the sailors on the ships, but I did not let them through. They went back, but I saw later that they were climbing the fence and were heading for the ships after all. What could I do? I pretended not to have seen anything.

The next morning a lad aged about seventeen came along and chatted with me. He wanted to volunteer to join the army. I advised him not to and described life on the Front to him in a way that made his hair stand on end. 'No, if it's like that, I would rather wait until I am called up.' 'Even then it will be too early,' I said. He thanked me and went away. I had the feeling that I had done a good deed.

On the following morning we lined up for a roll call with payment of wages. In Memel we were paid war wages at a rate of fifty three Pfennigs a day instead of the usual thirty three. When we had all been paid, the First Lieutenant called out: 'Musketeer Richert step forward!' I had no idea why, so I stepped forward and stood still. 'It is my duty,' he said 'to inform the Company of your brave and energetic behaviour while on sentry duty at the harbour. I wish to express my total appreciation. The duty officer observed the way in which you forced that rude brute of a harbour worker to show his pass.' I was totally surprised, but it certainly does not do any harm to be well in with your superiors.

One Sunday evening I was commanded to take part in a pub patrol, consisting of two men, led by an NCO. We had to carry our guns and wear our helmets. The NCO was a genial person with a head full of fun. He did not act like our superior, but like a comrade. We were tasked with going round the pubs after closing time to encourage the soldiers to go home and to write down and report the names of any soldiers who were there without permission. We visited more than twenty pubs. As soon as the landlord or landlady noticed our helmets they would call to the bar, order us a tankard of beer or a glass of cognac and encourage us to have a drink. By and by we got quite tipsy. If we encountered any soldiers in the street without permits, the NCO advised them to climb over the wall at the back of the barracks and take care not to get caught. The soldiers were very happy, because when we stopped them they expected that they would land in the clink. Then we landed in a brothel. My God, how frightened the half-naked prostitutes were when we walked in, because they knew that if they did not shut up shop after closing time their establishment would be closed. Our NCO acted as if he was going to report them. The prostitutes asked and pleaded and tried to flatter us and kiss us and do all kinds of things. The NCO really gave them quite a fright. Then he laughed, tore up the report he had started and told them not to worry. This pleased them and they put out two bottles of beer straight away, but we had drunk enough already so we went back to the barracks to sleep off our intoxication.

The next day we were told that a transport of replacement teams was to be sent from our Reserve Battalion to the Russian Front. That came as a real bombshell. Everyone was frightened of being sent to the Front. Everyone had a holy respect for the Russian winter, and it was just the end of November. I was quite sure, that I would be selected, as I was quite fit and looked it as a result of the good feeding I had received in hospital.

Then we were given another order: 'Everybody assemble.' The reserve battalion was to send twenty men to Pillau to join the First Reserve Machine Gun Company of the First Army Corps. 'Anyone who wants to volunteer to join the machine gunners should let us know!' I was one of the first to step forward because I thought, however it turns out, it's still better than being at the Front – and machine gunners never had to attack with bayonets – that is also worth noting! So it was decided that I should go to Pillau.

End of 1915 into 1916

With the Reserve Machine Gun Company of the 1st Army Corps in Pillau

The following day, the twenty of us travelled by train to Königsberg and on from there to Pillau. The town is located at the tip of a spit of land, about one kilometre wide and five kilometres long, which reaches out into the Baltic from the mainland. Pillau is surrounded by water on three sides: towards the northwest by the Baltic, towards the southwest by the entrance into the Frische Haaf, and to the east by the Frische Haaf itself. Pillau itself is a sea fortress. On a small hill behind the town lies the Fort of Stiele.

At the beach by the dunes were several batteries of heavy artillery in rotatable mountings pointing out to sea. Next to them were shell-proof casemates to protect the gun crews. From the station it took about a quarter of an hour to walk to the Company, which occupied single storey barracks with masonry walls. We had to assemble in front of them. The Company Sergeant, by the name of Hoffmann, a powerfully built man with a forehead like a bulldog and a neck like a bull, gave us a welcoming address – and how! I do not believe that criminals taken to Devils' Island[42] would have been spoken to in such an unreasonable way. Then we were allocated to rooms where we were given beds and lockers. Everything was painfully tidy and clean, which made it clear that strict discipline was the approach here, as it had been in the barracks before the start of the war. On the following day the instruction about machine guns started. It was not straightforward – you had to learn the names of all the big parts and the little parts and the way that they all worked together when shooting until you knew them well enough to explain them yourself. Exercising outside in the snow was much worse, and the ammunition boxes, which had been filled with stones, were very heavy to drag around.

The NCOs who had already been in the field treated us much better than those who had remained in the garrison and had become used to slave-driving and tormenting the soldiers. For a while I belonged to the

---

[42] Dominik Richert calls it Cayenne. He is referring to the island off the coast of French Guiana, which was used as a penal colony

group reporting to NCO Altrock who was a stupid creature, which helped him to plague us all the more. It sometimes put me off, but I consoled myself that at least I was not being shot dead here. Sometimes we had to crawl several hundred metres through the snow dragging the machine gun; the snow got up your sleeves, sometimes almost as far as your armpits. Your boots filled up too, and your hands got so cold that it became nearly impossible to grab hold of the iron on the gun and keep a grip. It was at its coldest when we had to practise on the beach while the wind howled across the Baltic.

The food was pretty good – better than in Memel. For lunch we were often given potatoes with sauce and two *Königsberger Klopse* (meat balls) which I enjoyed. Each person only got one portion, but several times I managed to get two, because I enjoyed having the second portion with the army bread in the evening. I made sure that I was one of the first when lunch was being handed out, ate up my portion quickly, and then joined the end of the queue. Once, the NCO who was supervising us as we collected our lunch caught me and reported me to the monstrous Sergeant Hoffmann. That will have consequences, I thought to myself! However I was so hardened to the situation that I was pretty indifferent, and Hoffmann could not eat me up. 'Richert should come to the orderly room!' they said. I went there. 'You thickhead, you must come from Polack country, thinking that you do not get enough in one portion. Do you want to land in clink?' This was all uttered in a way that caused the walls to shake. When he had finished, I asked for permission to speak, and explained to him that I came from the part of Alsace occupied by the French and that as a result I had no contact with home and was dependant upon the food in my barracks. 'Well, if that's the case, you might as well fetch yourself two portions!' So after all, Hoffmann seemed to have a little bit of humanity in his make-up! From then on I was able to have two portions a day. I normally kept one portion for the evening and warmed it up on the stove.

They once showed a film which annoyed me. It was called *Francs-Tireurs*.[43] In it they showed how French civilians used ruses and tricks to entice one or more German soldiers into their power, and then murder them. The purpose of this film was to fuel the hatred of the French, but I knew that there were no *Francs-Tireurs* in this war.

When the weather was reasonable I would go down to the sea to watch the waves. Quite often little pieces of amber were washed onto the sand. One stormy Sunday afternoon I was standing on the mole with some of my comrades watching the waves. The wind was blowing directly into the entrance to the lagoon with a result that the waves crowded into the whole entrance. Then we heard the sound of a ship's siren from out at sea. A large

[43] The term originally referred to irregular units who fought against the Germans in the Franco-Prussian War (1870–71).

freighter was slowly approaching the entrance, sounding its siren repeatedly to summon the pilots, who were the only people permitted to guide the ship into the channel or the harbour. Several pilots set out towards the ship on a little steamer. It was bobbing about on the waves like a nutshell. Several times the little steamer almost reached the ship, only to be caught by a wave and pushed back about one or two hundred metres. It was really interesting to watch. At long last, by a skilled manoeuvre the little steamer got alongside the big one and two pilots clambered up the rope ladder like cats, while the little steamer was washed away once again. Now the ship started to make its way in. We kept on watching it until it disappeared from view heading for Königsberg. In the harbour at Pillau they were busy completing an auxiliary cruiser. It was huge and it made me wonder how the water could carry such a monster. They were also busy repairing a damaged torpedo boat. On the other side of the harbour you could see several English steamers which had been detained when war broke out.

It was nearly Christmas. A beautiful Christmas tree was set up in a big room. To start with we sang some Christmas carols, followed by 'Deutschland, Deutschland über Alles' and Heil dir im Siegerkranz.[44] What stupidity! Captain Grosse from Alsace made a speech which was appropriate to wartime but not to Christmas. Then each of us was given a small present.

We had completed our machine gun training and our service was no longer so exacting. We often trained on the Schwalbenberg a sand hill on which some acacias grew. From this point we had a splendid view of the town, the harbour, the lagoon and the open sea. Sometimes we had target practise with the machine gun. To start with I got a bit nervous when the rattle started. When the machine gun worked well we were able to fire two belts – that is five hundred shots – in a minute. The targets were set up on the beach, so that the bullets landed in the water.

The soldiers in my room were very comradely, and my best comrade was an East Prussian called Max Rudat whose parents ran a large farm and often sent him parcels. He always gave me something from them. One fine day in the middle of January 1916 we had to assemble. The machine gun company of Infantry Regiment 44, which was stationed on the North Russian Front outside the Russian Fortress of Dünaburg, had asked for sixteen replacements. I had the misfortune to be one of the sixteen. My friend, who was not, asked the sergeant for permission to go to the Front with me, and they agreed to this.

On the following day we were fed up well for the journey. As the oldest soldier, I was put in charge of the group. After we had bid farewell to our

[44] *Heil dir im Siegerkranz* was the unofficial national anthem of the German Empire. It had the same tune as 'God save the Queen.' The *Deutschlandlied* (Song of Germany) became the German national anthem in 1922 and has remained so since.

more fortunate comrades, we went to the station. My God, how will it be this time! Now, right in the middle of winter, heading for the icy cold of Russia! At least I have a comrade with me, I thought to myself, and that consoled me a little.

The Journey to the North Russian Front – mid-January 1916

We boarded the train in Pillau and travelled to Königsberg. I asked when the next train to the Russian front in the direction of Dünaburg was due to leave. We had to wait until midday, then we set off. We travelled through Insterburg and Gumbinnen, crossing the border between Prussia and Russia at Eydtkuhnen. As soon as we crossed into Russia, the style of the buildings was poorer. Instead of tiles, more of the roofs were thatched. It was a boring journey – snow all around, and dismal pine forests. Between them, half snowed in, were houses, huts and villages. We passed the Fortress of Kovno and travelled along the Njemen, which was covered with drifting ice floes. The journey continued via Radsiwilischki, Rakischki and Abeli to Jelovka, where we arrived in the evening. We were able to sleep in barracks with lots of other soldiers, most of whom were on leave. As there was no heating, we froze, despite covering ourselves in our blankets. Each of us had been issued one at the garrison.

With the Machine Gun Company of Infantry Regiment 44

The next morning I asked the way to Regiment 44. A number of men from the regiment who had been on leave came along with us. We only made slow progress through the deep snow. Eventually, after walking for two hours we reached the Neugrünwald Estate. We heard the sound of sporadic shellfire from the Front. I reported to the Company Sergeant and informed him that the sixteen replacements from Pillau had arrived. Kaminsky, the Company Sergeant made a good, friendly impression on me. 'Well,' he said 'you will like it here.' He came out with me and I got the sixteen men to stand to attention according to the regulations. The sergeant asked each man for his name, where he was from and so on. Then he showed us a room where there was a stove and soldiers' metal cots. We were all satisfied about the reception in the Company as the mood was more friendly and comradely than in Pillau. The food that we were then given was good and the portions were generous. For the first two days our only duty was to fetch wood from the forest needed for heating.

The Neugrünwald Estate consisted of a large house with several stalls and outhouses. The walls were made of wood, which had been attractively carved. The roof was tiled. The Company's horses were kept in the stalls, and their drivers were in the room next to them. The reserve gunners, to which we belonged, occupied two rooms. The Battalion staff occupied the ground floor of the house. A company of 'shovels' – soldiers without weapons who were responsible for building reserve positions behind the front – occupied one of the buildings nearby. Their official name was fortification soldiers. In a small outbuilding they had set up a Company bath-house. Three baths were available, in which soldiers returning from the trenches could clean themselves. Anyone who wanted could go to a barber for a haircut or a shave – free of charge. It could not have been more comfortable. The railway line to Dünaburg ran along the side of the estate, but it had, of course, been destroyed at the place where it crossed the front. On both sides of the track – about five hundred metres to the left and one kilometre to the right – were attractive pine forests, which left a small hill exposed further on near the front. On this hill you could see the ruins of the small town of Illuxt, which had been shot to pieces.

On the third evening, as it got dark, we had to go to the Front as labourers. The route took almost an hour and led through gloomy pine forest. When we reached the edge of a wood we had to wait in a small hollow. Here I heard the first bullets whizzing past. 'Well, Max, how do you like this music,' I asked my friend Max Rudat, who had never been in the Field before. 'Quite honestly, Nickel,' he replied, 'I find it quite frightening.'

After we had waited for half an hour several men, led by an NCO, came towards us from the front through the snow. Now we had to carry heavy steel plates, measuring two metres long and one metre wide, forwards. It was a real struggle to get the plates onto our shoulders and, as we were forced to stand very close to each other, we could only take very short steps. We had to cross open country to reach the trench. The snow reached up to our knees. Whenever the Russians shot flares into the sky we had to stand still in order to reduce the chance of being seen. We put the plates down close behind the trench. We carried forward eight of them. When we were carrying the last one we were probably noticed by the Russians because we heard a lot of shots and a lot of bullets flew close to us. Each of us would have liked to fall to the ground, but this was impossible. Then I called out 'Look out! Throw it away!' The plate flew to the ground while we all jumped back from it to the left and the right. Then we raised the plate up and sheltered behind it. Crash, a bullet hit the front of the plate. What a noise! After a while the shooting stopped and we carried the plate forward. Then we hurried back to Neugrünwald, because we all had cold wet feet and wanted warm coffee.

On the following day a man at the front was shot in the arm. An ambulance man brought him back to Neugrünwald. I had to pack my things and take over his place in the position. At the front edge of the woods, the ambulance man and I went through the communication trench to the front position. I was quite astonished when I saw the position by day. I had really never seen anything like it before! Both sides of the trench were panelled with pine poles and on the base were so-called grills made from roof battens, so that your boots did not get dirty. Each infantryman had a gun port, and in the front wall of the trench, little boxes containing ammunition and hand grenades had been mounted. The trench almost seemed deserted, apart from the sentries who stood in covered sentry posts and observed the Russian position through trench periscopes. The other soldiers occupied warm shelters which were built in sloping towards the back. 'Your crew lives here,' said the ambulance man. 'You have a good NCO.' I went into the shelter. It was full of tobacco smoke like thick fog, and four men were sitting at the table playing cards. One other soldier was busy writing a letter. There was a little stove in there, which had been stoked so well that it glowed red in places. At the rear wall were two three-tiered metal cots. My first thought was: 'I could live here!' I stood to attention in front of the NCO and reported my arrival. 'Don't bother!' he said to me 'Here with me you don't need to stand to attention. You just need to do your duty. By the way, we are all comrades, what's your name?'[45] he asked. 'Richert,' I replied. 'I mean your first name,' he said, whereupon I said my name was Dominik. 'Eh, what?' they all called out, 'never heard anything like that before,' and started laughing at my name. 'Really,' said the NCO, 'I have never heard this name before!' 'Well, as far as I'm concerned, you can call me Nicki, like they do at home,' I said, smiling. 'Good, then we will just call you Nicki! Nicki, do you want something to eat?' asked the NCO. 'Have you got something?' I asked. 'Certainly, take what you want from what's up there on the bed.' I looked up and was quite surprised: several army loaves, cheese, lard substitute, German salami and butter were lying there next to each other. Beside them were two little boxes of cigars and cigarettes. 'No, I have never experienced anything like this since I joined the army,' I said.

In the afternoon I had to do sentry duty. Through the trench periscope I looked at the territory ahead of me. Directly beside the machine gun stand there was a communication trench which led to the listening post which was located in the barbed wire entanglement. Two broad wire obstacles protected the location from attack. There were two similar entanglements in front of the Russian line, which was about two hundred and fifty metres away. At various places over there I saw smoke rising, and the same was happening on our side. Every so often, a shot rang out. Each night we had to do sentry duty in pairs, spending four hours in the shelter, followed by two outside, and so on. At night, sentry duty was more boring than during the day, and it was severely cold, so that you had to always move and stamp your feet to stop yourself from freezing. The next day I had to go and fetch our food. The field kitchen drove up to a hollow at the edge of the woods behind our position. There I chanced upon my friend Max Rudat who had

[45] The NCO addressed him using the familiar 'du' form right from the start as a friendly gesture.

124

just arrived with all his kit. He was to join a machine gun team to replace someone who was on leave.

On the third day I was just standing on sentry duty from twelve o'clock until two o'clock in the afternoon. In order to pass the time, I was thinking about home, and all kinds of other things. It was completely quiet. Not a shot could be heard. Suddenly I heard an explosion louder than I had ever heard before. The ground shook and I nearly fell to the ground from fear. Then, about five hundred metres to my left in front of the German position, I saw a cloud of smoke more than one hundred metres high shooting upwards, while a huge number of clods of earth flew around. The Russians had detonated an underground mine in order to blow the German position there into the air. At the same moment I heard shells arriving. Directly in front of me four heavy Russian shells exploded in the barbed wire entanglement and tore large holes in it. This was followed by artillery fire so intense that you could no longer see or hear, and intense rifle and machine-gun fire started up from the place where the explosion had occurred, as the Russian infantry had rushed forward and taken control of the massive crater that had been created by the explosion. Soon a German counter-attack caused some of the Russians to flee, while the others were taken prisoner. The Russian artillery continued to fire, and shells landed in front of, or behind, or – every so often – in the trench. As soon as the first shots were fired the NCO came rushing out of the shelter with all the men, as they were anticipating an attack. We all ducked down on the ground in the trench in order to avoid being hit by splinters or clods of earth. Only the NCO looked round for Russians from time to time. While he was doing so, a shell splinter the size of a finger hit him above his ear on the edge of his cap, which caused him to sway and fall dazed to the ground, but there was no sign of a wound, only a bump. I quickly held a handful of snow against his forehead and he came to immediately. To start with he had no idea of what had happened, but after a few minutes he had recovered completely.

Right next to us was a dugout which was occupied by eight infantrymen. A short access trench led to the entrance, and beside the door a small window had been built in. One of the very first shells landed near the entrance, filling the trench with earth and preventing the door, which opened outwards, from being opened. From the inside, they pulled the window off, threw out their rifles, and then crawled out one after the other to take up their places in the trench. Just as the last one was crawling through the window a shell landed on the top of their wooden shelter. As a result of the pressure, the shelter gave way a bit and then collapsed. The infantryman, whose upper body and hands were outside the window while his legs were still inside, was trapped and could not move forwards or backwards. Fearing that he would die, he cried for help. Two of his comrades tried to pull him out, but they were not successful. As a result of the shells which were landing nearby they were both forced to look for better cover in the trench, so the poor chap hung there all on his own, scared to death, and trying to protect himself with his hands and his arms from the clods of earth that were flying around. Finally, after about half an hour, the artillery fire ceased and it was possible to try to free the poor soldier. As it was impossible to pull him in or out the only possible solution was to cut away the section of pine underneath him on both sides and remove it. The soldier, who was half dead from fear, was brought out, where it was quickly discovered that he was completely uninjured.

I asked the NCO for permission to go to Max Rudat to see whether anything had happened to him. The trench had been partially flattened, so I had to crawl at various places in order to avoid being seen by the Russians. A number of soldiers had been buried alive, and people were busy digging them out. There were also two dead soldiers in the trench. A number of people with more minor wounds had already cleared out. Three NCOs who had been playing cards in a dugout had been blown completely to pieces by a shell which penetrated the roof and exploded underneath. Max Rudat stood guard near his machine gun and made quite a strange face. The terror had still not completely left him. 'Well, Max, how did you like it this time?' I asked. 'Don't ask, Nickel,' he answered. 'I was lying flat out on the bottom of the trench and came very close to filling my trousers.' He showed me a number of new shell-holes very nearby. We were both happy to have come out of it unscathed.

After this it was quiet for several weeks without very much happening – sentry duty, fetching wood and fetching food, cleaning the machine gun – the same all the time.

One night I was on sentry duty and talking to the warrant officer, who was supervising our post. The moonlight made the surrounding area almost as bright as day. In order to stay warm, I was stepping from one foot to the other. Suddenly I heard a sharp crack from the opposite trench, followed by a loud ring by my right ear. The bullet had grazed my steel helmet on the right hand side at forehead-height and torn the paint off. I was pretty frightened. As the rear wall of the trench was sloping and covered with snow the Russian had probably seen the movement of my head against the white background and wanted to send me straight to the hereafter. From then on, I was much more careful.

Bit by bit the snow melted and winter gave way to spring. Life in the trenches became more pleasant. On sentry duty during the day you could enjoy the sunshine.

One day we were ordered to carry out a surprise attack, forcing our way into the Russian trenches in order to find out which regiment was opposite us. For this purpose a number of containers similar to buckets were set up in our trench and their contents were set alight at a time when the wind was

126

blowing towards the Russian position. Thick, almost impenetrable, clouds of smoke developed and were slowly carried towards the Russian trenches. About twenty infantrymen ran in the clouds of smoke towards the Russian position. They used wire cutters to open a way through the obstacles and forced their way into the Russian position. We listened anxiously, but there was no sound of firing. The Russians, who had probably thought that the clouds of smoke were actually clouds of gas, had evacuated this part of the trench. All the infantrymen came back safely. They brought back a Russian gun and a number of steel protective shields. One man had found a wallet containing military booklets in which you could find the number of the Russian regiment and of the division.

One day in May the Russian artillery fired consistently at one area in our wire entanglement until they managed to create a wide gap. We were certain that the Russians would make an attack the following night, and made our preparations. In our trench we set up three machine guns and reinforced our numbers in this part of the trench. From time to time we set off a flare, which flooded the area between the trenches with flickering light. Suddenly they said: 'They're coming.' Our machine gunners and infantrymen set off a thunderous wave of fire. Our artillery, which was informed by telephone and was at the ready, fired a steady barrage into the area between the positions. With the best will in the world, I could not see any Russians, even though the area was almost as bright as day thanks to the flares. They had hidden in the tall grass as soon as the shooting started. Then I suddenly saw some of them jump up and run back to their trench. All of a sudden it was crawling with fleeing Russians who disappeared into their trench. A few days later, I read in the papers: 'South of Illuxt a powerful Russian night attack was repulsed, inflicting heavy losses.' Well, that wasn't quite right, but every little event had to be trumpeted out loud as a great victory in order to maintain the people's motivation for war.

In May 1916 our machine gun team was transferred a few hundred metres to the right, to a place where the front line ran through a splendid forest of pines and birches. We were accommodated in a dugout which was of much poorer quality than the one we had been in. When it rained, we had to fill up lots of buckets of water each day and carry them out. In the morning we would find so much water in the shelter that it almost reached the lowest bunk. It was very unhealthy to live in such conditions. On warm May nights I often slept behind the shelter on the forest floor, where a heap of dry leaves had gathered. In order to improve our living conditions, we decided to build a new shelter to live in. We dug out a square hole about the size of a small room, went further back into the wood and felled strong pines, sawed beams and strong supports, and started building. It was a lot of heavy work but as we all did our utmost, we were soon finished. The roof consisted of six layers of pine beams lying criss-cross. The gaps were filled with earth. Of course, we could only work on the roof at night, and even then it could be dangerous when working on top without cover, as the Russian sentries used to shoot out into the night because they were bored.

The time came to fit out our shelter. We put six two-tiered metal bunks along one side. One of us was qualified as a bricklayer, and he built an attractive stove from bricks. A table and benches were constructed from boards, and behind the table we constructed a kind of sofa upholstered with dry grass. We undid new sandbags and used them to cover the sofa. As I had some skill in drawing and painting, I drew several pictures, framed them with thick birch bark, and hung them up in our shelter. We had carefully peeled off the bark of the pines which we had felled, and we used it to panel the walls. A comrade who was a gardener laid out a beautiful flower bed in the form of a star in front of the window, while another, who was a wood-carver, modelled a machine gun one and a half metres high out of wood. It was erected in the middle of the flower bed like a monument. When it was all done, we were very happy with our work, and so was our Company Commander, Lieutenant Matthes, who was a good, just superior, and praised what we had done.

Our machine gun was set up ready to fire in a concrete shelter with a gun port. It was guarded by one sentry during the day and two at night. It was not particularly dangerous here. While shells, shrapnel and small mines came flying across every day losses were seldom. We all hoped to be allowed to stay here until the end of the war. The food was no longer as good as when I arrived, but it was still bearable.

One day, several heavy mortars, bigger than any I had seen before were set up behind our shelter. The mines weighed two hundredweight.[46] As our side was planning a coup de main it was intended that these mortars, together with the artillery, should soften up the Russian position for an attack. Using two machine guns, our job was to fire alternately towards the Russian position to block their reserves from sending reinforcements to the front positions. In a period of twenty minutes we fired thousands of shots. The posts of the entanglements were completely shot to bits, and almost all the wires were torn in two. A number of young birch trees fell over; they were effectively sawn off by our bullets. The explosion of the two-hundredweight mortar shells was terrible. As a result of the massive blast, pines and birches swung to and fro. Then half a company of infantry advanced past us. After a quarter of an hour they returned unharmed with eight Russians they had found shaking in mortal agony in a dugout and taken captive without any resistance. The captives were visibly pleased to

[46] Dominik Richert is referring to German metric hundredweights. 1 hundredweight = 100 metric pounds = 50 kilograms.

128

know that they had now reached safety. The Russian artillery started to heavily bombard our position with shellfire and shrapnel.

I was standing behind the front of the concrete bunker with our senior lieutenant and two comrades when a small-calibre shell crashed down on it, exploded, and threw its load in all directions. Although we were almost sent flying by the shock, we were all unharmed, but a sergeant from the infantry who had been making his way along the trench was hit by a splinter in his stomach and died in hospital as a result of his serious wound. Our platoon leader, a lieutenant, had his arm torn off by a small mortar shell. Masur, a good friend of mine from Memel who was the lieutenant's orderly, was so seriously wounded that he died a few minutes afterwards. He was buried in our Regiment's cemetery which was located in the forest behind the Front.

One day in June our machine gun crew was relieved and we returned back to Neugrünwald. It was a real pleasure to be able to move about freely above ground and not be forced to live in trenches and dugouts almost like a mole. We were only given light duties – one hour of drill, one hour of training, and machine gun cleaning – that was all. We passed the time in wrestling matches and doing gymnastics on a high bar, or lazed around catching lice, as these beasts had made themselves at home among us once again.

One day, I was promoted to lance-corporal. The following day I had to go to Jelovka to report to the Commander of the Regiment. There, together with several soldiers and NCOs of the Regiment, I was awarded the Iron Cross 2nd Class. The Commander of the Regiment made a very warlike speech to us; we should all be proud of this decoration. However, that all left me cold, because I would have preferred to chuck in the whole thing and go home. When I arrived back at the Company I was congratulated and shaken by the hand by my superior and my comrades so much that my hand started to hurt.

After eight days in Neugrünwald we went back to face the enemy. At one place we passed many graves of fallen Russians, who had died during the war of movement at the end of 1915. That they were Russian graves could be seen from their caps, which hung half rotting from the ramshackle crosses. At some open ground near the railway there were also several graves of fallen German light infantrymen,[47] as could be recognized by the *shakos* hanging on the crosses. Further up, a communication trench led to the front position, where we relieved a team which returned to Neugrünwald for eight days rest and recuperation.

Once again the machine gun was located in a concrete dugout. The accommodation dugout was not bad but far less attractive and sturdy than

---

[47] The German word is *Jäger*, which has a particular cultural tradition and distinctive uniform that included a tall cylindrical cap, known as a *shako*.

the one we had built. It was also more dangerous here than in the previous position. As the wood lying next to the railway had been cut down for about one hundred metres and we were located in the open part, the Russians could observe our position and aim their artillery directly at us. Every day about twenty shells of calibre 12 would hit us, causing a massive pressure wave when they exploded. As soon as the first one hit we would run into the concrete machine gun post. One day I was busy reading a book in the accommodation dugout, while my comrades were playing cards, when one of the 12cm shells hit the top of the dugout, forced its way down to the lowest layer of the pine trunks which formed the roof, and exploded. The pressure shoved several trunks a bit apart, causing several wheelbarrow loads of earth to rush into the dugout. With the sudden shock we all flew to the ground, and then went head over heels out the door and into the concrete dugout until the shooting was over.

When it got dark in the evening we went to fill in the shell-hole at the top of the dugout; we threw the splintered pieces of wood which had been thrown out back into the hole and filled it up with earth. Then we fetched pine trunks and put them over the top. While we were doing this one of our squad, a friendly chap who was a watchmaker, was shot in the neck and collapsed onto the dugout. I could still see how he raised his hand and looked at me with a fixed expression as if he wanted to ask me to help him, but then his head immediately fell over backwards. He was dead. We were all shocked and saddened by the sudden unexpected death of our comrade. That same night we carried his corpse on a stretcher to the regimental cemetery where he was buried the following day.

Several days later a 12cm shell once again struck the corner of the dugout, knocking it out completely. Once again, none of us were injured because we had fled into the concrete dugout as soon as the first shells hit. An order came in for us to build a concrete bunker large enough to accommodate up to two hundred men next to the tracks in the forward trench. This was easier said than done. Both we and the infantrymen had to help with the work. To start with, we dug a hole, three metres deep, four metres wide and forty metres long. We had to heave the earth in sandbags for a distance of two hundred metres and then empty it out in the woods. That was a task and a half. Thousands and thousands of sacks were dragged away. When the hole had been fully dug out, the work of concreting started. With the help of a small military railway, cement and gravel were brought to about three hundred metres behind the front line. The substances were mixed at the place where they were unloaded and the resultant mixture was dragged to the front in sandbags. Each man had to fetch forty sacks a day. It was only possible to carry half a sackful as the mixture was very heavy and wet. In order to make the roof the railway tracks were unscrewed and two rows were laid across each other, then one metre of concrete was put on top.

In order to let in light and air, there were several small loopholes left in the walls.

In this way, the summer of 1916 gradually came to an end without anything special happening – alternately doing sentry duty by day and by night, collecting food, fetching food, stoking the oven and work duties – that was about it. The food got steadily worse, and soon we were down to two meat-free days per week. A day's rations consisted of one and a half pounds of army bread in the morning and in the evening, poor-quality black coffee – often without sugar – some butter or cheese, sometimes a bit of sliced sausage, lard substitute, but mostly jam, and a sort of grey lard which the soldiers called Hindenburg- or monkey-fat. At midday each man was given one litre of soup. Everything was used to put in soup – noodles, sauerkraut, rice, beans, peas, pearl barley, dried vegetables (called barbed wire by the soldiers), oatmeal, potato meal, and so on. Sometimes we were given green kelp fish: this muck was completely unpalatable and smelt like corpses that had been lying out in the sun for a few days. On meat-free days we usually got noodle soup with some raisins in it. There was never any sign of a bit of roast meat or salad, or anything like that.

In October 1916 we were relieved by a regiment which had come from the Western Front. We marched to Jelovka. On the way, people said that we would be transported to all possible fronts, but when we arrived in Jelovka we turned in a southerly direction and relieved a regiment about twenty kilometres to the south of our previous position. The Front crossed open hilly ground. We reached the front line through a long communication trench which ran through a hollow. Ahead of us, about four hundred metres away, was the ruined Schiskowo farm. The front went right past it. Our position – like the Russian position – was protected by three broad wire entanglements. There our machine gun company, which was under control of the regiment, was divided into three companies, and each was allocated to a battalion. I belonged to the second machine gun company and was put in charge of a gun. That is to say, although I was only a lance corporal I was acting as an NCO. I had a good team – all young, quick lads, including one from lower Alsace, Emil Fuchs from Erstein. The lads all had healthy appetites and there was never enough bread. One man from the team – the twenty-year-old Seedorf from Hamburg – always made us laugh. Each man was given a three pound loaf every two days. Seedorf would cut marks in his loaf with his pocket knife in order to divide it into sections. Up to the first mark was the portion which would last until the evening of the first day, the second was for the next morning, and so on. On the first evening he usually ate up to the mark for the next morning, in the morning he ate the piece for the following evening and the morning after that, and usually by the second day he did not have any bread left. Despite the food shortage, nobody ever stole any bread at all although it was lying out in the open on a shelf in the dugout.

131

My First Leave – end of October 1916

It was now my turn to go on leave. How good it would have been if I had been able to go home like the other soldiers. However, the Mattler family, who were refugees from Dürlingsdorf in Alsace living in Eberbach in the Neckar Valley, had written to invite me to visit them if I did not have anywhere else to go to. For a long time I was not sure what to do, but eventually I decided to visit them as I was keen to spend some time feeling free of the military yoke on my shoulders. I was also looking forward to the long journey, so I picked up my leave pass, together with some food, said goodbye to my comrades and headed off. I marched to Jelovka, boarded the train and off we went. I was overcome by a splendid feeling of freedom and security as we rolled further and further from the front. After a long journey, we crossed the German border at Eydtkuhnen. We all had to alight and go into the delousing station, because soldiers were not permitted to enter Germany without a document confirming that they were free of lice. The journey continued via Insterburg to Königsberg, where I boarded a train packed with soldiers on leave, heading for Berlin. The train went via Braunsberg and Elbing, and in Dirschau we crossed over the Weichsel on the biggest bridge I had ever seen. We continued on through Kreuz Schneidemühl, where we encountered large poor regions with sand – nothing but sand and the odd crippled pine tree about the height of a man. There was hardly a village or a farm to be seen. When we reached Lemberg and the fortress of Küstein the countryside became more attractive and fertile. As night fell, the train arrived in the Silesia Station in Berlin. I went into the town with a number of soldiers on leave who I had met on the train to see Berlin by night. The town was almost lit as bright as by day. We visited several restaurants, drank beer, and paid good money for an evening meal. We spent the night in the station waiting room and slept in a sitting position with our heads on the tables. In the early morning we drank hot coffee in a pub and went to the Anhalter Station. We obviously had to ask our way a number of times.

I boarded the express to southwest Germany and travelled via Lucken-walde, Halle, Merseburg, Naumburg, Weimar, Erfurt, Gotha, Eisenach, Fulda and Hanau to Frankfurt am Main. There I had to wait for a while. The journey from Berlin to Frankfurt was very beautiful and interesting. Almost all the time it passed through fertile densely populated areas. Both in town and country the houses were attractively built. How attractive it was here in comparison with deserted boring Russia! I could hardly believe that I had spent many months there living in dugouts in trenches. After I had had a look around the beautiful town of Frankfurt near the railway station I boarded the train again, and travelled through Darmstadt and Weinheim to the beautifully located town of Heidelberg on the Neckar. There I had to change trains again and travelled on to Eberbach, my final destination. When I arrived I asked after the Mattler family, who lived on the second floor of the Restaurant Koch.

Although I only knew Herr Mattler they all made me welcome. How glad I was, at long last, to be able to live for a few days like a normal human being. We all ate in the restaurant. The portions were not very generous, but they were in splendid contrast to the muck from the field kitchens. The bread was no better than army bread and quantities were limited, as indeed bread, meat and butter had already been rationed and could only be obtained using ration cards, with so much per head. I was particularly pleased to have a good bed, because I had not been able to undress and get into bed since January – nine months ago. All we could do there was sleep in the hard metal cots in the dugouts. Whenever there were good days, I went on excursions in the surrounding area – along the River Neckar, and up to the ruined castle of Eberbach, from which you had a good view of the beautiful valley. The days seemed to fly by. I got to know a number of refugee families from Alsace, who were all very friendly towards me. The refugee girls were extremely friendly and a number of them hinted that they would really like to be the sweetheart of a soldier from Alsace. I naturally enjoyed this and exchanged my address with a number of them, thinking that sending and receiving letters might bring some relief from the monotonous life in the trenches.

Altogether I was in Eberbach for ten days, after which I travelled for a day to the Rhineland to visit my former war comrade August Zanger from Struth. I could spend three days there and then take two days to travel back to the front. If you arrived at the Company only one day late, you could expect three days imprisonment in a dark dugout, and I did not want that.

I said goodbye to the Mattler family and the other families from Alsace with whom they were friendly and travelled back through Heidelberg, Darmstadt and Frankfurt. I changed trains there and travelled to Giessen where I had to change once again. Then I went to Marburg, Siegen and travelled along the River Sieg. My last stop was Schladern. Zanger lived in Dreisel about half an hour from Schladern. He had told me that he would meet me on the station in Schladern. By the time that the train arrived, it was pitch dark and it was drizzling. I left the station – there wasn't a soul in sight – and there was no sign of Zanger. 'That's good,' I thought to myself. Then, through the faint light of the gas lamps, I saw a woman with a boy coming towards me. I went up to her and asked the way to Dreisel. In an accent which I found very difficult to understand, she told me that she was going there and that I could go with her. While we were walking along she asked me who I was visiting. I said I was going to meet my comrade August Zanger. She did not know him. Then I told her that he was living with Theodor Gauchel's family. Now she knew where I was going, and took me there. Zanger was very pleased to see me again. He had expected me to be on the previous train and when I did not arrive he had assumed that I would not get there until the next day. The Gauchel family, consisting of the mother, a son called Josef and a daughter Maria, made me very welcome. Soon I felt quite at home. These good people fetched all that they had and served it up to me. Maria had taken care of Zanger in the military hospital after he was seriously wounded in 1915. They had fallen in love and planned to marry after the war (which they did). As the family was very religious, and in order to avoid gossip, Zanger did not sleep in the Gauchel's house, but had rented a room in a house nearby with a family called Batt. After we had chatted until late into the night, we went to bed. Then we talked to each other about our homeland and about our experiences until dawn.

The next day Zanger and I helped the Gauchel family with threshing using the threshing machine. I was not used to doing this kind of work any more, although I had done it often enough in the past. On the following day we travelled to Siegburg and we both had our photos taken and then sent some pictures home via Switzerland straight away. On the third day we went to the town of Eitorf about twenty kilometres away to find the grave of Josef Schwob from my home village. It was very sad for us both to find a good comrade from our homeland in such circumstances. After we had prayed at his grave for some time we went to the military hospital and asked to see the nurse who had taken care of him to find out how he had been wounded, and how he had spent his final days. Having found out we thanked the nurse and then travelled back. Then I only had one more night in a bed, and it would be over for God knows how long.

I was reluctant to leave Zanger and the Gauchel family after three days, but I had no choice. The good people had filled up my bread bag with all kinds of food and a bottle of liqueur, so I was well equipped for the journey. Frau Batt brought me a big salami too. The departure was very sad, as mother Gauchel cried as if I were her own son. It was also sad as you did not know whether we would see each other again or whether I would be shot dead out there, as the end of the war was not yet in sight. Zanger accompanied me to the station. I travelled to Cologne. As I had time to spare I had a good look at the splendid station. In Cologne I boarded the train to Berlin and spent two days travelling to the Front, first through the Ruhr area via Düsseldorf, Barmen, Elberfeld, Hagen and Dortmund. I had often heard people speak of the Ruhr area, but it was not as I had imagined it. It was one town after another, so that it was often impossible to see where the one finished and the next one started. In between there was nothing to see but mines and factories; as far as the eye could see masses of factory chimneys and pit heads jutted into the skyline. In between there was such a confusion of railway installations tracks and points that it seem highly likely that there would be frequent collisions. Eventually we left the Ruhr and the train rolled on through Paderborn, Halberstadt, Magdeburg, Brandenburg, Potsdam and Charlottenburg to Berlin. Without stopping, I went back to Russia along the same route as I had come. It was now the start of November and up in Russia the ground was covered with a light covering of snow. It made me shudder when I saw the snow, the miserable houses, the dismal pine forests and the badly-dressed inhabitants, and it made me shudder to think of the boring life in the trenches which I was facing once again.

End of 1916 into 1917

Back at the Front

From my final stop in Jelovka I was able to reach my troop on a waggon belonging to the battalion. I reported back from leave and immediately had to take over command of my machine gun. On arriving in the dugout, the soldiers told me straight away that Emil Fuchs from Erstein had fallen. He had been hit by a bullet from a Russian machine gun while performing sentry duty at night and had died immediately. I felt very sorry for him because he came from my homeland and was a good lad.

The days passed monotonously. Snow and fog followed by fog and snow – that was the extent of the change. Every day the Russians sent a few shells over, but they did not do much damage. One Sunday, two men from each machine gun were sent back for church service. I had to take the people back. In the forest, about one kilometre behind the front they had built a large hut which served as a place of worship. It filled right up with soldiers, and the army chaplain started the service. During the consecration we suddenly heard the impact of several shells from up at the front. The explosions became heavier and heavier. Some shells seemed to have exploded close by, as we heard fragments whizzing over the hut, and we all became very restless, but the chaplain continued the mass to the end as if nothing was happening. As we left the hut, the intensity of the Russians shooting increased. Our Company Sergeant gave us the order to return to our machine gun immediately. Two companies of infantry which had been in reserve were just marching forward, so we followed them. Then it started to snow, which reduced visibility to less than one hundred metres. On arriving at the edge of the wood I heard from the impacts that the Russian artillery were mainly firing at the communication trench which ran along the hollow behind our position. As I had the task of leading the churchgoers, I considered how best to reach our position and I decided to go up over the hill to get down to our position on the other side. We reached the top of the hill without any shells landing near us. When the snow suddenly stopped and we could be seen by the Russians as on a plate, we threw ourselves into the deep snow. What now? The communication trench and the position were

136

covered in thick clouds of shell smoke, and more and more shells continued to arrive. If we were to be seen by the Russian artillery observers or their machine gunners then we were as good as lost. It was impossible to stay where we were, so we had to either go about four hundred metres to the position or two hundred metres to the communication trench. We decided to hurry to the trench. 'Up! March! March!' I called. Straight away, we were all on our feet, and we ran as fast as we could towards the communication trench which ran through the hollow. A Russian machine gun started to rattle, but we could tell that it shot far too high as we could hear the bullets whizzing overhead. Almost out of breath, we made it to the trench.

When the shooting stopped for a moment we tried to make our way to the first aid dugout, which was located further forward next to the trench, as fast as we could. In places the trench was almost completely shot up. At one place lay three dead infantrymen; one of them was so mutilated that you would not have been able to recognize him. We were happy when we reached the strongly built first aid dugout. There was a fallen soldier lying on the floor. An ambulance man told us that the dead man had left the position that morning to go on leave. As he was making his way along the trench, several of the first shells landed ahead of him in the communication trench, so he had hurried back to the first aid post to wait for the shooting to stop. Then a shell landed at the back of the dugout and a small fragment of the shell penetrated the piece of pine wood that formed the lower part of the window frame and hit the unfortunate man in the forehead. He died immediately and fell off the bench. The poor chap, whose thoughts were certainly already focused on home, would never see his loved ones again.

The thundering and crashing of the shells had started again. At the next pause, each of us tried to reach his machine gun as quickly as possible, but once again projectiles whizzed over and we were forced to lie down, in order not to be hit by splinters and clods of earth. At long last I reached my dugout. My lads had fearful faces, as a light shell had exploded on the roof of the dugout – but without making its way through. Then I heard rifle and machine gun fire. I jumped out, took my binoculars and saw that behind the Schiskowo Estate the place was crawling with Russian infantry getting ready to attack. 'Come out everyone!' I yelled into the dugout. We heaved up the machine gun, which was standing hidden in a niche in the trench, and loaded it. I looked across towards the Russians and saw the last of them disappear into their trench. Above their position exploded a number of German shrapnel shells, which forced the Russians to withdraw before they had really started the attack. We were ordered to remain on the highest level of alert. Two men were to remain with the machine gun at all times, while the others were allowed to stay in the dugout but not to sleep. The day ended peacefully. As an attack by the Russians was still anticipated, a lot of flares were set off at night, so that it was almost always bright and the

Russians had no chance of creeping forward across the white snow. After midnight a machine gun started firing, and you could also hear rifle fire. Behind us a German searchlight lit up to one side, sweeping back and forth across no-man's-land between the positions, and then shone at full strength into a hollow which stretched from the Russian position to ours. We could not see into it. I fired off a number of flares, but I was unable to see any sign of Russians. Soon the shooting stopped again. As we then discovered, a Russian raiding party had been approaching our position along the hollow, but they were seen and driven back by the firing. A patrol was sent out and it found seven dead Russians and a seriously wounded one, whom they brought back with them. They placed him on a metal cot in the machine gun dugout and he came to his senses, but he had lost a lot of blood and had almost gone rigid, with the result that he died the following morning.

From then on we had peace. Apart from a few shells a day, the Russians did not bother us. As I was in charge of the gun, I did not have to do sentry duty any more, but I still took my turn so that it would be easier for my lads. As it got very frosty at night we had to warm up sacks filled with some dry sand on the stove in the dugout and tie them around the water jacket of the machine gun to prevent it from freezing. In the past this had not been necessary because the water had been mixed with glycerine, which, as is well known, does not freeze, but now there was a shortage of glycerine as well as most other things. It was difficult to keep the stove burning too, as we only had frozen green pine wood, which gave off terrible smoke and not burn well. You often had to almost blow out your lungs completely just to get a bit of coffee to the boil.

On Christmas Day while I was passing the canteen back in the woods I noticed that they were unloading several boxes of biscuits. That was exceptional, because all you normally got in the canteen was boot blacking, shoe polish, writing paper, pencils, military postcards, now and then a tin of sardines, and tinned fruit. I bought as many biscuits as I could and ate almost all of them one after the other, but I kept five rolls and took them back to my machine gun team. I still wonder now how I could have managed to eat so much. On Christmas Eve we were given bottles of sour Rhine wine as a Christmas present. Each three-quarters of a litre bottle had to be shared between two of us.

On New Year's Eve at the end of 1916, I was sleeping in the dugout when I was wakened by the Company Clerk. I looked at the clock. It had just turned midnight. Outside, the sentries were relieving the boredom by firing their guns to welcome the New Year. We both wished each other a Happy New Year. 'But,' I said to him, 'you didn't have to wake me for that.' 'I did not come up here for that reason,' he replied. 'I am bringing you an order from the Company Sergeant. You are to pack your things and report to him behind the lines in the camp in the woods.' I was quite flabbergasted, as I

138

had no reason why, and the clerk could not or would not give me any information. So I packed my belongings together and stumbled my way across the hard, frozen, crunching snow towards the camp in the forest. Then, ahead of me, I noticed another soldier carrying all his kit with him. 'Hey you! Wait a minute,' I called. He stopped and I recognized him as a man from Lorraine called Beck, who also belonged to my machine gun company. 'Where are you going to?' I asked. 'To the Company Sergeant,' he replied. 'The clerk said I should report to him.' When we arrived at the sergeant's dugout there were already a number of men from Alsace there, hopping from one leg to another, while some also swung their arms round their chests, to warm themselves up. I reported to the sergeant who was sitting alertly in his dugout, writing. He came out with me and pointed to an empty dugout which had neither a door nor a window and told us to wait for daybreak there. We went round the occupied dugouts stealing chopped wood to make ourselves a fire in our dugout, which was open to the outside and thoroughly frozen inside. As we sat round the fire, we cursed and raged and exchanged all kinds of ideas about what was happening. I said: 'Listen, we have been with Regiment 44 for a very long time. I reckon that we will be transferred.' My idea turned out to be true.

In the early morning the Company Commander lined us up and told us that the division to which Regiment 44 belonged was going to be transferred to the Western Front. According to orders from above, all the soldiers from Alsace and Lorraine were to remain on the Russian front and be allocated to other regiments. This gave rise to general grumbling – 'So, second class soldiers. They are obviously afraid that we will desert' – and so on. Then the Company Commander said: 'I would have been happy to keep you with the Company. I was very happy with all of you. But you know how it is, orders are orders and I cannot change it. At least you can count yourselves fortunate that you can stay here as it is much more dangerous on the Western Front.' Although we agreed with what he was saying, none of us said a thing. We marched to Jelovka and joined several hundred men from Alsace-Lorraine from our Division who had gathered there. Everyone was in the same mood. If the Prussians had gone where people wanted, then they would all have landed with the devil. In the afternoon the Commander of the Regiment held another speech and repeated that there was nothing to do about it as it came from above. We spent the night in barracks.

The next day, the 2nd of January 1917, we marched off. A first lieutenant rode alongside. This time we marched northwards. People were constantly grumbling out loud, or people called out loud. '*Épinal*,'[48] called one, while another called: '*Vive la France!*' Immediately the lieutenant rushed to the

---

[48] This town in Alsace was heavily fortified by the French.

unit in the column where the call had come from and wanted to know who had called out. He didn't have much luck. Some people said they had not heard a thing, while others laughed rudely in his face. Now people further forward and further behind him started calling *'Vive la France! Vive l'Alsace!'* He ground his teeth with rage but he could not find out who had called, because everyone stuck together. A chap at the back of the column started singing 'As long as there are flowers and *knefla*,[49] the Germans will not eat in Alsace.' Then the first lieutenant gave the order to sing. No sound could be heard. 'If anyone else is rude to me, he will get what's coming to him!' yelled the first lieutenant, who was very annoyed that his orders were not being followed. Suddenly one of the chaps from Alsace started to sing: 'O Strassburg, o Strassburg, you beautiful town!'[50] As if ordered, everyone started singing and the beautiful Alsace song rang out mightily in the icy cold winter air. The first lieutenant, who realized that he could do nothing, now rode along behind the column. We marched through splendid pine forests and stopped at a solitary farm. About two hundred men had to stay there, myself included, together with all the people from Alsace in the machine gun company, because we were always kept together. Now, led by a sergeant, we marched directly towards the Front.

With the Reserve Infantry Regiment 260 at the Russian Northeast Front – 2nd of January to the 14th of April 1917

A regimental headquarters of Reserve Infantry Regiment 260 was quartered on an estate. We were led there and detailed to the various companies. I asked to be detailed to the machine gun company, but when they phoned them, they said that they did not have any places free, so, together with about twelve others I was allocated to the 9th Company. Although night had fallen, we were taken out to the Company Sergeant of the 9th Company who had set up the Company Orderly Room in an attractive dugout in the woods. He was a friendly man, and we were really pleased with the way he welcomed us. He asked us straight away if we wanted something to eat, and got people to bring us bread and tinned meat. We had to spend the night in a cold dugout in which everything was frozen solid and white with hoar-frost. Although we laid a fire, we remained cold for a long time. The sector occupied by Regiment 260 seemed to be fairly dangerous, as we heard the roar of mortar and artillery shells all night long.

The following night, when we had already gone to sleep, the Company Clerk came and woke me up. Ahead of us, in the front line, the lance corporal

[49] Alsace noodles.
[50] This was a popular military song in Germany at the time.

in the group run by NCO Blau had been injured and I was to take his place. The clerk came with me through the woods for about twenty minutes. On the edge of the woods we reached a communication trench. The clerk told me I should go along this trench and would reach the 9th Company. I plodded on. The night was bitterly cold, and with every step the frozen snow crunched loudly. It was really a bit frightening to be all on my own in this unfamiliar trench. Sometimes I stopped and listened. I could not be far from our position, as I could hear the sentries firing nearby. Suddenly I heard a whistle which lasted for a second, followed by a flash and a roar: not far away from me a large shell had landed, causing the snow which had been blown into the air to float down on me, while some of the clods of earth flew right over me. I involuntarily broke into a run in order to get away from the dangerous place. I reached a place where the trench branched in three directions. One went off forward to the left, one forward to the right and the third went straight ahead. Eventually, after several hundred steps, I reach the front position. I asked the first sentry that I met what Company it was. 'The fourth,' he replied. It was a regiment from Silesia which was holding this part of the front. I had lost my way. 'Well then, where is Regiment 260?' I asked him. 'They are next to us on the right,' he replied. I thanked him and continued my search along the front trench. Almost all the sentries were moving around in order to keep warm. They had all pulled their head-covers over their chins and their noses up to their eyes, so that only a slit remained, so that they could see through.

After asking around for a while, I eventually found NCO Blau's dug-out, and reported to him. He asked me how long I had been a soldier, where I came from and so on. After a while, it was time to change the sentries. The NCO who was on trench duty called out 'Change!' down into the dugout. NCO Blau said 'Richert, you can go on guard right now.' I took the wounded lance corporal's gun. The NCO came along with me and showed me my post. Now I was left all alone in the unfamiliar position. Despite the darkness I was able to see the half snowed-in barbed wire entanglement, while beyond it there was only darkness, snow and fog. By and by I started to freeze, as the night was bitter cold. I got down from my lookout point, jumped from one leg to the other, and beat my chest with my arms. Then I went back up. Suddenly I heard a dull sound of firing from over there. I recognized the sound. It was a mortar. As I did not know where it would land, I jumped down into the trench and listened anxiously. Then I heard the mortar coming directly towards me, first quietly, and then loudly it went 'sh, sh, sh' as it made an arc through the air, hissing as it cut through the air. My blood froze with fear. I just had enough time to throw myself on the floor of the trench before the mine exploded less than two metres behind me, up on the top. Smoke, snow, clods of earth and splinters flew around. I had at least a wheelbarrow load of earth on top of me. I shook it off, jumped up and listened, because I was expecting a second mortar shell. I was not permitted to leave my post. Then NCO Blau came running along, because he had heard that the mortar must have hit near me. 'Are you injured,' he called. 'Whenever you hear a shot, you should go into the foxhole straight away!' 'What foxhole?' I asked. Then he showed me that there was a hole close by the sentry post which had been dug forwards from the foot of the trench. It was lined with wood and could comfortably accommodate one man. Boom, another shot came from over there. The NCO crawled into the foxhole. As there was no longer any room for me, I once again lay down on the floor of the trench. The mortar came whizzing over. This time it flew on a bit further over us. Blau went back to the dugout. Even more mortars came flying in but none of them got so close. Latterly I did not stay at my post at all; I just stayed in the foxhole until at long last it was time to be relieved. As it was so bitterly cold, we had to be relieved on an hourly basis. I went into the dugout, which was lit by a candle, and pulled off my boots, which were frozen solid, in order to warm up my feet a bit on the stove. My head-cover, which I had pulled up to cover my mouth and nose while I was outside, had iced up in front of my mouth to such an extent that a lump of ice and frost, almost the size of a fist, had formed. Once I had warmed up a bit, I lay down on a wire cot to sleep. How quickly the two hours passed until I was needed again! It seemed as if I had hardly fallen asleep before it was time to relieve the others. I had to do sentry duty six times a night. Naturally, it was no better for the other soldiers. The nights seemed to last forever.

Sometimes, when I stood there all alone in the cold night, I asked myself who or what really benefited from my being there. We soldiers from Alsace did not have a trace of love for the Fatherland, and sometimes I got furiously angry to think of what an easy life the people who had started this war were leading. I generally had a secret anger against all officers from lieutenant upwards, who lived in better conditions, were better fed, and, to top it all, were better paid, while the poor soldier had to go through the whole misery of the war 'for the Fatherland and not for the money, hurrah, hurrah, hurrah' as one marching song has it. In addition, with respect to the officers, you were not entitled to have an opinion. You had nothing to say, you just had to obey.

One day we were so bombarded with mortars that we did not know where to hide. Then we all ran into the concrete ambulance bunker. Huge finned mortars crashed in to the left and the right of it. The bunker was jammed full of soldiers like herrings in a tin. Suddenly there was a terrible din above our heads – a mortar had exploded right on top of the bunker. Cracks showed all round where the reinforced concrete roof lay on top of the walls. As a result of the enormous tremor the metre-thick roof had become detached. We looked fearfully at each other. Then there was another bang, which caused nearly all of us to fall on the floor. We had got another direct hit on the bunker. This time the entire cement cover had slid about a hand's breadth to the side. 'Karl, I'm not staying here!' I said to my comrade Karl Hetter, who was already a good friend. 'Where are you going to go?' he asked. 'Wait for the next hit. If you want to, then come along.' When the next mortar had exploded the two of us left the dugout and ran at the double along the front line to where a trench led forwards to the listening post, which was located in the barbed wire entanglement. We went straight in. Now we were completely safe, as all the mortar shells flew over our heads. We were able to have a good look at them as they flew in a great arc past us. The German artillery started to retaliate. Boom, boom, boom came the din of firing from behind us in the woods. They hissed loudly as they passed overhead to crash into the Russian position. We observed the hits on the other side through the trench periscope which was located in the listening post. It was a very exciting, interesting spectacle, which caused us both to forget the cold. The Russian artillery, who clearly wanted to show that they were not short of ammunition, now sent a good quantity of shells and shrapnel in our direction. It thundered and roared all around so that you could neither hear nor see any more.

The firing eased off towards evening. We went back into the front line. In places the trench had almost been flattened. We waited until dark, and then the trench was made passable and patched up. Several dugouts had been pounded to pieces, but only one of them had been occupied. Of the six soldiers in the dugout, four had been killed, while the other two had been seriously injured. It was a sad and difficult task to extricate the two seriously injured men and the four corpses from the frozen earth and the smashed-up tree-trunks.

On this section of the front, the Russians were becoming more and more impudent. If a bit of smoke rose from a dugout, they would bombard it with mortars and shells. From then on, we could only use charcoal in our stoves. The charcoal was burnt in the big forests behind the Front and then transported to the Front by the field railway. Each group got one large sack of it every two days. One morning NCO Blau sent me to collect charcoal. The sacks were located in a pile at the point where the communication trench merged with our position. A lot of the sacks had already been carried off. I was just in the process of putting my sack on my back when a shrapnel shell came and exploded above us. The whole load hit the wall of the trench less than a metre from us. At the same moment I felt a strong sensation of burning in my back. We all jumped head over heels into an old dugout nearby. There I asked one of the soldiers if he could see anything on the back of my coat. He discovered a hole the size of a pea. I told him that I had been hit by a small splinter, but felt that it was not really bad. I took off my coat. The splinter had forced its way through the little piece of leather which

143

holds your braces together on your back. As a result it had lost a lot of its force. The splinter, which was not quite as large as a pea, was just below the skin, and a soldier forced it out with his fingernails. I was pleased when the 'operation' was over, as my naked back was getting really cold. I took my sack in my arms and carried it to the dugout. I did not feel confident to carry it on my back as the top of the sack would have stuck out over the top of the trench and might have provoked a shrapnel attack.

The food got worse and worse and the portions became smaller. Very often, when you returned to the dugout from sentry duty in the early hours, there wasn't a bit of bread to be had, far less anything else to eat.

A Surprise Attack on the Russian Position – January 1917

One day we got the order: 'Tomorrow evening, after an intensive artillery preparation, the 9th Company is to attack, force its way into the Russian trench, and return with prisoners in order to determine which units we are facing. If possible, the Russian mortars should be destroyed!' When I heard this my heart almost sank into my boots, because I belonged to the 9th Company. I thought how terrible it would be to lie heavily wounded and helpless between the lines and slowly freeze to death in this cold weather. How much better it would have been if I had been with the machine gun company! Then I would not have had to take part in this attack!

The next night we had to cut passages through our barbed wire entanglements with wire cutters in order to be able to advance rapidly when attacking. Fortunately, the Russians did not observe us carrying out this work. The following day seemed to pass very slowly. We were all very despondent as none of us knew what would happen to him during the attack.

In the afternoon, the German artillery and mortars started a dreadful bombardment of the Russian defences, and wide gaps soon appeared in the Russian barbed-wire entanglements. The artillery fire stopped. Towards evening, we had to get ready. Each of us had to hang three grenades from his belt and fix his bayonet. We stood at the ready in the trench and waited, with our hearts pounding with anticipation. At this stage, everything was quiet. Quite abruptly, heavy German artillery fire started. The company and platoon leaders yelled 'Forwards!' We all climbed out of the trench and ran through the gaps in the barbed wire towards the Russian position as quickly as we could through the deep piles of frozen snow. As we approached the trench, the German artillery fired further behind the place where we were to attack, while the shells on the left and the right exploded in and around the Russian position, to prevent the Russians from shooting at our flanks. On reaching the Russian trench, a few hand grenades were thrown in and, after they had exploded, we jumped in. The trench was occupied by a small number of Russians who were taken completely by surprise. Some of them tried to defend themselves and they shot down two of our men and injured three others. The Russians were shot down like dogs, as were some others who were trying to escape. I felt sorry for the poor devils. The rest of them, about thirty men, surrendered. How afraid the poor chaps were! We let them fetch their belongings from the dugouts to take with them into captivity. On both sides of the place where we had broken through soldiers stood with hand grenades at the ready so that they could throw them at the Russians over the rim of the trench if they attacked – but no attack took place. My only wish was to get back to our position. It gradually started to get dark. The German artillery started to fire more heavily once again. That was a sign to us to withdraw under the protection of the artillery fire. The Russian artillery now started to fire on the German position, so that returning seemed to be becoming dangerous. We indicated to the Russians that they should get ready to move. We all climbed out of the Russian trench, put the prisoners in the middle, and off we went. Then a Russian flare went up, and they saw us. Several shots were fired – one man was shot in the arm, and one of the Russians was shot in the leg, but despite this everyone was dragged back, including the three men who had been wounded in the Russian position. On arriving in our trench, each of us tried to get into a dugout, as the Russian artillery was still sending some shells over. When the shooting was over, the Company had to line up in the trench. Eight men were missing. Two had fallen in the Russian trench, three had been wounded there, and one had been wounded on the way back, making six in all. Nobody had any idea what had happened to the other two. When it got light the next morning we saw one of them lying dead in the snow between the positions. There was no trace of the last man.

Thirty-eight Degrees of Frost – January 1917

The following night our Battalion was relieved. We marched about eight kilometres back and were accommodated in large bunkers. It started to get colder than I had ever experienced before – the thermometer fell to thirty eight degrees below zero. It was at its coldest in the morning at sunrise. It was so cold that the air shimmered. A rapid stream, which was about a metre deep, froze to the bottom, with the result that we were forced to melt lumps of snow and ice on the stove in our canteens if we wanted to prepare coffee or needed water for any other purpose. The bread and other food-stuffs, which were collected on sledges, were as hard as a stone.

If a man did not pull his head-cover over his nose, the tip of his nose would go whitish-yellow within five minutes, and he would lose all feeling in it. We were ordered to look out for each other, and each man was issued with a tin of frost ointment; it was to be rubbed in to the frozen place, which then had to be bandaged up. You often heard people saying 'Man, you've got a white nose!', whereupon the ointment would be rubbed into the affected nose, and it would be bandaged. The parts most easily affected were the nose, the ears, the skin on your cheekbones, fingertips, toes and heels.

After we had had a few days of rest, we had to go to the Front daily to help in building work. That was not so easy with this bitter cold. We almost always had to carry cement slabs through the communication trenches to the positions where they were used in building dugouts. On our way there and back we wore white snow shirts with hoods over our uniforms so that the Russians would not see us so well.

Back in Position – end of January 1917

At the end of January, when our rest period was over, we took up a position one kilometre to the north. Here, the Russian trench was less than fifty metres from ours. It is obvious that none of us was allowed to show his head. At night it was always necessary for half of the unit to be on sentry duty in order to be prepared for the possibility of being attacked, so every night each one of us had to spend eight hours outside in the bitter cold. People froze! It was seldom that you stood still for more than a few minutes. People stamped around and beat their chests the whole time. When you were relieved it took between half an hour and three-quarters of an hour to get a bit warm. Then you lay down on the hard metal cot for the rest of the hour. You had hardly fallen asleep before you had to go out again. It was strictly forbidden to take off your belts or your boots at night, so you had to sleep on your back with your full ammunition pouches on your stomach. The rifles were hung onto the beds so that they were immediately accessible if the alarm was raised. At least twice a week, practise alarms were carried out so that the officers could check how long it took to occupy the trench.

One morning I was sent to collect bread. I slung my cape over my shoulder, put my hands in my coat pockets and went to the distribution point, which was about three hundred metres away. I put as much bread as I could into the cape. Then I noticed that I had left my gloves in the dugout. I pulled the corners of the cape together, swung the bread on my back, and ran as fast as I could back to the dugout. My God, how my fingers began to freeze! I was hardly able to hold on to the cape. Eventually I reached the dugout and let the cape and the bread fall to the ground. Several fingertips were already frozen and whitish-yellow. My comrades immediately rubbed my hands with frost ointment and bandaged them up. I had almost no feeling of pain in my fingers, but I had such pain up my arms and especially in my chest that I rolled around on the bunks. After about a quarter of an hour the pain was almost completely gone again. I took the bandage from my hands and saw that the blood had returned to my fingertips.

At the start of February 1917 we were relieved once again and were quartered in the village of Kekeli, which consisted of a few wooden huts with straw roofs. Each day we had to work on a position outside the village which was made of snow. After about a week we went back to the front, and occupied the same position as we had before. Once more an order came to carry out a surprise attack on the Russian position. There was a call for volunteers. On completion of the attack, the volunteers would be awarded the Iron Cross. To my great surprise, twelve men volunteered. The following day, at dawn, the twelve men took up their positions in the trench, climbed out when commanded to do so and very quickly reached the Russian position. It all happened so quickly that not a shot was fired from the Russian position. We listened eagerly in the direction they had gone. Then some shots were fired. After about two minutes our machine guns started to rattle and swept closely over the Russian position to the left and the right of the place where the incursion had taken place. Our soldiers climbed out of the Russian trench and ran as quickly as they could back to our position. There were only eleven of them. Nobody knew where the twelfth man had gone. We assumed that he had remained there intentionally in order to be taken prisoner. The attackers told us that they had only killed one Russian. They had torn off his insignia and brought them back together with his briefcase.

The position we occupied was too close to the enemy and too dangerous, so we were to be withdrawn by about three hundred metres to a newly prepared position complete with dugouts over a stretch of about one kilometre. On the final night that we spent in the forward position we had to carry boxes of explosives there. These were distributed into the dugouts by the engineers and connected together with a wire. Then the entrances and windows of the dugouts were blocked with filled sandbags. At dawn the following morning we left the front position and occupied the newly built position further back. The detonation was due to take place at twelve noon exactly. We all looked eagerly ahead. Suddenly there was an explosion that caused the earth to shake. Ahead of us more than a hundred black clouds of smoke rose in the air and clods of earth and tree trunks – whole and in fragments – flew through the air and crashed loudly to the ground. Immediately a patrol of eight men was sent forward through the communication trench to find out whether all the dugouts had been destroyed. They encountered a Russian patrol of six men who surrendered immediately and they brought them back.

Now life went on as usual: sentry duty, bad food and tormenting lice. At the end of March 1917 we were relieved and were able to have a few days rest. The weather was somewhat milder, but there was still a massive amount of snow around. We had to exercise in the snow. The leader of our group was NCO Schneider, who, at the age of twenty-nine had already achieved a doctorate in chemistry, but did not have a clue about soldiering. The commander of our battalion, a very strict man, rode around in the battalion and observed the movement of the groups. When he stopped near us, NCO Schneider gave a number of wrong orders. The Battalion Commander yelled at him as if he had committed the greatest of crimes: 'How is it that an ass like you was promoted to be an NCO? You belong back in a recruiting depot to start to learn how to carry out your duty properly!' Then he said to me: 'You, Lance Corporal, take command of the group.' I stepped forward. As I had a powerful voice, and knew all the commands exactly after four years of service, it was easy to control the group. I got them to do several dispersed movements, take up positions several times, and then troop together again. The Battalion Commander, who had been watching, rode up and said 'Well done, Lance Corporal. How long have you been in the army?' 'Since October 1913!' I answered. 'How long have you been in the field? 'Since the start of the war, with a gap of about four to five months.' 'So, how does it come about that you are not yet an NCO?' 'I come from Alsace and for that reason I have had to change regiments four times. When you join a new regiment you are usually treated like a recruit'.

Then the Battalion Commander rode away and called our Company Commander, Lieutenant Kerrl, who was a good leader and got on well with me. I noticed that the two of them often looked at me and were obviously talking about me. When we had finished the exercise, the Regimental Orderly brought a report to our Battalion Commander. When he had read it he called out: 'The whole Battalion come here!' We all ran up and gathered in a circle round the Leader of the Battalion. 'Soldiers,' he started, 'The war on this Front is as good as over. A revolution has broken out in Russia. The Tsar has been deposed. The Garrison of St Petersburg – thirty thousand men – has joined the revolutionaries.'[51]

Our jaws dropped as we listened, and then we were allowed to go to our quarters. We exchanged all possible and impossible kinds of conjectures. While some people were dreading the prospect of having to tear up the filthy tracks of the military railway, others thought: 'Now we're off to Petersburg and Moscow.' Almost everyone was pleased that life in the trenches would soon come to an end. I was not really convinced, but I kept it to myself. From the Front, you could still hear occasional artillery shots being fired, so the Revolution had not had so much impact. Several days later, the true facts of the case became known. The Tsar had really been

[51] This was the February Revolution which resulted in the abdication of the Tsar.

148

deposed, but only because he had wanted to make peace. However, the war was to be continued anew under the dictator Kerensky.[52] That was quite, quite different from the first report.

At the start of April 1917 our Regiment was fully relieved. We marched back and were quartered in the little town of Subbat, which was completely occupied by Jews. Here, for the first time since my leave in 1916, I saw civilians. There was no food for sale, but everything else was available, and in the tearooms you could get reasonably good tea sweetened with saccharin instead of sugar. Then we marched to the railway station in Abeli, and were put on a train, but nobody knew where we were going. We travelled back via Radsiwilischki, Rakischki via Schaulen to Janischki. There we left the train and were accommodated in mass accommodation for two days, sleeping on the floor. I managed to purchase a dozen eggs and a pound of bacon on the quiet, giving two reasonable meals. When the three days were up, we travelled back to Schaulen. Together with another lance corporal, I was to be promoted to NCO. On arriving in Schlauen the order was given: 'All soldiers from Alsace and Lorraine are to leave the train!' I guessed the reason straight away. We had to line up on the platform. The Company Commander came to me and gave me a letter which I should hand to my new company commander. It was a letter of recommendation concerning myself and the other soldiers from Alsace who had belonged to the 9th Company. I thanked him, and then the Company Commander bade us farewell. We were unable to say goodbye to our comrades, as they were not allowed to leave the train. As we marched off, we waved them a last goodbye. The Regiment – in fact the whole Division – was transported to the French theatre of war, and the soldiers from Alsace were not permitted to go. We were quartered in a former leather factory in Schaulen for two days. Altogether there were about one thousand two hundred men. Here too people cursed and swore in the same way as when we were transferred from Regiment 44 to Regiment 260.

I was very curious to know what was in the letter of recommendation written by my former Company Commander. On the envelope it simply said: 'To the Company Commander'. I thought to myself: I can just as easily hand over the letter in an unwritten envelope – so I just tore it open and read the contents. This letter praised me very highly, and also praised Harry Runner, who came from Rufach, and the other soldiers of the 9th Company. It did please me that our Company Commander had thought so highly of us. I only told my comrade Harry Runner the contents of the letter. The next day I went to the town with Runner to see if we could buy anything to eat, but we were unable to find anything – except tea in the tearooms. We noticed that a lot of soldiers were going to or coming from a lane which was

[52] A prominent leader of the February Revolution, he became the second Minister-Chairman of the Russian Provisional Government.

off the beaten track. As we thought we might be able to buy something there the two of us went there as well. We went into the house where soldiers were going in and out like bees in a beehive. Yes, there certainly was something for sale. We had landed in a brothel where eight prostitutes were up to their mischief. In front of each door stood a whole line of soldiers, and they went in one after the other. The two of us turned back, ashamed of our countrymen, for all the soldiers came from Alsace.

The next day, we went back to the Front on the military railway, a distance of about sixty kilometres to the north. In the vicinity of Jakobstadt we left the train and were distributed among various regiments. Together with about two hundred other men I was allocated to Regiment 332. A sergeant led us to the Front – a distance of about fifteen kilometres. The sergeant got told all kinds of things and was glad when he could hand us over at the regimental headquarters.

We were immediately allocated to the battalions and taken to them. We had to fall in, and Major Zillmer, a man of about sixty-five, came to welcome us. Till then, there had not been any soldiers from Alsace in the regiment, so he only knew of them by hearsay, and from the way that he spoke it seemed that he had not heard much that was positive about people from Alsace-Lorraine. He started by walking past us all looking at each man's cap. The first sentence he said was: 'It's all right – I was expecting more second class soldiers.' (The second class soldiers – 'dangerous criminals' – were not permitted to wear cockades on their caps.) Then he continued: 'What's this I see? Some of you have even been awarded the Iron Cross!' He seemed so surprised, as if he had discovered something quite impossible. I would have loved to knock the old scoundrel down. He would have deserved it!

Now we were allocated to the companies. I had to go to the 5th Company although I asked to go to the Machine Gun Company. The Company Sergeant, whom I disliked as soon as I saw him, gave us a similar welcome. You've had it here, I thought to myself. I quietly resolved to defect to the Russians at the next opportunity, as it seemed it would be impossible to bear staying with this mob.

In Position with the 332nd Regiment

The following day I had to go to take up position at the Front, along with a number of other comrades. Most of our path took us through a swampy area. In places long bridges made from pine trunks had been built through the swamp to make the route passable. Eventually we reached the position. It did not consist of a trench dug in the earth; instead a wall of earth had been thrown up above ground level. Digging down was impossible, as the swampy ground meant that the trench would immediately have filled with water. Like the walls, the shelters that had been built above ground level were not well built and would not have offered much cover if attacked by artillery. However the position seemed quite peaceful and, as soldiers told me, there was only occasional shrapnel fire.

We had to report to our Company Commander, Lieutenant Pelzer. The lieutenant, who had a very hoarse voice and looked very washed-out and ill, looked at us in about the same way as you would look at repulsive cattle and ordered the sergeant who was with us to distribute us among the groups. Before this happened, I handed over the letter of recommendation from my previous Company Commander to him. The lieutenant opened the letter, read it, and simply said: 'You can go!' I shoved off and joined the group led by NCO Stein.

The discipline here seemed to be quite strict, as it was expected that when on sentry duty you had to look straight ahead like mad at the Russians. If an officer passed through the trench you had to stand still and, while still looking forward, report as follows: 'Lance Corporal Richert, at post number so and so, no news concerning the enemy!' When it came down to it, there was no need to fear the Russians in this position, as the great River Düna, which was about four hundred metres wide at this point, flowed between us and the Russians. A crossing during daylight would have been completely impossible. After about ten days we were relieved and lived in barracks which had been built about three kilometres behind the front, at the edge of a pine forest.

Hunger

The individual bread allowance was suddenly reduced from one and a half pounds per day, to one pound per day. The stock of food in Germany and the conquered territories had been calculated, and it was discovered that there would not be enough bread to last until the next harvest – so we got half a pound less per day. We had not even seen any potatoes for the last four months, never mind having some to eat, as the potato harvest in autumn 1916 had been very bad. Gradually all the soldiers got so hungry that we were getting beyond help.

Each morning and evening, the rations consisted of bad black substitute coffee without sugar together with a pound of bread a day, which was eaten straight away with the coffee in the morning. This was augmented with some butter, jam, liver sausage, or grey lard called 'monkey fat', but only a few grams per person – enough to feed a kitten but not young famished soldiers.

In addition, there were three meat-free days a week. Lunch consisted of one litre of thin soup – mainly semolina – or dried-vegetable soup. The field kitchen drove forwards to the position with the food. For those of us in the reserve platoon the soup was driven to us in a container on a little waggon. When it was about time for the waggon to come most of the soldiers went to meet it, because everyone hoped that in addition to his litre he might get a bit more, if some was left in the bottom of the container. The contents of the container were always cleanly scraped out with spoons. Sometimes when people wanted to follow the waggon to be there first, the driver would whip the horses into action and gallop to the distribution point, so that the people who wanted to be first ended up last. Despite this there were still stupid patriots who still believed in a German victory.

As it was now spring, lots of nettles were sprouting in the vegetable gardens of the ruined houses, in hedges and at the side of the road. As soon as they were big enough to hold, they were plucked and boiled in salt water and at midday they were added to the soup and consumed. In the same way, dandelions and saltbush leaves were collected, boiled and eaten. All things that crept and flew were eaten. Once, I succeeded in shooting down a wildcat from a tree. It tasted great. In the past, I would never have thought that I would sink so low as to eat cat meat.

We were ordered to go to the front every evening to build new barbed wire obstacles and dig additional trenches. We would march back to the barracks at daybreak. On the way back people could go as they pleased, in small groups of up to ten men. Ahead of us a hedgehog scurried across our path. About eight men jumped into the trench to catch it, but whenever anyone tried to catch it he would prick himself on the spines and let go with a yell. In this way the soldiers jostled each other in the trench – none of them wanted to let their prey go, but none wanted to grab it. I now jumped into the trench and saw the hedgehog, which had naturally rolled in a ball, lying in between the legs of the soldiers who were jostling each other. I pulled it towards me, took my cap off my head, and rolled it in with my foot. The hedgehog was mine! I roasted half of it, and used the other half to make soup. That was a real feast for me.

One morning, when we were returning from work, I saw about a hundred frogs, which were spawning in a pool of water. I went and caught them with one of my comrades, a gardener from Strassburg. When we were cleaning them, our Prussian comrades were so disgusted that they almost threw up, as they were not used to eating frogs. The two of us started to cook them in a pan on the stove. The day before, the gardener had been sent half a pound of butter from home, and, as is well known, frog's legs fried in butter produce a very pleasant aroma. One after another, the Prussians came along, attracted by the splendid smell, and looked longingly into the pan, saying 'Hey, I would like to try some of that!' The people who had been most revolted when we were preparing the frogs would now have been happy to eat the entire contents of the pan. But we just told them they should catch them and

152

cook them themselves. From then on, none of the frogs in the whole area was safe.

We kept hoping that the rations would improve, but we were disappointed. It was really almost unbearable. Never, not once, could you get enough to eat and what we did get was inferior substitutes.

I went with several other soldiers to the Company Commander to complain about the inadequate food. In his genuine Berlin dialect he simply said: 'Eat spinach too. I don't have anything different!' What could we do now? Nothing! The soldiers simply called boiled nettles and other greens 'spinach'.

One day, the battalion was mustered. We all had to line up. The Regimental Commander rode up. He inspected the parade. There was no question of putting on a smart goose-step – firstly because it had not been practised and secondly because nobody had the reserves of energy to lift their exhausted legs. Afterwards, the whole battalion had to form a semi-circle round the Regimental Commander. 'Comrades!' he started. 'We are starving; that's a fact.' (But in reality he had a face like a full moon and a big cushion of fat at the back of his neck.) 'Yes, we're starving, but England is starving too. Our submarines are the reason that hardly any ships can reach England without being sunk. France too is exhausted and is suffering from food shortages.' (However, two days before I had received a letter from my sister telling me that food was available in abundance and that there was no sign of shortages!) 'It is like a wrestling match,' he went on, 'in which the opponent has been forced to the ground but still has one shoulder up. We still have to force this shoulder down, that's why we have to hold out. Because we want to win, we have to win, and we will win!' That blockhead can afford to speak, I thought to myself. A number of patriotic soldiers naturally believed the Regimental Commander. Afterwards, when they started to speak about how England and France were starving, I got out my wallet and showed them my sister's letter. 'Gosh!' some said. 'If that's how it is, then we'll end up losing!'

In May 1917 our Regiment marched back and we were transported about one hundred and fifty kilometres further south on a military railway. At the town of Novo-Alexandrovsk we left the military railway and marched along a very good broad road towards the front. At Smelina, which consisted of a few huts and a church with a shot-off tower, we turned off to the left and reached the front-line position where we relieved the regiment which was stationed there. All their soldiers also looked miserable and emaciated: that showed us that hunger ruled here too.

My Company was based in a small wood on a spur of land between two lakes – the Medumsee on the right, and the Ilsensee on the left. The Russian position was about one hundred and fifty metres ahead of us. One night when I was on sentry duty, a Russian machine gun started to sweep our position. The bullets landed to my left and my right, causing the earth to land in my face. I took immediate cover and did not trust myself to look over the top for the rest of that night. The emplacement here was strongly fortified. Along the whole length of the trench there was a passage five metres deep which was connected to the trench by entrances with steps every fifteen metres. By and large, it was not a dangerous place, because although several artillery and shrapnel shells flew over each day, they did not do much damage. I was once again made group leader and did not have to do sentry duty. I just had to do one hour of trench duty each night, supervising the sentries. On a number of occasions on especially sticky nights I would come across sentries who had collapsed from weakness and were lying near their sentry posts in the trench. The soldiers who were totally exhausted were sent back to a convalescent home somewhere behind the front for two or three weeks in order to regain some of their strength.

I tried once again to join the Machine Gun Company of my Battalion. I went to the Company Commander of the Machine Gun Company and told him what I wanted. The Company Commander, a Freiherr von Reisswitz, was very friendly towards me and said that he would try to arrange a transfer from my Company. I went back to my Company. Two days later, the battalion order came: 'Lance Corporal Richert of the 5th Company is transferred to the 2nd Machine Gun Company.'

I was really pleased, said goodbye to my comrades, and went to the Machine Gun Company. The sergeant welcomed me and asked whether I could do telephone duty. Although I had not had much experience with the telephone, I agreed and became a telephonist. The telephone dug-out was built into a slope, close to the water of the Illensee, which looped round here and was covered from the Russians by a wood. There were three telephonists and each had eight hours of very simple duty per day. You sat in the dugout and waited until the phone rang, then you passed on the orders by telephone. In addition, every day came the military despatch from the big headquarters. This had to be written out and hung in a box attached to a pine tree so that the soldiers could 'feed themselves up' on the inflated reports of victory. Life here would have been very pleasant if only my poor stomach had had more work to do! The lack of provisions was a real problem – too little to live on, and too much to die! Once, the Gauchel family in the Rhineland sent me a one-pound loaf. The package had probably been left lying somewhere, because it had travelled for a fortnight before it arrived. Mrs Gauchel had probably packed the bread when it was still warm, because when I opened the packet there was nothing to see of the bread but green mould on the outside and the inside. It was impossible to eat it dry, but I could not throw it away, so I tried to make soup. I put water in my canteen, added some salt to it, cut up the bread and put it in. As it boiled, a lot of the

154

mould was released and I scraped it off the top. Then I ate the soup. It was very unpalatable, but I forced it down with utter disgust.

Close to the edge of the lake there was a large field, which was naturally now overgrown. In places there were some clumps of rye that were ripe for harvesting. With my pocket knife I cut myself a bread bag full of rye ears, and then I separated out the grains, blew away the chaff, and took a round stone and squeezed the seeds on a stone slab. I used this to make soup, which was not the best I had ever had. I did this for eight days, until there were no more ears of rye to be had in the surrounding area.

I often went looking for raspberries, to get something into my stomach. Right behind the dugout there was a round hill on which there were a lot of raspberry bushes. The front of the hill was exposed to the Russians; for this reason I started by only collecting the berries from the back of the hill. As it was warm, I took off my jacket. In my enthusiasm, I went round the hill without noticing that I was no longer covered. All of a sudden a shell came whooshing in and landed in the hill about three metres ahead of me. The Russians had seen me in my white shirt. I was naturally frightened by the sudden impact and ran as quickly as possible round the back of the hill in order to get into cover. While running, I caught my feet in the thorns and fell to the ground, which caused almost all the raspberries to tumble out of the canteen. I returned to the dugout with my canteen almost empty.

On the lake next to the dugout there was a little boat with two oars. Although it was strictly forbidden, the other off-duty telephonist and I went fishing on the lake with hand grenades. Sometimes we were successful in catching several lovely fish. We would take a hand grenade, activate it, and throw it into the water at a distance of about three metres. You would only hear a muffled bang, but the water moved so much that the boat started to rock. Some of the fish in the vicinity were killed, while others were only stunned. One time we were so keen that we went too far out on the lake, to a part which was not covered by the woods and was visible to the Russians. We were both busy, catching a number of stunned fish when a shell hit the water about thirty metres away. At the time, I was leaning far out over the edge of the boat while my comrade was standing up on the opposite side to keep the balance. When the shell hit, my comrade bent down, the boat started to rock, and I nearly fell head-first into the lake. Each of us grabbed a paddle and we tried to get behind the wood as quickly as possible. This did not go according to plan as we were not very good at paddling and in the commotion we often put the paddles in at the wrong time. The second shell flew just over our heads and exploded about thirty metres to our right. We got back to the landing place without any more bother. Several soldiers who were standing on the shore had a laugh at us and said we would lose our enthusiasm for fishing for a while – and they were right.

155

Not far from our dugout there was an old rubbish tip that was no longer in use. A potato must have got in there in the spring, with the result that a lovely plant had grown up. I thought of pulling it out to start with, but then I thought that there might not be any potatoes yet – or only small ones, so I left it to grow. I had not even seen a potato for more than half a year, let alone eat one! One day I had to take a report to the Battalion Headquarters, which was situated in a farmhouse behind the woods. Between the edge of the wood and the house was a potato field with a size of about 10–12 are.[53] As potatoes had already been stolen at night time on several occasions, sentries were posted to stand guard and patrol around the field. I went back to my dugout and said to my two comrades: 'Tonight we're having potatoes!' 'How? What?' they both called out at the same time. 'Yes, we really are!' I answered. 'Just leave it to me.' When it was dark, I headed off towards the Battalion Headquarters. The sentry was patrolling round the field. Whenever the sentry approached the field as he was doing his round I hid kneeling behind the bushes. Eventually there was only one bush between me and the path along which the sentry passed. I let him pass and then, when he had reached the other end, I crawled into the field on all fours and started to dig out the tubers with my hands and put them in the sandbag I had brought with me. Each time when the sentry went past I lay quiet as a mouse between the plants and, as soon as the danger was over, I resumed my digging. In this way, I gradually filled my sandbag and I estimated that my booty came to twenty-five pounds. I think that the sentry was being relieved at this time as I heard two soldiers speaking to each other at the bottom of the field. I used this opportunity to crawl back to the woods, after which I made off at the double.

On arriving in the dugout, I listened to make sure that the two telephonists were on their own. Then I opened the door of the dugout and threw the sack in. Now the rejoicing started! It was as if each of us had hit the jackpot! Immediately a good few were washed, peeled and boiled in salt water. The water was poured away and the potatoes were mashed with the handle of a bayonet. The other two wanted to start eating straight away but I said: 'Hang on a minute!' I went to my pack, fetched my iron rations, opened a tin, and mixed the meat in with the potatoes. As eating your iron rations without permission was punished with three days' arrest, my comrades were very surprised at my audacity and said: 'What are you going to do if there is an inspection?' 'Never mind. I will phone the Company Sergeant tomorrow and tell him that my iron ration has been stolen. I hope that he will send me a new one via the field kitchen.' My comrades laughed heartily and we ate this rare meal feeling thoroughly happy.

[53] 1 are $= 100$ m^2.

One day I got very severe toothache. As it lasted for several days I reported sick and the Battalion Doctor gave me authorisation to visit the dental unit in Novo-Alexandrovsk to have my bad teeth pulled. In the waiting room about twelve soldiers were sitting staring blankly into space. A soldier sitting opposite me looked familiar, but I just could not work out who he was. I soon noticed that he was looking at me in a similar way. I was just about to ask him if he came from Alsace, when he stood up, came up to me, offering his hand in greeting and said: 'You are Richert from St Ulrich!' Now I recognized him. It was Josef Schwob from Hindlingen. 'You too have got obese like me,' he said. And in truth, Schwob was terribly emaciated. That was the reason that I did not recognize him straight away. As you can imagine I too had turned into a walking skeleton just like him as a result of the way we were fed. We exchanged our news from home, with each of us telling what he had heard. Then Schwob was called into the dentist and was given a new set of false teeth. Without getting my teeth pulled, we went into the town in the hope of getting something to eat, but all we could get ourselves in a canteen was a glass of beer. I would have liked a second one, but each soldier was only allowed one in order to preserve supplies. We both found ourselves wondering how the poor inhabitants, who were walking around with hollow cheeks looking like skeletons, survived.

We went back to our posts and separated at Smelina. He told me that Thiebhaut Winniger from Fülleren was also stationed near him. I went looking for him later on. They were both soldiers without weapons – labourers or engineers.

The next day I went back to Novo-Alexandrowsk and two of my teeth were pulled, thus stopping the toothache. In mid-August 1917 I was relieved from my duties as a telephonist and was ordered to spend several days at the Tabor Estate. The sergeant pointed out the estate to me from the dugout. It was about six kilometres away on a hill, and from a distance it looked quite small. In between was undulating hill country. As I did not know the way, I set out across country, but I was mistaken, because when I reached the top of a flat hill I found that in a hollow there was a lake three hundred metres wide and three kilometres long which I had to pass. Eventually I reached the Tabor Estate. This was the place where the Company Orderly Room was situated, together with the reserve infantrymen, the drivers and the horses. As the Company Sergeant, by name of Laugsch, was a good person, we did not have a lot to do – just a bit of machine gun training and the cleaning of machine guns. One day the sergeant told me that the Company Commander had phoned him from his post to say that Lance Corporal Richert should report to him at once. Neither the sergeant nor I had any idea why. I went to the post feeling curious and reported to the Company Commander in his dugout. He smiled and said: 'Richert, you must be a good soldier!' As I did not know what he was getting at, I did not reply. 'Something has been sent for you,' he said, 'from the 9th Company of Infantry Regiment 260, to which you used to belong, didn't you?' I confirmed this, and he pulled down a box from a shelf, took out a bronze cross with a dark blue and yellow ribbon, and said, as he pinned the medal to my chest: 'I hereby award you the Brunswick War Merit Cross in the name of the 9./260.' Then he shook my hand. I was naturally surprised as I had had to leave Regiment 260 four months ago and had not had any written contact with the Company since then, except for keeping in touch with my former comrade Karl Herter. The Company Commander thought that I must have served for a long time with that Company, or had distinguished myself by some kind of heroic act. I replied that I had only spent three and a half months with the Company and had done nothing more than fulfil my duty as expected. I now left the Company Commander and returned to Tabor. On the way, I took the opportunity to bathe in a lake. The sergeant and all the soldiers looked at me like a marvel and congratulated me on the decoration I had received. As Regiment 332 was a Prussian regiment, they did not have any medals other than the Iron Cross, which I had received in 1916. The young lieutenants often looked at me jealously, as they had only been awarded the Iron Cross. If they had known what I had thought of this nonsense they might not have been as jealous, as I would have offered the cross together with its ribbon for sale in exchange for a loaf of white bread. The only pleasure that I had was that the 9./260 had held me in high esteem. I sent a polite letter to the 9./260 expressing my thanks, and a few days later I received a reply from the Company Sergeant wishing me all the best for the future and sending his greeting to all his loyal soldiers from Alsace who had previously been with the Company.

I had to return to the Front and take over a new machine gun. One day, a few kilometres to the south of us we heard continuous shellfire, mixed with the rattling sound of machine guns and the crack of infantry fire. Then came the order: 'The Second Platoon, guns three and four, led by Lieutenant Herbst should make ready immediately and report to the Battalion Head-quarters.' I was in charge of Gun Number Three, and NCO Kurtz was in charge of Gun Number Four. We got ready and carried our machine guns back together with the equipment. Under cover, two waggons were waiting for us. We were issued with rations for three days – back to one and a half pounds of bread a day, with the extra half pound issued as a supplement for those involved in fighting. Then we were ordered to move towards the Front along the main road. We were to report to a Battalion HQ located in a dug-out close to the road where we would receive further orders. That seemed to bode well! We reached the main road, which led through woods that seemed to go on forever. Straight ahead of us, not very far away we heard the rumbling of guns and the sound of shells landing. Suddenly there was a short whizzing sound followed by an explosion – a shrapnel shell had exploded in the bank of the road about a hundred metres ahead of us. Right afterwards came a second, which exploded a short distance from us. The horses and men became restless. 'Get the guns out!' shouted the lieutenant. We wrenched the guns and the equipment from the waggon. At the same moment, there was a whizzing sound over our heads and a shell hit the embankment about one hundred metres behind us. The drivers turned about and galloped back as quickly as they could. We would have preferred to advance parallel to the road but this was impossible as the woods on both sides consisted of thick impenetrable bushes. Each of us took the equipment allocated to him. Gunners 1 and 2 took the gun. Gunners 3, 4 and 5 took the ammunition boxes, while I, as gun commander, had to carry the water tank, the spade and the steam discharge pipe. The road was subjected to continuous Russian artillery fire. To get better cover, we often had to throw ourselves into the ditch, or jump behind the trunks of the trees at the side of the road. We were unable to find a dugout or any other cover like that. Then some lightly-wounded soldiers ran towards us. We asked them what was actually happening here, but they were so frightened and out of breath from running that they only gave us inadequate information as they ran past us. Eventually the road passed through a cutting; in the left embankment a tunnel had been dug. We left the machine guns and the equipment lying outside and fled into the tunnel. Here, in safety, you felt comfortable and at ease and could catch your breath again. Lieutenant Herbst, who was generally a reasonable person and obviously was not keen to die a hero's death either, said: 'So, whatever else, we will remain here until the shooting stops.' That met our heartfelt wishes exactly.

After about an hour the bombardment of the road finished. We took our things and eventually reached the Battalion HQ, and the adjutant immediately took us to our post, which was located in the forest on a hill near a number of dugouts. It was a reserve position. If the Russians were to break through, we were to stop them here. We quickly built emplacements for our machine guns and set them up ready to fire and then we set ourselves up in two dugouts. The artillery fire raged on with undiminished intensity. Several shells hit round about our dugouts but they did not cause us any harm. Ahead of us we suddenly heard the crackle of intense infantry fire, which continued for about half an hour. Lots of lightly wounded men passed us and told us that the Russians had broken into the German front line. Several companies of infantry advanced to counter-attack and force the Russians back. They all hung their heads and some said: 'You machine gunners have it easy! You can stay here safely under cover while we have to let ourselves be shot to bits!'

After about an hour the German artillery started a terrible bombardment. The Russians, who had gathered a lot of artillery here, did not fail to respond. Intense infantry fire told us that the counter-attack was in progress.

When the shooting stopped, a large number of Russian prisoners were led back past us, many of whom were doomed to a slow death from hunger. Many of the prisoners, organised in groups of four, were carrying seriously wounded Germans or Russians back in tents. Now things quietened down again.

On the following day we were ordered to return to our Regiment. We were all relieved to have survived the thing without casualties. When we returned to our Company we were told by several soldiers that we were going to be moved on, but nobody knew where we were going to. I went to my potato plant, which was still standing on its own in the old rubbish tip and had apparently not been discovered by anyone else. I pulled it out and four potatoes were attached. I washed them and boiled them in salt water. What a pleasure! They tasted better than the best festive meal I had eaten before the war or was to eat afterwards, because, apart from those I had stolen from the Battalion Headquarters, I had not eaten any potatoes for months.

Troop Displacement to the Riga Front

On the 26th of August 1917 our Regiment was relieved by other troops. After two days of marching we reached Jelovka. Our Company was quartered on the Neu-Mitau Estate, about half an hour away from Jelovka. A divisional headquarters was also based on the estate. The Divisional Guard consisted of hussars. There was a large orchard at the estate, bigger and more beautiful than any I had seen before. The trees were laden with the best kinds of apples and pears until they could hardly bear the weight. The early types were nearly ripe. We were strictly forbidden from intruding into the garden to fetch fruit. The fruit was intended as dessert fruit for the gentlemen officers. It was only natural that in addition to their large salaries and better food these gentlemen should also have dessert fruit. All the ordinary soldier has to do is to starve, to shout hurrah, to let himself be tortured by lice, and to let himself be shot dead for his 'beloved Fatherland'. For doing this he was rewarded with fifty three German imperial pennies pay per day, as well as food and clothing. Isn't that splendid? Always living in good quarters, and when the time came to go to sleep you just lay down on your back and covered yourself with your own stomach. Yes, I used to hear people sing 'a soldier's life is a happy one!'

The rectangular fruit garden was surrounded by wire mesh two metres high. During the day a hussar with a loaded carbine was posted at each corner, while at night patrols went round the garden as well. But come what may, I thought to myself, I must have apples. First of all, when it got dark, I went to one of the hussars' sentry posts and said: 'Listen, comrade, I really

160

would like to eat apples. I have not had an apple in my mouth for the past two years!' But that did not do any good. The hussar said: 'It's not on. If they caught me, then I would have to go to the trenches, and I do not want to jeopardize my safe posting to the Divisional Headquarters for your sake.' I agreed with him, but I still wanted apples. I went to my wagon, took the sandbag in which I had packed my belongings, emptied it out, unstrapped the wire cutters which were fastened to the wagon, and went round, avoiding the sentry post. As the night was dark, this helped my plan. Half way between the two sentry posts I lay down on the ground about thirty paces away from the fence and waited until the patrol had passed, then I crept to the fence, took the cutters and snip, snip, snip, I cut a slit in the wire, forced it apart and slipped inside. Then I closed the hole again. In order to be able to find the place again on my way out I put my cap on the ground. I went quietly into the garden, held on to the lower hanging branches and checked to see whether the apples and pears were soft, as well as picking up and biting into some fruit that had fallen to the ground. I searched around for a while without finding anything suitable. Eventually I found a tree with lots of fallen fruit. I took one and tried it – it was a good, ripe apple. I filled my sandbag to the top, tied it up with string and then made myself scarce. I searched for a while until I found my hat again and then I was able to creep out without being detected. I stuffed my pockets full of apples and put the sandbag back under the driver's seat in my waggon. Then I settled down with my unit and ate my fill of apples. I gave one of the lads who woke up some apples. 'Gosh! Where did you get them?' 'Quiet,' I replied, 'and you'll get more tomorrow!'

The following morning we marched to Jelovka where we boarded a train. We travelled all day and late into the night. Nobody knew where we were going. As we went through a larger station during the night I was able to make out the name Mitau. I knew that Mitau was south of Riga in the Kurland. After we had travelled for about two hours more we had to alight and march off straight away. Towards morning we had a two hour stop. Then we went on for the whole day with just a few short rest-breaks.

The Riga Offensive – Crossing the Düna at Üxküll on the 2nd of September 1917

During the night we entered a large forest, which was already occupied by many soldiers. Here we discovered that we were to break through the Russian front and take the offensive. Once again we were facing a happy prospect! We were all horrified by what the morning would bring. Two battalions of our Regiment were to remain in reserve in the forest, while the other one was to take part in the breakthrough. We were all anxious to know which battalion was to attack. It did not take long before it became clear.

'Second Battalion get ready!' What bad luck; that was my one. We got ready and groped our way forwards through the dark forest. It got a bit lighter and we reached the edge of the forest. The ground sloped downhill. Ahead of us lay dense white fog. Every so often a shell would come whizzing over or a shot would be fired from the enemy lines, but otherwise it was quite peaceful. We suddenly came to a trench that was full of German soldiers. We had to jump over it and after a few steps we stumbled across another trench, which was only lightly occupied. We had to form up there. More and more soldiers joined us until the trench was quite full. We were then ordered to fill up the trench to about three metres wide and stamp down the earth. I do not know why. I thought I could hear a quiet rustling and chuckling, and asked a soldier who was further forward in the trench what it was. 'That is the Düna,' he said. 'It is over four hundred metes wide here. The Russians lines are on the opposite bank.' 'And we have to attack here?' I said. 'That really will be something!' The soldier was also horrified of what the morning would bring.

The dawn came gradually. Hardly a shot was fired. It was the calm before the storm! As it became brighter I was able to see the water of the Düna, which was flowing quite quickly here. The Russian position on the opposite bank was not yet visible as white fog prevented us from seeing further. We were all tense about what was about to happen. All at once, the German artillery, which had been concentrated here, started to fire. The shells whizzed over us and exploded on the other side of the river with a booming din. A number of mortars, mainly heavy ones that shoot two hundred-weight shells, joined the dance. There was such a crashing, whizzing and roaring that my ears started to hurt. As the sun rose, the fog gradually disappeared and I was able to see the Russian position on the opposite bank. It was completely shrouded in black smoke, constantly and everywhere there were abrupt flashes and enormous clouds of smoke shot into the sky. There was also dense shell smoke at a number of places in the woods further back where the Russian batteries were probably situated, as these too were being given a real lathering by our artillery. Then the Russian artillery also started to fire, so that we were forced to duck down in the trench. A direct hit killed and wounded a number of soldiers not far from me. Straight ahead of us we suddenly heard an enormous impact; dense black smoke drifted over us and a huge number of clods of earth rained down on us. I looked ahead beyond the rim of the trench to where I could see the shell-hole. It was as big as a room and had in any event stemmed from one of the 28cm shells. Then once again there was a roar and at the same moment a terrible impact, this time behind us. The following heavy shells all hit the woods behind us. The barrage of the German artillery and mine throwers went on and on. In the middle of this din came the order: 'Get ready!' We looked at each other. 'We can't possibly swim the river!' said some of my neighbours. Then behind us we heard a yelling as if horses were being driven forward. I looked back and saw that the bridge train was arriving. They rapidly drove the waggons, which were laden with metal boats, across the places in the trench which we had filled in earlier and took them down to the river. A large number of sappers came up at the double behind them and in no time at all the boats were unloaded and in the water. Now we were ordered: 'Everybody out and into the boats!' We were quickly organized and twenty men boarded each boat. Six sappers rowed, and off we went across the river.

It was very frightening on the water. We all ducked down into the boats. The shells whooshed overhead while under and around us the water gurgled. Wherever I looked the whole river was seething with boats which were heading as quickly as possible to the opposite bank. Russian shells landed between the boats in the river throwing huge columns of water into the air. Another boat upstream from ours suffered a direct hit and sank in a few seconds. The occupants who had not been wounded fought with the waves for a short time and then all disappeared. It sent shivers up my spine. When I saw this I unstrapped my combat pack, opened the waist belt, and put my kit beside me in the boat so that I would be more able to swim if the same fate should befall us. I was afraid that we would suffer from Russian machine-gun and rifle fire, but apart from individual rifle shots it remained quiet on the other bank. Now we approached the shore, and our artillery moved the barrage further forward. Our boat ground its way into the sand. We all jumped out, happy to have firm ground beneath our feet again. Boat after boat arrived, and soon there were hundreds of soldiers standing under cover behind the steep bank, which was about three metres high. The current had carried our boat, and all the others, downstream. The bank, where the Russian infantry position was situated, and the barbed wire entanglement had all been torn to pieces by the barrage.

Now we had to storm the Russian trenches. That was an easy task. We did not encounter any resistance at all. The trench had largely been flattened. Mutilated corpses of the Russian infantrymen were lying around. Every so often you would encounter an unscathed Russian sitting in the corner of a trench and he would raise his arms in the air when we appeared, in order to surrender. There were also fallen Russian soldiers scattered behind the Russian position who had probably been hit while attempting to flee. I looked back towards the opposite bank and could see that the pioneers were already busy constructing a pontoon bridge. Single Russian shells continued to arrive, landing in the river or on the opposite bank. We were ordered to advance in skirmishing lines on the wood, which lay about six hundred metres ahead of us. To start with we were covered by a small extended hill, but when we advanced over the top we heard the rat-a-tat-tat of several Russian machine guns. The bullets whizzed frighteningly among us, and several men were hit and fell to the ground. On my command, my team jumped into a shell-hole close by. I quickly made an emplacement for the machine gun with the big spade, so that the barrel barely peeked over the surface of the earth. The Russians were firing like mad, with the result that a number of us were hit while digging in. We quickly loaded our machine gun, and in a period of three minutes I fired four belts – a thousand shots. I aimed at the edge of the woods, from where the firing was coming, and sprayed the bullets left and right, but the Russians' firing continued. In the meantime everyone on our side had managed to dig in, so that the Russian bullets could not do much more damage. It was clear that the Russians had erected hidden machine gun bunkers on the edge of the wood, which we could not deal with. The German artillery came to our assistance. They assailed the edge of the wood with shellfire and shrapnel. With the protection of the artillery fire we advanced and reached the wood without further losses. We forced our way into the wood and soon came across a battery of Russian field artillery which had been completely shot up. A bit further forward we came across an undamaged battery of four guns from which the Russians had removed the breechblocks. The wood here only consisted of scrubby pines, which found little nourishment in the sandy ground. On a poor sandy track we chanced upon two mighty guns. The Russians had obviously not been able to bring them any further forward. They both had a calibre of 28cm and were probably the guns which had made us so fearful in the early morning on the other side of the Düna.

It gradually grew dark. We had to spend the night in the woods. Powerful outposts were set up to ensure our safety. After we had eaten some army bread and tinned meat we lay down on the forest floor and fell asleep, as we were all dead tired. In the early morning the field kitchen arrived and brought us food, bread and coffee. The cook told us that the sappers had got the five hundred metre long pontoon bridge ready in three hours.

When we had eaten, we got the order 'Get ready, off we go!' Like all the others, I was afraid because we had no idea what the day would bring. After we had marched for a while we heard machine-gun and infantry fire up ahead – it was a new Russian defensive position. We carefully approached the edge of the woods. We had to go back carrying two machine guns in order to make our way round to a part of the wood which jutted out. When we got there we had to dig in the guns in the dense bushes at the edge of the woods without being observed. I crept out of the hole and looked forward while maintaining my cover. Ahead of me about five hundred metres away there was a large estate on a hill, consisting of a mansion, lots of farm workers' houses, and barns and stables. I could see Russian soldiers going backwards and forwards between the houses. A few shots fell from our edge of the woods. Then no more Russians could be seen – they had taken cover. We were ordered to open intensive fire on the farm when the attack started. As I continued to observe with my binoculars I discovered two Russian machine gun dugouts which were situated in positions which would allow them to sweep the entire attack area. I crept back to the machine gun and pointed it at the firing slit of one of the dugouts. Our artillery started to bombard the farm heavily and soon several fires started. In no time at all several barns were burnt down.

Our infantry started to attack. Large numbers of soldiers emerged from the woods and stormed towards the farm. The Russian machine guns started to rattle, and we returned the fire. We could see lumps of earth and grass fly up round the Russian firing slit, but we were unable to do them much harm as we were firing from the flank and could not reach their gun team. Suddenly a battalion rushed out of the woods above us and overwhelmed the farm and the machine gun posts from the side. The machine gun teams were killed by hand grenades which were thrown into the dugouts. The Russian infantry surrendered after only token resistance. The companies which had attacked the Russian machine guns directly had taken heavy casualties. Corpses and seriously injured men lay everywhere. We took over the farm and soon a wild slaughter of pigs chicken and sheep started. The starving soldiers were desperate to have enough good food for once. Lots of fires were lit and the food was roasted, cooked or grilled. There were plenty of potatoes to be had from the fields near the farm. Almost everyone ate too much with the result that they suffered from diarrhoea. We stayed in reserve at the farm all day and the following night. Towards evening we heard brisk firing up ahead.

The next morning we had to move on. We passed through the region where the battle had taken place some days before, and saw some Russian and German corpses lying around. The following night we camped in a wood. We built a big fire and almost the whole Company stood round it to get warm. Our Company Commander read out the orders for attack the following morning. That brought us down to earth with a bump. Each of us wondered what the morning might bring. Then one of the soldiers began to sing the song:

> *Out in the field on the hard stones*
> *I stretch out my weary limbs*
> *And send out into the night*
> *A thousand greetings to my love*
> *Nor was I the only one, Annemarie,*
> *At night the whole Company dreams of you!*
> *The whole Company.*
>
> *We have to fight the hostile horde*
> *In wild and dreadful battles*
> *And when we two shall meet again*
> *I really cannot tell you*

Maybe I will be with you soon, Annemarie
Or maybe tomorrow they will bury me
The whole Company.

At the last line of the song, I shuddered, as I am sure the others did too, because none of us could be sure that he would not end up being buried on the next day. We lay down, but it took a long time to go to sleep. I prayed until I was exhausted, and then fell asleep. I only woke when we had to get on the move. We drank coffee and then we were off. We marched for several kilometres and then had to lie down on the edge of a wood. The Russian position was well-hidden at a distance of three hundred metres on the edge of a wood opposite us. On the field in front of us were quite a lot of dead German infantrymen who had fallen on the previous day when their attack was driven back by the Russians. Not a shot was fired from the other side. This silence seemed suspicious. Before our artillery started to fire, a patrol was sent across. It found that the Russians had withdrawn from their position the previous night. 'Thank God,' I thought to myself, 'now our death sentence is deferred once again.' We marched on and stopped at a solitary farm. We took up quarters and the poor inhabitants were given six hours to leave their home. How they wailed and moaned. They were only allowed to take two cows with them – everything else had to be left behind. The offensive had reached its objective and we did not have to go any further.

This was good news for us. Every day we had to work on new defences. When we had eaten up all the cattle, pigs and smaller animals in the farm our first lieutenant, Freiherr von Reisswitz, assembled the Company. He selected the biggest rowdies and got them to stand forward. Two waggons were hitched up, and the gang were sent out to thieve. They came back in the evening led by the lieutenant looking like a robber baron. The booty was unloaded – there were about ten dead pigs, a large number of hens and geese, several sheep, a sewing machine for the Company tailor and a magnificent sledge for the Company Commander who apparently planned to take up sledging the following winter. We started cooking and roasting once again, and it lasted almost all night. The starving soldiers just kept eating and eating. When there was no more meat left, everyone went for the plentiful supply of potatoes from the surrounding fields. The soldiers found a mother pig living in the wild with about ten sucklings. They shot them cooked them and ate them. About two kilometres ahead there was a swamp roughly eight kilometres broad. The ground was almost completely covered with cranberry bushes, laden with berries. These were a welcome change for us. While I was busy picking berries with some of my comrades a few metres away a mighty stag jumped up and disappeared quickly into the bushes. This was the only time I had ever seen a stag in the wild.

After about ten days' break we had to get ready to march on again. We marched along behind the front for about fifteen kilometres to the village of Sunzel. We were quartered in a grocer's shop which had been completely ransacked. The rooms were jam-packed full of soldiers. Here too, we mainly had potatoes to eat. I felt that my strength had really improved recently, and I looked better too, as did the other soldiers. We had to build a powerful emplacement on a hill outside the village. We were secured by advanced outposts quite far ahead of us. We saw no sign of the Russians. By all appearances most of them had withdrawn a great distance. As we heard, we too would soon have to withdraw as well. The village of Sunzel, in which there was a wonderful castle, would then be burned down or blown up, as was the case with all buildings between the lines. No consideration was shown for the poor inhabitants.

One day I had to report to the Company Sergeant. 'Richert,' he said, 'it's your turn to go on leave again. You will get your eighteen days; if you want to wait for a couple of days, then we can travel together.' That was of course a pleasant prospect. 'Sergeant,' I said, 'would it not be possible for me to claim twenty-eight days of agricultural leave?' That made the sergeant, who was a friendly, honest man, laugh. 'But Richert,' he said, 'you will just be going to the refugee family in Baden and all their agriculture will consist of is a few flowerpots.' I laughed and agreed, then I showed him my pay book in which it said that I was a farmer and said: 'With a bit of good will I am sure it should be possible, and it is only the second time since the outbreak of war that I am able to go on leave.' 'Good, Richert,' said the sergeant. 'You can have your twenty-eight days. I will sort it out.' I thanked him and left.

My Second Leave

Two days later the two of us marched off. We often had to consult the Sergeant's map to find the right way. Eventually we reached the estate where our Regiment had suffered heavy losses on the second day of the offensive. The dead had all been buried in a mass grave at the edge of the woods. We went on and crossed the bridge over the River Düna. We still had to march for three hours to reach the first railway station. There was also a delousing station there. Every soldier on leave had to have a delousing certificate before he was allowed to travel on. As it was nearly evening, the delousing station had already closed. We would have to be deloused the following afternoon. That did not suit the sergeant, because he really wanted to get back to his wife and children as soon as possible. It did not matter so much to me, as I could not travel home. Quite by chance, the sergeant bumped into a lance corporal from his home who was a clerk in the delousing station. The sergeant told him his tale of woe. 'No bother,' said the lance corporal, 'I can soon get you the certificates', then he went into his office and brought them to us a few minutes later. We thanked him and boarded the train, which was ready to leave. On paper we were both free of lice but in reality we were so covered in these bugs that the biting never stopped. These darling creatures had multiplied amazingly during the offensive.

We travelled all night and crossed the German border at Memel. The journey continued through East Prussia. It was beautiful autumn weather and the farm workers were busy harvesting potatoes. Judging by the filled sacks, there had been a good potato harvest. In the meadows we could see herds of black and white cattle, which seemed to be of a superior breed, and some of the fields were being dug up by motor ploughs.

In Königsberg the sergeant took his leave of me, as he came from the Province of Posen and had to travel a different route from mine. I boarded a train heading for Berlin. In the compartment sat an old lady with her two pretty daughters. We started chatting about all kinds of things. They asked me where I had come from. I said 'From the Riga Front.' Then they asked me whether I had taken part in the offensive on Riga, and I told them I had. The three of them were quite enthusiastic as a result of the exaggerated reports of victory in the newspaper. I told them of my experiences during the offensive, what I felt about how the inhabitants had been robbed of everything, and that in my opinion the offensive would not have any influence on the end of the war. I also felt sorry for the five hundred thousand inhabitants of Riga who were now facing starvation. The three of them listened open-mouthed with astonishment. Their enthusiasm had suffered a mighty blow. For their part they now told me how foodstuffs were in short supply and that you could only get things using ration cards, so that those people who did not have the means to buy expensive food on the black market were hardly able to survive. Despite this, all three of them were convinced of a German victory, as our troops were all deep in enemy territory. I replied that it would be very difficult for Germany to win, as England had never lost a war, and they should not forget America. However, I was not able to change their opinion. After a while I fell asleep. When I woke again, several large lice were crawling around on my trousers, having probably crawled out though my fly. I was embarrassed in case the ladies had seen, but they spoke on quite harmlessly and I crushed the lice with my hands without them noticing. In Küstrin the ladies left the train. I went into another compartment where several soldiers were sitting. There I met a soldier from Berlin who belonged to my Regiment and was returning there because his wife had died and he had been given fourteen days' leave. The rest of the soldiers came from the Rhineland.

We left the train in Berlin. The Silesia Station was packed with people. I immediately noticed that the women and girls had narrow, pale, wretched faces and dark rings round their eyes. It is war here too, I thought, the war of hunger!

I went into the town with the three soldiers from the Rhineland. We visited the Imperial Palace,[54] the Siegessäule,[55] the Iron Hindenburg[56] and many other sights. By evening we were hungry, and none of us had anything to eat. We went into a brightly lit, large restaurant and ordered beer. My God, what an insipid drink that was! It was missing out on hops and malt! We asked for something to eat. 'Have you got tokens?' asked the waiter. 'What do you mean, tokens? How do you expect us to have them?' 'Bread, meat and potato tokens,' replied the waiter. 'If you do not have them I cannot serve you.' The chaps from the Rhineland started to grumble: 'That's how it is! If you have spent long enough fighting at the front then you can return to your homeland and starve!' We went on and tried our luck at three further restaurants. You could get as much beer as you wanted, but there was nothing to eat. A friendly Berlin civilian paid for two glasses of beer for each of us and told us that he would take us to a restaurant where we would be sure to get something to eat. No sooner said than done; we boarded the tram and travelled through the well-lit town for about half an hour. At long last, we got out. The man took us to a restaurant where you could get saddle of venison with potatoes. Game was the only kind of meat you could get without tokens. The portion consisted of six small potatoes and a small piece of venison, with a spoonful of sauce. It tasted excellent, but the plate was soon empty. Although I was not a glutton, I could happily have eaten eight to ten of these portions, but they were not allowed to serve more than one per person. The good-natured citizen paid for everything. We thanked him, and continued to stroll round the town. We were often stopped by prostitutes, or they nudged us with their elbows as we passed and gave us a look implying that we should go with them. But we just thanked them for their vulgar company and headed for the Anhalter Station, which we eventually found after lots of asking around.

I decided to make a detour to the Rhineland as I enjoyed travelling through areas I did not know. Towards the evening of the next day we reached Cologne. Here the chaps from the Rhineland bade me farewell. Then I travelled on along the Rhine to Koblenz, and from there I went along the Mosel to Trier, a beautiful journey. In Trier, I got out, as I knew that the Reserve Battalion of my Regiment was based there, and I was hoping to get a new uniform as mine was worn out. The troops were just getting a meagre lunch. I went to the duty NCO and asked his permission to take a portion as I had

---

[54] The Stadtschloss in Berlin was the residence of the Kaiser until 1918. It was bombed in the Second World War and the ruin was demolished in 1950. There are plans to reconstruct it.

[55] This monument to nineteenth century Prussian victories is still a Berlin landmark.

[56] This was a wooden statue to Hindenburg erected as part of a wartime fundraising effort. It was dismantled after the war.

just returned from the Front. I was in luck. Then I asked for the quarter-master's store and went there. However the sergeant in charge really yelled at me when I told him what I wanted. 'Anyone could come to me like this!' he said. I asked him where I could find the Battalion Commander, went there, and the lad told him I was there. I heard the major say: 'Come in!' I went in. The major was having his lunch. There was not much sign of shortages here. 'What do you want?' he asked me in a very friendly way. 'Major, I have just come from the front on leave and would like to request a new uniform from the Reserve Battalion of my Regiment here.' The major looked at me and suggested that while I was at home on leave I could wear civilian clothes, to which I replied: 'Major, I have no option but to wear my uniform as my home is located in the part of Alsace which is occupied by the French and I cannot go there.' The major said: 'Good, then you can have a new uniform', and wrote out a note for me to give to the sergeant. I went there and was given a new uniform, together with a cap. Then I bought new puttees in a shop and put them on. Now my outward appearance was acceptable again. I thought: the outside is fine but underneath it's filthy – it's crawling with lice! I visited the sights of the town; the old Roman gate[57] impressed me the most. I boarded a train again and travelled along the Saar to Saarbrücken and Kaiserslautern, crossing the Rhine near Ludwigshafen and then continued to Mannheim and Heidelberg. I had to spend the night in Heidelberg as the last passenger train to Eberbach had already left.

With great difficulty I managed to get two thin sausages and some potato salad in the station restaurant. A man from the Red Cross asked me whether I wanted to spend the night in Heidelberg, and I said I did. 'Come with me!' he said and led me to a hotel near the station. He gave me a room with a beautiful clean bed, then he asked me when I would like to be wakened, and left. I got undressed and lay down in the bed with my lice. God, what a feeling it was to be able to lie undressed in a good soft bed for the first time in more than a year! It made it clear to me what a miserable life we led at the Front. As I was very tired as a result of my journey, I fell asleep straight away. The next morning quite early I was wakened by the Red Cross man. I got up and put my clothes on. Then I thought: I would like to see whether I have lost any of my inhabitants in the bed. Right enough, there were about ten of the little blighters crawling around there. I thought of trying to catch them. Then I thought: why bother, the next chap can also feel what it's like. I then travelled to the Mattler family in Eberbach, who were very welcoming. I asked them to give me warm water, so that I could have a bath. In this way, I became lice-free once again.

---

[57] The Porta Nigra (black gate) is the largest Roman city gate north of the Alps.

I had some very pleasant days, but food remained a problem. You could never get enough to eat. As I did not have any handkerchiefs any more I went into a fairly big shop to buy two. The owner of the shop said: 'Can I have your coupon please?' I had no idea what he meant. Then the shop-keeper explained: he was not allowed to sell anything, anything at all, without getting a coupon, otherwise they would close down his shop. Coupons could be obtained from the town hall. But after we had talked for a while the man did agree to sell me the two handkerchiefs, but I had to promise him that I would not tell anyone.

1917 was a good year for fruit. On all my journeys I saw that the apple and pear trees were laden with fruit. The Mattler family's neighbour who ran an apple-juice factory asked me whether I would help him. He had too much work to do, and offered to pay me two Marks a day. But I did not want to; first of all, I was not used to working any more, and secondly, I had come on leave in order to recover a bit and not to end up totally exhausted. I had intended to spend the last six days of my leave with my comrade August Zanger in the Rhineland, but grandmother Mattler died and I decided to stay for the funeral.

On the day after the funeral I bade farewell to the family and travelled down to the Rhineland. I had a long stop in Wetzlar. Near the station there was a large prisoner of war camp. The prisoners were accommodated in barracks. High barbed wire fences surrounded the yards in which the captives were allowed to move about. As I had time to spare, I went to look at the prisoners. How poor they looked! Pale and gaunt, with half lifeless eyes, these poor unfortunate people were just standing around. They seemed to be quite jaded and indifferent as a consequence of their hunger. All races were represented here: Frenchmen, Belgians, Englishmen, Scotsmen with their short trousers,[58] Italians, Serbs, Rumanians, Russians, Indians, Arabs and Negroes. They had all had to leave their homes to make such a heavy sacrifice to the god of war.

I spent three very pleasant days with August Zanger and the Gauchel family. Then it was time to return to the Front. This time I travelled to Riga and was very surprised when I saw the town. I had not imagined that it would be so beautiful, with attractive streets, splendid squares and magnificent churches. I would have liked to have stayed for longer, but my leave was over and I had to find my unit as quickly as possible in order to avoid punishment. I went to an information bureau where I was told that Regiment 332 had moved and was based on the River Aa in Livland.[59] I would be able to travel to Rodenpois-Kussau, which consisted of lots of villas and restaurants hidden away in a very beautiful forest. From there I would only have a few

[58] Presumably these were actually kilts.
[59] Livonia, now divided between Latvia and Estonia.

kilometres to walk. At the present time the place, which was a favourite destination for excursions for the people of Riga, had been completely deserted by its inhabitants and was mainly occupied by German officers. I enquired where Regiment 332 was based. I had to follow the main road from Riga to Petersburg.

Along this road stood or lay a vast number of field kitchens and other vehicles which the Russians had abandoned as they retreated. I crossed a bridge over the Aa, a small river about thirty metres wide. Eventually I met some soldiers from my regiment who were able to direct me to my Company. On the way I met the infantryman from Berlin who had travelled on leave with me. He told me that when he arrived his wife had already been buried, and that he had only stayed in Berlin for six days. Then he returned to the Regiment voluntarily, because he would have nearly starved to death in Berlin.

The Company Sergeant, the drivers, reserve troops and the horses belonging to my Company were camping in North Wawer, a miserable little hamlet which only consisted of a few huts. I reported back from leave. The following day I had to help in building a dugout for the Company Commander. I was busy constructing a hand rail out of pine stems at the side of the stair leading down into the dugout when a voice said: 'Hi, Nickel!' I looked up in surprise and was really pleased to see Emil Winninger from my home village. I went up to join him and we went to a wood nearby and chatted about our home. Each told the other news he had heard of how things were there. Emil Winninger was also fed up with this miserable hungry existence, and we decided to desert to the Russians, as I had been informed from home that a number of people I knew, who had been taken captive as German soldiers by the Russians, were now in France. That is to say, the people from Alsace and Lorraine who were captured by the Russians would be transported to France. Emil was based several kilometres nearer the Front in an advanced outpost. He sketched it out on a piece of paper so that I would not miss the way.

Now I went to the Company Sergeant and asked permission to have the following day off to visit my 'cousin'. He wrote my leave form straight away and I had to then have it signed off by the Company Commander. In the canteen I bought a bottle of Rhine wine, which we could drink to give us courage, and a hundred cigarettes to distribute to the Russians when we arrived so that they would not harm us.

When night fell, a big fire would be lit in the yard so that the soldiers could warm themselves up, because although it was only the end of October the nights were already cold. I took Alfred Schneider, a good comrade from Metz, aside into the dark and told him what I was planning to do. Afterwards I bade him farewell. As I later discovered, we were observed by a sergeant who had happened to come out further back at the same time and had communicated his suspicion to the Company Sergeant.

172

My sleeping quarters were up above a stall, under a straw roof, in what had previously been a hen house. I shared them with a number of comrades. When I believed that they had all gone to sleep, I got up quietly, lit a candle, pulled on a second pair of underpants and second shirt and put a pair of socks in my coat pocket. A soldier named Geier from the Rhineland saw me do this and the sergeant heard about this too. When I went to go down the ladder in the morning in order to go to Emil Winninger the company clerk Krebs came and said: 'Richert, you had better stay here today!' I immediately noticed that something was wrong, but I just said, quite harmlessly: 'Then I will stay here.'

My comrade Alfred Schneider, who went off to Libau in the morning to fetch spares for machine guns, told me the following on his return the next day: 'Richert, they must have noticed what you were planning, because I had to go to the sergeant in the orderly room before I went to Libau. They asked me what you had secretly said to me that evening. I naturally lied to him.' He was a bright lad. The sergeant had questioned him further: 'Why did Richert bid you farewell?' He replied: 'I laughed and told him that you knew that I had to travel to Libau and you were jokingly bidding me farewell in case the train crashed.' Schneider had done well. Despite this I noticed from the look of the Company Sergeant that he did not really trust me and was permanently suspicious of me. I tried to look as harmless as possible and did my duty exactly as before.

One day we had roll call. The teams were lined up in two units. I stood in the row of NCOs at the front, as I was in charge of a gun. After the roll call the Company Sergeant said: 'I have something to say to the Company: If a man or his superior notes that a man or his superior is suspected of deserting to the enemy, he should report it to the orderly room immediately.' I naturally knew straight away that this speech was directed at me, but I managed to look as harmless as possible, as if the whole thing had nothing to do with me. The sergeant, who sneaked a look at me, did not know what to make of it.

Life went on as usual. The main things were work duty, hunger and lice. Near the huts in Wawer North there were some potato fields which had probably been dug over about twenty times, but people continued to search them in the hope of still finding some potatoes.

Quite suddenly a rumour went round: – And really, the rumour turned out to be true.[60]

Armistice with Russia

Our Regiment was to leave our position to be quartered in Riga for an indefinite period of time. This news was welcomed by all of us. I had to

---

[60] The armistice occurred on the 15th of December 1917.

march off straight away with a lieutenant and three other men to go to Thorensberg, a suburb to the south of Riga, in order to set up quarters for the Company. We boarded the train in Rodenpois-Kussau and travelled to Riga, where we spent the night in a hotel. On the following morning we found good quarters for the men and the horses in a large leather factory in Thorensberg, which had stopped work – like all the other factories in Riga – because of a shortage of raw materials. The Company arrived towards evening, and were pleased with their quarters. The men lived in rooms which had previously served as offices. We emptied them and set up metal bunks. The NCOs and sergeants lived in the director's villa and the orderly room was set up there too. The Company Commander Baron of Reisswitz lived in a small castle outside the factory.

End of 1917 into 1918

Life in Riga

The city of Riga is built on the river Düna. Its inhabitants are mainly Latvians, but there are also lots of Germans. Almost all the inhabitants can speak German. Apart from the poorest, most of the inhabitants were attractively dressed in modern clothes, so they did not really seem Russian. The Latvians are generally a handsome, strongly built race; their girls and women are almost all pretty and attractive.

Our duties in Riga were easy. In the morning we had two hours of training; in the afternoon we cleaned machine guns and played sport. Twice a week we would march out for combat practise. By and large, life was quite pleasant, if only the food had been better. You never got enough to eat. In the civilian population the hardship increased from day to day, and the poorest people could hardly get enough to survive. There was no source of income for the workers as all the factories were silent. The inhabitants often complained to us that we had caused their misery and asked why we had not occupied Livonia and Estonia, as these two agriculturally rich provinces, which lie to the North of Riga, would have been able to provide the town with foodstuffs. We soldiers could not do anything about that! Practically nothing could be delivered to the town from the parts of Russia that had previously been occupied by the Germans because they had used up so much that there was barely enough to keep the inhabitants alive. A large part of the population was seized by a limitless anger against the Germans because of the shortages, with the result that on several occasions German soldiers were murdered on outlying streets. We were not allowed to go out at night without loaded pistols. The suburb of Thorensberg is separated from the town of Riga by the Düna, which is about six hundred metres wide at this point. As the Germans feared an uprising in the town, traffic from the suburb to the town was often forbidden and the only available crossing over the Düna, a wooden bridge built by the Germans, was closed. People were often angry because they found it impossible to get home.

The city of Riga, which is located several kilometres upstream from the mouth of the Düna into the Baltic, could be reached by large ships. Before the war this town was the third largest trading port of Russia, but at this time all trading had stopped and only a few military transports, picket boats and coastal patrol boats used the harbour. The quay where the ships berthed was three kilometres long. The goods station was situated at the lower end of the harbour; formerly the goods taken from the ships were loaded into railway waggons there. The Russians had burnt down the buildings of the goods station before retreating. The road and railway bridge across the Düna, one of the most attractive bridges I had seen until then, had been detonated by the Russians. People were working day and night to raise the fallen sections of the bridge, which were made out of iron and weighed thousands of tons, using machines. I often stood and watched this work, which was interesting and new to me. I found it difficult to understand how it was possible to cut through the thickest iron beams using jets of flame. In the meantime, the winter had set in, and everything covered in snow and ice. The Düna was completely frozen over. Icebreakers – that is small powerful steamers with sharp pointed bows – broke the ice to enable ships to get to and from the Baltic.

At Christmas, the Company organised a small celebration. A beautiful Christmas tree was lit up in a large factory building and we sang some Christmas carols. Afterwards there was a small Christmas present for each man.

The next day I was promoted to be an NCO. I moved into the villa where I was quartered in a room with a stove which I shared with two other NCOs. We had metal cots, but they did not have paliasses and mattresses, so that you had to sleep with your clothes on at night time too. Despite this you could feel very fortunate living here, as there was no risk of being killed, and you could live and sleep in dry warm conditions. Generally, you almost forgot that the war was still on. As an NCO I now had two Marks pay per day. In addition, like all the other NCOs I had a batman who kept my clothes tidy, polished my shoes, brushed out the room in the morning, kept the stove going, and brought coffee and meals.

My duty was almost the same as I had had as a lance corporal, as I was previously in charge of a gun. On Sundays I always took leave until 1.00am in order to be able to visit the German theatre in the town. They almost always put on splendid pieces; best of all I liked *Around the World in Eighty Days*.[61] The town also had many modern cinemas, and I often also visited them.

As the Company did not provide coffee or anything else on a Sunday evening, I usually went to the soldiers' hostel where, with a bit of difficulty, you could get yourself a plate of bean, lentil or pea soup – naturally without any meat – for fifty Pfennigs. The congestion in the soldiers' hostel

---

[61] Dominik Richert may have been mistaken here. There was a film made in the USA in 1914, but there is no known stage version.

was such that you could hardly get in. At a counter you paid fifty Pfennigs and were given a plate and a token, which you had to hand in at the serving hatch where the soup was handed out. You had to take your own spoon with you. Then you had to join the queue. The line of hungry soldiers wound backwards and forwards through the large hall like a snake almost filling it to capacity. Sometimes there was not enough soup for everyone; then the last in the queue were given their fifty Pfennigs back and could leave without being fed. That happened to me once. I had stood in the queue for more than an hour. At long last I had almost reached the serving hatch and was looking forward to a plate of hot soup, as it was bitterly cold outside. There were only two men ahead of me. Then they said: 'The soup has run out!' I could leave with an empty stomach after I had got my fifty Pfennigs back.

You could not get anything to eat in the cafes and restaurants in town. All that was available was poor-quality wartime beer, and tea. The civilian population was suffering more and more from the shortage of foodstuffs. As a result of the hardship and lack of work many girls and younger women were reduced to prostitution[62] in order to earn a living in this sorry way. Many others had already been completely corrupted by the Russian army and now continued their trade with the German soldiers. Some soldiers who were addicted to this passion would hoard some of their meagre supply of bread and other foodstuffs in order to take them to their mistresses. The lance corporal on my gun, by the name of Westenberg, had also got to know one of these slags and took her some of the meagre supply of food which he got from the Company and should have used for himself. It is obvious that as a result of his starvation and poor moral conduct he became skeletal. I often warned him but my advice fell on deaf ears, as he was such a slave to his passion.

A good comrade of mine, NCO Kurz, had also got to know a girl and fallen madly in love with her. He would talk constantly of his Lola and praised her beauty and worthiness. One day I met the two of them. Lola was really a very pretty girl and made a very good impression. I walked along with them for a while and then went off on my own. One day, NCO Kurz told me that he had reached the goal of his aspirations. For this purpose he took overnight leave lasting until reveille. On the following morning we had drill at a sand school outside the town. NCO Kurz just arrived when we reached the sand school and reported to Baron von Reisswitz who had been promoted to captain. The Captain, who himself led a very loose life and who had earned himself the nickname of 'whoremonger' amongst the troops, simply laughed and said: 'Good, take over your machine gun. You seem to

---

[62] For reasons of propriety, Dominik Richert leaves the word out, using a dash instead, but it is obvious from the context.

have had a busy night's work. You look very pale.' Two days later, Kurz felt that he was suffering from a sexually transmitted disease. He was ashamed to report sick and hoped that the ambulance officer would be able to cure him. It turned out to be the opposite – his condition got worse and worse. Eventually he had to report sick and was sent to the hospital for diseased soldiers, which the soldiers called the 'knights' castle'. The illness had already contaminated his blood and he had to suffer the consequences for the rest of his life.

All in all, lots of soldiers contracted sexually transmitted diseases, so that the doctor started to run weekly roll calls. In addition, every soldier was given a packet containing things to protect them from getting ill. Most of the soldiers gradually got used to this low life as something to be taken for granted. I often heard people talking about Moat Street.[63] It was all go there! I too went there to the famed Moat Street with one of my comrades, NCO Kizmann from East Prussia. There really was a lot going on there: one brothel after another. The two of us went into one. In a fairly large room there were lots of soldiers sitting at tables all along the walls drinking tea. Three totally sordid blokes were playing dance music on their musical instruments. About eight prostitutes were dancing around with soldiers, moving their bodies in very vulgar ways. As a result of their slovenly life-style, almost all the prostitutes looked rough, but they hypocritically tried to give the impression of liveliness in order to ensnare the soldiers wherever possible. There was a counter in a corner; behind it sat an old shrew watching the action. Whenever a soldier wanted to go upstairs with a prostitute he would go to the counter, pay two Marks and get a ticket. He showed this to the prostitute he fancied, who then had to go up with him. We both considered this form of behaviour to be degrading. I noticed right away that one of the prostitutes did not make such a bad impression but her face showed deep suffering and worry. Kizmann said to me: 'That girl is only here reluctantly!' I replied: 'I noticed her too and I have the same impression.' As we had emptied our glasses, we asked her to bring us more tea. She brought it, and also brought a glass for herself, as seemed to be the custom in these houses. Then she sat down between us.

The two of us started a conversation with her, she spoke very good German. I said to her quite directly that she was not suited for this place and asked her how it had come about that she had ended up in this company. As soon as I asked her, she started to cry and, in order to hide her face and her tears, she turned her back on the old monster who was watching the events in the room. Then she started to tell us, sobbing quietly as she went on: 'I could never have imagined that I would have found myself in a situation

63 Grabenstrasse.

178

like this. I come from Petersburg and a year ago I got married to a Russian officer who was stationed here in Riga. In order to be with my husband we rented a flat here in Riga and were very happy.' She was so sad that she could hardly speak any more. When she had regained her composure, she went on: 'Suddenly the German offensive started. Before we could decide to leave, the town was surrounded by the Germans and my husband was taken off into captivity. As we had used up the Russian roubles which had previously been in circulation, all we had left was a sum of Kerensky – money that had no value after the Germans occupied the town. So there I was, with no money and with only enough food to last for a few days. When I had used the food up, I sold all the things I could do without, but we had not had many of those as we were living in a furnished flat. I walked round the town all day trying to get work as a carer, or a servant, or a part-time worker. It was no use, and everywhere I went was given the same reason: it was not possible to take on servants because it was not even possible to scrape together foodstuffs for their masters. I would have been satisfied with any kind of work, even the most humble task. As I could not pay the rent, I had to leave the flat where I had lived so happily with my husband. So there I stood on the street with no accommodation or money and feeling desperate. I thought of throwing myself into the Düna out of desperation, but I lacked the courage to do so. So I ended up here, as a last resort. I have often thought that it would be better to be at rest at the bottom of the Düna than to have to live like this. As I am not as degenerate as these terrible people, with whom I am hardly able to live as they are so revolting, the soldiers consider me the most desirable. You cannot believe how much effort it cost me each time I go upstairs and hear them insult me!' She started to sob again and continued: 'Oh, what would my kind parents or my husband think of me if they knew the circumstances I am now living in! In addition, I am expected to present a happy, high spirited appearance in order to bring in as much as possible for that wicked old woman, who has already threatened several times to throw me out if I look so sad!' 'That's terrible,' we both said. 'Is there absolutely no possibility of getting out of here?' 'I agonize over it the whole time,' she answered, 'but I can not find an escape.' We felt very sorry for the poor woman. The only way we could help her was to each give her two Marks, which she accepted gratefully. Then she was invited to dance by a soldier, who went straight up with her. On the stairs she gave us a desperately unhappy look.

'Now you see, Richert,' said my friend, 'what lies behind this superficial gaiety. I felt really sorry for that young woman. And there are still people who say that war is God's punishment. God wanted the war! But it's only the people who do not have husbands or sons who are liable to be called up and can benefit financially who say that.' We sat there for a bit longer and watched the goings-on. The Captain's servant came down the stairs with a prostitute. He made a face as if he had just won the jackpot. 'Do you see, Kizmann,' I said, 'the servant is following his master's example.'

We left the centre of vice and returned to our quarters. On the way we continued to talk about the fate of the unfortunate young woman. Yes, what such a terrible war brings with it: hunger, fear of dying, damp, cold, lying outside, lice, separation from home for soldiers at the front, the often terrible pain suffered by the wounded, the fear felt by those remaining at home for their sons and husbands, the tears and pain felt for the fallen, and then the thousands of identical or similar cases to that of the unfortunate woman. Really, the people who are to blame for such suffering deserve to be tortured slowly to death using all imaginable means.

As I heard, trains laden with potatoes had arrived at the goods station. I just had one wish: if only I could fetch myself a sack! As it got dark, I went there, gave a soldier standing at a side gate of the station office five Marks and asked him to let me fetch a sack of potatoes. 'Do what you like, sir,' he said good-naturedly, 'I simply can't see you!' I carefully made my way through underneath the waggons on the tracks, and reached the potatoes, which were piled up by the cartload. A soldier was patrolling round the heap of potatoes. I had to wait until he was at the opposite end of the pile. I quickly heaved the sack, which I would estimate weighed about a hundred-weight on my back and left the station as quickly as possible. I had just reached a dark side street when several civilians stopped me and asked me if I would sell them the potatoes. I did not want to have anything to do with this as I wanted to have a stock for a while and only someone who has had to do without potatoes for a long time knows what a sack of them is worth. Every few steps people asked me and harassed me to sell the potatoes after all! Eventually the sack became too heavy for me to carry, and I still had about half an hour to go before I would reach my quarters. In addition I was afraid that I might be noticed in the brightly-lit streets with the big sack, and that I would be stopped by officers and have to tell them where the potatoes had come from. I was busy trying to think this out when a young woman approached me once again. 'Now, soldier, do you not want to sell your potatoes?' 'How much would you pay me for them?' I asked. 'Twenty Roubles,' she replied. 'Good,' I replied, 'You can have half of them for ten Roubles.' I had to follow the woman to her flat, which was quite nearby. She lived on the second floor. Judging by her manner, her clothes, and her room furnishings, she seemed to be comfortably off. I emptied half of the potatoes into a box. Then the woman invited me to sit down on the sofa, and set about making tea. While she was waiting for the water to boil, she sat down close beside me, pressed her knee against mine, and, looking promisingly at me, said: 'My husband is away at the war!' Now I knew exactly how she wanted to pay for the potatoes, but I pretended that I had not understood at all and replied: 'Then your husband has the same misfortune as I do! Well, now that peace seems imminent, he will come home soon!' We chatted on for a while and she did not venture to return to her previous topic. After I had drunk my tea and was leaving she said that I could bring her as many sacks of potatoes as I wanted and that she would give me twenty Roubles for each sack.

I left the house with my half-empty sack of potatoes and the ten Roubles, made a point of noting the number of the house and the name of the street, and went to the nearest tram stop. There I threw my sack into the tramcar and travelled down towards the Düna. From there I only had a quarter of an hour's walk. On the bridge across the Düna an old woman went swaying past me, groaning continuously. I asked her what was wrong. 'Hunger!' she replied, with a tired, extremely sad look. She had a fairly large bag with her. I set down my sack of potatoes on the street and filled up her bag with about ten pounds. The woman could not thank me enough. I said 'Forget it, it's all right!' and went back to my quarters. The same night I boiled up a canteen full and shared it with my two room-mates.

I decided that I would fetch potatoes from the station the following night and take them to the woman, because twenty Roubles per sack was a tempting source of income. I took leave until twelve o'clock in order to be able to carry away as many sacks as possible. When I reached the gate to the station, the same soldier I had seen the previous night was on sentry duty. I promised him three Marks for each sack he would let me carry out. He agreed immediately. I went straight to the pile of potatoes, heaved a sack on my back, and was about to carry it off. I had not gone more than a few steps before someone held me by the shoulder. 'Stop, please!' came the order. I stood still and dropped the sack. 'What have you here?' the sapper NCO asked me, because that was who he was, on the so-called potato patrol, accompanied by two men. 'Potatoes,' I answered. Now I had to go with them to the guardroom. 'I will have to report you to your company,' said the NCO. 'Listen, comrade, to what I have to tell you,' I replied. 'It's obvious that people don't steal potatoes for pleasure; you know too, that we are all starving. I had no option but to use this way to improve on my situation. If you report me, they may punish me. That would be the first time in my military service, which is now more than four years. In addition, my home is located in the part of Alsace occupied by the French, so that I do not have a chance of being sent any money or packages from there. Just put yourself in my situation, comrade!' I finished. 'Yes, that's quite something,' said the sapper NCO. 'I tell you what. Just take your sack and go, but make sure you don't get caught!' Then he shook my hand. I went to my sack and put it back on my shoulders, paid the sentry his three Marks on the way out, carried the sack to the woman, and then went to the cinema with my twenty Roubles. I did not feel confident enough to steal any more potatoes. The potatoes which I had left lying in my heated room had previously been frozen like stones, and in two days they were totally rotten, so I was unable to eat them.

All that the soldiers thought about was getting hold of food by any possible means. Once I had to supervise potato peeling in a room next to the place where the field kitchen was situated. About twenty soldiers were busy peeling a big basket of potatoes. When the peeling was done, about half the potatoes were missing. 'Listen, soldiers! What you are doing now is over the top!' I said. 'Out with your potatoes, or I will be forced to search your pockets!' They all looked innocent, none of them owned up to having a potato. I checked their pockets and, to my surprise, I did not find a single one. I could not get wise to what had happened so I just got them to take the remaining potatoes to the field kitchen. The cook was not satisfied with the inadequate quantity, but there was nothing I could do about it. I noticed that several soldiers seemed to be secretly smirking and this indicated to me that they were actually in possession of the missing potatoes. I checked the room once again but could not find anything. The following day, my batman told me that if I did not tell anyone, he would explain where the potatoes had gone. I was very eager to know, and promised not to tell. 'In the room where the peeling took place there is a staircase with wooden steps. In the steps there is a hole the size of a medium potato. The potatoes are pushed through the hole. So that you do not notice, while they are peeling, several men stand in front of the hole. After you had gone, the boards were pulled out and the potatoes were taken out and distributed.' I had to laugh about the soldiers' cunning. They had followed the well-known saying 'necessity knows no law' – and I could not be angry with them.

One evening I happened to enter the room where my team lived, and was very surprised to find that the lads were busy eating a big cooking pot of meat. 'Gosh! Where did you get the meat?' They looked at each other and smiled and invited me to have some too. I still could not work out where the meat had come from. At the table sat a chap from Westphalia with an unpleasant face and red watery eyes. He was holding a piece of meat in both hands, bit some off, and chewed away with full cheeks. When I looked at him, it reminded me of the cannibals. 'Do you know what, Richert,' he said 'Yesterday evening out in the streets I shot a large dog with my pistol.' Then he pointed into the pan with his finger – they were eating dog meat. So the soldiers have sunk so low that they consume dog meat!

When I was on my own with my team, I did not want them to call me 'Sir', but they had to do so if there were officers in the vicinity. The captain once noticed that I spoke to a soldier in a familiar way.[64] He called me to the orderly room straight away and gave me quite a dressing down. He said, I should retain my authority. I thought to myself: Go to the devil, with your damned delusions of authority!

[64] Using the 'du' form.

One day I was duty NCO. As I was going through the yard Rifleman Anton Schäfer, who was a real Rhinelander, called to me in his unmistakable dialect 'NCO Richert, come here!' When I got there I said 'What's up Tünnes' (Rhineland slang for Anton). 'The whoremonger wants to talk to you in the office.' I naturally laughed out loud and even when I was standing in front of the Rittmeister it was a huge effort not to laugh in his face. He noticed this and said: 'Something must be amusing you, to make you grin like that!' Smiling, I replied 'Yes, sir'. He gave me my orders for the day and I left quickly.

One Sunday evening the Company organised a celebration in the Lithuanian Clubhouse. It was very merry. Each man was allowed six glasses of beer, at midnight we each got two sausages with potato salad, followed by tea with lots of rum prepared in the field kitchen. Eight musicians from the Regimental Band played dance music. There were lots of girls there, and soon everyone who could dance at all was whirling around in the large hall. As I had previously enjoyed dancing, I did not miss out on this opportunity and waltzed off in style. The Captain watched the events, smirking to himself. As I passed him, he said to me: 'What, you're dancing, Richert? I always thought of you as a good Catholic lad.[65] 'Well, captain, nobody can object to innocent happiness!' I answered, and I thought to myself: 'smell that, you old whoremonger!'

We often heard that our Regiment would soon be transported to the Western Front. We were all afraid of the prospect, but time passed, and we stayed on in Riga.

On Sunday the 18th of February 1918 I had been given night leave once again and returned home from the German Theatre with a number of comrades at 1.00am. I went straight to bed. At three o'clock my roommate Kizmann and I were wakened by the Company Sergeant Laugsch. 'Listen,' said the sergeant, 'the peace talks with the Russians have broken down and have been discontinued. We have to mount a new offensive. The two of you must travel with Lieutenant Herbst by train to the terminus in Hinzenberg and find quarters for the Company by the River Aa. They will march there on foot and arrive at nightfall.'

Brr! It sent the shivers down my spine again and again. The idea of mounting an offensive in this cold weather in such deep snow! Our leaders seemed to have gone mad. Now our pleasant life in Riga had come to an abrupt end. We packed up our possessions in our rucksacks, swung them on our backs and went to the station. I was terribly afraid of what the future would bring, because I did not know that the Russians would offer no resistance. The train stopped at Hinzenberg at dawn. We set up quarters

---

[65] The German word is *Marienjunge*.

for the horses and the men in the beautiful castle of Semneck. Towards evening, the Divisional Headquarters set up its quarters in the castle and simply threw us out. All the houses and huts in the area were packed full of troops and there was no free space anywhere. Then we found some old dugouts without doors or windows in the woods. Inside they were frozen solid, but free of snow. The men of Company, who turned up dead tired from their march, were very angry with us about the poor quarters. But we really could not do anything about it. The horses were placed close to each other, tethered to trees, and covered with blankets. The troops sat down in the cold dugouts as close together as possible and covered themselves with blankets and tents. Towards morning we got such cold feet that several people got up and collected fir branches to make a fire. We all missed our metal cots in Riga. At daybreak we were given coffee and bread from the field kitchen. How delightful a drink of warm coffee can be! We were all full of life again. Now we had to line up. The horses were harnessed to the machine gun wagons and we marched off to an uncertain future.

The Offensive against the Bolsheviks – Occupation of the Baltic Provinces of Livonia and Estonia

We marched through the crunching hard-frozen snow towards the Aa. We crossed the ice of the river, which was about forty metres wide, with men, horses and waggons. At Rodenpois-Kussau we reached the main road from Riga to St Petersburg and headed north towards Russia. We stopped at midday. The company commanders had to go to the Commander of the Regiment in order to receive orders. After his return, the Captain called the Company to assemble round him. 'Soldiers,' he started, 'the aristocrats and landowners of the Baltic Provinces of Livonia and Estonia have asked his majesty to liberate them from the Bolshevik hordes. So, forwards, soldiers to liberate Livonia and Estonia!' My first thought was 'Liberate!' it will once again be a beautiful liberation! In reality, the order meant: The workers and peasant farmers of Livonia and Estonia who had succeeded in liberating themselves for a few days from the yoke of the nobility and landowners are now going to be forced back into a situation of hunger and suffering once again by German militarism. The nobility and landowners have exploited the population ruthlessly since time immemorial. As generals and officers during the war they have been well paid for driving thousands of soldiers who had been forcibly recruited from the lower strata of society to their deaths. Generally, at every possible opportunity, the Germans tended to throw the word 'liberation' about. I just wonder that they do not write about how they wanted to liberate France from the French and England from the English! Although we heard all kinds of things, it was not possible to form a picture of the current circumstances in the Russian Army. We marched

184

through a large forest. At the end, the road led through a deep cutting. The road at this point was filled with drifted snow to a depth of more than six metres, so that the waggons could not progress any further. In the distance we saw a far-flung village, and the Russian position was said to be in front of it, at a distance of about one and a half kilometres away. We could just see a dark strip in the snow – this was the top of the Russian wire entanglement sticking up through the snow. We had to wait until dark and then everyone who had a spade had to shovel snow in order to clear the road. It must have been midnight or later before we completed this task. We spent the rest of the night in the forest, which was covered in deep snow. There was no chance of sleeping as it was so cold. We all tramped around and swung our arms around our bodies to try to warm ourselves up. They said we would have to attack the Russian position in the morning. At daybreak we were given warm food and coffee from the field kitchen.

The infantry had to line up at the edge of the wood. We had to get the machine guns and the ammunition boxes out of the carts and distribute them along the infantry lines. I impressed it upon my team that if they should encounter heavy fire from the Russians they should throw themselves down immediately and dig themselves in with their hands and legs in the deep snow to ensure that the Russians would not see them. It was a clear, cold winter's morning. When the sun appeared in the east we were ordered: 'Forwards march.' We left the wood, forming long lines in the snow field. Not a single shot came from the Russian position. I wondered whether they simply had not seen us, or whether the position was unoccupied. Then I noticed dark points in the snow beyond the Russian entanglement, first in small numbers, and then more and more. I took my binoculars and looked across. It was the heads of the Russians, which were covered with large fur caps. We slowly got closer. My team started sweating, as it really was not very easy to carry the heavy loads when your legs sank in the deep snow to above your knees at each step. We had got very close to the Russian position, and we could see one head after another looking at us. I raised my free arm in the air and waved to them. Immediately, on the other side, lots of arms were raised waving back at us. Not a single shot fell on either side. Where the road led through the Russian position, the barbed wire had been removed. The Russians came through there with their hands in the air, first individually, and then in large numbers. 'All form up on the road!' called our officers, so we headed in that direction, and set down our equipment when we got there. The Russians marched past us. They were young lads, hardly twenty years old, but they all looked smart. The older Russians had refused to stay in the trenches, and had either gone home or were wandering around in the villages and towns behind the Front. We marched on. At the head, there was a squadron of hussars on horseback, followed by a battalion of infantry and then came our machine gun company. To start

185

with we passed through some totally deserted villages. We stopped in one of these and spent the night there. We slept in living rooms, stalls and barns on the old straw that had previously been used by the Russians. The consequence was, that we all ended up being full of lice once again, but that was not so bad as we had long since got used to the darling creatures, and if you scratched hard, you would warm up a bit. On the following morning we went on in the same direction. On the way, a large number of soldiers in Russian uniforms went past us in the opposite direction. We all thought that they were Russians, but actually they were Russian prisoners who had been liberated by the Bolsheviks and were free to go wherever they wanted. A big-mouthed Berliner said: 'I'm fed up. I have been a captive since 1914!' But he looked well and did not seem to have suffered from any kind of shortage. I thought to myself: now he will get a few weeks of leave in Berlin. There he will get more fed up as a result of the hunger. Then he will head to the French front and will be completely fed-up.

Towards evening we approached the town of Wolmar where we were immediately quartered in the first houses. We heard some shots fired in the town. As we were tired we lay down and soon fell asleep. We stayed in Wolmar and had the following day off. I went into the town with some comrades. From a distance we noticed lots of soldiers standing together. We went there too and pushed through the crowd. What a spectacle greeted us there! There were six people who had been shot lying on the ground, all of them in Russian army uniform, lined up along a paling. Two lay there cowered up in the position they had assumed in mortal fear. One of them sat in the snow with his back to the fence. His head had been split from ear to ear down to his chin by a sabre blow. His face hung down on his chest, while the back of his head was raised up. A ghastly picture! We shuddered, turned away and went on, in the hope of being able to purchase some food. From a distance we noticed that several men had been hanged at the market place. We went there and looked at this gruesome spectacle. Altogether there were five men hanging there, four young ones and an older one; they were some of the people who had been liberated by the Germans, liberated from their lives! All five of them hung there with their arms, hands, legs and feet hanging limply down. Their heads were all leaning to the side, and the tips of their tongues were hanging at an angle between their lips. Beside them in the snow, a woman who had been shot was lying face down. On her feet, she was only wearing stockings. Her shoes had probably been stolen during the night. An older woman stood crying at the corner of a house. When the swarm of gawkers had wandered off a bit, the poor woman went to one of the people who had been hanged and crying loudly she stroked his leg as if she was caressing it. I pitied the poor pitiful mother to the bottom of my heart, but there was nothing I could do about it.

There were a number of Russian guns which had simply been abandoned in the market place. As no food was to be had in the town, I went with NCO Kipmann to a farm in the vicinity. The people understood German and gave us milk, potatoes and bread – raw black bread of the kind you got everywhere in that region. We tried to find out what sort of people had been hanged on the market place, but the people were careful and did not want to tell us to start with. When we told them that they had nothing to fear from us they told us that the people who had been hanged had all been citizens of the town. Two of them had returned from the army a few days ago. All five had been known as peace-loving people, and none of them had done the slightest harm. The dead woman was the mother of one of them, and she had struggled desperately to prevent her son's execution. The hussars had simply taken the first people they had found and hanged them to set a frightening example. How dreadful! I of course do not know whether these statements were correct, but I do consider it possible.

The next morning we went on. As we passed the market place, the poor people were still hanging there. We marched all day. Quite often German and Austrian soldiers who had previously been taken captive by the Russians went past us. Most of the Austrians looked very discontented. They would probably have preferred to stay in captivity, rather than face the prospect of being taken to a front once again. It was very difficult to march along the icy roads. Almost the whole time the rear wheels of the waggon slid to the side. The next evening we were quartered in a fairly large farmstead near the road. There were a lot of refugees staying there. When a sergeant went to a free-standing little stable to see whether there was space for a few horses, the refugees started to howl and moan. We did not know why. We soon found out, because in the stall the sergeant found the corpse of a smartly dressed elderly man. The refugees were mortally afraid that we would think of them as the culprits and shoot them, but we left them in peace, which made them very happy.

The day afterwards we went on. The area was fairly densely populated, the houses were better built than elsewhere, and the inhabitants were fairly smartly dressed. On both sides of the roads, and in the ditches lay many dead Russian horses, which were partly buried under the snow. We saw a town called Walk, and the hussars rode on ahead. Looking back, as far as you could see, the road was filled with German infantry, cavalry, artillery, machine gun companies and baggage trains. Suddenly we saw columns of Russian soldiers coming out of the town. We did not know what that meant. 'Guns at the ready!' shouted the captain. We heaved the machine guns from the waggons and brought them into position on both sides of the road on a slight rise. 'Load, range 900!' commanded the captain. 'As soon as you hear shots being fired from over there, fire continuously into their columns.' I felt quite horrified when I thought of how much devastation our machine gun would cause in the column. However, no shot fell. Then it sounded as if I could hear the sound of music being played. It was true! We could hear a Russian regimental band playing. Unbelievable! It was a Russian infantry regiment which was surrendering to us accompanied by a band. The troops laughed and waved to us as they marched past. They were followed by several hundred other soldiers who came into captivity with horses and waggons. Everywhere in the fields half-starved Russian military horses were wandering around, eating the bark off trees and the frozen twigs off bushes. Nobody took care of the poor animals.

We suddenly heard an enormous explosion in the town. We were all afraid and looked over towards the town. A massive heavy cloud had shot into the sky and lots of objects which we could not make out because of the distance were flying through the air. We heard that a munitions factory in Walk had blown up. We marched into the town. Thousands of Austrian prisoners of war stood at the roadside and watched us march in. I did not see many happy faces among them. They had all been liberated by the Bolsheviks and could now expect to be incorporated into German-Austrian militarism once again. The inhabitants reacted to our entry into the town with mixed feelings and were already afraid of the prospect of starvation, which seemed certain. In the square in front of the church the hussars had once again hanged two men. Nobody knows why. We were quartered in Walk. It was cold in the rooms as almost all the windows had been shattered by the massive explosion. Many Russian guns stood around in the streets and squares of Walk. The Russian soldiers had simply refused to obey and had run away.

A large Russian food depot, consisting of several large barrack-huts, was discovered on the evening after our arrival. Everyone was going there to get food. I too went there with three men from my team and went straight into the huts. On one side stood a number of small boxes containing candles, while on the other side there were high stacks with tins of canned goods packed in boxes. At the back there were lots of boxes of sugar, with a number of sacks containing sugar on top. Two of my men each took a box of tinned meat, and the third took a sack of sugar on his back, while I took care of the lighting by taking a box of candles. It went like a fair and the huts were emptying very quickly. We had hardly got away with our booty before several officers arrived on the scene. The soldiers were driven out and sentries were posted at the entrances to the barracks. We didn't mind as we had managed to get our booty to a safe place. Straight away we cooked up some of the tinned meat we had got away with and we five men ate an incredible quantity. We put so much sugar into our coffee that it was as sweet as honey and sticky too.

The following morning I went into the yard of a factory next to our quarters. Hundreds of Russian army horses had been herded together here, but there was no food for them – not a stalk of straw and no hay. The poor beasts were eating each others tails and manes in order to appease their hunger. Some small carts which stood at the side of the yard had been eaten down to the iron by the pitiful animals. Wherever there was wood it was gnawed away and eaten. In the vicinity of the factory, the horses for our machine gun waggons were accommodated in a stall. I went in there and fetched an armful of hay from the hay rack in order to take it to the captured horses. When I got through the gate and the animals saw the hay they galloped up to me from all directions. I got quite scared, let the hay fall and fled out through the gate. The horses bit each other for the small quantity of hay, which disappeared almost immediately. They looked at me as if they were pleading with me to fetch some more, but this was not possible as we only had a very limited supply for our own horses.

In the afternoon, the company sergeant called me to see him. 'Richert,' he said, 'the Commandant's Office of Walk has just asked for two NCOs and six men who are to be sent into the country, but I do not know what the purpose is. Would you be interested in going?' I replied 'why not, sir'. So then I went with NCO Langer and six men to the Commandant's Office and reported there. Then we had to go back to our quarters to fetch our things. In addition each of us had to be armed with a carbine and a semi-automatic pistol, together with sufficient ammunition. We arrived back at the Commandant's Office just as two Russians who were apparently Bolsheviks were being led in. The two people made quite a good impression, but they did not speak German. I heard how an officer said to them: 'Just you wait, you pigs; tomorrow you will have cold feet.' These two poor people had also been 'liberated'!

NCO Langer was now given the task of going to the castle in Hollerhof to protect its inhabitants from the Bolsheviks. I was ordered to take my three men and go to the castle of Ermes in order to protect the young woman who lived in the castle, as well as the parson in his parsonage, the schoolmaster and the stationmaster. We were also given the task of arresting Bolsheviks or people with Bolshevik attitudes and taking them to Walk, and of collecting any firearms belonging to the population in and around Ermes. That was quite a lot to ask of us: protect people, arrest others, and gather in weapons, using an armed force of three men! A number of farmers had been forced to wait outside the Commandant's Office with their horses and sledges to provide transport. NCO Langer and I were each given a map showing every farm and geographical feature in the surrounding area. We boarded the sledges and set off.

We had hardly left the town before we started to travel through a snow-covered pine forest which seemed to go on for ever. The sledge was pulled by a small unkempt horse which trotted on and on with unbelievable endurance. There was a wooden collar round the horse's neck, and underneath there was a bell which rang constantly. The farmer sat beside me in his fur coat, with a tall fur hat on his head. To me it seemed all in all to be a genuine Russian picture of the kind I had seen in calendars in the past. Only one thing was missing – the wolves! To start with I assumed that the farmer would not understand German. All at once he started a conversation with me. I immediately offered him a cigar, took one for myself, and lit them both. I asked him how far it was from the town of Walk to the village of Ermes. He told me it was 22 *versts*, which is about 25 kilometres. We passed through several villages. The inhabitants stared at us as we were the first Germans they had ever seen. In almost every village there was a beautiful castle. Normally a baron or a count would live there, and the whole village would have to work for him. But the workers here did have better cottages than in Poland or further south, and the people were dressed respectably. Towards evening we reached the village of Ermes. We travelled to the castle and got out. I wanted to report immediately to the lady of the castle. The caretaker told me: 'Her ladyship has gone away.' To be honest, I was glad to hear it. The castle cook immediately fried a pile of pork chops for us. The farmer, who had driven us here and who wanted to drive back straight away in the darkness, now had to eat with us and spend the night here. The four of us pitched in, as pork chops were something new to us. The consequence was that we ate too much and ended up with diarrhoea. The good thing was that none of us could have a laugh at the others' expense, because we all had the same problem. On the same evening we got a boy to take us to the school. I knocked – no answer. I knocked again and heard someone say something in Lithuanian. I answered: 'We are German soldiers who have been sent here from Walk to protect you.' It was the schoolmaster, who naturally spoke very good German. He carefully opened the door and lit us up with a candle. Then I noticed that he had a revolver in his right hand. I laughed and said to him that he had nothing to fear. He invited us in and was very friendly, as was his wife, who immediately ordered her servant girl to bring us tea and fine sugar buns. We spent about an hour talking, and then left to return to the castle to spend the night there. As we left, the schoolmaster invited us for lunch the next day, and we gladly accepted.

The next morning we went to the parsonage, which was located on a hill, and were made very welcome. The parson had a beautiful wife and three very pretty young children. We spent several pleasant hours there. We were treated very hospitably, and one of my soldiers, Lance Corporal Kessler from Berlin, played several beautiful pieces on the piano. We thanked them and went to the schoolmaster's for lunch. A schoolmaster in Lithuania is an important person, who is also a farmer as well as following his calling. Naturally he has workers to do things for him. We were given a meal, the like of which I had never had since becoming a soldier, it was almost too fine for us as our palates were only used to basic soldiers' food. After the meal we sat together comfortably smoking. Each of us had to talk about his home-land. When I said that I came from Alsace, the teacher said: 'So your home is the bone of contention which is probably to blame for the outbreak of war.' I now told the teacher of the beauty and fruitfulness of Alsace, and of the high level of culture and the many natural resources. Afterwards the school-master told me that he did not trust the Bolshevists, who were hostile towards him, and that this was the reason why he had asked for German soldiers for protection. I told him that we had been given the task of arrest-ing Bolshevists and people with Bolshevist sympathies and taking them to Walk. The teacher's wife suddenly got very involved. The teacher who lived in the upper floor had Bolshevist sympathies. She deserved to be taken away – and so on. She kept on and on trying to portray the teacher in an unbelievably bad light. I realized immediately that she had a deep hatred for the teacher, and I felt that her denunciation was very nasty. I tried to give her the impression that I was listening attentively and then said that I would go up and interrogate the teacher.

I knocked on the door that the schoolmaster's wife pointed out to me and entered when I heard 'Come in'. As I entered, the teacher got up from the sofa, offered me a seat, and immediately started to cry. She returned to sit on the sofa and continued crying, I sat down opposite her.

The teacher was a pretty, attractively dressed girl of about twenty to twenty-two years old. I started by saying: 'Why are you crying?' 'Oh God, you were down with the schoolmaster. How his wife hates me,' she sobbed. 'Listen, ma'am, you have nothing to fear from me. I am not bothered about what she may think. Maybe her opinions and mine might be different.' She looked at me with astonishment. 'Yes, believe me; I have also had to suffer greatly under the power of the military. My only wish now is to free myself from it in any way I can.' I told her that I had the task of arresting people with Bolshevist sympathies and taking them to Walk. 'You should feel lucky that you are dealing with me and not with an NCO with patriotic attitudes,' I said.

'Oh God,' said the teacher, 'if only I could get away from here and go to my parents.' I asked where her parents lived and she mentioned a village which was twenty kilometres away, to the south of the town of Dorpat. I thought for a bit and then I said: 'Don't you have someone here whom you can trust completely, who owns a horse and a sledge?' 'Certainly!' she replied, and pointed to the house where the farmer lived. 'Listen, miss, I will take you to your parents tomorrow. Would you please write me a note to give to the person you trust explaining our plan? I will go there tomorrow morning and give him the note. Then the two of us will arrive with the sledge. Be ready for me and I will pretend to arrest you. Cry for a bit, and then I will tell the schoolmaster that I am taking you to Walk, but we will head for your home instead. Do you agree?' I asked. 'Oh, how happy I am, you are a splendid

191

fellow. I will remember you all the days of my life!' After we had clasped each others' hands I went down to the schoolmaster's family and, looking serious, I said that I would take the teacher to Walk the following morning. I was revolted by the happiness which I saw on the face of the schoolmaster's wife. Then we went back to the castle and spent the rest of the day there.

The next morning I went and found the teacher's friend working in the stall. The man was frightened when I entered, and did not speak a word of German. I shook him by the hand and gave him a friendly nod. Then I took the note from the teacher and handed it to him. I was not able to read it, because although it was written using German letters, it was in Latvian. When the man had read it he looked at me with astonishment, and then looked at the note again. I smiled at him and indicated 'yes, yes' with my head, then I pointed in the direction of the teacher and waved my hand to indicate that we would leave. Then he believed me. I had to go into his living room and drink warm milk with him, while he put on felt boots and fur coat. The horse was harnessed and we went round to the schoolhouse. I went straight up to the teacher. She was very friendly but rather fearful. We waited for a minute, as I had to drink a cup of tea, then we went down. The teacher played her act well, holding her handkerchief in front of eyes, and sobbing. The farmer did not know what to make of it when he saw her sobbing. Then the schoolmaster's wife appeared below the window, her face radiant with joy. I curtly ordered the farmer to climb in, sat down next to the teacher in the back of the sledge, and we set off in the direction of Walk. When the schoolmaster's wife could no longer see us we turned off towards the north, heading towards the teacher's home. The three of us had a very jolly sledge journey. The teacher explained exactly what had happened to the farmer; he became very friendly to me, patted me on the shoulder, and said something in Latvian which the teacher translated for me. He said: 'If all the German soldiers were like you, you would have been welcome earlier!' I asked the teacher to explain to him that other German soldiers would have acted differently and that he should hide away a good stock of food, as the Germans would probably requisition almost all the cattle and all the food – which is to say, they would be stolen, and anyone who did not take pre-cautions would have to tighten their belts. The farmer was disheartened to hear what I had to say.

The inhabitants of all the villages and farmsteads that we passed looked surprised to see us. The horse galloped on and on. I found myself wondering where the small ragged horse got its strength from. The farmer's dog, a little rat-catcher, ran along behind the sledge with its tongue hanging right out as a result of the exertion involved. I indicated to the farmer to stop, got out and lifted it into the sledge. The teacher said that I must be kind hearted and that she could not imagine that I could have killed anyone in the war. To this I replied: 'I hope that all the people I have shot dead are enjoying good health!' which made us both laugh. She kept on thanking me for my help. At long last her home village could be seen. 'My parents live there,' she said. The village was still one and a half kilometres away. 'Listen, miss, we will have to part now!' 'No,' she said, 'you must come with me to my parents!' 'It's not possible,' I said, 'because nobody in your village must know that you were brought home by a German soldier.' As we were travelling through a small wood I got the farmer to stop and the young woman explained my decision to him. She climbed out and wanted to walk home. I said she should continue in the sledge, and that I would wait there until the farmer returned. Now we said goodbye. 'How can I thank you?' she kept repeating, and suddenly, in an upsurge of sincere gratitude she put both her arms round my neck and gave me two hearty kisses on the mouth, which I reciprocated equally heartily. She tore herself away, climbed back on board the sledge, shook my hand for the last time, and the sledge drove off. She waved goodbye to me until she was close to the village. I felt very strange, the whole thing had affected me, and it took me some time to forget the girl. It took a while before the farmer came back. At long last, the sledge came from the village. When I had climbed on board, the farmer gave me an attractive picture of the teacher. On the back she had written: 'To my dear rescuer, as a keep-sake, Olga Anderson.' Now the farmer got out a large piece of cooked ham, some bread and a flask of warm tea. I enjoyed what he had brought and invited him to have some too. He laughed, pointed back to the village and indicated with his mouth as if he was eating. So he had eaten at the teacher's parents. Now I fed the dog which was sitting beside me and became very trusting. In this way, the three of us travelled happily back to Ermes. When we got there I told my three soldiers the whole story; they all agreed with my standpoint and approved of what I had done.

We all went across to the parson on the sledge, and I asked him to make it known that all the weapons owned by the population were to be handed in at the castle. Towards the evening the inhabitants came from all directions bringing Russian and Japanese rifles, revolvers of all kinds, new and ancient hunting rifles and bayonets. Gradually we filled up an unoccupied room completely with weapons. The next morning we got a man with his horse and sledge to take us to outlying farmsteads to collect weapons. He spoke fairly good German. He asked if it was true that our bread was only made of wood-shavings and how we could bring ourselves to eat the cooked fat of the fallen Russians, Englishmen and Frenchmen. 'Listen to me, my good fellow,' I replied. 'It is true that shortages are severely affecting the German army and the population, and you will find some wood chippings in bread, but what you have heard about corpses is a complete lie. But I will tell you something. It will not take long before you too will suffer great shortages, because most of what you have will be taken from you. You would be well advised to hide away foodstuffs straight away. Pass on the word to the

193

people that you know!' Now we went round from one house to another. We were welcomed almost everywhere, and people immediately served up tea or milk. We knew that the Latvian for 'Good Morning' was 'Lalies'. With this greeting we went into the houses and said 'Flint-Revolver', whereupon they brought them to us. In the case of several farmers I noticed that they were reluctant to part with their old hunting blunderbusses and I gave them back to them, and indicated that they should hide them. They were very pleased to hear it. In many of the houses we encountered old fashioned cottage industry – looms and other machines I could not give a name to. As this was all new to us, we often spent time watching what they did. In a number of farms we came across people slaughtering large cattle or pigs. When we turned up they would usually be frightened because they thought that we would take away the meat. I gesticulated to them that they should simply hide the meat away well, to which they nodded their assent. In farmsteads like this we were invited into their best rooms and served milk, tea and food. Naturally enough, on days like these we could not eat everything that was offered to us. Our only wish was to stay here for as long as possible. In comparison with the past, we lived like princes here.

As we were approaching another farmstead we heard the sound of an accordion. We went in. In addition to the family, there were eight strongly-built young men in the living room who were obviously Russian soldiers, even though they were wearing civilian clothes. Some of them did not have a trustworthy appearance. We were given a sign to sit down at the table and drink tea. My soldiers wanted to just lean their carbines against the wall. I told them: 'Keep your weapons in your hands!' Then I noticed that the door to a small adjoining room was slightly opened and in the room I saw two men who were observing us through the gap. I waved to them to come in, and they did so. I now said 'Flint-Revolver' and indicated that they should fetch them. They just shrugged their shoulders. I showed them using my fingers that a large number of German soldiers would come and if they found weapons then the men would be taken to Walk as captives. To make it clear to them, I put my hands over each other as if they were bound together. They went into the barn and returned with ten Japanese rifles. We loaded them onto the sledge and returned to Ermes, where I released the farmer from his duties. Then we went to the Post Office; the woman spoke very good German and her three daughters could play very beautifully on the zither and the mandolin. As we were leaving the Post Office two Russian soldiers were coming along the street. We had been ordered by the Commandant's Office to take all the Latvian soldiers who did not have discharge papers issued by the Germans to Walk to record their details. The two men were frightened when I stopped them. I indicated to them that they should show me their papers. Each showed me a form on which I was unable to read a single word. I took them to the woman in the Post Office and she translated for me. The soldiers told us that they were only ten kilometres from home and that they had not seen their families for two years. I asked the woman to tell them that as far as I was concerned they could happily return home; we too would be glad to go home. The two of them were very pleased. I gave each of them a cigarette. They went on and waved back at me several times.

The next day we travelled by sledge to Hollerhof Castle where NCO Langer from my Company had been sent with four men. My God! What a state the castle was in! In all the halls and rooms all the furniture had been smashed, cut up and demolished. Tables, couches, mirrors, cupboards, sideboards and beds formed a desolate heap of rubbish. Even the duvets had been slit open and the feathers had been scattered around. 'Who did that?' I asked the cook, who spoke good German. 'The Russian Bolshevik soldiers,' she replied. 'Why did they do it?' I asked. The owner of Hollerhof Castle had been a Russian general who had often callously driven his troops into useless attacks which had cost thousands of them their lives. She believed that the general had been murdered. About four hundred Austrian prisoners of war lived in houses next to the castle. Two of them spoke German. The Bolsheviks had liberated them at the start of the revolution.

We were ordered to return to Walk immediately and arrived late at night. The next morning our Battalion marched northwards. Everywhere we encountered the same scene – snow, pine forests, and snowed-up villages and farmsteads. At the roadside there were many dying horses, together with abandoned artillery pieces, field kitchens, and ammunition and baggage waggons. We reached the town of Dorpat which had already been occupied by the Germans. There were more Russian soldiers than Germans here. They were all Latvians and Estonians who were waiting to be discharged. As there was a lack of clothing, they were allowed to continue to wear their Russian uniforms, but they had to remove the cockades from their hats and their marks of rank. The next day we went further north. Ice and snow started to melt and we moved forwards in a dreadful mess, with wet cold feet. We spent the night in a small town. The very next morning we were relieved by a Territorial Army battalion and marched back for several days to Wenden, where we boarded a train. It was said that we were going to a German military training area and from there to the Western Front. So once again we had the happy prospect of being allowed to die a sweet heroes' death[66] for our dearly loved Fatherland.

The Journey from Russia to France

After the horses, waggons and troops had been loaded, the train set off in the direction of Riga. On the road, which was close to the railway, I noticed

[66] This is a reference to the line from Horace: *Dulce et decorum est pro patria mori.*

herds of cattle being driven southwards by soldiers – so the 'liberation' of the Latvian and Estonian farmers had begun. We soon reached Riga, and waved to the population. They waved back – and how! They waved: 'Away with you!' To the south of Riga the snow had already melted in places; we were no longer used to seeing land free of snow. We travelled through East Prussia and then West Prussia to Brandenburg. There are lots of poor sandy regions there. We travelled through Berlin just as the first reports of victory from the West arrived. This news seemed to have given the half-starved population new courage, because everywhere we were cheered loudly; train after train packed with soldiers and munitions rolled from Russia towards the West. People believed that the armies which had been freed-up in Russia would be able to break through the English-French front and achieve victory after all. As night fell, we all fell asleep in the waggons.

About midnight, the train stopped in a badly lit little station. 'Everybody out!' Horses and waggons were unloaded and hitched up, and then we travelled to a village called Schweinitz. Our quarters had already been arranged for us. NCO Krämer, who came from the Rhineland, and I were quartered with a Frau Sanftenberg, who got up in the middle of the night to make hot coffee for us – but naturally it was ersatz coffee. We lay down in a room on a pile of straw and soon fell asleep. On the following morning I asked the lady where we were. She told us that the village was located next to the large military training area of Altengrabow, not far away from Magdeburg. The Division was accommodated there. The ground was very sandy and I wondered how the farmers could eke a living from this poor soil. We had drill in the morning, and the afternoons off. I helped Frau Sanftenberg by removing the harmful caterpillars from the trees, and then pushed a wheelbarrow full of dung into her vegetable garden for her. Like me, her husband was a serving soldier. They had three young daughters, Ida, Maria and Gretel, aged sixteen, twelve and eleven respectively. Every evening, with the exception of Good Friday, there was dancing in the two village pubs. As a result of the continuous billeting, most of the girls were abysmally corrupted and ran after the soldiers like dogs. Many parents, brothers and sisters and wives came from all over Germany to visit the soldiers they were related to. For many of them, this was the last time they would see each other.

On Easter Sunday the alarm was suddenly raised: we were to be loaded onto a train at Nedlitz station five kilometres away in an hour's time. We harnessed up, piled things higgledy-piggledy into the machine gun cart, said a quick farewell, and off we galloped to Nedlitz. In a few minutes, everything was loaded onto the train which was waiting for us. Our journey took us through the Ruhr district via Düsseldorf to Cologne. There we were fed, and then we travelled on to Belgium. There were lots of agricultural workers in the fields. We waved to them. They almost all made a cut-throat sign and pointed towards the Front. As we approached Laon, four aerial bombs exploded near the train, the first greeting from the Western Front, but they did not cause any damage. We were supposed to leave the train in Laon, but we had to get out at the station before as the town was suffering a bombardment of heavy French shells. We marched to La Fère and spent the night in the little town which had been half shot to pieces. From the Front we heard the firing of the guns. Everyone looked serious.

The next morning we went towards the Front, passing through the area in which the big summer battle had raged in 1916. Within a sixty kilometre radius there was hardly a house standing – nothing but rubble and ruins. The fields were covered with overgrown shell-holes. Between them were the crosses of the fallen. If you had not seen it yourself, you would not be able to form a picture of the damage. Several of the villages had completely disappeared. There was only a sign on which was written in English: 'This is ——' and the name of the village. We reached the Somme at the former village of Brie and camped in corrugated iron barracks that had been erected by the English. We went down to the Somme, which is fairly wide and boggy but not deep at this point. A bridge led across the river. It had been repaired by German engineers. To the west of the bridge, I could see the first dead English soldiers. From up ahead came the continuous thunder and boom of the artillery. On all our faces you could read a dread of the future. People call us 'heroes,' a wonderful name which seldom – and in a manner of speaking, never – reflects reality.

We also came across the corpse of an airman which lay beside a burned-out aircraft which had broken up as it crashed into the edge of a trench. The pilot's body was burnt; there was nothing left of his clothes apart from his shoes and a strip of his trousers and underpants. Hundreds of midges sat on his partially charred body. We could tell by the machine gun that it was not a German airman. Then I noticed a chain with an identity tag on the charred arm. I tried to see who the dead person was. The chain had melted at the point where it was soldered together, so that I was able to get hold of the identity tag. I was only able to make out 'Canada' and 'protestant'. It was obviously a Canadian airman who had found a gruesome death thousands of kilometres from his home. To the east of the bridge lay nine partially blown-up English tanks, which had no longer been able to travel back across the bridge once it had been destroyed by shellfire during the German attack. On the back of one of them, the steel plate had been pushed in. A part of a German belt and a fragment of field-gray fabric were jammed in the crack. On the inside was a severed left hand which looked completely dried out, and on the second smallest finger there was a wedding ring. The only way I could explain this was that German soldiers crossing the Somme had sought shelter behind the tanks and had been killed by German shells falling short.

We crossed the bridge. It was the same on the opposite bank as it had been on the other side: shell-holes and old trenches. About sixty dead Englishmen had been gathered together here awaiting burial. There were dead English-men lying all around. A number had gold fillings which you could see as their mouths were often wide open. In larger shell-holes we found the wreckage of four English field-guns: in the case of two of them the corpses of the entire gun crews lay dead next to them, with some of the bodies torn apart. Next to each gun lay a number of shell-cases, indicating that the English gunners had fired a lot from this position. We spent the next night back in the corrugated-iron huts, and this time we were not bothered by aircraft.

The following morning we marched on in the direction of the Front. There was nothing but rubble and in places there were villages which had almost completely disappeared. In the vicinity of the town of Harbonnières we spent the night in a small poplar wood. Nearby lay several dead English soldiers whose uniforms and faces had been eaten away in places. Next to them there were two shell-holes; the ground around them was splashed with green and yellow. So in this case the Germans had used their feared green and yellow cross gas.

About five hundred metres from the wood was an English military rail-way station, with a large number of locomotives and waggons. Next to a ruined factory there was an English ammunition dump of a kind I had never seen before. There were thousands and thousands of shells of all calibres, from the biggest to the smallest. The dump was criss-crossed by walls of earth so that the whole thing was divided into squares about ten metres wide. That meant that if the dump were bombed, only the shells in one of the squares would explode.

We spent two days lying in the woods. On the first evening I went into Harbonnières to purchase a bottle of wine in a canteen. The town was almost completely undamaged, but I could not see any inhabitants. When I returned to the wood, the Company was standing at attention and the Captain was reading a divisional order. I stood behind a waggon and listened in. The contents of the order almost made my hair stand on end: tomorrow evening we were to go to the Front. We were to dig ourselves in at a particular place, and on the following morning, after an intensive German artillery prepara-tion, we were to attack and break through the English positions and reach the western edge of the village of Cachy. Several divisions were to execute the attack, and more than eight hundred German guns were to bombard the English positions with destructive fire. In addition, four German tanks were to be deployed to prepare the way for the infantry. Attacking a large well-fed army equipped with all possible and impossible instruments of murder – that was quite something! At any rate, this order was a death sentence for many poor soldiers. Nobody knew what he was facing and the mood was, as everyone can imagine, very gloomy. When the Company had been dismissed

I stepped out from behind the waggon and was very surprised and pleased to meet Joseph Hoffert from my village back home. He was a warrant officer in a territorial regiment and at the time he was stationed in the village of Rosières. Hoffert had bumped into a soldier from my regiment and had noticed that his insignia carried the number 332. As we wrote to each other often, he had my address, but believed that my Regiment was still in Russia. He had come to my Company with the soldier straight away, with the result that we met. We told each other the latest news from home, which each of us had heard by post sent through Switzerland. Hoffert also had a picture in which you could see the young men and girls from our village who went to evening classes. Good God! How surprised I was! They were still children when I last saw them and now they were grown up young men and young women. We stayed together until late in the night, and then I accompanied him for part of the way to Rosières. When I left, I asked him to greet my parents and my sister if I should fail to return home. At this moment, I was nearer to crying than to laughing. After shaking hands again we parted. I went back to the Company and lay down to sleep in the wood. We were soaked by a heavy shower as we had failed to put up our tents. The next day we had lovely weather so we were able to dry our clothes. Up in the sky there were two fierce dogfights causing two aircraft to crash to the ground in flames. These pilots die a hero's death three times over: first they get shot dead, then they get burnt, and last of all they get smashed up when they hit the ground.

The artillery fire from the Front roared continuously, louder at some times than at others. The day drew slowly to a close. The order 'Get ready!' was given, and we packed up. Each of us had the same serious facial expression. Then the machine gun teams were reorganized. I got Alex Knut from Berlin as my chief gunner, gunner Lang from Wermelskirchen, and two men from the Rhineland whose names I have now forgotten. Sergeant Bär from Berlin was Platoon Commander. As the sun set we set off, with a gap of 40 metres between each waggon and the one in front. A number of English planes circled above the road. Suddenly we heard the well-known whistling sound. Immediately everyone, apart from the drivers and their horses, was lying in the roadside ditches. Crack, boom, crack! The bombs exploded next to the road without causing any damage. Only the horses shied so that their drivers could hardly control them. It started to get dark. As the area was almost completely flat, we could see the shrapnel shells exploding ahead of us. Fires which had broken out ahead coloured the sky blood-red. We passed large artillery pieces which were mounted on railway waggons and fired off occasional shots. Then we approached the village of Marcelcave, in which the fires had broken out. Every few minutes a heavy English shell would fly into the village with a terrible howl and light it up for a moment as it exploded. We stopped outside the village, and took the machine guns out of the waggons which then turned back. At this moment I would have given anything to be a driver and be able to turn back. We headed down the village street. We went one gun at a time, with about twenty metres between each one. What a state the village was in! Many houses were almost completely shot away, while others had been torn open at the front, with the result that bedsteads and other furniture were hanging out. The village had been in the hands of the Germans for about a month. Another heavy shell zoomed in; everyone ducked involuntarily. The shell hit the village on the other side of the road. A few minutes later another one came and crashed into a house at the side of the road, blowing the whole thing apart by the force of the explosion. A soldier from Lorraine who was running past was knocked down and buried by the debris. We all rushed forwards without helping the soldier. We all wanted to get out of the village and out of range of the shellfire. On the far side of the village we followed the road for about two kilometres. Individual shells fell in the fields everywhere but none of them came in our immediate vicinity. The moon rose and illuminated the area brightly. Behind a wall of earth I saw a number of the fallen, some of whom had their ghostly hands stretched towards the sky. Ahead, at the front, flares rose steadily into the heights; you heard individual shots being fired, or the rattle of machine guns. The German artillery only fired individual shots; they whizzed as they hurtled over us. The English artillery patterned the area with crackling attacks of fire, switching from place to place. Suddenly a particular place would be subject to intensive fire lasting for two or three minutes, after which it would stop as suddenly as it had started. We turned off the road down a farm track. Soon we were told 'Halt!' and had to dig ourselves in. My team and I dug two holes about 1.2 metres deep and got into them. The work had made the soldiers thirsty, and they started to drink. Each of them had been issued with two canteens of coffee (one and a half litres). I told them to be economical with the coffee as they might well be thirstier tomorrow.

Gradually we fell asleep in the damp holes; you had the feeling that you were buried. I was wakened by the hum of an English aircraft, but I could not see where it was although the moon was shining. All of a sudden, a large flare attached to a parachute floated over us, brightly illuminating our surroundings. 'Everybody stay in your holes!' All at once, four bombs came whizzing down. It was clear that the pilot had discovered the dark holes and the freshly dug mounds of earth. Then the hum of the aircraft's engine diminished in the direction of the English front. I immediately told my team: 'Watch out, comrades, they will be firing at us soon!' I urged them once again to stay loyal to each other and said that nobody should let a comrade down. If one of us should be seriously wounded then we would leave the machine gun and the kit that went with it behind and, if possible, get the wounded man back, because there were enough machine guns but each man had only one life to lose. Everyone immediately agreed with this

200

suggestion. We chatted on. Suddenly there was a short whoosh, followed by a flash and a bang, and then splinters and clumps of earth rained down on us. A shell had impacted a few metres from us in between the holes. Then came, the second, third, fourth; there was an uninterrupted whooshing and booming all round us. Large and small clumps of earth continually rained down on our helmets and packs. Crouching, we squatted in the holes and started with fright whenever a shell landed nearby. From time to time a very heavy shell, bigger than all the others, would arrive, falling nearly vertically. I raised my head for a moment and saw that the area round about was covered in thick shell smoke. Suddenly I heard the call 'G-a-a-s!' Everyone repeated the call. Each of us pulled off his helmet, yanked his gas mask out of the tin and put it to his face. Gradually the firing almost stopped completely. We took of our masks and asked around whether there had been any casualties. Three men who had been lying together in a hole had suffered a direct hit and been blown to pieces. Two others had been wounded in the face by flying splinters; they cleared out straight away. So our Company had got off lightly. The losses in the machine gun teams were immediately replaced by reserve gunners who had been waiting with the platoon commanders.

The dawn came slowly. A light fog developed so that you could only see about three to four hundred metres. The Captain, who seemed fairly agitated, went round the teams again, encouraging us to do our duty whole-heartedly. While he was speaking to us, a number of shells came flying over and exploded nearby. The Captain jumped into our hole to take cover. 'Captain,' I said, 'I do not understand what's going on. Where are we? Where is the English front? Who is ahead of us?' The Captain took his detailed map which showed the area and the plan of the positions. Our division was covering a stretch of five hundred metres width. The other regiments of the Division were dug in ahead of us. Our Battalion was planned to be in the last stage of the attack. We were to pass the edge of a wood and then go directly towards the village of Cachy. Now I knew.

24th of April 1918, Day of Battle – The Attack at Villers-Bretonneux[67]

Half past six in the morning. All quiet, with only the occasional artillery shot. The silence is spooky. It seemed to me as if both parties had stopped to recover their breath and their strength before they plunged at each other in order to tear each other apart. At seven o'clock on the dot the German artillery started the barrage. At a blow, more than eight hundred guns sent over their iron greetings and then went on and on; for a full hour the guns thundered

[67] This was known as the Second Battle of Villers-Bretonneux.

and roared. The shells flew over us continuously. From the other side you could hear the individual shell bursts. It was almost impossible to communicate with each other. You had to shout the words into the other person's ear. The English soldiers were not lazy either and covered the whole area with shells. The general attack was to start at eight o'clock. The hand on the clock moved round towards the fateful moment – slowly, but far too quickly. At five minutes to eight I put my head up and looked out. It looked dead. I could only see two or three heads, and the impact of the English shells. Then, behind me I heard the muffled clatter of powerful engines. It came from four German tanks, called assault vehicles. They were the first German tanks[68] I had seen. They were quite different from the French and English tanks, like a steel house pointed at the front, on which you could not see the tracks or anything else. Armoured machine guns pointed out in all directions. Two of the tanks were also equipped with two small guns. As identifying marks they had a big Iron Cross painted on each side.

'Get ready!' With our hearts pounding we all got ready. 'Forwards! March!' We grabbed hold of our machine, left the security of the hole and walked forwards. The artillery fire continued unabated; we could now hear the crackling of the rifles as well. The attack was in full swing. Wherever you looked it was crawling with German soldiers pushing forwards. Infantry, machine guns, small and medium-sized mortars were all moving forward. A swarm of German aircraft flew low over us in order to contribute to the success of the attack with bombs, hand grenades, and machine-gun fire. As we approached the corner of the wood there were already a number of dead lying on the churned-up ground.

We were suddenly showered with a hail of artillery and mortar shells, and all jumped into shell-holes or holes that had been dug by the men. We ducked down as low as possible to avoid being hit by the whizzing splinters and clumps of earth. 'We can't stay here!' I shouted out, and raised myself up to look for suitable cover. At the same moment, a mortar shell landed in a hole about three metres away from me in which three infantrymen were cowering. Their mutilated body parts flew in all directions. I told my team: 'I will go first. Someone keep an eye on me. If I find better cover, then I will hold up the big spade, and then you come running to join me as quickly as possible!' No sooner said than done. About fifty metres away I found a large shell-hole which offered good cover. I jumped in and held up the spade. My team came running across immediately. In this way we went on from one hole to the next. As I was bounding across a field of clover a shrapnel shell exploded above me. It felt like a miracle that I remained unscathed. I looked down at my body, because I thought that I had to be bleeding somewhere.

[68] These would be A7V tanks. A total of twenty-one were made.

To start with I was agitated, but now, despite the continuous explosions, a cold feeling of peace came over me as it had done in the most dangerous moments in the past.

We passed the edge of the wood, from which the first German waves of attack had stormed out towards the English positions, which were stretched out across open ground. There were lots of dead infantrymen lying on the ground, some of whom had been terribly messed up by artillery fire. Lots of lightly wounded men ran back past us, as did English prisoners who had had to surrender during the first attack. The English soldiers were made to gather in a particular place, where the whole ground was covered with khaki uniforms. These poor devils had to endure staying there under heavy fire. When we made it to the first English trench we jumped in. We found lots of empty bullet-cases there, a sign that the English infantry had defended their position bravely. In the trench were two dead Englishmen, with the one lying on top of the other. Up in the open was another English soldier, who was in his death throes. About three metres behind the trench lay another who kept calling imploringly 'German Fri-itz'. I put my head up and waved to him to crawl to us. He pointed to his back and I saw that he had been hit by a bullet there, as a result of which his legs were paralysed. I would have liked to fetch him into the trench, but I did not want to risk going out as the English were now continuously sweeping the area with their machine guns, causing their bullets to whizz over our heads in large numbers. We tied three carrying straps together and I threw one end towards the English soldier. He held tight with his hands, and in this way we pulled him slowly to the edge of the trench, after which we put him down on the trench floor. I took a pack from one of the fallen, and put it under his head and gave him some of my coffee to drink. As a result of pain and blood loss he now lost consciousness. One of the dead English soldiers had a packet of cigarettes sticking out of his pocket, so I took it for myself.

A machine gunner from another regiment came along the trench and asked me: 'Sir, can I join your machine gun team please?' I realized immediately from his accent that he came from Alsace, so I asked: 'Where are you from?' He replied: 'I was with my company in the first wave at the edge of the woods. The English, who must have noticed us, bombarded the edge of the wood terribly using light artillery. My whole team were killed while lying down. My assault pack, my canteen and my haversack were all torn to shreds by shell fragments.' He showed me these things, and they were completely in shreds. 'Listen, comrade,' I said, 'if you are wise, you should stay lying here in the trench.'

In the meantime, the trench had filled up with advancing soldiers. Some lieutenants made an unholy din to drive us forward. I climbed out of the trench, looked for cover, and waved with the spade once again. My team came running to me. Then I noticed that one of my lads from the Rhineland let out a scream, dropped his ammunition box and came running towards me. He had been shot through the shoulder. We bandaged him up straight away, and he ran back to the English trench which we had previously left. Ahead of us the English laid down a fearful barrage across a width of about eighty metres. Shells fell continuously in a line to prevent the last attacking units from advancing – and we were expected to go through! My platoon leader gave me a reserve gunner to replace the wounded Rhinelander. I noticed that there were little pauses between the arrivals of the shells, caused by the need to reload the guns. We advanced to the edge of the area where the shells were hitting and lay down. 'Listen, comrades,' I said, 'We will wait for a particular moment. Just as soon as a round of shells has exploded, we will run through as fast as possible. Maybe we will get out of the area being shelled before the next round comes over.' As soon as a round had exploded we got up and ran forwards as fast we could, given that we were carrying our machine gun. The next round whizzed closely past us and exploded a few metres behind us. We hurried on quickly to get away from the danger zone. Many corpses of the fallen were lying on the torn-up area which was subject to the barrage. Even in death, many of the corpses continued to be flung hither and thither and lacerated.

Suddenly a large number of machine gun bullets started whizzing about our ears. We threw ourselves to the ground, left our gun where it was, and crawled on our stomachs to a large shell-hole nearby in which about twelve to fifteen people were cowering. We lay down on top of the heads, shoulders and backs of the soldiers in the hole, with the result that the ones lower down nearly suffocated, but we could not move away as the machine gun bullets were whizzing just over our backs. Suddenly there was an impact in close proximity. We were almost completely covered with earth. Everyone was frightened to death. I raised my head and saw that there was only about half a metre of earth between our shell-hole and the new one. If the shell had landed one metre further, then all eighteen of us would have been torn to shreds. My team and I immediately jumped into the new hole. When the fire let up for a moment we crept to our gun and hauled it into our hole. We set the machine gun up ready to fire at the front of the hole.

Our hole soon filled up with infantrymen. The NCO in charge of our ambulance men was there too. An infantryman who had been shot through one of his toes ran back towards us. As we were as crowded in the hole like sardines, Lance Corporal Alex Knuth, who was always a particularly good-natured chap said: 'I'll make a bit of space', and crawled to another shell-hole nearby. When more and more infantrymen arrived in our hole, I said to one of my gunners: 'Go and see if that hole has some space; if so, we'll go there.' He crawled there and shouted: 'There's only a corpse here. God, it's Alex!' I crawled across straight away. Poor Alex had been shot in his fore-head above his left eye with an exit wound in his left temple. Alex was not yet dead, but he was not conscious. We tried to make him comfortable and I bandaged his head using his gauze bandage. I spoke to him by name, but he could not hear or see any more. He started to rattle. The rattle became weaker, and then his whole body started to shake; he stretched himself, and was dead. We moved some earth out of the way at the side of the shell-hole, laid him down, and covered him up. You can imagine how we felt while we carried out this work. Then I took his bayonet, pushed it through its leather scabbard in the form of a cross, and put it on his grave.

The firing of the guns, machine guns and so on raged on at the same intensity throughout the morning. As we were burying poor Alex I thought I heard, in the midst of the din, the loud crack of a pistol close by. When I crawled back to the shell-hole where the machine gun was situated I saw that one of the soldiers from the Rhineland had been shot in the hand. One of the gunners was in the process of bandaging up his hand. The wounded man told me that he had been trying to fasten the steam discharge pipe to the front of the machine gun's water cooling jacket when he had been shot. I did not believe him, as his shamefaced look told me that he had shot himself in the hand in order to get back to the field hospital. He was quite right to do so, but I did not trust myself to tell him. Now I had two wounded men and one dead one at my machine gun. It was pretty grim. As a result of the enormous losses the attack had ground to a stop. Everyone had sought cover in the numerous shell-holes. The whole area was constantly covered in black shell smoke. All at once officers and orderlies ran around the occupied holes and shouted: 'Divisional orders: The attack must be continued!' We were all appalled. Individual groups who had been driven out of their holes started to jump forwards. Our Captain got out of a hole near us and ordered us to advance. What choice did we have? We had been given a reserve gunner, so I too went forward with my four men. The English firing intensified terribly and we were forced to take cover in shell-holes once again. An infantry private, whom I had known since we were in Riga, knelt down beside my hole in order to light a cigarette while advancing. Suddenly he fell headfirst to the ground and did not move any more. We dug in our machine gun ready to fire, with only the barrel looking out over the earth, and then we ducked down in the hole.

I noticed two infantrymen running back as fast as they could go, with their faces full of fear. I looked up and saw that the whole area was full of infantrymen running back. I shouted: 'What's wrong?' 'Tanks!' was the reply. The Battalion Commander, Captain Berthold, with his pistol raised, tried to force the infantrymen to stop, causing some to obey, while others ran on. Lots of the fleeing men were mown down by the furious machine-gun fire of the tanks. I looked forwards and saw a number of English tanks advancing towards us firing steadily. In training we had been told that two bullets of steel core ammunition fired at the same position would penetrate a tank's iron wall. The English tank was driving straight towards our hole, firing continuously with its machine gun. 'Comrades, now we will use steel core ammunition!' I shouted. One of the gunners passed me the belt immediately. I loaded, aimed accurately at the middle of the front of the tanks, and fired off the belt, which contained two hundred and fifty shots. The tank drove on. I shot three further belts of steel core ammunition – so that was one thousand shots in all aimed at the same point. Nothing did any good. I grabbed my binoculars and saw that the tank looked completely white at the place where it had been shot, but we were unable to harm it. 'Take full cover!' I called. So we all crouched down in the hole and awaited the moment when the tank would come and shoot us dead. Then, behind us, I heard several shots being fired and the clatter of an engine. I raised my head and saw a German tank coming, continuously firing with its small gun. Then, looking forwards I saw that the English tank was standing stationary and had a number of gaping holes. The German tank immobilized two further English tanks and then advanced into the English lines and drove about two hundred English infantrymen out of their holes using machine-gun fire. The English soldiers had no option but to surrender to us with their hands in the air. I got three men who were passing to come into our hole. They were gasping from running and shaking with fear of dying. They offered us their money, but we naturally did not accept it. Next the German tank was shot at by the English artillery to such an extent that it nearly disappeared in the clouds of smoke from the shells, and suddenly came to a stop. After several minutes it started to wobble again and drove back past us.

The English pilots were incredibly brave and flew at about house-height above us, dropping bombs and hand grenades into the holes occupied by us. I saw four planes crash. One of them hit the ground only about forty metres away from us, boring itself into the ground with its engine, so that the tail end stuck up in the air. The pilot, who seemed to be dead and must have been strapped in, was hanging with his upper body sticking out of the cockpit. Just after the crash the plane caught fire and burnt down to its metal skeleton.

The reserve gunner Martz, who came from lower Alsace, was looking forwards when a gas shell landed directly in front of us and surrounded him with the densely concentrated gas. He only breathed once, and then he was stunned and collapsed down between us. I too felt the gas from my nose to my throat while breathing in, and blew it forcefully out again. Then I held my breath, yanked the gas mask out of its tin and put it on in a flash. I could now feel that some gas must have made it to my chest after all, because it started to tickle and I felt nauseous. It burned so much in my nose and my throat that my eyes started to water. I needed to cough and found it difficult to breathe with the mask on. All this happened in a matter of seconds. As he was incapacitated, I pulled out Martz's gas mask and put it on him. Then I crawled on all fours to the Platoon Commander as I knew that the NCO in charge of the ambulance men would be there with the safety equipment (a device for administering oxygen). He came crawling after me straight away and we set up the safety equipment up for poor Martz. After a quarter of an hour he came to, but he was stunned.

Now our Captain crept into our hole. 'Well, Richert,' he said 'are you still fit?' 'Yes, I am,' I replied, 'but Alex Knut is dead and two men are wounded. Hermann's team had worse luck. All six men were killed by a direct hit'. The Captain was very jumpy because it was the first big action he had seen. He had been on the general staff before he came to our Company, and he was to go back there soon. Now I remembered the English cigarettes I had in my pocket. First I offered the Captain one, and then shared them with my team. How good an English cigarette tasted compared with the German ones, which consisted solely of abominable substitute tobacco – mainly beech leaves! After about half an hour the Captain said to me: 'Richert, give me another of those English cigarettes, and then I will go to check up on the Reserves.' I gave him two and then he climbed out and ran back. It was about four in the afternoon. The artillery fire had reduced in intensity, but shells were still falling. We heaved a sigh of relief. 'If only we could get out of this mess!' was the general feeling. My soldiers had all drunk their coffee and were desperately thirsty, while I had drunk less than half of my canteen. When they asked, I gave each of them a gulp.

It gradually became evening, and soon the darkness hid the suffering. What would the night bring? I expected a counter-attack by the English troops. My only wish was to be taken captive. There at least, my life would be safe. Then an orderly came into our hole and said that the people who were to collect the food should get ready and come with him. Since it had got dark, the English maintained a fearful barrage about four hundred metres behind us, in order to prevent reinforcements from being brought up and to prevent any contact with the rear. As I did not want to order any of my gunners to go for food, I asked for a volunteer. Nobody volunteered. I said: 'Good, then we will eat our iron rations!' In addition, each of us had a piece of army bread in his haversack. If only we had had more to drink! So we all stayed in the hole.

The orderly left us. The small number of infantrymen who were lying spread out in shell-holes ahead of us now had to come back and take up position in our line. In this way we once again formed a firm front. The other machine gun belonging to the unit had to be built in three metres beside us. The platoon leader Sergeant Martin Bär was a few metres behind us in a shell hole. The English shells continued to shoot howling over us to explode, mainly in the barrage line. I went to sleep in the hole. One man had to stay awake and look ahead from time to time. I was suddenly jolted awake by a clattering hail of shells. Aha, I thought, preparation for a counter-attack. We were still relatively fortunate, as only a few shells exploded near us. They whizzed just over and past us and hit the ground further back. Tz-tz-tz, a huge number of machine gun bullets whizzed over us, so that none of us dared to raise his head to see what was happening. When the machine-gun fire eased off, I fired off a flare and observed the territory in front of us. I thought I could see movement in several places and fired off several more flares. At the same moment I heard people calling to the left and right of me: 'They are coming! They are coming! Alarm!' And it was the case. Now the whole area in front of us was crawling with English soldiers. The first of them were possibly still a hundred and fifty metres away. Bending down fearfully, they jumped from hole to hole. If I set things up right, thirty, forty or fifty of these poor people would be hit. I quickly decided not to fire, and to surrender to them when they got close. I jumped to the gun, loaded a belt, pressed on the top spring, picked up a pinch of earth in my left hand, and sprinkled it inobtrusively into the machine gun's mechanism. Then I fired. The bullet in the barrel went off, and then it stopped. The slide mechanism was blocked by the bit of earth. 'What will we do now?' the gunners asked anxiously. 'Put your hands up, if they come!' I said. 'Get your pistols out,' I told them, 'if they decide to massacre us then we will defend ourselves with our pistols for as long as possible.' Then we took off our webbing and threw it into the back of the hole. Then sergeant Bär came crawling: 'Richert, Nicki, man, why are you not firing?' 'Jammed,' I replied. 'We have taken off our kit.' 'That's the best thing to do,' replied the sergeant and then he too took off his webbing and threw it on the pile. The night was now lit as clear as day by a hundred flares. Lots of red flares requesting protective barrages from the German artillery shot straight up into the sky. Lots of light and heavy machine guns and infantrymen had started defensive fire. Masses of German shells whizzed over us and landed among the English troops. The English soldiers, who suffered great losses, now crawled away into the shell-holes and we had to put on our kit again. At this moment, I was very angry with the English troops as they had not caught us. Despite the darkness, I cleaned the machine gun so that nobody would see that there was earth in it. Then I loaded it and fired off a belt. Afterwards we slept until near morning in the damp hole.

25th of April 1918

At daybreak the English started to shoot like mad again, for about an hour. Afterwards, everything was fairly quiet. It was the start of a beautiful spring day, the sun shone down bright and clear. What a contrast: nature awoke to new life, and this poor maddened humanity mutually slaughtered each other – and yet everyone wants to live! But hundreds of thousands of people have to submit to the stubbornness of a few powerful people. There was no means of changing this. If you refuse to obey, then you will be shot. If you obey, you may also be shot, but you also have a prospect of surviving. So you obey, however reluctantly.

About ten in the morning a soldier from the Company came crawling and reported that the Captain had just been found seriously wounded. He had been lying alone and forlorn among the reeds of a drainage trench since about four o'clock yesterday evening. Anyone who volunteered to take him back would be promoted up a level and awarded the Iron Cross. Gunner Lang from my team and Lance Corporal Beck from the other machine gun volunteered. 'If I get back there in one piece,' said Lang, 'I will not come back here!' 'That's obvious,' I replied. So the two of them crept back. The Captain must have been wounded yesterday evening when he left us to go to the Reserves.

Towards midday we developed an agonizing thirst. I had drunk part of my coffee and shared out the rest among the gunners. Not far away from us we noticed a massive shell-hole. One of the gunners crawled there with his canteen and discovered, as he had correctly presumed, that some water had gathered in the deep hole. He disappeared down the hole, reappeared soon afterwards with his canteen, and crept back again. But what sludge he brought back with him! It was pure silt mush. We now put a handkerchief on top of another canteen to let the water filter through and get a bit cleaner. Then each of us slurped a few mouthfuls of this revolting sludge.

Sheltering behind the dug-in machine gun, I had a look around. Everywhere you could see torn-open earth and shell-holes. Scattered between them were the prone corpses of the fallen. Ahead of us was the burnt-out aircraft, the shot-up English tank was a bit further away, and about one kilometre away was the shot-up village of Cachy. We were supposed to capture it yesterday and take control of its western edge – that's on the opposite side. So our attack had failed although we had forced our way about eight hundred metres into the English position and, as they told us, taken two thousand prisoners. I was now convinced that there was not much chance of breaking through the English-French-American Front. To the inside right about two kilometres away was the town of Villers-Bretonneux, which was only a pile of ruins. I looked with my binoculars in all directions towards the English Front. I could not detect the slightest sign of life apart from the clouds of smoke rising from the German shells. Above our heads a fierce dogfight was taking place, involving more than thirty aircraft. Three of them crashed, two on fire, while the third plunged down as swiftly as an arrow.

The team on the other machine gun asked us whether we had anything more to drink, as they were dying of thirst. One man from my team replied that some water would have gathered in the big shell-hole once again, and that we had already collected some from there. Gunner Schröback, a cheeky Berlin lad, crawled there and disappeared into the hole. He soon reappeared with a full canteen and was about to leap across to the hole where his team were based. Just at that moment a shell whizzed over our heads and exploded less than two metres behind our hole. The shock made us duck down as low as we could. When I raised my head again, I saw that Schröback was lying motionless about two metres on the other side of the new shell-hole. As I did not know whether he was dead or unconscious, I crept over to him to check. He was beyond all help. He had been hit in the stomach by a number of shell splinters so that his entrails were hanging out. Schröback was dead.

Quite unexpectedly, our artillery fired a barrage between the two lines so that the frequent impact of the shells, the smoke and the flying lumps of earth formed a wall between us and the English. Gradually the fire reduced in intensity. At about four o'clock in the afternoon a German shell fell short and landed less than three metres from us. Directly afterwards another one came and landed right next to the hole occupied by the other team, almost covering them with earth. How angry that made us! It was worse than if twenty English shells had landed. Then another one came, followed by yet another. I told my team: 'Put your packs on your backs and take your helmets and your gas-masks! We will crawl back, because I have no desire to be shot dead by our own shells!' Then we crawled back on our stomachs, but still more shells came, so that we were forced to creep back about two hundred metres. Now we crouched in a shell-hole while our machine gun was up front. In the meantime, all the soldiers who had been located at the front had crept back without the English noticing anything. I did not feel comfortable that we had come back without our gun. I said to my lance corporal, Fritz Kessler, who had joined the team during the night: 'Fritz, will you come and help fetch the machine gun?' 'Why not?' he answered. We put on a carrying strap and were just about to leave when the Adjutant of the Battalion, Lieutenant Knapp crawled up to us and asked us where we were really planning to go. I told him that we wanted to fetch our machine gun, which we had left at the Front as a consequence of being bombarded by our own artillery. He warned us to take care. Then we slid our way forwards on our stomachs. It was difficult crawling over the churned-up ground, and we had to avoid the numerous corpses of fallen soldiers. Eventually we reached our gun. After having a rest in the hole, we pulled the gun backwards onto the ground. I fastened two ammunition boxes to the sledge and then we fastened the carrying straps and hauled the load behind us, crawling all the way. Eventually we got back to the others, tired and dripping with sweat. Lieutenant Knapp crawled back past our hole and saw that we had our machine gun again. He asked for my name and put a cross beside it. What he intended was that I should be awarded the Iron Cross, First Class.

It gradually became evening, then a dark night. I hoped that we would finally be relieved by other troops during the night. But hour after hour

210

passed, and we waited in vain. The English artillery once again shot a massive barrage behind us. They did not seem to be short of ammunition. Then it started to rain, slowly at first, and then heavier and heavier. I did not think it would be a good idea to put on my coat, because it would have got in the way if we had been forced to flee. By and by, we all got soaked to the skin, and a sticky sludge developed in the hole. We started to shiver from the wet, but we did not feel safe to warm ourselves up as shells fell periodically, and the English often swept the field with a machine gun. Eventually I fell asleep. One man in the team had to stay awake at all times. Suddenly the soldier who was on duty woke me and said: 'The relief has arrived!' I got up straight away and thought: thank God! But I was still afraid of making my way back across the open terrain as we had to pass through the English shellfire further back. The soldiers who were relieving us got us to hurry up as they wanted to get into the protection of the hole. I now gave the order: 'The ammunition boxes and the gun-sledge stay here. We will only take the gun and share the task of carrying it!' My soldiers were very pleased that they did not need to carry the heavy things.

As it was fairly dark and continued to rain, we often stumbled over dead bodies or fell down into shell-holes. We kept together by calling to each other. Everywhere you could see the silhouettes of people scurrying back, as the remains of the whole Division were being relieved. Then I heard, fairly far away, a moaning voice: 'Comrades, for God' sake, take me with you! I have a wife and three small children at home.' The poor wounded soldier, who was lying helpless there, had obviously heard the soldiers as they ran back. I said to my team: 'We'll take this chap with us!' When I could not hear him any more, I called out: 'Where is the wounded man?' 'Here,' came the reply. One of the other soldiers and I bent down to pick up the poor wounded man. Just at that moment four large English shells landed very near us, with the result that we were nearly floored by fright and by the shock wave. We ran through the hail of lumps of earth as quickly as possible to get away from the danger area. We had left the poor wounded man where he was. We had been separated by the explosion. I only had one man with me. By calling to each other, we met up again. Then I heard a call from the side: 'The Second Machine Gun Company of Infantry Regiment 332 should meet up here!' It was the voice of Lieutenant Strohmayer. We went there. When the remainder of the Company had assembled, the lieutenant, who was totally demoralized, gave the order 'Go back in this direction,' and marched parallel to the Front instead of backwards. 'Sir,' I said, 'we have to go back this way. The fire that we can see is the village of Marcelcave and we have to go there!' The lieutenant, who was almost at the end of his tether replied: 'Do what you want!' The next moment, everyone was flat on the ground, as four heavy shells had hit nearby. 'Is anybody wounded?' I called. 'No,' came the reply. Now I called out: 'The Company will obey the command of NCO

Richert. Everyone is to go back as quickly as possible in the direction of the fire! Keep in touch by calling to each other!' We hurried back as fast as we could. Lieutenant Strohmayer toddled along behind me like a drunken man. Although shells often landed close to us, we all got back safe and sound. Progress was slow because the ground had been softened by the rain and the sticky mud stuck to our boots.

Eventually we reached the road leading to Marcelcave and followed it. I heard someone calling 'Fritz, Fritz!' from the ditch, together with some words which I did not understand. I realized that there must be a wounded Englishman lying here, said 'Tommy' and went into the ditch. I was right, there lay an English soldier with his leg bandaged; it would appear that he had dragged himself here and was unable to go any further as a result of exhaustion and weakness. I gave one of my soldiers my pack to carry and then I signalled to the Englishman to climb onto my back, and knelt down in front of him. The Tommy understood me straight away, climbed onto my back, and held on with his arms around my neck, while I grabbed hold of his knees with my arms. The Englishman was quite a slight lad, who, in my opinion, probably weighed less than 100 pounds. Despite that I soon felt hot carrying my burden. Then I heard the sound of a waggon behind us. When the waggon was near us I put the Englishman on the ground, grabbed the horse by the reins, and stopped the waggon. 'What's up?' asked the two ambulance men who were sitting on the box. 'You could take this wounded man I have here with you.' They replied that they did not have any more room, as the waggon was crowded with seriously wounded men. I replied that the wounded man had only been shot in the leg and certainly could sit at the front on the box. I took the Englishman and heaved him onto the waggon, where the ambulance men received him. Only now did they realize that it concerned an Englishman.

I ran after the Company and caught up with them. As we were approaching Marcelcave, lots of English shells flew over us, with some of them exploding in the village and some at the edge. 'Second Machine Gun Company, halt!' I called. 'We must go round the village to the right in order to avoid the shellfire.' Once again we had to make our way across the dirty damp farmland. At least we could now see where we were going, because it was gradually getting light. Ahead of us we suddenly heard a detonation so loud that we almost all instinctively threw ourselves to the ground. A heavy German battery, which was hidden in the wood, had just fired a salvo. That was the reason for the loud bang. At the far side of the village we reached the road leading further back, which was still in range of the English artillery. We moved briskly to get to safety at long last, and passed another village in which most of the houses were undamaged. Then we passed through a wooded area. The Company Sergeant and the horses and drivers of the Company were camped there. They gave us hot coffee, food, schnapps and smoking material. But we looked filthy and were soaking from head to foot! The sergeant said: 'You seem to have been through a lot! As I have been informed, the Captain has died of his severe wounds.' Then the leader of each gun had to report the losses in his team. We spread our tents out in a sunny area, took off our wet jackets, slipped on our coats, lay down, and were soon fast asleep. We had all slept very little during the last forty-eight hours and were totally exhausted as a result of the stress.

In the afternoon, two very heavy English shells suddenly landed in front of us at the edge of the woods. For God's sake! Had we still not reached safety? Soon afterwards more shells came howling in. This time they exploded about one hundred metres away. 'Lads,' I told my team, 'pick up your helmets and your gas masks, we are right in the firing line.' We ran away immediately. One of the next shells hit the waggons, destroying a machine gun waggon completely. The following two shells flew right over the wood and killed two horses and an artilleryman who was minding the horses in the meadow. There were no further shots for a long time so we went back to the Company. However, you were left feeling uncertain the whole time because new shells could arrive at any moment. The two dead horses were skinned by the soldiers; the meat was cut off and made into mince, mixed with salt and eaten.

Towards the evening I saw the Battalion Messenger coming through the woods towards the Company. As he knew me well, he waved to me and said: 'What do you think: this evening you will have to take up the reserve position up front.' 'What?' I said. 'But we only just got back here this morning!' 'It's definite,' said the messenger. 'I have the order here.' I cannot begin to describe to anyone how I dreaded the prospect of going back to the Front. The reserve positions were the most exposed to shellfire. Up ahead the guns roared without stopping. I went to Sergeant Bär and NCO Peters and told them what was coming up. They were both rigid with fear. We tried to think of a means of ducking out. You could not run away, yet we did not want to take part. Then I saw a bucket near the field kitchen that was full of miserable schnapps. I told the others: 'I know a way out!' Then I fetched my canteen and dipped it inobtrusively into the bucket. I had almost two litres in my canteen. We went to the bushes and got so drunk that we could hardly stand up and walk. We lurched our way back to the Company and lay down on the ground. The Company had to fall in. The sergeant read out the order. When the three of us did not stand up the sergeant immediately noticed what was wrong, but did not say much. However, Lieutenant Strohmayer, who had now taken over command of the Company, went on and on at us. NCO Peters got up, grabbed hold of one of the big spades, and lurched towards the lieutenant. Raising the spade, he yelled: 'If Mr Strohmayer gives another stupid order like last night, I'll smash his head in!' The lieutenant reached for his pistol, but then kept ducking out of the

213

way of Peters, who stumbled, fell down and lay there. As the Company marched off, we three heroes lay asleep in the woods. The following morning we got up feeling the worse for wear. The Company Sergeant felt that we had behaved badly, to which I replied: 'They asked too much of us!' He agreed with me completely. The Company returned. They had been lucky, as they had only had one person die, while three had been wounded.

We spent the whole day until after dark in the wood. Then we heard that we were to go to quarters in Harbonnières. I told my Lance Corporal Kessler: 'Fritz, take over the machine gun and I will go on and try to find something to eat or somewhere to stay.' I set off, taking NCOs Peters and Schulz with me. It was pitch dark and quite often when we met soldiers we had to ask them the way. Eventually, when we reached Harbonnières, we found that the place was overcrowded with soldiers as the remains of our Division were quartered there, together with another division that had just arrived from Russia. Eventually we found an empty kitchen. I heard voices in the room next door and went in. They were lorry drivers from the supply train. I asked them if they had anything for my two comrades and I to eat. They gave me a cheeky answer. One word led to another and when I called them lazy base wallahs it nearly got violent. But the fact that I had a pistol, and that the two other NCOs, Peters and Schulz, joined me, held them back. Where could we sleep now? We did not fancy sleeping on the cold stone slabs on the kitchen floor. We took the old kitchen cupboard, put it on its side, removed the shelves and lay down in it. We all had to lie on our sides as our 'bed' was too narrow.

When we had slept for a while, I had to go for a pee. I took my torch and went out the back door. There I noticed a small building like a washhouse. It seemed to me that I could hear loud snoring from inside there. I went quietly to the door, which had windows in it, and pressed on the handle. It was locked. Then I noticed that a corner of the glass had been broken and I shone my torch inside. I almost bounced back with joy. On the table, directly opposite the door was a batch of bread in a stack, next to which were several three-pound tins of liver sausage, and a tin of cigarettes and cigars. That was certainly the food store for the supply train. I went quietly back to my two comrades and woke them! 'We have to move on,' I said. 'You must be mad!' was the answer. Then I told them what I had found. By this stage, both of them had got up. We quietly got ready and tiptoed to the door. I reached through the hole in the glass and shoved the bolt back. I slowly opened the door, tiptoed in and handed out three loaves and two packets containing a hundred cigarettes each, then I took three tins of liver sausage. Then we disappeared the way we had come. The man sleeping there, who continued to snore, will have been quite surprised the following morning when he noticed that the things were missing. After looking for a while we found accommodation in an attic room used for storing chaff. By the light of a candle we now ate some of our booty.

The following morning we went looking for our Company, and eventually found it quartered in a shed. My team was a bit annoyed as I had deserted them, but when I brought out the bread and a tin of liver sausage they were all pleased and pitched in valiantly until both bread and liver sausage were gone. Then I gave each of them ten cigarettes as well.

During the day gunner Lang, who had helped to carry the Captain back, returned to me as well. He told me that the Captain had still managed to recognize them. To start with they had put him on a tent and crawled along dragging him back. Then they had found a stretcher in a hollow with a dead man on it. They had put the corpse on the ground, heaved the Captain onto the stretcher, and carried him like this to the doctor in Marcelcave. By the time the doctor arrived, the Captain had already breathed his last. After that, Lang and his three comrades had hung about in the rear until the Company was relieved.

In the afternoon the Company was ordered to attend the Captain's funeral, which was held in the Military Cemetery in Harbonnières, where thousands of the poor victims of European militarism lay buried. As was to be expected, a speech was given in which the following featured prominently: Fatherland, hero's death, honour, he can be certain of the deepest thanks of the Fatherland, and so on. In reality that is all a pack of lies, because in my opinion the only people who really fall for the Fatherland are the ordinary soldiers up to the rank of sergeant. The upper ranks are paid and die for the sake of money.

After the funeral, Joseph Hoffert came looking for me, as he did not know how I had got on at the Front. I told him that Sergeant-Lieutenant Orschel, who had been a border guard in our home village, was in the First Machine Gun Company of my regiment and that I had often talked with him. We both set off to try to find him. We soon found the First Machine Gun Company. There we were told that Orschel had been seriously wounded by a shell, and that he had survived for a day before dying. He was just being buried at the Military Cemetery. We went there, but Orschel had already been buried. His grave is just next to the grave of my Captain, Baron Götz of Reisswitz. The bodies of more and more victims were brought to the cemetery; some of them looked ghastly.

The Division's losses during the attack were made known. Sixty-five per cent of the overall number had been lost. Of the thirty-two officers of my Regiment who had taken part in the attack, twenty-two had fallen. Of the forty-four men serving in the Mortar Company of my Battalion only four were left, while the rest were killed or wounded. My Company had been relatively lucky, as more than half the contingent returned safely.

215

The next day was regimental roll call. The remains of Regiment 332 had to fall in at a meadow near the town. The Divisional Commander, General von Adams, who had a very unpleasant face and was hated by everyone for his brutal ruthlessness, rode up. 'Attention, eyes right!' Now we all had to look at this human being. He greeted us with: 'Good morning, children!' I thought to myself. You damned mass-murderer calling us children! The ruthlessness of this paid scoundrel in insisting that the attack be continued had resulted in many pointless deaths. He then gave a speech oozing with nationalism, militarism, hero's death, and so on. Even though we did not reach the objective of the attack, at least we had shown the British what German courage and bravado could achieve. The truth is that there is no such thing as courage. Fear of death exceeds all other feelings, and only frightful coercion drives soldiers on. I would like to have seen, for example, what would have happened if all the people who wanted to go home had been given permission to leave, while those who wanted to stay could do so. I do not think that a single man would have been left at the front of his own free will. Nobody would have bothered about the Fatherland; they would only have sought to save their lives and to live as human beings again.

After the roll call, medals were handed out. About sixty men in the Regiment were awarded the Iron Cross, Second Class. Two first class Iron Crosses were also awarded. They naturally went to two officers, because it's obvious that if you get a high salary you also get a high award. Afterwards we could go back into our quarters in the shed. During the night I heard the hum of several English aircraft over the town. I recognized them immediately by the high, singing sound of the engines. You expected to hear the whoosh and explosion of the bombs. There was no sense in running away; it was best just to stay lying were we were. If you got a direct hit, it would be over. If the bomb did not land nearby, it would do you no harm. Suddenly we heard the familiar whooshing and whistling of the bombs. We all pulled our heads closer to our shoulders, and then it went crack, crack, crack. Fortunately the bombs did not fall near us.

The next morning we learned that a number of men and horses had been killed. Until now, Harbonnières, which was fifteen kilometres behind the Front, had been spared from bombardment by artillery. Then, in the afternoon of the 30th of April two of the heaviest calibre of shells whizzed in and exploded in the centre of town, making a horrible din. Everyone immediately became indescribably agitated. Two more of the monsters came whizzing in straight afterwards, increasing the confusion. We were ordered: 'Get ready to move on!' Everything was packed away quickly, the horses were hitched up to the waggons, and off we went further back. In the streets it was crawling with soldiers, officers, horses and waggons as everyone tried to reach safety as fast as possible. The things kept flying in, blowing up a

216

house or tearing a huge hole in the ditches. Eventually we left the town and the danger behind us. It was like a mass migration on the road to the rear.

The order was given: 'The Second Machine Gun Company will move to Framerville.' The village of Framerville is situated about five kilometres behind Harbonnières and was half-ruined since the summer battle of 1916. It is situated on the edge of the region in which the summer battle raged. Not a single house remained habitable between Framerville and Le Fère, a distance of seventy kilometres. Everything had been shot up or blasted by the Germans during the withdrawal in 1917. Our Company was quartered in Framerville Castle. The castle was however half destroyed and had no doors or windows any more. When it rained we were forced to put up tents in the rooms. The village filled up with army. The English, who seemed to know this, sent their squadrons of aircraft to bomb us almost every night. It was almost impossible to sleep peacefully.

8th of May 1918 – The Divisional Sports Day

Our Division now organised a sports day to cheer up the soldiers and raise their morale. Everyone who believed he could achieve something was free to enter. I signed up for grenade throwing, long jump with springboard and the obstacle race. The evening before, I went with a number of comrades to familiarize myself with the obstacle course and to practise. From the starting point you had to run about fifty metres to the first obstacle – a wall of boards with four identical gaps. The soldiers were expected to run in groups of four at a time. As I am quite slim, I did not have any difficulty in getting through one of the gaps. After about twenty metres there was a wire obstacle, but the wire was not barbed. After a further twenty metres there was a trench two and a half metres wide. We had to jump across this. Twenty metres after that was the most dangerous obstacle. This was a smooth wooden wall whose top could be reached by jumping up. I tried every possible way of getting across. Pulling yourself up took too long. The best way was to jump up, hold on to the top with your hands, drag yourself up a little and support yourself against the wall with your left leg while swinging your right leg up and over the top. Once you were sitting on top it was easy to get the other leg over and jump down. I needed no more than six seconds for this manoeuvre. The whole thing was pretty strenuous, as we had been weakened by under-nourishment and our irregular lives.

The sporting demonstrations were due to start at nine o'clock in the morning. Lots of officers and soldiers came to see the events. A senior officer made a speech. The sports ground was situated behind a small wood, so the massed meeting was not visible from the English observation balloons. A German fighter squadron flew above the place the whole time to defend against possible attacks by English aircraft.

217

First of all there was a race. It was won by a man from the Rhineland who had always given me the impression of being stiff and clumsy. We were all surprised at how fast he ran.

Lots of people had entered for the obstacle race. People went off in groups of four, and the time taken by each person was recorded. I ran in the fourth group. I immediately noticed that two of them were excellent runners, and they got to the first obstacle about two paces ahead of me, but I got through before them. The fourth contestant fell over in the wire and was out of the race. The three remaining contestants reached the final obstacle at the same time. As I had worked out the best way of crossing the wooden wall the previous evening, I crossed it in a few seconds, while the others took longer to get across. I now ran like the wind to the finishing line and was only two steps ahead when I got there. I was quite exhausted and lay down to have a rest. It took a while until the obstacle race was completed. Then I had to do the long jump, but I did not jump off correctly and did badly.

Next came the high jump. This was followed by grenade throwing. The target was forty-five metres away and consisted of a scarecrow dressed as a soldier. We naturally did not throw live hand grenades – we used training grenades instead. I landed my hand grenades close to the target and was hopeful of winning one of the prizes which had been offered. We almost laughed ourselves to death in the sack race which followed. Then we had to try to climb up two smooth poles. The person who got the highest would get the first prize. In the next event, first two, then three and even four gym horses were set up and people had to vault over them. It is clear that only the best gymnasts could participate in this. The exercises were all very interesting, and you almost forgot that you were in the middle of a war. Afterwards the prizes were handed out. I won the sixth prize in the obstacle race – a bottle of cognac containing about three-quarters of a litre. In grenade throwing I won the eighth prize – an attractive cigar case containing good cigars. Gradually the place emptied and people went back to their quarters. On the way back, you were reminded by the rolling thunder of the guns that it was still war.

The following day a Battalion of infantry was training in the waste ground near the Somme when it was bombed by a squadron of English bombers. Several men were killed. In Framerville there were about a hundred captive French and English soldiers who had to do various tasks. The French could not stand the English and blamed them for the fact that the war was not yet over. I often gave the French cigarettes, for which they were very grateful.

It was now announced that anyone who had lead, copper, brass, sheet zinc and so on should bring it to a collecting place in the village where they would be paid a certain amount per kilogram. You cannot imagine the wave of destruction caused by this announcement! All the brass door handles and window latches were unscrewed or chipped off. All the copper cooking utensils and anything consisting of copper was also removed. Entire sheet zinc roofs were removed and hauled to the collection posts. Some soldiers were paid several hundred Marks for their robbery. There were even some people who specialised in searching the occupied territories looting the bells of churches. I said to Lieutenant Strohmayer, who was standing beside me and watching the process: 'I think it is wrong to misappropriate church property.' Strohmayer said: 'What do you want to do? Necessity knows no law.' Yes, necessity knows no law, that's the German excuse.

One day, each team was tasked with digging itself in and getting ready to fire, making sure that it could not be seen from the front. When we were ready the new Company Commander, whom I had not yet got to know, inspected the guns from the front and concluded that my team had hidden itself best. The whole Company now had to come and learn from our example how to dig themselves in. The Company Commander gave me two good cigars, and from then on I was, so to speak, well in with him.

After we had been in Framerville for about twelve days, replacement troops came from Germany and we heard: 'Tomorrow evening we are going back into position.' We were all frightened by the prospect. Right next to the village was an airfield, at which about fourteen aircraft were based. These were used in aerial combat with the English and as night bombers. In the afternoon before we were due to go into position I went with Lance Corporal Fritz Kessler to the pilots' canteen to buy a stock of cigarettes which I would take with me to the Front. On the way there we saw and heard two large shrapnel shells explode high above us. This was the first time that an artillery shot had come so far back. 'Fritz,' I said, 'take care, they will hit us here.' 'That's quite possible,' said Fritz, 'but we're out of here this evening and will have to get used to something quite different anyway.' We bought our cigarettes and went casually back towards the Company. It was a splendid day in May, with the air so clear, warm and fragrant that it was a joy to be alive. 'How beautiful it could be now in the world,' said Fritz, 'and we stupid people kill each other.' Suddenly we threw ourselves to the ground. We registered the gurgling whoosh of two large shells, and almost instantaneously we heard the dreadful explosions. One of the shells had landed in among the aircraft, causing the wreckage to fly in all directions. The other one had landed in the yard of a house in which the military band of an artillery regiment was quartered. Afterwards we heard that several men had been wounded and killed. In a mad rush, everyone left the village. We ran at the double to our Company. The horses had already been harnessed. My gunners had packed Kessler's things and mine, and loaded them on the waggon. Now we hurried out of the village. Behind us we heard the booming impact of the heavy shells. In a sunken road we waited for the evening.

219

Back to the Front

Then we headed off towards the Front. We went along a very good broad road towards Amiens, which was called the Roman Road. As it started to get a bit dark, I noticed that in the distance ahead of us lots of shrapnel shells were exploding. So, things were happening here too. We got to the village of Warfusée-Abancourt. There we had to take down our machine guns and equipment from the waggons and carry them. Two guides from the Front were waiting for us. We avoided going through the village which was often a target for the English artillery. The guides took us along a hollow leading past the village in which several German batteries had been mounted. As it was not yet dark, some of the English observation balloons were still up, and they stayed there until night-time. The people in charge of the batteries were angry with us and swore at us, saying that we would be to blame if the English discovered where their batteries were located.

It got really dark, and we had trouble sticking together. In this unfamiliar environment you felt as stupid as a calf leaving the stall for the first time. Every few steps you fell in one of the many shell-holes. The soldiers, who were sweating as they carried the load, started to get bad-tempered and complained. You were often blinded by the flares going off up ahead. In the night sky behind the English front you saw a large number of jerking flashes, followed first by a whizzing which lasted a second, followed by the explosion of the shrapnel and artillery shells. These were the localized attacks practised by the English, and greatly feared by us, that lasted two or three minutes, after which there would be a pause and another area would be targeted. Having passed the village, we rejoined the road. As we were about to cross it, we found ourselves in the middle of an English barrage. As fast as lightning we all lay down in the roadside ditch. I pushed myself against the slope and held the two water tanks and the big spade over my head in order to protect myself as much as possible from the splinters. How it whizzed and boomed all around us! You felt you would be hit at any moment. The feeling you have in a moment like that can only be imagined by someone who has been in the same situation. A number of the shells hit the road, tearing out lots of stones which also buzzed around in the air and hailed down on us. Suddenly, as abruptly as it had started, the shooting stopped. We heaved a sigh of relief and asked whether anyone was hurt. Miraculously, nobody was injured.

We went on to the Front, which was being defended in depth. Defence in depth means a band six to eight hundred metres wide along the front is held by soldiers scattered everywhere – infantrymen, light and heavy machine guns, which occupy the machine gun nests, grenade launchers, mortars and so on. The soldiers shelter in shell-holes or in holes they have dug for themselves. It would have been almost impossible to maintain a continuous trench here as it would soon have been discovered and it would have been bombarded by the hostile artillery until hardly a man would have been left alive. Defence in depth means that the enemy artillery is forced to scatter the whole field without any target or plan. This, however, naturally leads to casualties since there are no dugouts, or barbed wire entanglements, and there is no good cover. All the soldiers cowering in the holes asked what Regiment we came from, or whether they might not be able to leave and go back soon. The all had their knapsacks on, so that they could run back as soon as possible when ordered to do so. We often had to lie down on the ground as the English swept the field with machine guns, but we reached the Machine Gun Nest Owl without suffering any losses. No sooner had we arrived, than the soldiers who had occupied the nest crept out of the hole and disappeared backwards in the darkness. We were happy to get some cover in the hole.

In Machine Gun Nest Owl

Machine Gun Nest Owl was simply a shell-hole which had been dug out to make a square, with a stand for the machine gun dug in at the front. In the darkness it was impossible to get your orientation. Nobody had told us whether we were at the outermost edge of the Front, how far away the English soldiers were, or what was going on. You felt that you had just been dropped in. I shot a flare up into the sky. But what did I see? Nothing but a field strewn with shell-holes – as if we were the only ones here, and yet, all around us were thousands of soldiers in the holes. We also had the misfortune that we got the new Company Commander in our hole. Naturally this made things less cosy, because these chaps always want to command something or to bully people. The other machine gun of the platoon led by NCO Krämer was only about four metres away from us and also belonged to Machine Gun Nest Owl. Towards the morning several shells hit quite close, which caused us some anxiety as a direct hit means nothing but shreds. The prospect of being torn to shreds is naturally very unpleasant and makes you anxious.

When it was day, I briefly stuck my head up to orientate myself. I saw nothing but the shot-up field and could not determine where the edge of the German Front was, or where the English were located. The road was about one hundred metres to our left, and about eight hundred metres away was the town of Villers-Bretonneux, which was now only a heap of ruins. Further left was the shot-up village of Cachy, which we were supposed to conquer during the attack on the 24th of April. I also saw a number of shot-up tanks lying around. Behind us I saw the village of Warfusée-Abancourt, which had been shelled to pieces. That was all. A number of English tethered balloons rose into the sky; we counted twenty-eight in all.

Our Company Commander thought that we should dig him a better shelter. He wanted us to dig four or five steps down from the hole and then dig him out a hole like an oven, in which he would live. I would really have liked to hit the scoundrel on the head with the big spade. It did not bother him whether we had any shelter – all that mattered was that his valuable life should be saved. I said: 'Sir, in my opinion it is impossible to dig during the day, because if we throw out earth, we will bring the English artillery fire onto us.' That seemed to make sense to him. There were a lot of new sand-bags in the hole, which had probably been left behind by the previous team. Now the lieutenant got us to fill the sacks during the day and empty them in the shell-holes at night time. What were we to do? We just had to do what he wanted, so we filled the sacks.

During the day terrible air-battles frequently took place; it was horrifying and interesting to watch. Out on the field there were lots of crude wooden crosses, which had been erected by the comrades of the fallen on their graves. Directly behind our hole there were three such crosses on a filled-up shell-hole. If we had not been so hardened, we might have found it unpleasant to be camping so near to the dead. In the following night we experienced the same bombardments and machine-gun fire as the night before. One man from each machine gun had to go to fetch food. These people dreaded the prospect of risking their lives for a bit of dog food. We emptied the sandbags in the shell-holes. It was too dark to bury it. During the day I had noticed a telephone pole standing by the road. I borrowed a saw from the neighbouring gunners and cut it into pieces about one and a half metres long. Then we carried the wood to the machine gun nest. There we dug in the pieces to a depth of about half a metre, forming a square in the base of the hole. I fetched a number of thin pieces of corrugated iron which came from the English, put them on top of the wood, shovelled some earth on top, and had cover against splinters and rain. We also fastened one of the sheets of corrugated iron on top of the lieutenant's hole. The following day, we finished the lieutenant's oven. Now this fellow spent the whole time in his hole. He did not speak much. He was too proud for that. The battalion messengers brought him the battalion, regimental and divisional orders. If we could only get rid of this chap, I thought to myself.

In the evening, when it got dark, we had to take his orders to the other machine guns, a task which always brought us into mortal danger. On our fourth evening in the nest, he called me down into his hole. 'Richert,' he said, 'a regimental order has come that each night between twelve and two a machine gun should go forward, report to the Commander of the Infantry Company, and fire one thousand five hundred shots at the crossing behind the English front, as people suspect that there is a lot of activity there at night. It would be good, Richert, for you to start this process tonight.' I said: 'That's just what I need. We would have to cover more than four hundred metres to reach the most advanced German infantry. You know sir, as well as I do, that we would constantly be in great danger of losing our lives. In addition, you could easily break a limb in these shell holes in the dark. I just wish that the person who gave this order would carry it out himself!' 'Richert, do not be abusive. Orders are orders. I too would prefer you to stay here, but we have no choice. Go, for God's sake, and come back safely.'

My gunners, who had heard the conversation, were terrified. Each of them was afraid that I would give them the order to go with me. I quietly said something to them. They were immediately consoled. 'Right, get ready!' I said loudly, so that the lieutenant would hear it in his hole. 'We will leave the sledge here. I will carry the machine gun; Kessler will take the stand and a box of ammunition. Thomas, you take the two other boxes of ammunition, to make up the required number. Right! Then off we go, for heaven's sake!' We climbed out of our hole and simply went to the other hole four metres away, which was occupied by Krämer's machine gun team. I told him how it stood. 'You would be mad if you went! These pig-headed people can lick our arses! They ought to go themselves!' said Krämer. We took the one thousand five hundred shots out of the belts; I threw them into a shell-hole and buried them. Then I blackened the recoil booster at the front by the barrel of the gun using a candle so that it looked as if it had been fired. We stayed almost three hours in the hole with NCO Krämer. 'Tomorrow night it's my turn,' said Krämer. 'We'll just go to any old shell-hole.' 'Oh,' I said, 'feel free to stay in your hole. This cowardly lieutenant is not brave enough to make the five exposed steps from his hole to check whether you have really gone or not.' Every few minutes the field was swept by the English machine guns, and ping, ping, ping went the bullets as they whizzed over the holes. When it went quiet for a moment, I said: 'Right, let's jump back to our hole, and leave the rest to me. I will manage to deal with the lieutenant.'

I took the machine gun, Kessler and Thomas took the empty ammunition boxes, and we jumped back into our hole; we panted as if we had almost run ourselves to death. We put down the gun. Then the lieutenant came up and said: 'Did you all get back?' 'Yes,' I replied, 'but I tell you frankly that I never intend to do this again. It's a miracle that all three of us have got back safely, as the machine gun bullets frequently whizzed at a hair's breadth past our ears, and in the darkness we could have easily lost our way and ended up among the English troops.' I lied. 'Well, the main thing is that you made it back. I was worried that something might have happened to you.' I thought to myself: if only he knew! My team, which was always loyal to me, now thought even more of me as I had, as far as possible, not put their lives – or my own – at risk.

It was very boring, sitting in the hole all of the time, and we could not talk freely because the lieutenant was there. One day, when I remarked that I was convinced that Germany would lose the war, the lieutenant called me down into his hole. 'Richert,' he said forcefully, 'what have you been saying! You are generally too friendly with the teams. Instead, you should show your authority as their superior, and say nothing which might disturb their confidence in victory.' 'I cannot speak against my conviction, sir,' I replied. 'You can see as well as anyone, sir, that for every fifty German shells that are fired, three hundred English shells come in response. Our planes seldom risk crossing our front, while the English planes whizz above us in large numbers. Our attack of the 24th of April has shown sufficiently that the English Front is solid. And, sir,' I continued, 'I have now been a soldier for almost three years and know what I think of a strict, unreasonable superior; I am convinced that you can make more headway with the men on the basis of comradeship and fairness, and that in an emergency you will perform better. And if, for example, I were wounded, I would be certain that my people would not abandon me. That would be much more likely if I treated them roughly and let them feel my authority too much in an inconsiderate way.'

'You may well be right,' replied my lieutenant, 'but you should not damage your teams belief in victory.' To this I replied: 'It would soon be all the same for all of us how the war ends, as long as we can just keep our lives and return home as soon as possible.' Now the lieutenant nearly got furious: 'What's this you're saying? You don't care how the war ends? Just think of the consequences which defeat would bring with it for us!' 'Sir,' I answered, 'the war can end any way it likes. If I live to the end of the war, I am certain to be among the victors.' 'How come?' asked the astonished lieutenant. 'It's quite simple,' I replied. 'I come from Alsace. If Germany wins, Alsace will continue to be German and we will be with the winners. If the others win, then Alsace will become French and we will also be with the winners!' 'Really,' said the lieutenant. 'I hadn't thought of that. But of course you would prefer a German victory, rather than a victory of the enemy!' To this I replied: 'Sir, I am a farmer, and will have to cultivate the fields one way or another. I couldn't care less whether I have to pay my tax to the one lot or the others.' 'Listen, Richert, you are speaking in a way which is not appropriate. At the moment you are a German NCO and your loyalty should be to Germany. You can go!' I climbed up the four steps and joined my team in the hole. My soldiers quietly asked me what had actually happened, and I told them quietly what had transpired in my talk with the lieutenant. They all had to laugh.

As it was not possible to relieve yourself outside the hole during the day, you had no choice but to relieve yourself down in the hole. For this purpose we had an empty tin can which we peed into. We then just chucked out the urine. Similarly, we would defecate onto a spade covered with a little bit of earth and then throw the stool out of the hole. By and large, it was not a life fit for human beings any more, but we could not do anything about it. One day the lieutenant came out of his hole for a pee. Just as he finished, a shrapnel shell suddenly exploded above us. A bullet penetrated the thin corrugated iron and hit the lieutenant on the forehead above his left eye. As a result of fright and stupefaction, he fell down backwards with a scream. That caused the urine in the tin to pour over his face and his chest. I jumped quickly down to him, as I did not know whether he was seriously wounded or not. He soon got up, pale with fright. The piece of shrapnel had only knocked a round dent in his forehead, after which it had fallen out. The blood ran down the lieutenant's face. I bandaged his forehead with his two gauze bandages. When the evening came, the lieutenant ran to the rear, fast as a hare. Now he had a better future to look forward to than us. My gunners had a good laugh about the fact that he had splashed himself in the face with his urine as he fell backwards. The main thing for us was that we had got rid of him.

During the night I ran back to Machine Gun Nest Vulture where Lieutenant Clemens was the platoon leader. He now took over command of the whole Company. Lieutenant Clemens was a good superior officer and was popular in the whole Company. When I brought him the report that the Company Commander had been wounded, he immediately gave me two good cigars. Afterwards I ran back to my machine gun nest. The English shot more than usual during the night and twice I was forced to throw myself down to avoid their machine gun bullets. The English artillery attacks also came more frequently, and we often had frightening minutes as the artillery shells rained down and the shrapnel shells exploded overhead. You were often dazzled. Despite it all, we remained lucky, and up until now none of my team had been injured during our stay in the 'owl'.

The night after the Company Commander was injured, Gunner Thomas had gone up out of the trench to relieve himself. An English machine gun suddenly started to rattle. A bullet went through Thomas' boot and cut off his little toe as it slanted through it lengthwise. With a cry of pain, he came tumbling back into the hole as quickly as he could, given that his trousers were down, preventing him from walking properly. We picked him up. 'Ouch!' he cried. 'They got me!' 'Where then?' I asked. 'On my leg, on my foot,' he replied in great distress. I took my torch and saw from his damaged boot where the injury was located. I quickly used my pocket knife to cut his boot off his foot and then I pulled off his sock and bandaged his wound while one of the gunners shone the torch on it. Thomas was in a lot of pain as the tendon in his toe was severed and the bone in his toe was splintered. 'If only I could get back!' he kept moaning the whole night, but he did not feel confident to hobble back in the darkness, as he was afraid of tumbling into one of the many shell-holes. As it got light we got his shirt out of his knapsack, fastened it round his foot as well as we could, and tied it up with string. At the first light of dawn Thomas hobbled as quickly as he could towards the rear where he soon disappeared in the darkness and morning fog, never to be seen by us again.

We were all hoping to be relieved, but it seemed as if we had almost been forgotten. In the afternoon, four heavy English shells flew in and exploded about one hundred metres in front of us. I was afraid that they were aiming at us, as our machine gun nest was located on a barely visible rise above the surrounding landscape. The English would assume that a machine gun nest would be positioned here. A few minutes later, four more shells arrived, exploding less than thirty metres ahead of us, causing the lumps of earth that had been thrown into the air to come rumbling down onto our bit of cover, and into our hole. I was hoping that the battery might sweep the field in a straight line. Soon, all too soon, we became convinced that the shells were being aimed at us. With a nerve-shattering whoosh the next shells, which were probably calibre 21,[69] flew just over our heads and exploded with a fearful roar just behind our hole. The following salvo exploded directly ahead of us. The battery had homed in on us. 'Richert!' called NCO Krämer from the next hole. 'This time, we've had it!' 'Not yet,' I called back. 'Maybe they will stop again soon!' But I was mistaken. Salvo after salvo rained in, one every five minutes. The shells crashed in front of us, beside us and behind us, with the result that our hole was soon a quarter full of the lumps of earth that had fallen on us. Pale and trembling we lay huddled together in the hole. All of us lit up cigarettes to calm our nerves a bit. Each time the five minutes were up we listened in suspense. Then we heard, to our unspeakable horror, the boom, boom, boom, boom of the distant firing, then nothing more for several seconds, until the shells came whizzing in. Involuntarily we hugged the ground as hard as we could, as each time we were certain we would receive a direct hit. 'This time we almost had it,' called Krämer, 'a shell has hit right beside our hole.' After the next salvo, a mutilated leg landed in our hole. Some infantrymen who were occupying a hole not far from us had suffered a direct hit, tearing them apart. We were also assailed by the smell of rotting corpses. I looked up and soon saw the cause of this smell. One of the shells had hit in the grave behind us and had torn up and thrown out the corpses, which were already decomposing. It was almost unbearable in our hole. Right next to us were lumps of this sickening human flesh. The next round landed very close to us. We were nearly frantic. There was no chance of running away, because the moment you showed yourself you would have been sprayed with machine-gun fire. After the next salvo we heard gruesome screams of pain. Once again a shell had hit a hole occupied by infantrymen, killing some and seriously injuring others. Despite their moaning, nobody went to help them.

Finally, after about two hours, the shelling stopped. We heaved a sigh of relief. The cigarette which I had lit after the first salvo had soon gone out,

[69] These were probably 8-inch mortar shells (20.3cm rather than 21.0cm).

and I had almost chewed it to the end without noticing it as a result of the tension. A large number of German shells whizzed over our heads. I raised my head and was able to see their impact in the territory occupied by the English. At that moment, I felt that they deserved to suffer too. While I was watching the impact of the German shells, I noticed an English observation balloon going down in flames. I took my binoculars and saw a German aircraft, which looked quite small in the distance, flying towards the next balloon. As soon as he reached it, the balloon also caught fire and crashed. A third balloon suffered the same fate. Then the German plane, surrounded by little clouds from shrapnel shells, returned unharmed to the German lines.

When it got dark, we immediately got to work to put the evil-smelling remains back into the grave and cover them up. As we were unable to discover any of the crosses, it was impossible to mark the grave. Next to us we heard people speaking and working. They were infantrymen who were burying their fallen comrades. They told us that three of the holes that were occupied had suffered direct hits, as a result of which their Company had suffered twelve deaths and one person seriously wounded. All round the Machine Gun Nest Owl there were huge new shell-holes and it hardly seemed possible to them that all the people from both teams had survived unscathed.

After dark, the English attacks started again. As I was about to send people away to fetch food, the Company Messenger came and told us that we would be relieved by another regiment belonging to the Division in half an hour's time. We were naturally very pleased at the news – and yet we were afraid of having to make our way back out in the open. We fastened our knapsacks on our backs, unscrewed the machine gun from its sledge and waited. At long last, figures scurried past us. They were infantrymen who had to relieve troops stationed further forward. Ratatatata crackled the English machine guns. They all threw themselves down, and then after the shooting they picked themselves up and went forward as quickly as they could. Our patience was sorely tried. Eventually we heard people calling out softly: 'Where is Machine Gun Nest Owl?' 'Here,' I replied. Soon the relief team appeared and put us under pressure to get out of the hole. We left the ammunition belts and only took the machine gun, the empty boxes, the big spade, the steam discharge pipe and the emptied water tanks. We hurried back as quickly as our equipment would allow. Twice we were forced to throw ourselves to the ground because of machine-gun fire. We only came under shellfire as we passed the batteries in the hollow, but nobody was injured. When we reached the big road behind the village I heard the call: 'The Second Machine Gun Company 332 gather here!' We went there; the whole Company had soon assembled. For about two kilometres we followed the road, and then we were led off to the left across the fields.

A Rest at Long Last

Soon we reached a deep ravine. The Company was here – drivers, horses and everything. We had a meal and then stretched ourselves out in the bushes to get a peaceful sleep once more. When I awoke, the sun was already high in the sky. It was now possible to work out where we were. The ravine was possibly twenty metres deep, and about thirty metres wide at the bottom, and the two embankments were partially covered with dense bushes. At the lower end of the ravine the Somme flowed gently by. Next to it lay the village of Morcourt, on a hill to the left was the village of Méricourt, and about three kilometres behind us lay the large village of Proyart. All these villages had been partially shot up and deserted by their inhabitants. There were two other battalions of infantry camping in the ravine with their baggage. Until now, the ravine had not yet been bombarded by the English. Despite this, we dug holes in the slope facing the Front so that we would be able to crawl in and take cover if we came under shellfire or were bombed from the air. As it was the end of May and we were enjoying beautiful warm weather, we felt comfortable. All too soon we received an order to move back into position.

This time my team and I had to occupy Machine Gun Nest Eagle. Our Company's machine gun nests were all named after birds of prey: owl, vulture, eagle and hawk. The team ahead of us had started to dig a tunnel in the ground shored up by boards. We continued this work. We did the digging during the day and filled a lot of sandbags with earth, and in the evening we emptied them into nearby shell-holes. Every night, as we were finishing the work we would scatter white dry earth over the fresh, damp earth in order to hide the fact that we had been working here from the English pilots. The days passed slowly, while the nights passed even more slowly. It was always the same: fill the sandbags and sit around in the hole during the day, and fetch food and drag over boards for the tunnel in the evening, accompanied by English machine-gun fire and artillery bombardments. A number of times the English bombarded us with gas shells, containing either a visible gas or an invisible one which smelled like garlic. We were forced to keep our gas masks on, often for hours at a time.

One night I was detailed to lead the people who had to collect the food to the field kitchen, which drove up to near the village of Abancourt at night time. On the way back we suddenly came under a massive artillery attack. In the darkness ahead of me I saw a hole. 'Come here!' I shouted. We all went straight into the hole. Then I noticed that a passageway went diagonally down into the earth from the hole. I felt my way along the dark passage and told the others to follow. I felt a tent, which seemed to be blocking off the passageway. I pushed it back and shone my torch inside. On one side, I saw three men wrapped in blankets. 'What do you think you are doing

228

here?' a voice snarled at me. 'What are we after? Cover, nothing else,' I answered. 'Get out of here straight away!' 'As soon as the shelling stops,' I replied. 'Do you know who I am?' this man wrapped in blankets shouted at me. 'No,' I replied. 'I am in charge of the food collectors of the Second Machine Gun Company 332 and I consider it my duty to bring them back safely if it is in my power to do so, and you take cover wherever you can find it.' Now this man became a bit friendlier. 'You are with the KTK of the Battalion.' KTK[70] means Commander of the Fighting Troops, and Major von Putkammer held this post for the Third Battalion. As the firing now ceased, we crept out of the hole and ran hurriedly to our machine gun nests.

As our Company was weakened once again, a platoon from the machine gun company of the territorial regiment to which Joseph Hoffert belonged was ordered to provide reinforcements. One team was very unlucky. As they were approaching the nest which had been allocated to them, one man fell to machine-gun fire. The next day they suffered a direct hit in their hole which killed all but one of them – a young man from Berlin. As he was now on his own, he joined another team in the platoon. After two days, they were relieved by another platoon in their company. Two days later, the soldier from Berlin was ordered back into position, although most of the teams in his company had not yet been in the front line, since his territorial regiment was based in the villages behind the Front. He said to his sergeant that it was not yet his turn, and that he would only go back when it was. Really, he was in the right, but he seemed to have forgotten that he was expected to be a submissive tool of Prussian militarism. 'So you are disobeying my order,' said the sergeant. 'I will go when it's my turn,' the soldier replied. He said the same to the Company Commander. It was reported up the line of command. The Divisional Court Martial met and sentenced the poor young man to death by firing squad for disobeying orders in the face of the enemy. The sentence was carried out the next day. This poor lad was used by those in power to warn the other soldiers, because they were aware that most of them were only obeying their orders reluctantly.

The English started firing shells with delayed-action fuses, that is to say, they did not explode on impact with the ground, but only when they had gone deep into the ground, so that they would cause any tunnels nearby to collapse. We called these dangerous things tunnel breakers. Lots of these shells went so deep into the earth that they were not powerful enough to burst the earth above them, and they only forced up the ground like a bubble. These shells caused may tunnels to collapse, which buried the soldiers, causing them to suffer a horrible death by suffocation. The poor soldiers were killed in all kinds of ways, and yet they had to keep going on or they

---

[70] The *Kampftruppenkommandeur* was in charge of the forward battalion as part of the strategy of defence in depth.

would end up like the lad from Berlin. Gradually I developed a deadly hatred of all those who were well paid to force the unfortunate soldiers to endure the conditions at the front and to die.

One evening Gunner Konkel from my team, a twenty-year-old lad from Danzig, was due to go to fetch our food. He took the canteens and left. But Konkel did not come back. Lance Corporal Kruchen, a Rhinelander from Cologne, went missing as well. We all believed that they had fallen. Naturally, that day we really suffered hunger and thirst.

The following night we were relieved once again. As it was quiet, I said: 'Let's go along the street through the village. It's shorter and easier than going through the field, and I'm interested to see how it is in the village.' We all agreed to go. On reaching the village, as the moon shone brightly, we were able to see the horror of the devastation. Almost all of the houses had been blown apart by the heavy English shells. Often, the ruins lay right across the road. Only a small road way had been cleared. At one point there was a wrecked field kitchen with two dead horses hitched up in front. A few steps further on lay two dead soldiers and two dead horses hitched to a waggon laden with boards for tunnels. We hurried to leave the village. When we were about half way through suddenly several very heavy shells flew into the village with a deafening whoosh. The force of their explosions was so strong that you felt you were being lifted into the air. As a result of the blast tiles and timberwork fell from the damaged houses. The four of us ran as quickly as we could to get out of harm's way. But the shells were quicker than us. The next ones exploded close behind not far from us. The enormous splinters whirled their way past us overhead. We hurried on! We were almost breathless with running and agitation. Sch-sch-schr-crack-crack – two of the monsters flew over us and exploded ahead of us, while several exploded behind us. Now we were right in the middle. The hail of clods of earth never seemed to stop. More and more shells flew in and exploded all around us. We did not know where to turn.

Eventually we reached the end of the village and immediately ran to the left across the field as we realized that the fire was aimed mainly at the road. Now we were running through splendid wheat fields that had been partially torn up by shells. When no more shells landed near us we stopped; we were so tired and out of breath that we had to lie down for a while to catch our breath. Suddenly pandemonium broke out at the Front. The English artillery pounded the German positions. The fire was returned by the German artillery with all calibres of shell. Towards the Front you could see nothing but the continuous twitching and flashing of the exploding artillery and shrapnel shells. Hundreds of flares shot up. The machine guns started to clatter. 'Something's up there!' we said to each other, and we were really glad that we had been relieved. We saw lots of red flares rising up, requesting barrages from the German artillery. These started immediately.

Spellbound, we watched and listened to this flashing and banging until the impact of a shell not far from us told us that we should get a move on as quickly as possible. We now approached the ravine, but we did not go to the Company as we were afraid that we would be alerted and ordered to go forwards to provide reinforcements. Gradually the fire dwindled and it became quiet. Then we went to the Company. We thought we were the last, but we were the first team back. The following morning we heard that the English had carried out a night attack and that they had forced their way into the German positions in places and taken prisoners; then they had withdrawn again.

Start of June 1918 – At Rest Again

On our first rest day a dreadful aerial battle involving fifty-two aircraft took place high above us. Six of them crashed. One of them, an English aircraft, crashed less than fifty metres away from us in the ravine. We all thought it was going to land right on top of us. At that moment, you did not know how to escape. The impact with the earth was terrible. The aircraft was shattered and immediately caught fire. Nobody could get near it because of the jets of flame, which were caused by the fuel, and because of the explosion of the heated ammunition. When everything had burnt out, the charred body of the pilot was released from the wreckage and buried up on the field.

On the second rest day an English plane flew down at great speed from high up and, using only a few shots, set the observation balloon which was quite near us alight. The observer was able to save himself by jumping out with his parachute and swinging gently he descended safely to the ground. The next day a new observation balloon had already replaced the old one. An English pilot flew over it and threw out something which was quite new to me. You saw lots of little strips of smoke falling from the plane. This was probably a burning liquid that was intended to set the balloon alight, but it was pulled down immediately.

Every day all the company sergeants in the Battalion went to Morcourt to receive orders and to be told the password. They were standing in a yard waiting for the Battalion Commander, when suddenly a shell landed in the middle of them. They were all torn apart with the exception of our company sergeant, Laugsch, who survived, only suffering from a torn-off calf. As soon as he had heard the sound of the shell, he had thrown himself to the ground immediately. We were all sorry to lose this man, as he was good and just and a real company-mother.[71] From this day onwards, the village of Morcourt was bombarded every day.

---

[71] A traditional army term for a company sergeant.

One day about forty English planes circled above the village. Only a single one approached our ravine. The order came: 'Take cover!' We sat in front of our holes, hidden by the bushes, and observed the pilots' movements. One of the pilots suddenly fired a flare; at the same moment we heard the bombs whistling down and their detonation in the village of Morcourt sounded like a barrage. Soon afterwards, the village was shrouded in black smoke. Suddenly we heard bombs hurtling down, followed by four detonations. We all crawled into the holes at lightning speed. The soldier who shared the hole with me said 'I've been hit!' A splinter the size of a nickel had penetrated his bottom. I was able to remove it. He only had a flesh wound and was given several days of recuperation by the battalion doctor. A driver belonging to the battalion baggage train had his throat torn away by a splinter. He still managed to dismount from the waggon, ran with his hands in the air and mortal fear in his eyes for a few steps, collapsed, picked himself up again, fell into the arms of several soldiers who were coming to his aid, and died. His corpse, the front of which was completely covered with blood, looked dreadful, but we had been so blunted by our experience that we could not feel very much. When, when at long last would this murder come to an end? There was no prospect of peace soon. I felt how sad it would be if, after all the terrible horrible things that I had been forced to take part in, I would end up being killed! This uncertain future was almost the most unpleasant aspect.

The food was somewhat better and more substantial than in 1917. We were given an additional combat food allowance, but even so you only had one meal a day which was sufficient to satisfy your hunger. One day I was very surprised to see Gunner Konkel and Lance Corporal Kruchen returning to the Company, accompanied by two soldiers. We thought that they had fallen about ten days ago while collecting food. In fact, they had deserted and had boarded a train in Péronne which took them to Cologne. Konkel, who was unable to find food anywhere, found himself forced to report to the authorities, while Lance Corporal Kruchen was apprehended in his wife's flat. They were now returned to their unit, to be sentenced by the Divisional Court. Each of them was sentenced to five years in prison. Together with two soldiers, I was given the task of taking them to the prison in Cambrai. We marched as far as Péronne, passing through devastated territory all the way. There were a number of English aircraft circling over the station. As we were afraid of being bombed we all hid between the tracks under a railway waggon which was loaded with pit props. The bombs came whizzing down but missed their targets and landed near the station. Then we travelled on a train carrying soldiers going on leave to Cambrai. Not a single occupied house could be seen. Everything was shot up, destroyed or blown up. To the west of Cambrai, about one hundred English tanks which had been shot up during the fighting in 1917 were lying in the fields. In Cambrai I had to hand over the two men to the officer who ran the prison. 'How are things at the Front?' he asked me. 'I don't think they are going very well,' I replied. I told him that the English were greatly superior in terms of aircraft and artillery, and certainly also in terms of foodstuffs, and that in my opinion the Americans would tip the balance. 'Yes,' said the officer, 'you have the same opinion as I do.' This was the first time I had found an officer who was willing to say that Germany would lose the war. The two soldiers and I went to look round the town. It had been spared the worst of the war and only a few houses had been destroyed by bombing. I was really impressed by the town hall (Hotel de Ville), the likes of which I had never seen before. Then we went to the soldiers' home where we were able to get a beer – something that did not happen often. Although it was only insipid wartime beer we made the most of it. We spent the night in the Cuirassier barracks. The next morning we caught the train to Péronne and returned to the Company by foot from there. How lucky the soldiers who served in the rear echelon were. They never had to risk their lives! When I reported back to the Company I discovered that half of them had moved up into position the previous night. This time our regiment was further north.

After three days, I had to go with my team to relieve a unit at the Front. We went through the village of Morcourt, following a road which ran in the valley along the bank of the Somme and passed the ruined villages of Cerisy and Chipilly. Then we turned off along a war-damaged cart track heading towards the front. The route led through a communication trench which was bombarded by the English artillery day and night and led to the most advanced part of the Front. We went past a wood that had been completely shot up. Only a few tree trunks were left standing like telephone poles. The tactic here was defence in depth, and there was only one trench – right at the front – which ran through a wheat field. As the wheat limited visibility, the troops in the trench used to trample it down during the night in order to be able to have a clear field of view. I could not tell how far away the English troops were. The remains of the villages of Hamel and Hangard were located in and around the defences. Near Hangard was the infamous Hangard Wood. Thousands of soldiers on both sides lost their lives fighting to gain control of it. The position was constantly under fire by heavy English mortars. In the places where they landed the grass did not grow any more. They had an incredible explosive power. All day we looked into the sky towards the front to see whether one of these shells was coming, as it was easy to make them out. If you really paid attention, you could often quickly avoid them. Single English aircraft, relieved by others, flew constantly over our positions. They watched for every movement and as soon as they saw anything they dropped four bombs or shot down on us with machine guns. We called these pilots grave inspectors.

We were relieved at night after five days without any major incidents. When we were on the way back through the ruined village of Cherisy we were suddenly bombarded by a terrible English shell and mortar attack. The powerful explosions crashed and thundered without stopping. Equally suddenly English shells held the road leading along the side of the Somme under fire. We hurried to a tunnel that had been dug into an embankment nearby. 'It's rattling up front,' was our general opinion. From the Front we suddenly heard rifle and machine-gun fire, but not much of it. 'Listen, the English soldiers have reached our positions!' I said. On the road about thirty metres away from us marched dark infantry columns advancing as reinforcements. These poor devils would also have palpitations, as they had to make their way through shellfire to the Front. If the English were in the German positions they would have to attack and attempt to drive them out, which would never happen without heavy losses. We decided to stay in our tunnel until the shooting up front had stopped.

Towards morning it became more peaceful. I saw a number of lightly wounded soldiers hurrying back along the road in nervous haste. I ran over to find out what had happened. My team joined me as well and we marched back with the wounded men. They told us that they had been suddenly assailed by English mortar and artillery shells. They had lain down on the trench bottom for cover. All of a sudden the English shells flew further back; just at this moment the English troops jumped into their trench and started to slaughter everyone. They had managed to climb out of the trench and had been wounded while fleeing. They did not believe that any of the men who had remained in the trench would still be alive. I inwardly thanked God that we had been relieved half an hour before, and felt deeply sorry for the two teams from our machine gun company who were in the front trench, as I was very concerned about their fate. On arriving at the ravine the Company Sergeant Bukies asked us what had happened, so I told him what I had heard.

In the course of the morning, about twenty seriously wounded people were brought back. Some of them had terrible wounds, mainly bayonet and stab wounds, or wounds caused by hand grenades. One of the wounded was Lance Corporal Reinisch from my Company. A hand grenade had torn off both his heels, and he also had splinters in his calves and his thighs. These seriously wounded people were transported to the rear immediately. Then two unwounded men from my Company arrived. One of them, a handsome Rhinelander, was shaking so much that he was hardly able to say a word. The other one, who was also a Rhinelander by the name of Panhausen, told us that he had been the platoon leader's orderly and was going with him to the other machine gun during the heaviest mortar fire. Suddenly the mortar shells went further and just at the same moment the English troops jumped into the trench in front of him. One of them held a bayonet to his chest. Panhausen, who was a good Catholic, crossed himself and then held his hands up. The English soldier got Panhausen to cross himself again, which he did. A second English soldier who stood behind the first one tried to get past him to bayonet Panhausen. He hit him in the chest. The bayonet went through his jacket, his braces and his shirt, and penetrated his body to a depth of about one centimetre. Panhausen would certainly have been run through if the Englishman standing next to him had not prevented the blow. The two Englishmen now had an argument; the one wanted to kill Panhausen, while the other would not permit it. Panhausen used this moment to climb out of the trench and disappear to the rear among the wheat. The platoon leader had cleared out straight away. Panhausen also believed that there had been many dead in the trench, as he had heard many death cries. 'I am certain,' he concluded, 'that making the sign of the cross saved my life.' The other Rhinelander had by now recovered sufficiently that he was able to relate what he had experienced. During the artillery and mortar fire he lay down in a small hole in the trench to get cover. The English troops had jumped suddenly into the trench and bayoneted three infantrymen who were lying next to him in the trench although they had wanted to surrender. Their ghastly cries of pain and their death cries nearly drove him mad. He expected to be discovered and bayoneted at any moment. 'Those were the most terrible minutes of my life,' he continued. 'After they had killed all the Germans they could reach, the English troops ran backwards and forwards in the trench for a while, without finding me. Eventually they left the trench again, and returned to their own positions.' As the attack had been so surprising the Germans had hardly been able to offer any resistance, so that the English had suffered almost no casualties.

During the following night three waggons from the Battalion transport had to come forwards to collect the corpses. They were to be buried at the large soldiers' cemetery in Proyart. The next morning the waggons laden with the dead were standing in the ravine. What a sight! Piled high, this way and that, intertwined and on top of each other, they lay there with mortal fear still showing on some of their faces. I once read: 'Our soldiers die for their Fatherland with a smile on their lips.' What a brazen lie! Who would feel like smiling if he is facing such a terrible death! All the people who invent and write such things deserve to be sent right to the front. There they would be able to see on themselves and on others what an infamous lie they have launched upon the public.

The burial of the unfortunate victims was to take place in the afternoon. About twenty men from my Company were ordered to go to the burial. In groups of three we made our way from the ravine across open country to Proyart. The day before, Proyart had been attacked by English artillery, so we were only allowed to leave in small numbers in order to avoid becoming targets. We reached the cemetery before the waggons carrying the dead arrived. The mass grave had already been dug. Lots of soldiers had already found their last rest here, far from home. I went through the rows of graves and read the names written on the crosses. On one of them stood: 'Reservist Karl Krafft, 5th Company, Infantry Regiment 332.' I knew Krafft, who came from Berlin and had been a landlord in a pub there, very well because we were in the same group in the 5th Company. He was a likeable comrade, just a bit too patriotic. He had, as he had told me earlier, a wife and four small children at home. I felt very sorry for poor Krafft and for his family. In the same row where Krafft was buried, a number of airmen had been buried.[72] These could be recognized by the broken propellers, which had been stuck in the earth next to the crosses. In the meantime the waggons with the bodies had arrived. They were taken down from the waggons and piled three deep. First their boots and jackets were removed and then they were covered with so-called corpse paper – thin frilled paper. Then the padre who was present prayed some burial prayers. An officer held a short talk, which did not contain anything apart from patriotic lies. Then the grave was filled in. These poor soldiers now had their rest, but what about their parents, sisters, wives and children? We left again, in small numbers, as we had come, returning to the Company in the ravine.

In the evening I had to go back into position, relieving NCO Peters' team. The machine gun nest was not in the outermost trench, but about three hundred metres further back on the corner of a wood that had been completely shot up. This was a high point from which it was possible to get a good view of both the German and the English position. NCO Peters told me that at night time it was the most dangerous place far and wide, as five or six fearful artillery attacks could be expected every night. Peters left the dangerous place at the double. Fortunately for us the engineers had built a tunnel about six metres deep in the chalky cliffs, in which you could be fairly safe. The tunnel first went straight into the earth, and then made a bend as it went down lower, in order to prevent splinters from flying into it. We set our machine gun up at the top of the tunnel while we sat down at the bottom on the stairs. I had brought a number of candles with me so we did not have to sit around in the dark all the time. One of the soldiers had to stay under cover at the entrance up above in order to hear what was happening if something should start out front. Until this time, although the artillery on both sides had been firing, nothing had come in our direction. But suddenly, at a stroke, it started. It thundered and crashed above us and round about us. As a result of the pressure caused by the shells exploding very close to us the tent which we hung outside the entrance blew away, so that our candle went out several times. It thundered and roared above us as if the Day of Judgement had arrived! We had a number of picks and spades down in the

---

[72] 4,643 German soldiers from the First World War are buried in this cemetery. There is a Karl Kraft (note different spelling) buried there.

tunnel in case the entrance got blocked and left us buried alive. As suddenly as it had come, the firing stopped again. Although we had not been in direct danger, we heaved a sigh of relief. We had to survive four more bombardments during the first night. It gradually grew light. Everything quietened down. We went out of the tunnel to the entrance trench, and had a look at the surrounding area from this beautiful viewpoint. All around, everything you could see was ruined or spoilt. A bit off to our right was the village of Hamel, which had been completely flattened. On this side were the Germans; on the other side were the English positions. If there had been an English attack, we would have been able to wipe them out wholesale with our machine gun, but in a case like that we would have been bombarded so intensively by artillery that none of us would have risked leaving the tunnel. The next three days passed without anything significant happening. Almost every day we would see large and small examples of aerial combat, which almost always led to aircraft crashing. In several cases, English squadrons which had been operating behind the German front were attacked by small German aircraft on the way back. They would separate the last aircraft from its squadron and shoot it down. Sometimes up to three English aircraft would be brought down in this way.

We were relieved on the third night and returned to our Company in the ravine. While making our way back we often had to throw ourselves to the ground as the English often shot at the lines of communication. As we got near to Morcourt we heard an English aircraft zooming low overhead, but we went on calmly as he could not see us. Suddenly our environment was brightly lit. The pilot had fired a parachute flare, which enabled him to see us, and his machine gun started to rattle. Lots of bullets rained down on us and one of the riflemen got a grazing shot on his arm. We jumped into the trench at the side of the road and didn't move. The plane flew on and we eventually reached the Company. On one of the following days, our ravine was bombarded with gas shells. As we put on our gas masks straight away the gas did not do us any harm, but nineteen infantrymen further up the ravine who had been asleep were killed by the gas.

Start of July 1918 – The Spanish Flu and the Journey to Metz

Some soldiers had started to feel unwell for several days without anyone knowing what was wrong with them. Then we read in the newspapers about a new illness called the Spanish flu, because it had started in Spain. Now we knew. More and more soldiers were infected and shuffled around looking half-dead. Although they reported sick, hardly any of them went to hospital, as it had been declared that no more people should be classified as having minor illnesses or having been lightly wounded – there were only the seriously wounded and the dead. As our undernourished bodies, which had been weakened by all the exertions we had had to make, were unable to put up any resistance to the illness, it only took a few days before half of the team was ill. There was no question of providing them with care. We had to make do with the lousy grub from the field kitchen. Up until this point, I had remained free of illness.

One day the sergeant got all the NCOs who were present in the ravine to fall in. He said: 'An order has come from the Battalion that an NCO from the Machine Gun Company should go with a soldier from the 6th Company to Metz to bring a soldier, who deserted from the 6th Company and was apprehended there, back to his unit. Whom should I send, as I know that each of you would like to go?' I stepped forward and said: 'Sergeant, as I have not been home for four years, I would like to ask to be allowed to go.' 'Ah yes, but of course, Richert, you should go. I trust that you are all agreed?' he asked the others. They naturally all agreed. I was really pleased to get away from the Front for a few days. I was also looking forward to the change, as I had never travelled this route before.

The next morning the infantryman who was to accompany me reported to the Company, and the two of us headed off on foot. Before leaving we had been given a travel voucher and a food voucher by the sergeant. We boarded the train in Péronne. The young soldier kept addressing me formally as NCO this, NCO that. I told him to leave off, as we were simply comrades. He told me that he came from Metz. 'So,' I said, 'then you will have a chance to visit your parents.' 'I do not have any parents any more. They died. Only my married sister, whose husband is a prisoner of war in France, lives in Metz,' he replied. 'What do you think? Don't you think that he is luckier than we are?' I asked. 'Certainly,' replied the lad, 'he will not be shot dead there, and at all events he will be given better food.'

From Cambrai we travelled in a train, packed with soldiers going on leave, via Neufchâteau and Rethel to Sedan. Between Rethel and Sedan I felt the first waves of fever, alternating from glowing hot to cold shivers. Now the flu had hit me too. I became very thirsty and when the train stopped in Sedan, I got out and drank quite a lot of cold water from the station drinking fountain. The journey continued via Montmédy and we crossed the border into Lorraine at Fentsch. This area was a centre for the iron and steel industry, with a varied mixture of coal mines, enormous blast furnaces, workers' housing and factories. What enormous wealth existed here, both above and below ground! We travelled on through the main industrial centre of Hayingen and everywhere we saw the same picture – enormous blast furnaces, larger than anything I had seen before. At Diedenhofen we had to wait for two hours before catching a train to Metz. The two of us went into the town. Near the station the walls of a number of houses had been damaged by bomb splinters, as the town was often attacked by French aircraft at night. We went into a restaurant and were able to order quite a reasonable Mosel wine, but I did not feel completely well, as I kept feeling feverish. It was getting dark by the time that we boarded the train to Metz. When we got there, we went to the canteen at the station and on showing our food voucher we were each given a helping of food. The day was marked on the voucher so that you could not get two meals on the one day. After eating, we went to visit the soldier's sister. The whole town was shrouded in darkness in order to hide it from French aircraft. The soldier's sister had already gone to bed when we knocked at the door. She asked, 'Who's there?' and was surprised and happy to hear, 'Just me, your brother, and a comrade.' She opened up straight away and they embraced each other. Then she made us black coffee. We chatted on for a bit about why we were here, and so on. Afterwards we went to bed. God, what a pleasure to take off your clothes and sleep in a bed! Once again it had been three-quarters of a year since I had taken off my clothes and slept in a real bed.

The sergeant had given me three days for the journey: one day there, one day in Metz and one day for the return journey. On the first day in Metz I had to go with the soldier to visit his relatives. We were welcomed everywhere and people served up the little that they had for us. At midday I was supposed to go to my comrade's sister for lunch, but as I knew that she did not even have enough for herself, I went to the canteen at the station and was given two portions on showing the voucher which had been made out for two men. You ate in a hut. Two Italian prisoners had the job of tidying the dishes and clearing the tables. They both looked appallingly wretched. As one of them carried out the dishes I saw that he wiped them on the inside with his finger and then licked his finger. Oh dear, I thought. These poor people here in the canteen are half starving. I called them over and gave them one portion, which they ate up straight away. They nodded thankfully to me. In the afternoon I looked round the town, and in the evening I went to a cinema on the esplanade. Then I drank a few glasses of beer and went back to join my comrades. The next morning I went to a fast photo studio, but the picture did not turn out very well as I looked even worse than usual as a result of the flu.

In the afternoon the two of us went to the prison office and showed our authorisation. The sergeant there issued us with an authorisation to take the prisoner. I got him to make it out for the next day, as I wanted to sleep in a bed for another night. Then I went back to the canteen. The two Italian prisoners recognized me immediately once again and gave me a friendly nod. I fetched two portions again. As I had lost any hunger as a result of my flu I only took a sausage from one portion and gave everything else to the to Italians, who wolfed it down. Now I went to the urinal. Another Italian prisoner came in and bent down. I looked over and was quite surprised. The Italian picked up a cigarette end that was lying in the urine in the gutter, probably because he was intending to dry it and smoke it. How low people

239

can sink! He had probably been a passionate smoker in the past, and now, in captivity, he did not get anything to smoke. As I still had some cigarettes in my pocket, I gave them to him. How he thanked me – as if I had given him the largest of presents!

The next day we took our leave of the lady who had provided us with our quarters and went to fetch the prisoner. He was only nineteen years old and also came from Metz. I asked him whether he wanted to say goodbye to his relatives. He replied: 'Only my mother lives here and I don't want to see her as she is an old bag.' What ideal family circumstances! We went to the station. On the way I saw cherries, big black cherries, on sale in a shop. I purchased six pounds without delay, and the three of us ate them up straight away in the train. I really enjoyed this food that I had missed for so long! It was exactly four years since I had last eaten cherries. We travelled down though the beautiful Mosel Valley, through which we had travelled at night on the way there. Then we followed the same route back to Northern France. I was quite surprised when I heard an announcement in a station before Cambrai that everyone belonging to my Division should disembark. I asked what was up. Our Division had been relieved from the Front and was temporarily in quarters. I went to the information bureau and was told that the Second Battalion, Infantry Regiment 332 was in quarters in the village of Bévillers. We had to walk about six kilometres. On the fields we saw lots of French girls who were being forced to work under the supervision of German soldiers. On arriving in Bévillers, I handed the prisoner over to the Battalion Headquarters and went to join my Company.

In Quarters in Bévillers

I was allocated to quarters where three other NCOs were already living. This was my first contact with French civilians, as the villages at the Front had all been deserted by their inhabitants. The family with whom I was now quartered was very friendly. Father, mother and their nineteen-year-old daughter Lidga, a pretty girl who had already learnt to speak German well.

I went to report sick immediately as the flu had now got worse and I had become quite hoarse. There were about a hundred men standing outside the house where the doctor examined people. NCOs were examined first. You could hardly call it an examination. You were asked what was wrong. When I had answered, the medical NCO gave me a peppermint tablet about the size of a penny and the doctor said: 'Make some tea for yourself. Next please!' So I could go. Make some tea for yourself! That's about the same as saying die or kick it! I felt so inwardly angry that I hardly knew what to do. Make tea! I didn't even have a lump of sugar, nothing at all! I went back to my quarters and told the daughter about the result of the examination; then she went and spoke to her mother in French. Although I was not able to understand them,

I could see that they were talking about me. Then the girl came, led me to a room, and said that I should go to bed. Then she went down; her mother came and, smiling, spread a duvet over me, indicating in a friendly way that I should sweat it out. After a while she came to me with hot sugared tea and made sure that I drank it. Then she got me to drink another cup. Now I started to sweat. My whole body just dripped with sweat. NCO Peters came to see how I was doing. I asked him to fetch my other shirt from my knapsack. He did so, and when I had sweated enough I put on the fresh shirt and got up. Then the woman came up; she quickly changed the bed-clothes and made me get back into bed. How grateful I was to these good people! How good it was for me that someone cared for me again! After a while the woman brought me a little piece of roast meat with sauce, together with a piece of white bread, followed by a cup of cocoa. After that I did not feel like staying in bed any more. I got up and went downstairs.

In the evening, the family invited us all to have a cup of cocoa with them. The inhabitants of the part of France and Belgium occupied by the Germans were sent foodstuffs from America, to prevent them from starving. The Germans had to promise to distribute these foodstuffs and not take any of them for themselves. As a result, these people had sugar, cocoa, meat and white bread, in short: everything you need for a reasonably decent life. If only we could stay here for longer! That was my most fervent wish. But then we were ordered: 'Go to the station tomorrow and board the train; the destination is unknown.' So the next morning we had to bid farewell. I offered to give the good woman ten Marks to thank her for her efforts, but she firmly refused the money. I exchanged addresses with her daughter, so that we would be able to let each other know how we were getting on. Then I thanked her mother once more, and left.

As I felt weak and wretched, I sat on a machine gun waggon until we reached the station. We travelled back along the same line on which I had returned two days before. I was hoping that we might be transferred to the Front in Alsace, because it was quieter than in the north, and I would have loved to see my homeland again – but I was wrong. The train stopped in Conflans, not far from the border to Lorraine. We left the train and marched southwards towards the Front. In Mars-la-Tour I stayed behind as my condition had worsened during the journey. I went to the treatment station there and reported sick. After the examination the doctor said: 'The flu has really got to you.' 'I certainly think so,' I replied. 'You should stay here for the time being,' the doctor told me. I was allocated to a hut which was already occupied by eight men who sat around feeling bored. We had metal bunks to sleep on, with straw mattresses full of lice on top, and the food was pure misery for ill people. In the morning we got black coffee, which was naturally coffee substitute without any sugar, and a slice of army bread with jam on it. Even a pig would have refused the soup made from dried

241

vegetables which we were given at midday. In the evening we got the same as we had in the morning. I was very fed up with it. In order to get some diversion, I asked the doctor for permission to go out, and he allowed me to do so. On the second afternoon I went to a cinema which had been set up by the army in Mars-la-Tour. There were two good features shown, followed by a comedy film which, despite my miserable state, made me laugh heartily and forget the war, the soldier's life and the flu. As soon as the performance was over, it was back to gruesome reality. The next morning I asked the doctor if I could be transferred to a military hospital, but he could do nothing – everything was full up.

The next day I went out for a walk and came across an enormous memorial. It was on the battlefield of Mars-la-Tour at the place where the famous death-ride of the German Cuirassiers and Uhlans took place during the war of 1870. The French Cuirassiers brought them to a halt and the remaining German riders were driven back. Carved in stone on one side of the memorial was a depiction of the collision of the French and German cavalry, while on the other side was a depiction of French infantry lines under fire. On the other two sides were inscriptions in French, which I was unable to understand. Underneath the memorial you could go down to a room like a cellar without a door. This contained skulls and human bones – presumably remains which had been gathered from the fields. By going up a small hill I was able to get a splendid view across the broad plain, dotted with villages and surrounded in the distance to the south and the west by a range of seemingly blue hills. From far in the distance, scarcely perceptible, came the boom, boom of the artillery – at Verdun and at the fortress of Toul, which was further south.

As the food in the treatment station did not improve, I reported that I was well again, because I wanted to return to the Company rather than stay there. 'Well, lad,' said the doctor, 'there's no question of you being well again. Why are you saying that you are well?' 'Because I don't like it here and the food is too poor. I think it would be better with the Company. When I get there, I will be able to stay with the waggons behind the front until I get well again.' 'Well, if you really want to!' said the doctor, and signed my discharge paper. I fastened my knapsack with my belongings in it onto my back and marched off in the direction my Regiment had taken. The Front was still about thirty to thirty five kilometres away. Of course I did not know where my Regiment was, but I was not worried about it. It was a pleasant summer day without being too hot, round about the tenth of July 1918. Behind me I heard the sound of hooves and saw a troop of emaciated horses approaching, accompanied by a soldier. I waited and asked the soldier if he would let me ride on one of the horses as I had the flu and was not able to walk very well. Only two of the horses had saddles. I mounted the horse – a new experience. Anyway, the horse was surprised by my riding skills.

Gradually I got used to it and was able to match my movements to the horse's pace. As I went on I chatted to the soldier who was walking beside me. I must have looked odd, because I have never seen a soldier riding a horse with a pack on his back. On the way, a major asked me what right I had to be riding a horse. I explained that I was ill with the flu and was on my way to find my Regiment. I had mounted the horse because I was feeling weak. I was allowed to continue my journey. I did not want the horse to trot in case I fell off. The horse seemed happy to walk. Towards evening we reached the village of Jonville, which was the destination for the horses. I continued on foot and reached the town of Thiaucourt, where I spent the night.

The next morning I met some soldiers from my Battalion who told me that my Regiment was in position. After asking around for a while I eventually found my Company about three kilometres from Thiaucourt based in a camp in the forest which consisted of huts and dugouts. The teams were in position. Only some reserve gunners, the drivers, the horses, the Company Sergeant, the Company Clerk and the Company tradesmen were there. I reported back to the Company Sergeant Bukies, who was a good friend of mine. 'Well, Richert,' he said, 'you don't look well.' 'I'm not but I could not stand it any longer in the miserable treatment station where I was.' 'No bother,' said the Sergeant, 'you can just stay here until you have recovered.' So I stayed and found myself a place in a dugout where I lay about and the Company Cook took care of it that I got somewhat better food than the rest of the people. Ahead of us at the edge of the woods a road was being built using Italian prisoners. How poorly these poor people looked, yellow, more gray-yellow with collapsed faces, in short: half-starved. It was pitiful. They kept scanning the bushes looking for berries or whatever they could get hold of. Whenever one of them saw something, he would rush to get it and eat it. These people were not at the Front, but despite that they suffered terribly.

After I had spent about six days in the camp the Sergeant came to me and said: 'Well Richert, how are you coming on? NCO Peters is due to go on leave. Would you be able to take over? I also want to tell you that you will soon be promoted to Senior NCO. The application has already been made.' 'I will give it a try,' I said, 'it is fairly quiet in position here.' So I headed off the next morning. The sergeant had shown me the way on the map. On a hill I passed through the ruins of the village of Viéville-en-Hay. Well hidden in the ruins of the last houses was a German battery. It disgusted me to see the cursed game of war once again. Behind the French Front I saw a number of French observation balloons hanging in the sky. I passed the corner of a wood and encountered two batteries quite close to each other. Then I found a communication trench which went in a zigzag to the front line. When I encountered a machine gun from my Company I asked for NCO Peters; I was told that I could find him about two hundred metres further to the

243

left. I looked over to the French position and was overcome with a powerful longing. If I could just get over there then I would be saved, I would be in touch with home, and would certainly be able to see my relatives again soon! At this moment, I resolved that if it were possible, I would desert. I went along the trench, which was very sturdily built and had bomb-proof dugouts. I soon found Peters. 'I am supposed to relieve you, Joseph! You are to go on leave!' At this moment I thought that I might be seeing Peters, who was a good loyal comrade of mine, for the last time. On bidding him farewell I pressed his hand more firmly than usual and looked straight in his eyes. 'Nicki, watch out, there is a lot of barbed wire here. By the way, I wish you luck!' I was rather dismayed that Peters, who was a bright lad, might have read my thoughts. Although I knew that I could trust him implicitly I did not say any more about my intentions.

'One more thing, Nicki,' he continued. 'We have got a revolting blighter as a platoon leader. He's sitting down in the dugout. I have already had a real go at him. Do not let this greenhorn step on your toes!' We shook hands again. 'Goodbye and good luck!' Then Peters disappeared round the next traverse.

Now I was curious to get to know the new Platoon Leader and went down the stair which led to the dugout. I had to climb down thirty steps until I reached the dugout, which was lit using electricity. Each day when the food was collected they also brought a battery, which was sufficient for twenty-four hours. The new sergeant, a lad under the age of twenty, was sitting at a little table. I unhurriedly swung off my knapsack, undid my webbing, and said that I was here to replace NCO Peters. I saw straight away that my relaxed approach did not suit this young lad. He would have preferred me to stand to attention and report to him formally. He asked me for my name and then said: 'There doesn't seem to be much discipline around here!' I simply replied: 'It's not needed either. With a few exceptions, we live in the Company on as comradely a way as possible. In my opinion it is not at all necessary for a person in charge to make his subordinates feel his position of power.' 'I am not used to this,' replied the sergeant. 'If you are in charge you must always be treated with respect!' 'If you take this approach, you would soon be hated by your subordinates instead of being respected, and in certain circumstances your life might be dependent upon whether people love you or hate you!' 'What do you mean by that?' he asked in astonishment. 'Just imagine that you were seriously injured in a battle and could not move. If you are popular, then your subordinates would hardly leave you in the lurch, but if you are hated nobody would risk themselves to save you and you would have to die miserably. Have you never been at the Front before?' I asked. 'No,' he said, 'I am a one-year volunteer and until now I have always been in a garrison. I have to spend six weeks at the Front and then return for officer training. Afterwards I will be a lieutenant.' 'Do you see, sergeant, in my opinion that shows the biggest injustice in the

German army, that one year's service is sufficient to become a lieutenant, even if the person concerned almost doesn't have a clue about military things. In other words: if a father has the money to enable his son to study, the way is opened to him to become an officer after only one year's service or less. On the other hand, the door is closed to other soldiers who have served actively and have been in the field for four years. They can't become officers, even though they would be better suited to lead a company than all the one-year volunteers put together.' The young sergeant had to agree with me but I could see that he felt offended.

Then I went up to my team. They were standing round in the trench having a smoke and enjoying the sunshine. They had all been in my team before and I knew they were good lads. We always talked informally to each other.[73] NCO Gustav Beck's team was based in the same dugout as mine. He came from Lorraine. In 1916 he was in Regiment 44, then in Regiment 260, and now he was in Regiment 332 – just the same as me. We were good friends too. I looked out over the cover to see what it was like – everywhere you could see the horror of devastation. The Front had been situated here since the end of September 1914. Everything was dug up – full of holes and overgrown with thistles, thorns and old scrawny grass with patches of green in between. There were rusty old barbed wire obstacles stretching every-where – between the lines I counted twelve barbed wire entanglements. It was really not going to be that simple to make a break for it! However, I was determined to go and was just waiting for the right opportunity. The ground sloped gently down from the position and then it seemed to go down steeply. You could see where the shell-damaged top of the church steeple from the village of Régnieville protruded over the horizon, but you could not see the village. However, it had been shot to pieces. I fetched the map from the sergeant to orientate myself better. Off to the right were the ruins of the village of Lironville, while even further to the right were the villages of Flirey and Essey where I had had to take part in heavy fighting in September 1914 with Regiment 112. I could not recognize anything any more as both the villages and the woods – in short, everything – had been shot-up and destroyed. Beyond the village of Régnieville the ground sloped gently upwards. The enemy positions were situated there. It was full of trenches and wire entangle-ments so that you could not tell which position the enemy was actually occupying. The sentries who served in the listening post at night believed that the enemy forward posts were located in the village of Régnieville, as they had often seen a fiery glow when someone lit up a cigarette or a pipe. That was all very interesting to me as these details would be to my advantage in getting over safely. If only I knew who was facing us! Some

[73] Using the '*du*' form.

245

people said it was the French, some said it was black troops, while yet others said it was Americans. I spent hours every day looking across with my binoculars but I could not see French, black or American troops; it all looked empty and deserted. Only now and then you could hear artillery firing from the wood behind their position. Then the shells would whizz over us and explode in the woods behind us, somewhere near the German batteries. Sometimes, especially at night, shells also landed near us. Then everyone would rush down into the dugout, where we were perfectly safe.

All the time I kept thinking: if I could only get over there! But where to begin? And to try it on my own seemed too reckless, especially as I did not speak a word of French. On the fourth morning I noticed that, on a position to the right, three French observation balloons had gone up where they usually only had one. We soon found out why. The German position was suddenly subjected to a fearful hail of shells, which lasted for almost an hour. Then the firing subsided; we heard that the French had forced their way into the German trench and taken prisoners before withdrawing to their own trenches again.

In the afternoon we heard a rumour that the French and the Americans had started an offensive on the Marne and made progress. We were to leave soon and move there. All the soldiers were more than a little frightened at the prospect of landing in a hell like that. My resolution to make the attempt to desert soon increased.

Preparation for Defection

On the following Wednesday, the 23rd of July 1918, we once again had a miserable lunch – burnt dried vegetables. NCO Beck and I were standing on our own up in the trench shovelling down the terrible muck. Suddenly, in an abrupt outburst of rage, Beck took his canteen and its contents and flung it against the traverse near him. 'Goddamit!' he raged. 'I've just about had enough of this!' I pointed across towards the French front as if to say: 'What do you think, Gustav?' He suddenly looked at me and said: 'Would you be willing to come?' I said yes, and Gustav now told me that for several days he had thought of little else but defection. But how – that was another matter. If we went north we had the pleasant prospect of being killed. If we got over safely here, we would be saved. If we were killed while deserting, then all our suffering would be over.

Just at that moment an infantry lance corporal from Lower Alsace by the name of Pfaff, whom we both knew well, walked past. He was a little energetic fellow who persisted in growing a royale beard,[74] much to the

[74] A pointed beard made fashionable during the reign of Napoleon III in France.

annoyance of the officers, although he was often ordered to shave it off. As he was walking past he suddenly stopped close to us and asked quietly: 'Will you come with me tonight?' 'Where to?' I asked. 'Across,' he replied tersely. 'How are you planning to do it, Pfaff?' I said. 'Tonight I am on sentry duty and have to go to the listening post. There's quite a good chance of disappearing from there.' 'Listen, Pfaff, we have just agreed to desert. We just didn't know how.' 'Let's do it like this,' said Pfaff, 'as soon as it gets dark come to the outpost and we'll work out how to get away.' We promised to go there, and Pfaff left us. 'Listen, Nickel,' said Beck, 'how are we going to get away from our machine gun without catching attention. We are under orders not to leave the machine guns. You know what a crazy zealous poser our platoon leader is.'

I thought for a while and after making certain that nobody noticed I took several ammunition boxes with their contents and threw them over the top of the trench into the long grass. 'What are you doing, Nickel?' asked Beck. I said: 'In the evening I will tell the sergeant that several ammunition boxes have been pilfered from us – probably by the infantry, who have the light machine guns. I will volunteer to get us some replacements.' 'That might just work,' replied Beck.

It gradually grew dark. What would the night bring – life or death? As the sun set on the horizon behind the distant defences of the Fortress of Toul I thought: if I see you again tomorrow then I will be saved. If not, then it's all over. I felt a very unpleasant sensation in my chest as the uncertainty of our venture was a torture to me.

I went down into the dugout. I inobtrusively put my handkerchief and my soap into one rear pocket of my jacket and a piece of army bread into the other and then reported the 'theft' of our ammunition to the sergeant. 'My God!' he flared up. 'What are we going to do now? It would not be a good idea to report this to the Company Commander.' I said: 'Sergeant, I know a means which does not involve reporting it to the Company Commander. We will just go and steal the missing boxes from the light machine guns.' 'Would you manage to do that?' asked the sergeant. 'It should be simple, but I will need some help. I cannot carry four boxes on my own.' 'Good, take someone else with you.' I said: 'I would like to take NCO Beck with me. He's a smart fellow.' 'That's not on – that both gun commanders are away at the same time' said the sergeant. I replied: 'The lance corporals can take charge of the machine guns for the time involved; in any case it's quiet and we'll be back in half an hour.' 'Well, go if you like.'

As we were not allowed to move about the trench without weapons I put on my webbing with my bayonet and my Mauser pistol, loaded with nine shots. I had already put two clips of nine bullets each in my jacket pocket, and had also folded a new newspaper and shoved it in the sleeve of my jacket in order to have something white to wave with. Then each of us hung

247

a couple of hand grenades on our webbing and we left the dugout. The first step towards our peril or to the route to life and freedom had been taken. I felt sorry that I had to leave my team and all my comrades without being able to say goodbye.

The Night of the 23rd to the 24th of July 1918 – Defection to the French

We made our way along the trench: as it was already getting dark there were sentries posted every few yards. When we reached the communication trench leading to the outpost we turned into it and soon got there. It was about two hundred metres long. The outpost was occupied by a group of eight infantrymen and an NCO, and had a sturdy dugout. We chatted with the NCO for a while and then we went to see the listening posts, which were about thirty steps further on. Pfaff followed on without catching attention. We had still not spoken to him. The listening posts, which were not occupied, were surrounded by a chaotic barbed wire entanglement. Beck and Pfaff were just about to get their legs up to get through the wire when I heard steps in the trench. 'Psst,' I went quietly and then I said out loud 'nobody will be able to reach the men listening here' and jumped back down again, followed by Beck and Pfaff. We chatted with the NCO again and went back to the outpost. Two men went into position in the listening posts. The First Lieutenant of the 5th Company, who was responsible for the outpost, turned up to check up on it. When he saw Beck and I he curtly asked 'Who's this then?' I straightened up and said: 'We are two NCOs from the heavy machine guns and we wanted to see where the outpost was situated so that if the enemy were to attack we would not shoot the men in the outpost in the back.' 'Good for you,' said the first lieutenant. 'If all the soldiers had the same interest as you do we would have won by now.' I thought to myself: 'if only you knew and understood our intentions!'

Now Beck and I went back into the communication trench. We were both convinced that we would be unable to do anything this night. Pfaff came running up behind us and murmured 'Off we go!' Before we knew it he was out of the trench and had disappeared in the tall grass. The two of us climbed after him and found him waiting in an old shell-hole. We were in between two lines of barbed wire. The one behind us hid us from the sentries in the main trenches. We crawled along the line of barbed wire ahead of us and found an opening, formed by two shells that had landed one behind the other. We crawled through the barbed wire there, tearing our clothes slightly in the process. We carried on, crawling on all fours, making our way through a deep old trench and then we came to a halt behind a mound of earth. Here we quietly promised each other not to leave anyone behind,

248

whatever happened. I put up my head for a moment and saw the two tree stumps that I had seen ahead of me when I was in the listening post about thirty paces to the left. I quietly told Pfaff that we were about thirty paces to the right of the listening post. 'We need to go closer to the listening post,' he said, 'because there is a passage through the broad barbed wire entanglement, where the top wires have been cut to enable patrols to get through.' My God, I thought, what will become of us? So we crawled several metres further to the left towards the listening post. Right enough, we found the passage in the entanglement. Pfaff got up and went crouching through the wire. When he was nearly through I heard the sentries speaking less than twenty metres ahead, and bang bang went two shots. We had been discovered! Pfaff had disappeared on the other side of the wire. Now Beck got up and overcame the obstacle as quickly as possible. They fired four shots at him. He too disappeared on the other side of this obstacle.

Now I crept into the gap, but as it was only the upper wires which had been cut, I got caught and had to free myself with my hands. When I reached about the middle of the wire I got really caught up. As soon as I moved, the wire grated all around me. What should I do? Creeping through was impossible. If I got up, there was a risk that I would be shot, because the sentries had already become aware of my position. I got pretty anxious, freed myself from the wire as best I could, and stood up. Rip, I had holes in my trousers and my jacket. I had hardly stood up before two shots were fired. I rushed forwards as quickly as I could, and at the moment when I threw myself to the ground on the far side of the wire another shot was fired. I ran on all fours as fast as I could, following the grass which had been trampled down, then I stopped for a moment and called out quietly: 'Beck! Pfaff!' A few steps ahead of me I could see an arm held up holding a cap. I crept to them as quickly as possible. We quickly confirmed that none of us had been injured. We were all in one piece, but we all had a few scratches from the wire. Pfaff said: 'We must get away as quickly as possible, because the First Lieutenant will certainly get the people in the outpost to try and catch us.' We could not risk the possibility of being taken captive, because in that case we would be court martialled and shot. In this circumstance we would have had to defend our lives against our own soldiers. We climbed through three further wire entanglements. By now our uniforms were terribly torn, and the scratches in our skin caused by the rusty barbed wire were painful.

We reached an old trench that led towards the French. It got deeper and deeper and then stopped abruptly; it was like being in a sack. I put my back to the wall. I folded my hands together and Pfaff climbed onto them and from there onto my shoulders, then he held tight to the grass and climbed out. Beck did the same. Then I stretched my hands in the air. The two of them, lying on their stomachs, grabbed hold of me and pulled me up, while I pushed with my legs to help. Then we got going again. We climbed over two further narrow wire obstacles and saw the ruined village of Régnieville lying below us. There was no further obstacle on the way down to the village. We had now survived the danger from the rear; now the danger came from ahead.

As Beck and Pfaff spoke French, I suggested that they should call to the people in the French outpost situated in the ruins. 'We can't do that, otherwise the First Lieutenant who is following us will know where we are!' So we ran down the slope towards the ruins. I was afraid that at any moment that we would see a flash in the ruins and that we would be hit. Nothing of the kind occurred. We reached the ruins; everything was dead quiet, nothing moved. We continued to listen for a while; nothing, nothing at all. Pfaff jumped into an old trench which led round the church. He landed on a piece of corrugated iron lying in the trench, which caused a great din. We listened once again – it was as quiet as could be. Then the French artillery started to fire. The shells flew over us in high arcs and impacted behind the German positions. As a result of the stress and the running we were all bathed in sweat. It was a mild summer's evening, and the moon lit everything almost as bright as day. We went carefully along the trench, which led towards the French position and gradually led uphill. Every so often we stopped and listened. Nothing could be heard other than some rifle shots, the odd rattle of a machine gun and the sound of some close and some distant single artillery shots. It was very unpleasant not to know who was ahead of us, or where they were located. So we went carefully on, stopping every so often to listen. We passed old tunnels and dugouts, which seemed to yawn darkly towards us. We reached a position which crossed with the communication trench. There was a board fastened to a pole, but it was not bright enough to be able to read what was written on it. I shone my torch into the trench. We saw from the many footprints that the trench was used frequently. We went on and came to another position which, like the previous one, crossed the communication trench. Pfaff said: 'I am certain that we have passed through the French infantry positions and have just not encountered a sentry.' 'Don't believe it!' I replied quietly. I asked the two of them to call out to the French, or whoever it was in the trenches, but they still did not trust themselves to do so for fear of the pursuing Germans. With our pistols at the ready we went carefully on. We came to a so-called Spanish rider[75] in the trench. That is what the portable wooden obstacles covered with barbed wire were called. Now I was convinced that we had to be near the French. We worked our way past the obstacle. A few steps further there was a structure like a tube in the trench, surrounded by plain wire. We crawled through on all fours, one after the other. While doing so our backs touched some empty tin cans, which banged against each other causing a

---

[75] The term used in English is based on French: *Cheval de frise.*

250

ringing sound. That was certainly an alarm signal for the French sentries. Once again I said quietly to my comrade that they should, for the love of God, call to the French. They still did not want to, and they went on, stopping and listening behind the next traverse.

I was a few steps behind them and noticed a French soldier jump up beside the trench on the other side of the traverse; he got out of the trench and ran back. I immediately thought: that was the man from the listening post, who has now gone to warn the outpost. I went to the others and called in a low voice: 'Call now! I have just seen a Frenchman running back!' The three of us were very stressed at this moment. The two of them were just about to call when we heard shots from ahead and the bullets hit the trench behind us. Now the French shouted, while they continued to fire. Now Beck and Pfaff called out: 'We are three men from Alsace who want to join you! *Vive la France!*' but in the wild shooting that now started the French could not understand what they said. Pfaff, who was unbelievably brave, went round the traverse towards the French. Beck wanted to follow him. At the same moment I heard a small click. This click was made by the spring in a hand grenade when it is released on being thrown. 'Beck!' I called, 'stand still! They have thrown a hand grenade!' and I pulled him into cover behind the traverse. Boom went the hand grenade on the other side. At the same moment it went boom once again. A second had grenade had exploded. Then we heard Pfaff scream. In any event, he had been hit. Now the smoke from the hand grenades came round the traverse and enveloped us completely. When I looked round, Beck had disappeared. He must have gone round the traverse.

I also was about to go round the traverse when someone called to me in French from above. I looked up. There stood a Frenchman who held up a hand grenade in a threatening gesture. I immediately dropped my pistol, pulled my newspaper out of my sleeve and put my hands up calling: '*Alsacien, deserteur!*' The Frenchman called: '*Combien?*' I understood the word: How much? I thought 'three' was the same as '*treize*' and called '*treize!*' instead of '*trois.*' The Frenchman bent down and seemed to be looking to find the thirteen men. However when he did not see anyone else but me in the trench, he called again '*Combien?*' whereupon I held up three fingers to him. He reached down to me; I quickly undid my webbing and let it fall, then I reached up my hand to him, he pulled, and I climbed out of the trench. Thank God! I thought to myself. Now I have survived it, and lowered my arms. The Frenchman, who did not seem to really trust me, jumped back from me and raised the hand grenade threateningly again. I put up my hands again and repeated: '*Alsacien, deserteur.*' Now the Frenchman shook me by the hand and patted me on the shoulder. I can't describe how happy I was at this moment.

251

I now immediately thought of Pfaff as I heard him groaning quietly. I said to the Frenchman *'Kamerad blessé'* and pointed to myself and into the trench. The Frenchman signalled to me that I should just go. I jumped back in at the same place where I had climbed out and went round the traverse meaning to go to Pfaff. There were lots of Frenchmen there who were talking to each other in a lively confused way. Like lightning one of them held his pistol to my forehead so that I felt the cold muzzle. Equally quickly another one pointed his bayonet at my chest. Like the wind my arms shot up in the air again and I said my little piece: *'Alsacien, deserteur!'* They immediately let go and I heard someone say: *'C'est le troisième.'* Beck had actually told them already that there was a third man in the trench. All this since the first shot had taken less than three minutes.

I went to Pfaff straight away – he was lying unconscious at the foot of the trench and he groaned lightly with every breath. I pushed the Frenchmen who were caring for him aside and felt his uniform all over, because the light of the moon did not reach the bottom of the trench, so you could not see where Pfaff had been wounded. When I was feeling his left thigh I noticed it was damp and at the same time I felt warm blood, which sprayed jerkily into my hand. Shot in the upper thigh – artery hit flashed through my head. The best treatment was to tie up the thigh to prevent him from bleeding to death. I quickly undid the belt holding up his trousers and opened his trousers and his underpants. Beck helped me to raise up his body a bit. Then we pulled down his trousers. I went to pull off my necktie in order to use it to tie up his leg. Crack, the old washed-out thing had torn in half. One of the Frenchmen who were standing around watching gave me a piece of strong string, which I then tied loosely round his thigh above the wound. Then I broke a piece of wood about thirty centimetres long from the trench planking, put it out-side the thigh between the string and the leg, and turned the wood. In this way the string was tightened so much that it cut into the flesh of the thigh and pressed the artery shut. The bleeding stopped immediately. The French-men patted me on the shoulder and said that I had done it well. Pfaff was still unconscious. Beck wanted to give him a piece of sugar in his mouth. One of the Frenchmen took the piece of sugar from his hand, poured a fluid smelling strongly of alcohol onto it, and then shoved it into Pfaff's mouth. He came to immediately. The first words that he said were *'Moi mourir pour la France!'* which I did not understand, but Beck translated it for me. I then said to Pfaff that he was not so seriously wounded and that his leg had been bound up. The Frenchmen were very friendly towards us. They all wanted to shake our hands. Some of them gave us cigarettes, while others gave us a piece of chocolate or offered us wine from their canteens. I drank a few mouthfuls as I had got very thirsty as a result of the stress. This drink seemed very strange to me, because when serving with the Prussians all we got was stale substitute coffee to drink. Then one of the Frenchmen lit me up a cigarette which I was hardly able to smoke as it was so strong.

We were guided through the French position by a young officer and two soldiers. As the whole complement of men in the trenches had been put on alert, they stood one after the other in their firing positions. As we passed them, they all said friendly words, which I naturally did not understand. As we were going to the rear through the communication trench two ambulance men carrying a stretcher passed us on the way to fetch Pfaff. Beck chatted with the soldier ahead of him. The young officer who was walking behind me suddenly spoke to me in Alsace dialect with a strong French accent: 'Where do you come from?' Without thinking, I replied in High German. 'You are a German, you don't speak dialect,' to which I replied in dialect: 'No, I am from St Ulrich near Dammerkirch.' 'So, you're from there,' said the officer. 'Tell me, who is the mayor in Dannemarie?'[76] With the best will in the world, I did not know. I told him that I did not know and that I had been away from home for five years and had forgotten all this sort of thing. 'Well then, who is the bookbinder who lives in Kriz Street?' he asked. 'It used to be Hartmann,' I replied. 'That's right,' said the lieutenant, 'I often went through St Ulrich when we marched to Seppois-le-Bas.' I asked him if St Ulrich had been damaged. He did not think so, but he was not able to remember exactly how it was.

We chatted on about this and that until we arrived at a camp in the woods. He told me that he came from Rosheim in Alsace. In the camp lots of soldiers who wanted to see us came out of their dugouts. Beck could not keep up with all the questions they asked him. They pretty well left me in peace as they saw that I did not understand anything. What struck me most about these soldiers was how lively they were and that they had fat round faces – quite different from the half-starved gaunt Germans, almost all of whom had yellowish faces. Beck had to go to the Company Commander in the dugout where he was interrogated. My gas mask was taken from me. Several soldiers brought me wine and cigarettes. I drank two tumblers full, and was expected to drink more, but I decided not to as it was going to my head. I was really not used to drinking wine any more. My back was cold too, as I had a soaking wet shirt as a consequence of sweating. Some people brought me white bread and cheese. I reached into my jacket pocket and gave them my army bread. They smelled it and went 'Brrr', as if it were not possible to eat something like that, while during the last two years we could simply not get enough of it. I started to eat the white bread straight away and stroked my stomach to show them how much I liked it. They all laughed and although we could not make ourselves understood by a single

[76] The French name for Dammerkirch.

253

word we were the best of friends. Then a Frenchman came and asked me in German: 'What do people think of Hindenburg and Ludendorff?' I told him that people loved Hindenburg and hated Ludendorff. He then asked if we knew that the Germans had been repulsed on the 19th to the 20th of July on the Marne and that the big French-English-American offensive had started. I gave him the new German newspaper, for which he was very grateful. In the meantime, Beck's interrogation was over and we were led further to the rear by two soldiers. When we reached a road in a wood, which crossed another road near a railway bridge, the French indicated to us that we should run through at the double. They explained to Beck that this place was often bombarded by the Germans at night. Naturally we ran as fast as we could, as we did not want to get hurt at this stage. Then the two Frenchmen told us that there was no more danger.

Saved! Further and Further from the Front

I can't describe how happy I was to know that my life was safe and that I had put the miserable life at the Front and the starvation behind me. I believe that however much pleasure anything else in my life may give me, I will never be able to feel such a deep sense of well-being again. When I thought of my parents, and my mother in particular, I knew how happy they would be when they heard the news that I was safe and that I would be able to write to them. I wanted to let them know as soon as possible. Beck said: 'Our Platoon Leader, the snotty brat, will have to wait for a long time for his ammunition boxes. He will certainly get into trouble since both his NCOs have scarpered.' We both had to laugh as we imagined his expression on discovering that that we had both left for good. We marched along a road that ran past a wood on one side of the Front. There were a large number of batteries mounted there. Further forward, hundreds of soldiers were busy building more mountings for guns. 'Look, Gustav,' I said to Beck, 'It won't take long before it goes crazy here.'

We were taken to a large hut in the woods which was occupied by the Regimental Headquarters. It was about three o'clock in the morning and it was still dark. Beck had to go in first then it was my turn. There was only a clerk there, but he spoke very good German. 'Ah,' he said, 'you have obviously had enough black bread and wanted to try some white bread.' I laughed and said: 'You're not quite right there, because for the last two years I have hardly ever had enough black bread to eat because I wasn't given it.' He laughed too and then asked me in a friendly way: 'Would you be so kind as to put everything you have in your pockets on the table.' I started to dig out and put all my belongings onto the table. Wallet, pencil, pocket knife, handkerchief, clock, pocket mirror, comb, towel, torch and compass. The clerk took my wallet and gave me back the thirty Marks that were in it. He kept the wallet and the compass. He let me take everything else back, and then I was allowed to leave. Two soldiers, who took bicycles with them, led us further back. At daybreak we went through a village. All the barn doors were open, and in each barn stood a tank.

By the time it was fully light we reached another village in which the Brigade Headquarters were based. As the gentlemen were still asleep, we had to wait for an hour. A regiment of Moroccans came marching into the village in full marching order. I thought to myself: 'It doesn't seem to be so comfortable being on the French side if you have to march like that so early in the morning.' The Moroccans spread out into the barns. An officer cursed and swore at them and when two of the Moroccans came to the well with a kettle he went up to one of them and kicked him hard twice. I was quite flabbergasted. I had only seen something like this once on the German side. Lots of the Moroccans came to us, as did some Frenchmen who belonged to the Moroccan regiment. They were all very friendly and gave us cigarettes. One of the Frenchmen pulled my sleeve and said to me in quite genuine Mülhausen Alsace dialect: 'Hey, listen for a minute. What is the situation – is there anything left over there?' 'There's not much left,' I replied. He then asked 'Man, how much longer can they hold out?' Not much longer. The soldiers do not want it any more nor do the people at home,' was my answer. He then told me that he came from Mülhausen, and that he too had almost had enough, as the Moroccans were always in the thick of the fighting. They had come from Villers-Bretonneux outside Amiens on the 24th and 25th of April, and from then on they had been forced to take part in terrible events. So we had been opposite each other in Villers-Bretonneux, what a coincidence. All of a sudden the angry officer came running up and snarled at us in French. I stood still; I did not understand what he was saying. He looked at us and said something of which I only understood the word 'Boches'. Beck later explained to me that he had said that even if we were from Alsace we were just the same Boches as the Germans. Well, if he had gone to where I wished him to go! Oh dear, now Beck was to be interrogated! I did not have to go in. Then we went on. This time we were accompanied by two old soldiers. On the way we encountered a number of Moroccans who had collapsed at the side of the road. We reached an inn where the Divisional Headquarters were based. It was the same here as on the German side – the higher your salary, the further back you were, and the safer you were. The office of the general in charge of the division was in a large hut. Beck had to go in first. It lasted at least half an hour until he came out again. Then it was my turn.

I went into the hut and stood to attention in front of the general in charge of the division. He beckoned me forward and asked me in broken German: 'Why have you come to us now?' The question was a bit tricky. I answered:

'Because in the past I either lacked the courage or the opportunity, because I was starving, because I did not want to shoot at the French, and because generally I had had enough of war.' He now asked: 'Why did you not want to shoot at the French?' I answered: 'Because I preferred them to the Germans and because my parents, who lived in the part of Alsace occupied by the French, had only good things to report of them.' 'Right,' said the general, 'now come here.' He led me to a map which occupied the full length of the wall in the hut and represented the section of the Front covered by his division. This map really astonished me. I had never seen anything like it before: each detail, each dugout, each battery, and each footpath – in short, everything was recorded. Now the general of the division asked me where I had crossed over. I told him that I had headed straight for the church in the village of Régnieville. He asked me: 'You were with the machine gun company?' to which I answered 'yes'. Then he showed me the dugout in the German position where I lived and it was, without a doubt, accurate. Now he said that I should tell him what I knew about the German position, where the batteries were located, where the Machine Gun Company's waggons were located, and so on. As I had deserted to save my life and not to betray my former comrades I told him that I had been ill in the sick bay with the flu, that I had rejoined the Company in a wood somewhere behind the German lines towards evening and that I had been taken into position by a guide the same night. I had not been able to see in the darkness, and as I was in charge of my gun I had orders not to leave it, so with the best will in the world I did not know any more. The general looked at me searchingly and said: 'You do not want to betray your former comrades. We know it all already anyway.' Now he showed me all the batteries which I had seen as I had gone into position, the place where the Battalion Commander was based, where the Battalion Canteen was situated, the route the food collectors took – in short, everything – and it stood there as if it had fallen from the sky. I thought: 'Why don't the French shoot everything to pieces if they know where everything is. The general saw how I was thinking and told me what I had thought, adding: 'Just you wait!'

I was allowed to go. We were taken into a kitchen and were given coffee, white bread, cooked ham and butter. How good the coffee was! That was coffee as I remembered it, strong and sweet. I had not had coffee like it for several long years. Then a car drove up to the kitchen. We had to get in and off we went. Beck and I were the happiest people in the world. This beautiful journey by car on a splendid summer's morning was taking us further and further from the Front, and each of had a slice of bread and cooked ham to eat! What more could you wish for? We soon reached the Fortress of Toul. We stopped in the street in front of a large building. Beck was led in. I had to sit outside supervised by a soldier. Lots of inquisitive civilians came along to look at me. I really looked splendid! My jacket and trousers were all torn. One of my puttees was in tatters, while the other one was completely missing – it had probably got torn in two by the barbed wire and had then rolled up and fallen off, without me noticing, while I was running. I did not look very good either, especially as I was just recovering from the flu. I also started to feel sleepy. But despite that I felt as happy as a lark! The soldier told people that I came from Alsace and had deserted. The onlookers' attitude changed immediately. Some of them shook me by the hand and said things to me which I did not understand. A number of them gave me cigarettes. They laughed out loud to see me holding my piece of white bread in my hands like a treasure. Then I had to get into the car on my own. As I left, I waved goodbye to the people, and they waved back.

We went along the Maas valley to the village of Flavigny where the Army High Command was located. I was led into a large barn. A gendarme stood guard at the door. I had to climb the steps to the empty hayloft. There were a number of German prisoners there. The people from Alsace and Poland were on one side, while those from Germany were confined on the other side in a kind of wire cage. The people from Alsace wanted to ask me all kinds of questions, but I was too tired. I lay down on a bunk bed and fell straight off to sleep. I was immediately awakened again. When I first woke up, I had no idea where I was. A cook had brought me lunch. Good God, how amazed I was; I got a container of meat soup with bread, another with potatoes and gravy and a chop on top, with a salad on the lid, together with a quarter of a loaf of white bread and a quarter of a litre of wine. It was like being in heaven. On the German side you did get meat soup with bread, but you never got potatoes with gravy, or anything roasted, or a salad, far less white bread or wine. Although I was not hungry at all, I got stuck into these splendid things and demolished almost everything. A person leading a normal life cannot imagine my state of mind at that time. I was like a famished abandoned dog who thinks he should eat up anything edible that comes his way. When I was replete I gave the crockery back to the cook, who had smiled as he watched me, and then I lay back down on the bed and fell asleep immediately. I was soon wakened once again, a gendarme waved at me to go with him. I got up and went with him. He led me into a castle where I was interrogated by an officer who spoke very good German. He spoke to me in a familiar way.[77] I immediately thought, you can't catch me by speaking in this way, because I had made up my mind not to reveal anything about our position as I did not want my former comrades to lose out because of me. I answered his questions as I had answered the questions put by the general of the division. He asked how long I had been a soldier. I said that I had served since the 16th of October 1913. 'So,' he said, 'you are

[77] The officer used the 'du' form.

still on active service. What Regiment were you in when you went to war?' I told him that I had been with the First Company of Regiment 112. He immediately asked me: 'Were you also involved on the 26th of August 1914?' 'Yes,' I replied. He now asked me what I knew about the events of the 26th of August. I told him that on that day General Stenger had given the order that we should take no prisoners and that we should kill all the French who we took captive, whether they were wounded or not. I said that I had seen with my own eyes how a number of wounded who were lying on the ground had been shot dead or stabbed to death like pigs. I had personally protected a Frenchman and saved his life. 'Are you willing to swear to what you have told me?' 'Yes, sir,' I replied. The officer then asked me in detail about where I had served since the start of the war, and what I had experienced. After about two hours I was returned to the barn. I showed the gendarme the scratches in my skin which I had got from the barbed wire while I was defecting and indicated that they were painful. He led me to the infirmary, where a medical orderly painted all the scratches with iodine to disinfect the wounds and prevent them from festering. The iodine stung me for a while, but then it soon wore off.

24th of July to the 3rd of August 1918 – Life in Flavigny

On returning to the barn I was very pleased to meet Gustav Beck, who had arrived while I had been away. The next morning we were taken to a de-lousing station, and while we washed off the dust of the front in the bath, our clothes were deloused. You felt as if you were reborn. It was something quite new for both of us to sleep right through the night having bathed, eaten properly, and got rid of our lice. Beck was now put in charge of ten German prisoners and tasked with cleaning the streets of the village. I was put in the company kitchen to help out there. I was really astonished when I saw the plentiful supply of good food. It was the kitchen of the Guard Company, which had to post the guards for the Army High Command. The three cooks were all over forty, had red heads fit to burst as a result of the good eating and drinking, and were as high-spirited as conscripts.[78] They were all very friendly towards me – they pointed at my gaunt cheeks, then they puffed up their own cheeks and indicated to me that I should get cheeks like that while I was there. 'Not bad,' I thought. For breakfast they gave me half a pound of cooked ham, cheese, jam, bread, and I was allowed to drink coffee or wine with it – whatever I felt like. In the mornings I had to slice bread and put it into bowls for the Company. Afterwards bouillion was poured in. Before the Company fetched their food the head cook called me

[78] In Alsace conscription was traditionally seen as the stage at which young men became adults – and it was celebrated accordingly.

over to the cooking pot, took a soup plate and filled it half full of bouillion and then added a glass of red wine to it. That was for me. It tasted great! These cooks always cooked something better for themselves. I always had to eat with them, and they preferred it when everything was heavily seasoned. I was not used to this, and sometimes I felt that the spicy stuff was tearing my mouth and throat open. After lunch we washed all the dishes for the Company. Then in the time before the evening meal I had to peel onions and garlic and prepare and wash salad. I could easily have got all my day's work done in four hours. One of the soldiers had nothing to do but saw wood and chop it up for the kitchen. I helped him sometimes, even though I did not have to do so. He took me into the kitchen to where a fresh keg of wine was delivered each day and set up on a low trestle. The soldier took a beaker and put it in my hand. Then I had to put it under the tap on the keg, fill it up with wine and drink it. He indicated that if I were thirsty I should just help myself, but he waved his hand in front of his forehead and then laughingly pointed his finger at me to say that I should take care not to get drunk.

Several days after I had arrived there, the young soldier who had come with me to Metz about three weeks before turned up. At that time we had stayed with his sister for three days. 'Did you abscond as well?' I asked. 'Of course I did! I thought, if Richert has gone, then I will go too!' he replied. In the place we were living, French infantry had been put into quarters temporarily. He happened to meet his brother who had joined the French army, so he joined up too and was able to stay with him. He told me about how the soldiers from Alsace in our Division were no longer permitted to go into the front trench, as nobody could be trusted, and that a divisional order had been read out in which Richert, Beck and Pfaff had been sentenced to death by the Divisional Military Court for desertion. Good – everything is the wrong way round in war. Because we did not want to kill and did not want to be killed we were quite simply sentenced to death. But there is an old saying which goes: 'In Nuremberg they don't hang anyone until they have caught him', and I felt quite relaxed even though I had been sentenced to death. But I did get angry when I thought of how a few well-paid senior officers who might never have been under fire themselves had the right to pass the death sentence on poor soldiers who had borne the misery of war for nearly four years and only wanted to save what was left of their lives. In reality, didn't people like that who drove soldiers to hold out at the front and made them take part in attacks incurring heavy losses deserve to die more than I did? These were the people who always went on about the dearly beloved Fatherland, got paid to lead a comfortable life into the bargain, filled their chests with medals they had not earned, and let the poor soldiers be killed for nothing, absolutely nothing. But the main thing was that they could do me no harm.

In Flavigni I encountered people of all races. Lots of American troops passed through the place, together with Negroes, Arabs, Moroccans, Indo-Chinese and Italians; I never stopped looking at them. In the barn where I slept there were also a few Frenchmen, several Moroccans, two Negroes and four Chinese workers who were imprisoned for various crimes and were awaiting sentencing. They were all locked up in small cells which had been erected on both sides of the barn floor. None of them was permitted to have a knife or braces, and at night time they had to put their shoes out in front of their doors. The four Chinese were suspected of having raped and murdered a young girl. When they ate on the barn floor they all went down on their knees round the food bowl and stayed like this until they were finished.

Gradually I felt my strength returning. I just wanted to stay here for a long time, but after nine days I was told: 'Tomorrow morning you have to travel on!' The following morning I bade farewell to the cooks, who gave me meat and bread to take with me, and thirteen of us – half of us from Alsace and half from Poland – were led to the nearest station. We boarded the train and travelled to the town of Neuf-Chateau. There, wherever you looked, it was swarming with American soldiers – young lads full of the joys of life whose faces and eyes were still free of the traces of war. We were led to a high hill outside the town, and suddenly came upon the entrance to a fort. Above the gate stood the name: Fort Burglemont.

Life in Fort Burglemont

We crossed the moat via a drawbridge and were led to an office inside the fort. We had to go in one after another. I was last. An officer from Alsace, who appeared to be a Jew, asked about my regiment and my home and so on. Then I had to give him my money. He told me I would get it back on my arrival at the camp for men from Alsace in St Rambert. Then I was allowed to go. We were accommodated in a casemate of the fort. On either side of us lived the garrison of the fort – all soldiers over the age of forty. In another part lived lots of German prisoners. We, as soldiers from Alsace and Poland, were given the same food as the French soldiers, while the Germans had to make do with poor food. Life here was lazy and boring. In the four weeks that I was there the most I did was to help unload four trucks carrying bread with eight other men, and to go into the woods twice to fetch brushwood. We passed the time with gymnastics and wrestling and things like that. One day we were asked whether one of us would volunteer to take the food to the officers who were imprisoned in the fort. Beck volunteered. Each day he brought the food into our room. There we ladled the fat out of the meat soup intended for the officers and put it in ours, and we swopped their best bits of meat for our poorest bits. We emptied half of their wine into our jug and made up the difference with water. 'So,' we said, 'they have eaten up the best things for long enough. Now we're changing things round.' The German officers were supposed to get the same food as the French soldiers and us.

After four weeks there we had to travel on. We went by train via Langres to Dijon. We marched through the beautiful town and continued for about half an hour to a fort in which a large number of German prisoners were accommodated. They had almost all been in captivity since the start of the war and were wearing bright pre-war uniforms which had been sent to them via Switzerland. There were all kinds of uniforms here: light infantry, Uhlans, Hussars, Dragoons, and Artillery – in short, almost all the uniforms which were worn in the German Army before the war. A lot of the prisoners there had recovered from serious wounds and were awaiting repatriation via Switzerland.

On the second day of my stay there, a proclamation in German was posted; it stated that German prisoners would no longer be exchanged and sent home because it was known to the French that many of the people exchanged had been sent to Rumania as occupying forces, in order to free up soldiers capable of fighting for the offensive against Amiens. The prisoners who were waiting to be exchanged, who were already back home in their thoughts, hung their heads. In this fort we were given the same food as the German prisoners. Rice in the morning, rice at midday, and rice in the evening. The same again on the following day, and on the third and fourth day. You could certainly eat as much as you wanted, but always the same – that was pretty steep! The rice was cooked until it was fairly thick, and on the top they sprinkled rendered American bacon. The bread was black as coal, old and mouldy. The Germans told us that you would get nothing but rice for fourteen days, followed by fourteen days with nothing but beans, and then fourteen days of peas or lentils – but no other changes. We were happy when, on the fifth day, we were sent on.

We marched back to the station in Dijon, boarded the train and travelled steadily southwards. We went through the splendid Saône Valley in which we could see a large number of vines. Beautiful grapes, which were already starting to turn blue, were hanging from them. I really liked the area. In the evening we had to leave the train in the town of Macon and we were locked into a dark cellar. That did not suit us. It was already very dark when we were brought to the cellar. We discontentedly lay down on the plank bed which ran along the walls. Then I heard someone speaking Alsace dialect on the other side. There was a voice speaking the exact dialect of my home town. I got up, went over, and asked if one of them came from the vicinity of Dammerkirch. 'Yes,' said one of them, 'I am from Fülleren.' I quickly lit a match and recognized him immediately. It was Emil Schachrer from Fülleren! He did not recognize me even though we lit up my face with several matches. I told him who I was, to which he said that I had altered a great deal. We talked on for a long time about our home until we eventually fell asleep. The next morning we were pleased to travel on and leave that dark, damp hole. We were not given anything to eat in the morning or during the whole day. At a station where we had to change trains, there were some big pieces of fine American bread lying near the platform; they had probably been thrown out of a train by American soldiers. I wanted to quickly pick up one of the best pieces. Then the gendarme who was accompanying us knocked it out of my hand, saying that I should ask his permission if I wanted to pick up the bread! I felt quite angry, and I would rather have starved than give this scoundrel the honour of asking for his permission. Eventually we could board again, and a train full of men on leave stopped next to ours. Beck heard the soldiers saying: 'They are luckier than we are – they will not get shot dead any more!' One of them, who knew a few words of German tried to speak to us. Beck replied to him in French and then told him that we had not had anything to eat all day. The soldier gave us a big piece of bread and a number of soldiers passed us their canteens which were filled with wine. These were front-line soldiers – they were all friendlier than the lazy base wallahs!

We travelled on and after journeying for several hours we reached Lyon. This town lies in a splendid location at the place where the Rhone and the Saône meet. On both sides of the river, even far from the town, the hills are covered with splendid villas and mansions. We had a long stay in the main station in Lyon. We still were given nothing to eat. To ease our hunger we drank water from the drinking fountain in the station. A number of trains carrying front-line soldiers, probably from the Italian Front, passed through the station. The soldiers all looked good. Beck heard how two young girls who were walking backwards and forwards past us said to each other: 'These ones don't look like Boches, and this one here (she meant Beck, who was a handsome chap) would suit me well as a husband.' Beck could not help smiling, and he said to her in French, that he quite fancied her too. How she blushed! Beck asked her for her address, and she wrote it on a slip of paper and gave it to him. Then our train came in and we had to travel on.

It was night before the train pulled in to the station of St Étienne. We had to alight and were led into a barracks. On the way we passed lots of restaurants whose many guests were sitting on chairs on the pavements having a good time drinking beer or wine. Looking at them, I felt a great urge to be free. We were hoping that we would get something to eat in the barracks – but we were out of luck! We were simply locked into the detention room. We were furious, and we had forgotten all the good things the French had done for us. The sympathy for France, which we had all felt so much had fallen below zero, and you could hear all kinds of things, but not 'Vive la France'. Our predecessors must have been a lot angrier than we were, because the plank beds in the detention room were all smashed up and the boards were lying all around the room. In addition there was human excrement in the corners. It was pitch black. With the aid of matches I eventually found a place where Beck, Schachrer and I were able to sit. The next morning we went on, without having anything to eat or drink. Eventually we reached our destination, the station of St Just. From there we had to walk for twenty minutes to reach the Alsace POW Camp in St Rambert. The road crossed the Loire on a suspension bridge. At long last we reached the camp.

In the Alsace POW Camp at St Rambert sur Loire

The POW Camp was located in a former monastery, situated on a low hill near the village of St Rambert. There is a big building on one side which is similar to a barracks. On the side facing the road a high wall separates the monastery from the world. On the other side there are stables and farm buildings. The monastery church is built next to the large monastery building. At the entrance gate there was always a French soldier on duty – but he was not armed. We were not allowed to go out without permission. In the buildings and in the yard it was full of soldiers from Alsace, some of whom had been captured, but most of them had deserted. We were accommodated in a former stable in which there were tables, benches and bunks. You could immediately tell that you were with people from Alsace due to their terrible bad habit of swearing. Where once the prayers of the monks rose up to heaven they had now been replaced by these terrible curses!

Immediately after we arrived we were fed beef and rice, together with a big piece of bread and a quarter of a litre of wine. As we new arrivals were starving, we soon polished off the meal. I would have gladly written home, but I did not have any centimes in my pocket to buy paper. I went through the big yard and encountered someone I knew from home – Hoog from Manspach. After greeting each other I said to him: 'Listen, Hoog, I am going to have to do something now which I have never done in my life before. I am going to have to ask you to lend me some money.' He laughed and said: 'There's no point, as I only possess five Sous.' I told him that I wanted to write home but I did not have any money to buy writing paper. He gave me three Sous, which was enough to buy paper. I wrote home straight away and asked for money. Although I had written home more than twenty times I had still not had a reply and had to assume that none of my letters had arrived. In the afternoon we had to go to an officer to be interrogated. We stood in the corridor and waited. He came out and asked if one of us came from the area round Dammerkirch. Emil Schachrer and I told him that one of us came from Fülleren, while the other came from St Ulrich. The officer decided that I should come to his office at 2.00pm. I went there. He ordered a bottle of wine to be brought. Now the officer told me that he knew my parents well, and asked me, when I looked at him in amazement, where we had bought our leather shoes from in the past. I said: 'At Klötzlen's in Dammerkirch!' Now he said: 'I am Klötzlen's son, but here I am known as Tuchart.' We talked about our home, and when I told him that I had gone to war with Regiment 112 he asked me in detail about the events on the 26th of August 1914, and in particular about General Stenger's order which had called on our soldiers to kill all the French troops who fell into our hands. I repeated what I had said at the previous interrogations. At the end Klötzlen said that if I felt like becoming a gendarme then he would arrange it that I would be transferred to the gendarme station in Lüre. I thanked him for his helpfulness but I did not want to go as I had been in uniform for far too long already. However I did ask him to write to my relatives, as it seemed that nothing from me was getting through. He promised me that I would get an answer from home within seven days. I bade him farewell and returned to the stable. This life did not please me. The lack of activity made it boring.

On the second day we were given different uniforms and turned into French soldiers. I was given red trousers, blue puttees, a short dark blue jacket, and a large dark blue cap for my head with protruding points like horns at the front and the back. When I looked at myself in the mirror I had to laugh. I thought: 'In these clothes you would not look bad on a cart-load of monkeys!' On the sixth day I was standing outside the stables with Schachrer, Beck and a number of other comrades enjoying the sunshine, when the clerk came along and said that he needed six men who were able to do agricultural work. I volunteered first, and Beck and Schachrer were second and third. A whole string of people had soon volunteered. They all wanted to get out of the Camp. Now the clerk counted: '1, 2, 3, 4, 5, 6'. The first six were sent to get our things. It did not take long to pack. All I had was what I was wearing, and a blanket. A brake[79] drove up. The six of us got on board and we left the monastery. We travelled for about three hours far into the hills. The man who collected us was a POW from Lorraine called Barbier who was in charge of a detachment of about thirty-five men from Alsace who were working in and around the little town of St Heand – mainly for farmers. Barbier told us that he had a good life; he lived in the Hotel Thevenon in St Heand and his only responsibility was to fetch the payment in kind for the workers, which came in the form of clothing and shoes, from the stores. If someone did not like where he was working, he would find him a different job. We stopped up in the hills and Barbier said: 'This farm needs three men. Who would like to go?' I volunteered straight away. Beck and Schachrer each wanted to go to a separate farm instead of the three of us going together, so I went with Joseph Meier from Obersaasheim and a chap called Alfons from

---

[79] This was probably a horse-drawn shooting brake, which typically had space for six passengers.

Erstein. There were already three chaps from Alsace there, and they made us welcome. They told us that we had made a good choice and that we would like it there. The farm, which was called Poizat, belonged to the mayor of St Heand who lived about half an hour away in a palace and was a multi-millionaire. The farm was run by a manager and his wife; he was about forty-eight and she was about forty. They both gave us a friendly welcome, and said a few words to us, none of which we understood.

On the Poizat Farm near St Heand (Loire)

The three men from Alsace had already been at the farm for one and a half years and it seemed, as far as I could tell, that they could speak French well. They all liked it there and were hoping to stay there until they could return home. We were well fed, and that was the main thing as far as we were concerned. We arrived at the farm on Saturday afternoon. We spent most of the Sunday in the garden, from which we had a splendid view down into the beautiful Loire valley. The Loire looked like a broad silver band. Across the entire width of the valley was a scattering of villages and small towns, and in the background rose the mountains of the Massif Central. With the naked eye you could make out hundreds of farms, which looked a bit like cubes, in the mountains. Over to the left, at a distance of about seven kilometres, in a hollow was the large industrial town of St Étienne. There were lots of coal mines there. It was particularly beautiful to look down on St Étienne at night time when the thousands of electric lights were turned on. Towards evening the owner came over from his castle in order to get to know the three new arrivals. He asked us how we were for money, and someone translated for us, to tell him that none of us had any. He immediately reached in his pocket and gave each of us twenty Francs. 'That's good,' I thought, 'before we had done any work at all.' Then he asked us how we were doing for clothes. We told him that the clothes we were wearing were all we had. The very same evening a man from Alsace who worked in the castle brought us clothes, so we were able to discard our ill-fitting uniforms. Now, at long last, we were dressed as civilians. Over the following days we had to mow the second crop of grass which was growing in the meadows in the ravines. That was something completely different. We were not used to this kind of work any more and at the start we sweated dreadfully. But we soon got into the swing of things. The owner was very satisfied with our work.

At long last I heard from my family. They were very pleased to hear that I was no longer at the front, and sent me money straight away. As soon as they could get a *'Laisser-passer'* (ticket)[80], they would come to me

---

[80] It actually means a pass, rather than a ticket.

and bring my clothes. I was very pleased to think I would see them again. I was given back the money which I had had to hand over in the fort at Neuf-Chateau. At the current exchange rate, I was given nineteen Francs for my thirty Marks. After we had brought in the grass I had to go with my comrade Joseph Meyer to a neighbouring farm to harvest potatoes as the whole family apart from the father were ill in bed with the flu. Afterwards we had to spend a few more days harvesting potatoes at the farm near the castle. I really liked it there. The farm manager there had lost a leg during the war. I learned how to milk a cow. Then we went back to the farm in Poizat. My five comrades were given the task of making bundles of sticks in the woods, while I had to stay at the farm and help tidy up and to work in the large vegetable garden. I got on well with the manager and his wife and this was to my advantage. When I was working in the garden the manager's wife often called me into the kitchen where she would give me a glass of wine or, if the weather was fresh and cold, a sweet coffee laced with cognac, together with a piece of cake. I was also often given chocolate. It suited me better and better and if I had been homeless then I would certainly have stayed on there. When the work in the garden and on the farm was over, I had to join the others in the woods to make bundles of sticks. Each of us made sixty a day. Both the manager and the owner were very pleased with our work. After the first month, each of us was paid a wage of one hundred Francs, although our owner was only obliged to pay us forty per month. In addition, I was given a further eight Francs because I had been an NCO.

As I have already said, the food was very good. In the morning, as soon as we got up, we were given a cup of strong black coffee and a piece of cake. Then each of us went to make his bed and we cleaned out the bedroom. Breakfast consisted of ham soup, ham, jam, cheese, bread and wine. Each midday we got two courses, always followed by cheese or jam as a dessert, and often a piece of chocolate as well. In the evening we usually got soup, potatoes, meat or sausage, followed once again by cheese and jam. Our farm had thirty-two nut-trees and a number of sweet chestnut trees. Each of us had a sack of nuts and chestnuts by his bed. In short, we led a very comfortable life!

At the end of September, my father and my sister came to visit me. I was busy propping up a hedge when my comrades told me they had arrived. We were very happy to see each other again, but I could see straight away that my father and my sister had grown older – after all, four and a half years is quite a long time. They also found that I had changed a lot. We spent an hour in the farm, and then went to the Hotel Thevenon in St Heand, where we stayed and ate for the next three days. These were three lovely days. We had invited my comrades and Emil Schachrer to spend the evenings with us, and they were glad to do so. My father and my sister had brought my clothes with them and we bought anything else I needed. It made me feel like a human being again. All too quickly the three days were over and my father and my sister returned home. Although I was doing well, I would very much have liked to go with them. I would manage well now, as father had really padded my wallet. We went to St Heand every Sunday, and spent almost the whole day in restaurants and cafes. Almost every Sunday the thirty-five men from Alsace in the detachment met in the Hotel Thevenon and it often got lively.

At the start of November we heard that peace would come soon. On the 10th of November there was a rumour that it would only take two or three days until the armistice. On the 11th of November we were busy in the woods bundling sticks when we suddenly heard trumpets blaring in the little town of La Fujus down below us, while we could hear artillery being fired in St Etienne. Here and there we heard bells being rung and shots being fired, and then, from La Fujus we heard a clamour in which it was impossible to tell whether people were laughing or crying. 'Peace has come,' we said to ourselves, and we all cried, because we imagined that we would be allowed to travel home in the next few days. We stood together and called out 'Vive la France!' three times, so that the echo echoed round the hills. 'Today we will not work any more!' we said, and we made our way towards the farm. We were all pleased that the French had won the war, because, if the Germans had won, Alsace would have continued to be part of Germany and we, as deserters, would never have been able to return home. When we arrived at the farm the manager and his wife kissed each of us twice and said that we were now Frenchmen like them. The manager's wife cooked a very good lunch to celebrate the day and we were all in a very happy mood. In the afternoon we all went to St Heand, where we drank, celebrated and danced right through the night until dawn the next day. Then we went back to the farm feeling hung over and had the whole day off to recover. We heard that the Kaiser had run away to Holland. As soon as a scoundrel like him experiences a little bit of danger he abandons everything and scarpers, while we had to spend four years in need surrounded by death for absolutely no good purpose. If you want to save your little life, you are sentenced to death. They even sent him on a heap of money even though without a doubt he was one of those to blame for the ghastly slaughter. Yes, as the old saying goes: 'They hang the little people and let the big ones go free!'

Now we went to St Heand every Sunday. Occasionally we went to the church in the morning. We had collected money to buy an accordion. Our comrade Michael Strub, who was the son of an innkeeper in Obermodern in Lower Alsace, knew how to play it expertly. We would go from one pub to another and danced like mad. Lots of the young girls from St Heand who enjoyed dancing would follow us round from one pub to another. We seldom went home before two in the morning.

The only problem was language, you often got stuck and sometimes you came out with things that made everyone laugh, but the people were so decent that they never laughed directly at us, even if we said things completely wrong. Often peculiar things would happen. One time the manager's wife wanted to cook noodles. She needed four eggs. She said to my comrade Alfons: '*Alfons, va vite chercher quatre oeufs a l'autre ferme. J'en ais besoin pour faire le diner.*' (Alfons, go quickly to fetch four eggs from the other farm. I need them to make lunch.) Good Alfons, who believed that he had understood correctly, said: '*Oui Madame!*' and headed off. It took a while and still Alfons had not turned up. Eventually his wife indicated that I should go to see where he had got to. I went and as I was heading down the steep road into the ravine I saw Alfons leading four yoked-up cattle. As they were not used to him they did not want to move, and Alfons stood there sweating and poking at them with a long stick with a nail at the end. I had to laugh and waved to the manager's wife, who was standing on the steps at the front door, to come and see. She came and when she saw stressed Alfons with his four cattle she fell on the ground laughing. She laughed until the tears ran down her cheeks. Alfons was given a couple of glasses of wine and had to take the cattle back. It was all because he had misunderstood what she had said. He only understood '*vite chercher quatre*' and instead of '*oeufs*' he had understood '*boeufs*' and '*diner*' and had interpreted the sentence as follows: 'Alfons, fetch four cattle from the farm, and make sure you are back for dinner'. Another time he went to fetch scissors. He said '*Madame, six sous*'. The lady gave him six sous, but that's not what he wanted. '*Pas comme ça, pour couper!*' Then the woman understood and gave him the scissors. Similar things happened every day and we never stopped laughing. Each of us bought a dictionary and we eagerly started learning French. Gradually we got so far that we could make ourselves understood in broken French.

Quite a lot of the men from Alsace who were able to speak French well had found themselves girlfriends. That was not too difficult here as there were no male inhabitants here between the ages of seventeen and forty-five, and lots of girls wanted boyfriends. Emil Schachrer and I often travelled down to St Etienne with the narrow-gauge railway where we met up with Peter Koegler and Joseph Huber from Fülleren for an enjoyable Sunday afternoon. There were people of all races in St Etienne, mainly Chinese and Arabs who worked in the factories, while there were also enough Negroes and Americans.

When we still had not had an order to return home by the New Year we started to believe that if we did not go back to the camp at St Rambert then we might have to wait for a long time before we were returned home. So we decided to leave the farm and go to the camp. The manager's wife cooked us a good farewell lunch, and then my comrades bade them farewell. I waited until they had gone and then thanked the couple once again. When I shook hands for the last time they both started to cry, because they were very fond of me. Now we went to St Heand and loaded our cases and trunks onto the waggon which we had ordered and said goodbye to our acquaintances. It seemed to be the custom there that people would kiss each other when they said goodbye, so the kissing seemed to go on and on, until it seemed too silly. Singing, we left this place of which we had grown so fond. The whole population had rushed onto the street to wave to us. On leaving the town we waved our caps and shouted 'Vive St Heand' three times. Then we headed for St Rambert.

We were not made welcome there as we had returned to the camp without being ordered to do so. The camp was full to overflowing. Everything was occupied – the corridors, the attics, all the rooms and halls, the stables, sheds – in short the whole place was occupied by people from Alsace and Lorraine. The food was not very good but we all had money so we were able to fend for ourselves. Each week we were allowed to go out for two afternoons. It got busy in the pubs. The people who had money would buy themselves food to take back into the camp. We were lucky to have been allocated to a room which was well heated by the central heating. We did not have to work, apart from peeling potatoes for a few hours each week. We passed the time dancing, wrestling, telling stories, and all kinds of tricks. I met lots of people from home – more than twenty – who couldn't wait for the day when they would be allowed to go home. I met Albert Dietsch from Merzen who had just returned from Saloniki and had no money, so I lent him twenty Francs to help him out. One day it was announced that there would be a Rosary Service in the Cloister Chapel and all Catholics would be welcome to come. I went there and was very surprised to find that less than twenty men were taking part in the service. That is the way that the war 'improved' people.

On the 25th of January we were all issued with French uniforms. There were about one thousand two hundred of us. 'Tomorrow,' they said, 'a transport will take you home.' We were glad that at long last we would be able to get home and see our families. On the morning of the 26th of January we went to the station in St Just. We were all as happy as could be. Three large French flags were paraded at the front. We followed on, singing. At the end of the line came a number of waggons on which the cases and trunks were transported to the station. Now we were organized into sections, got on board, and off we went. Thank God, we were going home. The journey went via Lyon, Dijon, Lure and Epinal. It was dark by the time we reached Epinal. We went on via Luneville. Between Luneville and the border to Lorraine I looked out of the window. We were just passing through the Front. I shuddered to see the empty snowed-up trenches, the barbed wire entanglements and the dugouts. I could almost not imagine that I had spent years of my life in an environment like that.

At Arricourt we reached my homeland at long last, and then we went on via Laarburg where I had been made to take part in the big battle four and a half years before, to Zabern, Strassburg and Colmar. We arrived in Colmar early in the morning and were taken to huts next to an army barracks where we had to wait for our discharge papers. Eventually at ten o'clock in the morning I was free. As it was cold, Emil Schachrer and I went into a restaurant and had something to eat. We were not used to hearing women and girls speaking the language of our home. Then we went back to the station where we checked in our luggage. We missed one train and had to wait until the evening before we could travel in the direction of Mülhausen. From there the train was heading more in the direction of Altkirch so we had to spend the night in the waiting room. The following morning we caught the first train to Dammerkirch. I was quite surprised when I saw that Altkirch, which was so near to the Front, had not been more badly damaged, since this would have been possible with the smallest calibre of field artillery, and I thought to myself, the war did not reach here. Carspach looked different, but still most of the houses had been left standing. Now we travelled through the trenches, shell-holes, barbed wire entanglements and shot-up trees. At Dammerkirch the railway had been diverted to bypass the viaduct which had been partially destroyed (the Baraweg Bridge). At long last we arrived in Dammerkirch. Off we went across the Mittelfeld towards home. I said goodbye to Emil Schachrer at the Black Barn.

Up on the hill in the Altenach Woods at long last I saw my home village, which I had left in October 1913, almost five and a half years before. All of a sudden, my eyes filled with tears. I hurried on to get home. How surprised I was to see the young people in the village; how they had grown. I cannot describe how it was when I saw my mother again. We were so happy that we could not speak. Now at long last I was home again. Although I had often doubted that it would happen, I had achieved the one and only thing I had hoped for throughout the war.

Appendix: Place Names

As Alsace, Ukraine, Poland and Lithuania have undergone massive changes in the last century, it is not surprising that many place names have changed. My policy with regard to place names has been to retain the original names where relevant – thus I have written Mülhausen rather than Mulhouse, but Vienna and not Wien. The following table consists of a list of most of the places mentioned in the book whose names have changed.

There are a few of the entries with question marks. It was not completely clear from the text whether I had identified the correct location.

Readers with access to the internet may find it helpful to look at the map which can be found at http://goo.gl/maps/hZFAF to follow Dominik Richert's movements.

Name used in text	Present-day name	Name used in text	Present-day name
Arricourt	Avricourt	Givenchy	Givenchy-lès-la-Bassée
Pillau	Baltiysk	Gumbinnen	Gusev
Brzeżany	Berezhany	Hardwald	Harthwald
Braunsberg	Braniewo	Hayingen	Hayange
Pressburg	Bratislava	Hénin-Liétard	Hénin-Beaumont
Brest-Litovsk	Brest	Grubeschow	Hrubieszów
Brie	Brie-Comte-Robert?	Üxküll	Ikšķile
Brünn	Brno	Illuxt	Ilūkste
Bühl	Buhl-Lorraine	Hinzenberg	Inčukalns
Wenden	Cēsis	Jaroslau	Jarosław
Insterburg	Chernyakhovsk	Jakobstadt	Jēkabpils
Eydtkuhnen	Chernyshevskoye	Mitau	Jelgava
Fraustadt	Wschowa	Janischki	Joniškis
Kurland	Courland	Königsberg	Kaliningrad
Dammerkirch	Dannemarie	Kovno	Kaunas
Düna	Daugava	Memel	Klaipėda
Dünaburg	Daugavpils	Küstrin	Kostrzyn/Küstein?
Dürlingsdorf	Durlinsdorf	Libau	Liepāja
Jelowka	Eglaine	Lörchingen	Lorquin
Elbing	Elbląg	Lüre	Lure
Ermes	Ērģeme	Lemberg	Lviv
Fentsch	Fontoy	Ménil	Ménil-sur-Belvitte
Framerville	Framerville-Rainecourt	Méricourt	Méricourt-sur-Somme
Livländische Aa	Gauja	Mörchingen	Morhange

Name used in text	Present-day name	Name used in text	Present-day name
Munkács	Mukachëvo	Heydekrug	Šilutė
Mülhausen	Mulhouse	Tilsit	Sovetsk
Njemen	Neman	Strassburg	Strasbourg
Neuenburg	Neuenburg am Rhein	Sunzel	Suntaži
Pfalzburg	Phalsbourg	Dorpat	Tartu
Schneidemühl	Piła	Dirschau	Tczew
Posen	Poznań	Thiaville	Thiaville-sur-Meurthe
Radsiwilischki	Radviliškis	Diedenhofen	Thionville
Rieding	Réding	Thiess	Tisza
Richebourg	Richebourg-Saint-Vaast	Tucholka	Tukhol'ka
Rakishki	Rokiškis	Walk	Valka
Rodenpois	Ropaži?	Wolmar	Valmiera
Rosières	Rosières-en-Santerre	Weichsel	Vistula
Laarburg	Saarebourg	Volodawa	Włodawa
Zabern	Saverne	Novo-Alexandrovsk	Zarasai
Obersept	Seppois-le-Haut	Zurawno	Zhuravno
Schaulen	Šiauliai